THE 80x86

IBM PC

& COMPATIBLE

COMPUTERS

THE 80x86 IBM PC & COMPATIBLE COMPUTERS

VOLUME I: Assembly Language Programming on the IBM PC, PS and Compatibles

Muhammad Ali Mazidi

Janice Gillispie Mazidi

REGENTS/Prentice Hall
Englewood Cliffs, NJ 07632

Library of Congress Cataloging-in-Publication Data

Mazidi, Muhammad Ali.
    Assembly language programming on the IBM PC,PS, and compatibles/
Muhammad Ali Mazidi, Janice Gillispie Mazidi.
    p. -- (The 80 x 86 IBM PC,PS, and compatible computers series;
vol.1)
Includes biographical references and Index.
ISBN 0-13-036286-7
1. Intel 80 x 86 (Microprocessor)--Programming. 2. Assembler
language (Computer program language) I. Mazidi, Janice Gillespie.
II. Title III. Series.
QA76.8.I292M39 1993
005.265--dc20   92-38826
                                                                    CIP

Editorial/production supervision: Mary Carnis
Cover design: Marianne Frasco
Manufacturing buyer: Ed O'Dougherty

Published by
REGENTS/Prentice Hall
A Division of Simon & Schuster
Englewood Cliffs, New Jersey 07632

Printed in the United States of America
10 9 8 7 6 5 4 3 2 1

ISBN 0-13-036286-7

Prentice-Hall International (UK) Limited, London
Prentice-Hall of Australia Pty. Limited, Sydney
Prentice-Hall Canada Inc., Toronto
Prentice-Hall Hispanoamericana, S.A., Mexico
Prentice-Hall of India Private Limited, New Delhi
Prentice-Hall of Japan, Inc., Tokyo
Simon & Schuster Asia Pte. Ltd., Singapore
Editora Prentice-Hall do Brasil, Ltda., Rio de Janeiro

knowledge is a veritable treasure for man

Bahá'u'lláh

DEDICATIONS

This book is dedicated to the memory of Muhammad Ali's parents, who raised 10 children and persevered through more than 50 years of hardship together with dignity and faith.

We feel especially blessed to have the support, love, and encouragement of Janice's parents whose kindness, wisdom, and sense of humor have been the bond that has welded us into a family.

In addition, we must also mention our two most important collaborations: our sons Robert Nabil and Michael Jamal who have taught us the meaning of love and patience.

CONTENTS

PREFACE TO THE SERIES   xix

PREFACE TO VOLUME 1   xx

CHAPTER 0: INTRODUCTION TO COMPUTING   1

    SECTION 0.1: NUMBERING AND CODING SYSTEMS   2

        Decimal and binary number systems   2
        Converting from decimal to binary   2
        Converting from binary to decimal   2
        Hexadecimal system   3
        Converting between binary and hex   4
        Converting from decimal to hex   4
        Converting from hex to decimal   4
        Counting in base 10, 2, and 16   6
        Addition of binary and hex numbers   6
        2's complement   6
        Addition and subtraction of hex numbers   7
        Adding hex numbers   7
        Subtraction of hex numbers   7
        ASCII code   8

    SECTION 0.2: INSIDE THE COMPUTER   9

        Some important terminology   9
        Internal organization of computers   9
        More about the data bus   10
        More about the address bus   10
        CPU and its relation to RAM and ROM   11
        Inside CPUs   11
        Internal working of computers   12

    SECTION 0.3: BRIEF HISTORY OF THE CPU   13

        CISC vs. RISC   14

CHAPTER 1: THE 80x86 MICROPROCESSOR   18

SECTION 1.1: BRIEF HISTORY OF THE 80x86 FAMILY   19

Evolution from 8080/8085 to 8086   19
Evolution from 8086 to 8088   19
Success of the 8088   19
Other microprocessors: the 80286, 80386, and 80486   19

SECTION 1.2: INSIDE THE 8088/8086   21

Pipelining   21
Registers   22

SECTION 1.3: INTRODUCTION TO ASSEMBLY PROGRAMMING   23

Assembly language programming   24
MOV instruction   24
ADD instruction   25

SECTION 1.4: AN INTRODUCTION TO PROGRAM SEGMENTS   26

Origin and definition of the segment   27
Logical address and physical address   27
Code segment   27
Logical address vs. physical address in the code segment   28
Data segment   29
Logical address and physical address in the data segment   29
Little endian convention   31
Extra segment (ES)   32
Memory map of the IBM PC   32
More about RAM   32
Video RAM   33
More about ROM   33
Function of BIOS ROM   33

SECTION 1.5: MORE ABOUT SEGMENTS IN THE 80x86   33

What is a stack, and why is it needed?   33
How stacks are accessed   34
Pushing onto the stack   34
Popping the stack   34
Logical address vs. physical address for the stack   35
A few more words about segments in the 80x86   36
Overlapping   36
Flag Register   37
Bits of the flag register   38
Flag register and ADD instruction   38
Use of the zero flag for looping   40

SECTION 1.6: 80x86 ADDRESSING MODES   41

Register addressing mode   41
Immediate addressing mode   41
Direct addressing mode   42
Register indirect addressing mode   42
Based relative addressing mode   43
Indexed relative addressing mode   43
Based indexed addressing mode   44
Segment overrides   44

CHAPTER 2: ASSEMBLY LANGUAGE PROGRAMMING 49

SECTION 2.1: DIRECTIVES AND A SAMPLE PROGRAM 50

Segments of a program 50
Stack segment definition 51
Data segment definition 51
Code segment definition 52

SECTION 2.2: ASSEMBLE, LINK AND RUN A PROGRAM 54

.asm and .obj files 55
.lst file 55
PAGE and TITLE directives 56
.crf file 56
LINKing the program 57
.map file 57

SECTION 2.3: MORE SAMPLE PROGRAMS 57

Analysis of Program 2-1 58
Various approaches to Program 2-1 60
Analysis of Program 2-2 62
Analysis of Program 2-3 62
Stack segment definition revisited 62

SECTION 2.4: CONTROL TRANSFER INSTRUCTIONS 64

FAR and NEAR 64
Conditional jumps 64
Short jumps 64
Unconditional jumps 66
CALL statements 66
Assembly language subroutines 67
Rules for names in Assembly Language 67

SECTION 2.5: DATA TYPES AND DATA DEFINITION 69

80x86 data types 69
Assembler data directives 69
ORG (origin) 69
DB (define byte) 69
DUP (duplicate) 70
DW (define word) 70
EQU (equate) 71
DD (define doubleword) 71
DQ (define quadword) 72
DT (define ten bytes) 72

SECTION 2.6: SIMPLIFIED SEGMENT DEFINITION 73

Memory model 74
Segment definition 74

SECTION 2.7: EXE VS. COM FILES 76

Why COM files? 76
Converting from EXE to COM 77

CHAPTER 3: ARITHMETIC AND LOGIC INSTRUCTIONS 82

SECTION 3.1: UNSIGNED ADDITION AND SUBTRACTION 83

Addition of unsigned numbers 83
CASE 1: Addition of individual byte and word data 83
Analysis of Program 3-1a 84
CASE 2: Addition of multiword numbers 85
Analysis of Program 3-2 86
Subtraction of unsigned numbers 87
SBB (subtract with borrow) 88

SECTION 3.2: UNSIGNED MULTIPLICATION AND DIVISION 88

Multiplication of unsigned numbers 88
Division of unsigned numbers 90

SECTION 3.3 LOGIC INSTRUCTIONS AND SAMPLE PROGRAMS 93

AND 93
OR 93
XOR 94
SHIFT 95
COMPARE of unsigned numbers 96
IBM BIOS method of converting from lowercase to uppercase 99
BIOS examples of logic instructions 100

SECTION 3.4 BCD & ASCII OPERANDS AND INSTRUCTIONS 101

BCD number system 101
Unpacked BCD 102
Packed BCD 102
ASCII numbers 102
ASCII to BCD conversion 102
ASCII to unpacked BCD conversion 102
ASCII to packed BCD conversion 103
Packed BCD to ASCII conversion 104
BCD addition and subtraction 104
BCD addition and correction 104
DAA 105
Summary of DAA action 105
BCD subtraction and correction 105
Summary of DAS action 107
ASCII addition and subtraction 109
Unpacked BCD multiplication and division 109
AAM 109
AAD 110

SECTION 3.5: ROTATE INSTRUCTIONS 110

Rotating the bits of an operand right and left 110
ROR rotate right 110
ROL rotate left 111
Rotation through the carry 112
RCR rotate right through carry 112
RCL rotate left through carry 112

CHAPTER 4: BIOS INT 10H AND DOS INT 21H PROGRAMMING   118

SECTION 4.1: BIOS INT 10H PROGRAMMING   119

Monitor screen in text mode   119
Clearing the screen using INT 10H function 06H   120
INT 10H function 02: setting the cursor to a specific location   120
INT 10H function 03: get current cursor position   121
Changing the video mode   121
Attribute byte in monochrome monitors   122
Attribute byte in CGA text mode   122
Graphics: pixel resolution and color   124
INT 10H and pixel programming   125
Drawing horizontal or vertical lines in graphics mode   125
Changing the background color   126

SECTION 4.2: DOS INTERRUPT 21H   127

INT 21H option 09: outputting a string of data to the monitor   127
INT 21H option 02: outputting a single character to the monitor   127
INT 21H option 0AH: inputting a string of data from the keyboard   128
Inputting more than the buffer size   129
Use of carriage return and line feed   131
INT 21H option 07: keyboard input without echo   133
Using the LABEL directive to define a string buffer   133

CHAPTER 5: MACROS   139

MACRO definition   140
Comments in a macro   141
LOCAL directive and its use in macros   144
INCLUDE directive   147

CHAPTER 6: SIGNED NUMBERS, STRINGS, AND TABLES   152

SECTION 6.1: SIGNED NUMBER ARITHMETIC OPERATIONS   153

Concept of signed numbers in computers   153
Signed byte operands   153
Positive numbers   153
Negative numbers   153
Word-sized signed numbers   154
Overflow problem in signed number operations   155
When the overflow flag is set in 8-bit operations   155
Overflow flag in 16-bit operations   156
Avoiding erroneous results in signed number operations   157
IDIV (Signed number division)   158
IMUL (Signed number multiplication)   159
Arithmetic shift   161
SAR (shift arithmetic right)   161
SAL (shift arithmetic left) and SHL (shift left)   161
Signed number comparison   161

SECTION 6.2 STRING AND TABLE OPERATIONS   163

Use of SI and DI, DS and ES in string instructions   164
Byte and word operands in string instructions   164
DF, the direction flag   164
REP prefix   165
STOS and LODS instructions   165
Testing memory using STOSB and LODSB   166
The REPZ and REPNZ prefixes   166
SCAS (scan string)   168
Replacing the scanned character   168
XLAT instruction and look-up tables   169
Code conversion using XLAT   169

CHAPTER 7: MODULES, MODULAR AND C PROGRAMMING   172

SECTION 7.1: WRITING AND LINKING MODULES   173

Why modules?   173
Writing modules   173
EXTRN directive   173
PUBLIC directive   173
END directive in modules   174
Linking modules together into one executable unit   175
Analysis of Program 7-1   176
SEGMENT directive   177
Complete stack segment definition   177
Complete data and code segment definitions   177
Analysis of Program 7-2 link map   179
Modular programming and the use of the new segment definition   180

SECTION 7.2: SOME VERY USEFUL MODULES   182

Binary (hex)-to-ASCII conversion   182
ASCII (decimal)-to-binary (hex) conversion   183
Binary-to-ASCII module   184
ASCII-to-binary module   186
Calling module   186

SECTION 7.3 PASSING PARAMETERS AMONG MODULES   187

Passing parameters via registers   187
Passing parameters via memory   187
Passing parameters via the stack   187
Stack contents analysis for Program 7-9   188

SECTION 7.4 COMBINING ASSEMBLY AND C PROGRAMS   189

Why C?   189
Inserting 80x86 assembly code into C programs   190
C programs that call Assembly procedures   191
C calling convention   192
How parameters are returned to C   193
New assemblers and linking with C   194
Passing array addresses from C to the stack   195
Linking assembly language routines with C   196

CHAPTER 8: 32-BIT PROGRAMMING FOR 386 AND 486 MACHINES 199

SECTION 8.1: 80386/80486 MACHINES IN REAL MODE 200

General registers are pointers in 386/486 201
386/486 maximum memory range in real mode: 1M 203
Accessing 32-bit registers with commonly used assemblers 203
Little endian revisited 205

SECTION 8.2: SOME SIMPLE 386/486 PROGRAMS 205

Adding 16-bit words using 32-bit registers 205
Adding multiword data in 386/486 machines 207
Multiplying a 32-bit operand by a 16-bit operand in the 386/486 208
32-bit by 16-bit multiplication using 8086/286 registers 208

SECTION 8.3: 80x86 PERFORMANCE COMPARISON 210

Running an 8086 program across the 80x86 family 210

APPENDIX A: DEBUG PROGRAMMING 214

SECTION A.1: ENTERING AND EXITING DEBUG 214

SECTION A.2: EXAMINING AND ALTERING REGISTERS 215

SECTION A.3: CODING AND RUNNING PROGRAMS IN DEBUG 216

A, the Assemble command 217
U, the unassemble command: looking at machine code 218
G, the go command 218
T, the trace command: a powerful debugging tool 220

SECTION A.4: DATA MANIPULATION IN DEBUG 222

F, the fill command: filling memory with data 222
D, the dump command: examining the contents of memory 223
E, the enter command: entering data into memory 224

SECTION A.5: EXAMINING THE STACK IN DEBUG 227

Pushing onto the stack 227
Popping the stack 228

SECTION A.6: EXAMINING/ALTERING THE FLAG REGISTER 228

The impact of instructions on the flag bits 229
Hexarithmetic command 229
Procedure command 229

SECTION A.7: ADDITIONAL DEBUG DATA MANIPULATION 231

M, the move command: copying from one location to another 231
C, the compare command: checking blocks of data for differences 232
S, the search command: search a block of memory for data 232

SECTION A.8: LOADING AND WRITING PROGRAMS 232

W, the write command: saving instructions on disk 232
L, the load command: loading instructions from disk 233
N, the name command: used to load a file from disk 233

APPENDIX B: 80x86 INSTRUCTIONS AND TIMING   236

SECTION B.1: THE 8086 INSTRUCTION SET   236

SECTION B.2: INSTRUCTION TIMING   259

APPENDIX C: ASSEMBLER DIRECTIVES AND NAMING RULES   272

SECTION C.1: 80x86 ASSEMBLER DIRECTIVES   272

SECTION C.2: RULES FOR LABELS AND RESERVED NAMES   284

APPENDIX D:DOS INTERRUPT 21H LISTING   287

APPENDIX E: BIOS INTERRUPT 10H LISTING   311

APPENDIX F: ASCII CODE   317

INDEX   321

ABOUT THE AUTHORS

Muhammad Ali Mazidi is a Ph.D. candidate in the Electrical Engineering Department of Southern Methodist University. His dissertation topic is RISC-based massively parallel processing machines. He is a co-founder and chief researcher of Microprocessor Education Group, a company dedicated to bringing knowledge of microprocessors to the widest possible audience. He also teaches microprocessor-based system design at DeVry Institute of Technology in Dallas, Texas.

Janice Gillispie Mazidi has a Master of Science degree in Computer Science from the University of North Texas. After several years experience as a software engineer in Dallas, she co-founded Microprocessor Education Group, where she is the chief technical writer, production manager, and is responsible for software development and testing.

Please write to us at the following address if you have any comments, suggestions, or if you find any errors.

Microprocessor Education Group
P.O. Box 381970
Duncanville TX 75138

PREFACE TO THE SERIES

"I think that Intel has some of its greatest times ahead of it. That's because they are driving microprocessor design technology and enjoy the largest installed base of software in the world. If you're going to learn only one instruction set, it's going to be the Intel X86." *

Philippe Kahn
Chaimman, president and CEO
Borland International Inc.

It is currently estimated that there are over 100 million 80x86-based (8088, 8086, 80286, 80386, 80386SX, 80486, 80486SX) IBM and compatible computers in the world and this number is growing by 10 to 15 million units a year. The alliance of Intel, IBM, and Microsoft brought about a revolution in the computer industry by creating a unified system that became the standard for desktop computers. Intel provided the 80x86 microprocessors and Microsoft developed the DOS operating system, but it was IBM who set the revolution in motion by making the architecture of the PC open for cloning. In the absence of such a role by IBM, we would have desktop computers with four or five different architectures and operating systems, all incompatible with each other. This would have been more like the tower of Babel than the friendly world of IBM PCs and compatibles that we have known and enjoyed since 1981 when the first IBM PC was announced. The fact that the newer-generation 80x86 CPUs are achieving the power of minicomputers will assure the survival of the 80x86 well beyond the year 2000. These facts explain why many companies such as Sun Micro and Next have made available an 80x86 version of their operating systems.

Why this series?

It is our belief that many computer hardware and software concepts are much easier to learn if one has access to a system whereby these concepts can be experimented with hands-on. Undoubtedly, the 80x86-based PC is the most affordable tool to achieve this objective. The steadily decreasing price of PCs has made these tools available to schools, students, individuals, and small businesses.

Although there are many fine books that deal with various hardware or software aspects of the PC, this series is designed to provide a systematic and comprehensive introduction to both the software and hardware of the PC. We have embarked on the task of creating this series of books which will provide a guide to those wanting to become proficient in the PC. The range of topics selected and their degree of coverage have been designed based on over ten years of classroom experience introducing these concepts to students. Emphasis has been placed on providing information in such a way as to enable the student to gain hands-on experience quickly in order to master the concepts as they are presented.

More about the series

Both the software and hardware of 80x86 computers fall into two categories: 16-bit and 32-bit systems. Therefore, Volumes 1 and 2 emphasize 16-bit systems while the later volumes cover systems with 32-bit architecture.

Volume 1 of this series provides an introduction to Assembly language programming on the PC, and Volume 2 covers the hardware design and interfacing of 80x86 systems

---

* "The Empire Strikes Back", *Upside*, June 1992, p. 42.

PREFACE TO VOLUME 1

Purpose

This book is intended for use in college-level Assembly language programming courses. It not only builds the foundation of Assembly language programming for students in computer science curricula, but also provides a comprehensive treatment of 80x86 instructions, programs, and their use for students in engineering disciplines who want to develop microprocessor-based systems.

Prerequisites

Readers should have a minimal familiarity with the IBM PC and the DOS operating system. Knowledge of other programming languages would be helpful, but is not necessary.

Contents

A systematic, step-by-step approach has been used in covering various aspects of Assembly language programming. Many examples and sample programs are given to clarify concepts and provide students an opportunity to learn by doing. Review questions are provided at the end of each section to reinforce the main points of the section. We feel that one of the functions of a textbook is to familiarize the student with terminology used in technical literature and in industry, so we have followed that guideline in this text.

Chapter 0 covers concepts in number systems (binary, decimal, and hex) and computer architecture. Most students will have learned these concepts in previous courses, but Chapter 0 provides a quick overview for those students who have not learned these concepts, or who may need to refresh their memory.

Chapter 1 provides a brief history of the evolution of 80x86 microprocessors and an overview of the internal workings of the 8086 as a basis of all 80x86 processors. Chapter 1 should be used in conjunction with Appendix A (a tutorial introduction to DEBUG) so that the student can experiment with concepts being learned on the PC. The order of topics in Appendix A has been designed to correspond to the order of topics presented in Chapter 1. This allows the student to begin programming with DEBUG without having to learn how to use an assembler.

Chapter 2 explains the use of assemblers to create programs. Although the programs in the book were developed and tested with Microsoft's MASM assembler, any Intel-compatible assembler such as Borland's TASM may be used.

Chapter 3 introduces the bulk of the logic and arithmetic instructions for unsigned numbers.

Chapter 4 introduces DOS and BIOS interrupts which allow the student to get input from the keyboard and send output to the monitor.

Chapter 5 describes how to use macros to develop Assembly language programs in a more time-efficient and structured manner.

Chapter 6 covers arithmetic and logic instructions for signed numbers as well as string processing instructions.

Chapter 7 discusses modular programming and how to develop larger Assembly language programs by breaking them into smaller modules to be coded and tested separately. In addition, linking Assembly language modules with C programs is thoroughly explained.

Chapter 8 introduces some 32-bit concepts of 80386 and 80486 programming. Although this book emphasizes 16-bit programming, the 386/486 is introduces to help the student appreciate the power of 32-bit CPUs. Several programs are run across the 80x86 family to show the dramatic improvement in clock cycles with the newer CPUs.

The appendices have been designed to provide all reference material required for this course so that no additional reference sources should be necessary.

Appendix A provides a tutorial introduction to DEBUG.

Appendix B provides a listing of Intel's 8086 instruction set along with clock cycles for the instructions.

Appendix C describes assembler directives and gives examples of their use.

Appendix D lists the most commonly used DOS INT21H function calls.

Appendix E lists BIOS INT10H function calls.

Appendix F provides a table of ASCII codes.

Acknowledgments

This book is the result of the dedication, work and love of many individuals. Our sincere and heartfelt appreciation goes out to all of them. First, we must thank the reviewers who provided valuable suggestions and encouragement: Mr. William H. Shannon of The University of Maryland, Mr. Howard W. Atwell of Fullerton College, Mr. David G. Delker of Kansas State University, Mr. Michael Chen of Duchess Community College, and Mr. Yusuf Motiwala of Prarie View A&M University.

Thanks also must go to the many students whose comments have helped shape this book, especially Daniel Woods, Sam Oparah, Herbert Sendeki, Greg Boyle, Philip Fitzer, and Adnan Hindi. Last but not least we would like to thank Mr. Allen Escher whose encouragement set the making of this series into motion. For the last 25 years, his dedication and love of microprocessor education have been a source of inspiration to many.

Finally, we would like to thank Holly Hodder and Mary Carnis of Prentice Hall for their whole-hearted support of this series.

CHAPTER 0

INTRODUCTION TO COMPUTING

OBJECTIVES

Upon completion of this chapter, you will be able to:

» Convert any number from base 2, base 10, or base 16 to any of the other two bases
» Count in binary and hex
» Add and subtract hex numbers
» Add binary numbers
» Represent any binary number in 2's complement
» Represent an alphanumeric string in ASCII code
» Explain the difference between a bit, a nibble, a byte, and a word
» Give precise mathematical definitions of the terms *kilobyte*, *megabyte*, *terabyte*, and *gigabyte*
» Explain the difference between RAM and ROM and describe their use
» List the major components of a computer system and describe their functions
» List the three types of buses found in computers and describe the purpose of each type of bus
» Describe the role of the CPU in computer systems
» List the major components of the CPU and describe the purpose of each
» Trace the evolution of computers from vacuum tubes to transistors to IC chips
» State the differences between the RISC and CISC design philosophies

To understand the software and hardware of the computer, one must first master some very basic concepts underlying computer design. In this chapter (which in the tradition of digital computers can be called Chapter 0), the fundamentals of numbering and coding systems are presented. Then an introduction to the workings of the inside of the computer is given. Finally, in the last section we give a brief history of CPU architecture. Although some readers may have an adequate background in many of the topics of this chapter, it is recommended that the material be scanned, however briefly.

SECTION 0.1: NUMBERING AND CODING SYSTEMS

Whereas human beings use base 10 (*decimal*) arithmetic, computers use the base 2 (*binary*) system. In this section we explain how to convert from the decimal system to the binary system, and vice versa. The convenient representation of binary numbers called *hexadecimal* also is covered. Finally, the binary format of the alphanumeric code, called *ASCII*, is explored.

Decimal and binary number systems

Although there has been speculation that the origin of the base 10 system is the fact that human beings have 10 fingers, there is absolutely no speculation about the reason behind the use of the binary system in computers. The binary system is used in computers because 1 and 0 represent the two voltage levels of on and off. Whereas in base 10 there are 10 distinct symbols, 0, 1, 2, ..., 9, in base 2 there are only two, 0 and 1, with which to generate numbers. Base 10 contains digits 0 through 9; binary contains digits 0 and 1 only. These two binary digits, 0 and 1, are commonly referred to as *bits*.

Converting from decimal to binary

One method of converting from decimal to binary is to divide the decimal number by 2 repeatedly, keeping track of the remainders. This process continues until the quotient becomes zero. The remainders are then written in reverse order to obtain the binary number. This is demonstrated in Example 0-1.

Example 0-1

Convert 25_{10} to binary.

Solution:

		Quotient	Remainder	
25/2	=	12	1	LSB (least significant bit)
12/2	=	6	0	
6/2	=	3	0	
3/2	=	1	1	
1/2	=	0	1	MSB (most significant bit)

Therefore, $25_{10} = 11001_2$.

Converting from binary to decimal

To convert from binary to decimal, it is important to understand the concept of weight associated with each digit position. First, as an analogy, recall the weight of numbers in the base 10 system:

$$740683_{10} =$$

$$
\begin{array}{rcr}
3\times10^0 & = & 3 \\
8\times10^1 & = & 80 \\
6\times10^2 & = & 600 \\
0\times10^3 & = & 0000 \\
4\times10^4 & = & 40000 \\
7\times10^5 & = & \underline{700000} \\
& & 740683
\end{array}
$$

By the same token, each digit position in a number in base 2 has a weight associated with it:

$$110101_2 =$$

$$
\begin{array}{rclcrr}
 & & & & \text{Decimal} & \text{Binary} \\
1\times2^0 & = & 1\times1 & = & 1 & 1 \\
0\times2^1 & = & 0\times2 & = & 0 & 00 \\
1\times2^2 & = & 1\times4 & = & 4 & 100 \\
0\times2^3 & = & 0\times8 & = & 0 & 0000 \\
1\times2^4 & = & 1\times16 & = & 16 & 10000 \\
1\times2^5 & = & 1\times32 & = & \underline{32} & \underline{100000} \\
& & & & 53 & 110101
\end{array}
$$

Knowing the weight of each bit in a binary number makes it simple to add them together to get its decimal equivalent, as shown in Example 0-2.

Example 0-2

Convert 11001_2 to decimal.

Solution:

Weight:	16	8	4	2	1
Digits:	1	1	0	0	1
Sum:	16 +	8 +	0 +	0 +	$1 = 25_{10}$

Knowing the weight associated with each binary bit position allows one to convert a decimal number to binary directly instead of going through the process of repeated division. This is shown in Example 0-3.

Example 0-3

Use the concept of weight to convert 39_{10} to binary.

Solution:

Weight:	32	16	8	4	2	1
	1	0	0	1	1	1
	32 +	0 +	0 +	4 +	2 +	$1 = 39$

Therefore, $39_{10} = 100111_2$.

Hexadecimal system

Base 16, the *hexadecimal* system as it is called in computer literature, is used as a convenient representation of binary numbers. For example, it is much easier for a human being to represent a string of 0s and 1s such as 100010010110 as its hexadecimal equivalent of 896H. The binary system has 2 digits, 0 and 1. The base 10 system has 10 digits, 0 through 9. The hexadecimal (base 16) system must have 16 digits. In base 16, the first 10 digits, 0 to 9, are the same as in decimal,

---

and for the remaining six digits, the letters A, B, C, D, E, and F are used. Table 0-1 shows the equivalent binary, decimal, and hexadecimal representations for 0 to 15.

Converting between binary and hex

To represent a binary number as its equivalent hexadecimal number, start from the right and group 4 bits at a time, replacing each 4-bit binary number with its hex equivalent shown in Table 0-1. To convert from hex to binary, each hex digit is replaced with its 4-bit binary equivalent. Converting between binary and hex is shown in Examples 0-4 and 0-5.

Converting from decimal to hex

Converting from decimal to hex could be approached in two ways:
1. Convert to binary first and then convert to hex. Experimenting with this method is left to the reader.
2. Convert directly from decimal to hex by the method of repeated division, keeping track of the remainders. Example 0-6 demonstrates this method of converting decimal to hex.

Converting from hex to decimal

Table 0-1: Decimal, Binary, and Hex

Decimal	Binary	Hexadecimal
0	0000	0
1	0001	1
2	0010	2
3	0011	3
4	0100	4
5	0101	5
6	0110	6
7	0111	7
8	1000	8
9	1001	9
10	1010	A
11	1011	B
12	1100	C
13	1101	D
14	1110	E
15	1111	F

Conversion from hex to decimal can also be approached in two ways:
1. Convert from hex to binary and then to decimal.
2. Convert directly from hex to decimal by summing the weight of all digits. Example 0-7 demonstrates the second method of converting from hex to decimal.

Example 0-4

Represent binary 100111110101 in hex.

Solution:
First the number is grouped into sets of 4 bits: 1001 1111 0101
Then each group of 4 bits is replaced with its hex equivalent:

$$\begin{array}{ccc} 1001 & 1111 & 0101 \\ 9 & F & 5 \end{array}$$

Therefore, 100111110101_2 = 9F5 hexadecimal.

Example 0-5

Convert hex 29B to binary.

Solution:
$$\begin{array}{cccc} & 2 & 9 & B \\ = & 0010 & 1001 & 1011 \end{array}$$
Dropping the leading zeros gives 1010011011.

Example 0-6

(a) Convert 45_{10} to hex.

Solution: Quotient Remainder
$45/16$ =   2   13 (hex D)   (least significant digit)
$2/16$ =   0   2   (most significant digit)

Therefore, $45_{10} = 2D_{16}$.

(b) Convert decimal 629 to hexadecimal.

Solution: Quotient Remainder
$629/16$ =   39   5   (least significant digit)
$39/16$ =   2   7
$2/16$ =   0   2   (most significant digit)

Therefore, $629_{10} = 275_{16}$.

(c) Convert 1714 base 10 to hex.

Solution: Quotient Remainder
$1714/16$ =   107   2   (least significant digit)
$107/16$ =   6   11   (hex B)
$6/16$ =   0   6   (most significant digit)

Therefore, $1714_{10} = 6B2_{16}$.

Example 0-7

Convert the following hexadecimal numbers to decimal.

(a) $6B2_{16}$

Solution:
6B2 hexadecimal =

$$
\begin{aligned}
2 \times 16^0 &= 2 \times 1 &= \quad\ 2 \\
11 \times 16^1 &= 11 \times 16 &= \ 176 \\
6 \times 16^2 &= 6 \times 256 &= \underline{1536} \\
& & \quad 1714
\end{aligned}
$$

Therefore, $6B2_{16} = 1714_{10}$.

(b) $9F2D_{16}$

Solution:
9F2D hexadecimal =

$$
\begin{aligned}
13 \times 16^0 &= 13 \times 1 &= \quad\ 13 \\
2 \times 16^1 &= 2 \times 16 &= \quad\ 32 \\
15 \times 16^2 &= 15 \times 256 &= \ 3840 \\
9 \times 16^3 &= 9 \times 4096 &= \underline{36864} \\
& & \ 40749
\end{aligned}
$$

Therefore, $9F2D_{16} = 40749_{10}$.

Counting in base 10, 2, and 16

To show the relationship between all three bases, in Figure 0-1 we show the sequence of numbers from 0 to 31 in decimal, along with the equivalent binary and hex numbers. Notice in each base that when one more is added to the highest digit, that digit becomes zero and a 1 is carried to the next-highest digit position. For example, in decimal, $9 + 1 = 0$ with a carry to the next-highest position. In binary, $1 + 1 = 0$ with a carry; similarly, in hex, $F + 1 = 0$ with a carry.

Table 0-2: Binary Addition

A + B	Carry	Sum
0 + 0	0	0
0 + 1	0	1
1 + 0	0	1
1 + 1	1	0

Addition of binary and hex numbers

The addition of binary numbers is a very straightforward process. Table 0-2 shows the addition of two bits. The discussion of subtraction of binary numbers is bypassed since all computers use the addition process to implement subtraction. Although computers have adder circuitry, there is no separate circuitry for subtractors. Instead, adders are used in conjunction with *2's complement* circuitry to perform subtraction. In other words, to implement "$x - y$", it takes the 2's complement of y and adds it to x. The concept of 2's complement is reviewed next, but the process of subtraction of two binary numbers using 2's complement is shown in detail in Chapter 3.

Decimal	Binary	Hex
0	00000	0
1	00001	1
2	00010	2
3	00011	3
4	00100	4
5	00101	5
6	00110	6
7	00111	7
8	01000	8
9	01001	9
10	01010	A
11	01011	B
12	01100	C
13	01101	D
14	01110	E
15	01111	F
16	10000	10
17	10001	11
18	10010	12
19	10011	13
20	10100	14
21	10101	15
22	10110	16
23	10111	17
24	11000	18
25	11001	19
26	11010	1A
27	11011	1B
28	11100	1C
29	11101	1D
30	11110	1E
31	11111	1F

Figure 0-1. Counting in 3 Bases

Example 0-8

Add the following binary numbers. Check against their decimal equivalents.

Solution:

```
        Binary    Decimal
        1101        13
        1001         9
    +  10110        22
       101100       44
```

2's complement

To get the 2's complement of a binary number, invert all the bits and then add 1 to the result. Inverting the bits is simply a matter of changing all 0s to 1s and 1s to 0s. This is called the *1's complement*.

Example 0-9

Take the 2's complement of 10011101.

Solution:

	10011101	binary number
	01100010	1's complement
+	1	
	01100011	2's complement

Addition and subtraction of hex numbers

In studying issues related to software and hardware of computers, it is often necessary to add or subtract hex numbers. Mastery of these techniques is essential. Hex addition and subtraction are discussed separately below.

Addition of hex numbers

This section describes the process of adding hex numbers. Starting with the least significant digits, the digits are added together. If the result is less than 16, write that digit as the sum for that position. If it is greater than 16, subtract 16 from it to get the digit and carry 1 to the next digit. The best way to explain this is by example.

Example 0-10

Perform hex addition: 23D9 + 94BE.

Solution:

```
  23D9
+ 94BE
  B897
```

LSD:	$9 + 14$	$=$	23	$23 - 16 = 7$ with a carry to next digit
	$1 + 13 + 11$	$=$	25	$25 - 16 = 9$ with a carry to next digit
	$1 + 3 + 4$	$=$	8	
MSD:	$2 + 9 = B$			

Subtraction of hex numbers

In subtracting two hex numbers, if the second digit is greater than the first, borrow 16 from the preceding digit.

Example 0-11

Perform hex subtraction: 59F – 2B8.

Solution:

```
  59F
- 2B8
  2E7
```

LSD:	8 from $15 = 7$
	11 from 25 $(9 + 16) = 14$, which is E
MSD:	2 from 4 $(5 - 1) = 2$

ASCII code

The discussion so far has revolved around the representation of number systems. Since all information in the computer must be represented by 0s and 1s, binary patterns must be assigned to letters and other characters. In the 1960s a standard representation called *ASCII* (American Standard Code for Information Interchange) was established. The ASCII (pronounced "ask-E") code assigns binary patterns for numbers 0 to 9, all the letters of the English alphabet, both uppercase (capital) and lowercase, and many control codes and punctuation marks. The great advantage of this system is that it is used by most computers, so that information can be shared among computers. The ASCII system uses a total of 7 bits to represent each code. For example, 100 0001 is assigned to the uppercase letter "A" and 110 0001 is for the lowercase "a". Often, a zero is placed in the most significant bit position to make it an 8-bit code. Figure 0-2 shows selected ASCII codes. A complete list of ASCII codes is given in Appendix F. The use of ASCII is not only standard for keyboards used in the United States and many other countries but also provides a standard for printing and displaying characters by output devices such as printers and monitors.

The pattern of ASCII codes was designed to allow for easy manipulation of ASCII data. For example, digits 0 through 9 are represented by ASCII code 30 through 39. This enables a program to easily convert ASCII to decimal by masking off the "3" in the upper nibble. As another example, notice in the codes listed below that there is a relationship between the uppercase and lowercase letters. Namely, uppercase letters are represented by ASCII codes 41 through 5A while lowercase letters are represented by ASCII codes 61 through 7A. Looking at the binary code, the only bit that is different between uppercase "A" and lowercase "a" is bit 5. Therefore conversion between uppercase and lowercase is as simple as changing bit 5 of the ASCII code.

Hex	Symbol	Hex	Symbol
41	A	61	a
42	B	62	b
43	C	63	c
44	D	64	d
45	E	65	e
46	F	66	f
47	G	67	g
48	H	68	h
49	I	69	i
4A	J	6A	j
4B	K	6B	k
4C	L	6C	l
4D	M	6D	m
4E	N	6E	n
4F	O	6F	o
50	P	70	p
51	Q	71	q
52	R	72	r
53	S	73	s
54	T	74	t
55	U	75	u
56	V	76	v
57	W	77	w
58	X	78	x
59	Y	79	y
5A	Z	7A	z

Figure 0-2. Alphanumeric ASCII Codes

Review Questions

1. Why do computers use the binary number system instead of the decimal system?
2. Convert 34_{10} to binary and hex.
3. Convert 110101_2 to hex and decimal.
4. Perform binary addition: $101100 + 101$.
5. Convert 101100_2 to its 2's complement representation.
6. Add 36BH + F6H.
7. Subtract 36BH – F6H.
8. Write "80x86 CPUs" in its ASCII code (in hex form).

SECTION 0.2: INSIDE THE COMPUTER

In this section we provide an introduction to the organization and internal working of computers. The model used is generic, but the concepts discussed are applicable to all computers, including the IBM PC, PS/2, and compatibles. Before embarking on this subject, it will be helpful to review definitions of some of the most widely used terminology in computer literature, such as *K, mega, giga, byte, ROM, RAM,* and so on.

Some important terminology

One of the most important features of a computer is how much memory it has. Next we review terms used to describe amounts of memory in IBM PCs and compatibles. Recall from the discussion above that a *bit* is a binary digit that can have the value 0 or 1. A *byte* is defined as 8 bits. A *nibble* is half a byte, or 4 bits. A *word* is two bytes, or 16 bits. The following display is intended to show the relative size of these units. Of course, they could all be composed of any combination of zeros and ones.

```
Bit                                         0
Nibble                                   0000
Byte                           0000      0000
Word          0000    0000     0000      0000
```

A *kilobyte* is 2^{10} bytes, which is 1024 bytes. The abbreviation K is often used. For example, some floppy disks hold 356K bytes of data. A *megabyte*, or meg as some call it, is 2^{20} bytes. That is a little over 1 million bytes; it is exactly 1,048,576. Moving rapidly up scale in size, a *gigabyte* is 2^{30} bytes (over 1 billion), and a *terabyte* is 2^{40} bytes (over 1 trillion). As an example of how some of these terms are used, suppose that a given computer has 16 megabytes of memory. That would be 16×2^{20}, or $2^4 \times 2^{20}$, which is 2^{24}. Therefore 16 megabytes is 2^{24} bytes.

Two types of memory commonly used in microcomputers are *RAM*, which stands for random access memory (sometimes called *read/write memory*), and *ROM* which stands for read-only memory. RAM is used by the computer for temporary storage of programs that it is running. That data is lost when the computer is turned off. For this reason, RAM is sometimes called *volatile memory*. ROM contains programs and information essential to operation of the computer. The information in ROM is permanent, cannot be changed by the user, and is not lost when the power is turned off. Therefore, it is called *nonvolatile memory*.

Internal organization of computers

The internal working of every computer can be broken down into three parts: *CPU* (central processing unit), *memory*, and *I/O* (input/output) devices (see Figure 0-3). The function of the CPU is to execute (process) information stored in memory. The function of I/O devices such as the keyboard and video monitor, is to provide a means of communicating with the CPU. The CPU is connected to memory and I/O through strips of wire called a *bus*. The bus inside a computer carries information from place to place just as a street bus carries people from place to place. In every computer there are three types of buses: *address bus*, *data bus*, and *control bus*.

For a device (memory or I/O) to be recognized by the CPU, it must be assigned an *address*. The address assigned to a given device must be unique; no two devices are allowed to have the same address. The CPU puts the address (of course, in binary) on the address bus, and the decoding circuitry finds the device. Then the CPU uses the data bus either to get data from that device or to send data to it. The control buses are used to provide read or write signals to the device to indicate if the CPU is asking for information or sending it information. Of the three buses, the address bus and data bus determine the capability of a given CPU.

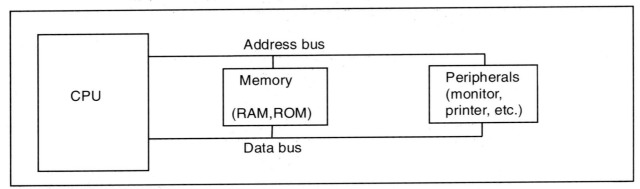

Figure 0-3. Inside the computer

More about the data bus

Since data buses are used to carry information in and out of a CPU, the more data buses available, the better the CPU. If one thinks of data buses as highway lanes, it is clear that more lanes provide a better pathway between the CPU and its external devices (such as printers, RAM, ROM, etc.; see Figure 0-4). By the same token, that increase in the number of lanes increases the cost of construction. More data buses means a more expensive CPU and computer. The average size of data buses in CPUs varies between 8 and 64. Early computers such as Apple 2 used an 8-bit data bus, while supercomputers such as Cray use a 64-bit data bus. Data buses are bi-directional, since the CPU must use them either to receive or to send data. The processing power of a computer is related to the size of its buses, since an 8-bit bus can send out 1 byte a time, but a 16-bit bus can send out 2 bytes at a time, which is twice as fast.

More about the address bus

Since the address bus is used to identify the devices and memory connected to the CPU, the more address buses available, the larger the number of devices that can be addressed. In other words, the number of address buses for a CPU determines the number of locations with which it can communicate. The number of locations is always equal to 2^x, where x is the number of address lines, regardless of the size of the data bus. For example, a CPU with 16 address lines can provide a total of 65,536 (2^{16}) or 64K bytes of addressable memory. Each location can have a maximum of 1 byte of data. This is due to the fact that all general-purpose microprocessor CPUs are what is called *byte addressable*. As another example, the IBM PC AT uses a CPU with 24 address lines and 16 data lines. In this case the total accessible memory is 16 megabytes (2^{24} = 16 megabytes). In this example there would be 2^{24} locations, and since each location is one byte, there would be 16 megabytes of memory. The address bus is a *unidirectional* bus which means that the CPU uses the address bus only to send out addresses. To summarize: the total number of memory locations addressable by a given CPU is always equal to 2^x where x is the number of address bits, regardless of the size of the data bus.

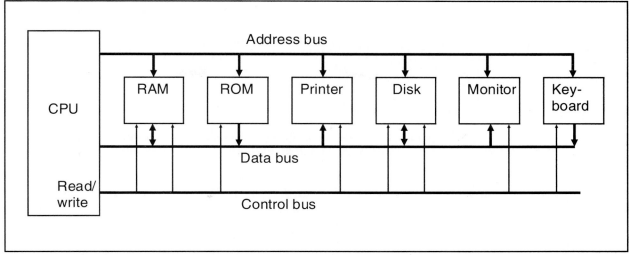

Figure 0-4. Internal organization of computers

CPU and its relation to RAM and ROM

For the CPU to process information, the data must be stored in RAM or ROM. The function of ROM in computers is to provide information that is fixed and permanent. This is information such as tables for character patterns to be displayed on the video monitor, or programs that are essential to the working of the computer, such as programs for testing and finding the total amount of RAM installed on the system, or programs to display information on the video monitor. In contrast, RAM is used to store information that is not permanent and can change with time, such as various versions of the operating system and application packages such as word processing or tax calculation packages. These programs are loaded into RAM to be processed by the CPU. The CPU cannot get the information from the disk directly since the disk is too slow. In other words, the CPU gets the information to be processed, first from RAM (or ROM), and only if it is not there does the CPU seek it from a mass storage device such as a disk, and then it transfers the information to RAM. For this reason, RAM and ROM are sometimes referred to as *primary memory* and disks are called *secondary memory*.

Inside CPUs

A program stored in memory provides instructions to the CPU to perform an action. The action can simply be adding data such as payroll data, or controlling a machine such as a robot. It is the function of the CPU to fetch these instructions from memory and execute them. To perform the actions of fetch and execute, all CPUs are equipped with resources such as the following:

1. Foremost among the resources at the disposal of the CPU are a number of *registers*. The CPU uses registers to store information temporarily. The information could be two values to be processed, or the address of the value needed to be fetched from memory. Registers inside the CPU can be 8-bit, 16-bit, 32-bit, or even 64-bit registers, depending on the CPU. In general, the more and bigger the registers, the better the CPU. The disadvantage of more and bigger registers is the increased cost of such a CPU.
2. The CPU also has what is called the *ALU* (arithmetic/logic unit). The ALU section of the CPU is responsible for performing arithmetic functions such as add, subtract, multiply, and divide, and logic functions such as AND, OR, and NOT.
3. Every CPU has what is called a *program counter*. The function of the program counter is to point to the address of the next instruction to be executed. As each instruction is executed, the program counter is incremented to point to the address of the next instruction to be executed. It is the contents of the program counter that are placed on the address bus to find and fetch the desired instruction. In the IBM PC, the program counter is a register called IP, or the instruction pointer.

4. The function of the *instruction decoder* is to interpret the instruction fetched into the CPU. One can think of the instruction decoder as a kind of dictionary, storing the meaning of each instruction and what steps the CPU should take upon receiving a given instruction. Just as a dictionary requires more pages the more words it defines, a CPU capable of understanding more instructions requires more transistors to design.

Internal working of computers

To demonstrate some of the concepts discussed above, a step-by-step analysis of the process a CPU would go through to add three numbers is given next. Assume that an imaginary CPU has registers called A, B, C, and D. It has an 8-bit data bus and a 16-bit address bus. Therefore, the CPU can access memory from address 0000 to FFFFH (for a total of 10000H locations). The action to be performed by the CPU is to put hexadecimal value 21 into register A, and then add to register A values 42H and 12H. Assume that the code for the CPU to move a value to register A is 1011 0000 (B0H) and the code for adding a value to register A is 0000 0100 (04H). The necessary steps and code to perform them are as follows.

Action	Code	Data
Move value 21H into register A	B0H	21H
Add value 42H to register A	04H	42H
Add value 12H to register A	04H	12H

If the program to perform the actions listed above is stored in memory locations starting at 1400H, the following would represent the contents for each memory address location:

Memory address	Contents of memory address	
1400	(B0)	the code for moving a value to register A
1401	(21)	the value to be moved
1402	(04)	the code for adding a value to register A
1403	(42)	the value to be added
1404	(04)	the code for adding a value to register A
1405	(12)	the value to be added
1406	(F4)	the code for halt

The actions performed by the CPU to run the program above would be as follows:

1. The CPU's program counter can have a value between 0000 and FFFFH. The program counter must be set to the value 1400H, indicating the address of the first instruction code to be executed. After the program counter has been loaded with the address of the first instruction, the CPU is ready to execute.
2. The CPU puts 1400H on the address bus and sends it out. The memory circuitry finds the location while the CPU activates the READ signal, indicating to memory that it wants the byte at location 1400H. This causes the contents of memory location 1400H, which is B0, to be put on the data bus and brought into the CPU.
3. The CPU decodes the instruction B0 with the help of its instruction decoder dictionary. When it finds the definition for that instruction it knows it must bring into register A of the CPU the byte in the next memory location. Therefore, it commands its controller circuitry to do exactly that. When it brings in value 21H from memory location 1401, it makes sure that the doors of all registers are closed except register A. Therefore, when value 21H comes into the CPU it will go directly into register A. After completing one instruction, the program counter points to the address of the next instruction to be executed, which in this case is 1402H. Address 1402 is sent out on the address bus to fetch the next instruction.
4. From memory location 1402H it fetches code 04H. After decoding, the CPU knows that it must add to the contents of register A the byte sitting at the next address

(1403). After it brings the value (in this case 42H) into the CPU, it provides the contents of register A along with this value to the ALU to perform the addition. It then takes the result of the addition from the ALU's output and puts it in register A. Meanwhile the program counter becomes 1404, the address of the next instruction.

5. Address 1404H is put on the address bus and the code is fetched into the CPU, decoded, and executed. This code is again adding a value to register A. The program counter is updated to 1406H.

6. Finally, the contents of address 1406 are fetched in and executed. This HALT instruction tells the CPU to stop incrementing the program counter and asking for the next instruction. In the absence of the HALT, the CPU would continue updating the program counter and fetching instructions.

Now suppose that address 1403H contained value 04 instead of 42H. How would the CPU distinguish between data 04 to be added and code 04? Remember that code 04 for this CPU means move the next value into register A. Therefore, the CPU will not try to decode the next value. It simply moves the contents of the following memory location into register A, regardless of its value.

Review Questions

1. How many bytes is 24 kilobytes?
2. What does "RAM" stand for? How is it used in computer systems?
3. What does "ROM" stand for? How is it used in computer systems?
4. Why is RAM called volatile memory?
5. List the three major components of a computer system.
6. What does "CPU" stand for? Explain its function in a computer.
7. List the three types of buses found in computer systems and state briefly the purpose of each type of bus.
8. State which of the following is unidirectional and which is bidirectional.
   (a) data bus   (b) address bus
9. If an address bus for a given computer has 16 lines, then what is the maximum amount of memory it can access?
10. What does "ALU" stand for? What is its purpose?
11. How are registers used in computer systems?
12. What is the purpose of the program counter?
13. What is the purpose of the instruction decoder?

SECTION 0.3: BRIEF HISTORY OF THE CPU

In the 1940s, CPUs were designed using vacuum tubes. The vacuum tube was bulky and consumed a lot of electricity. For example, the first large-scale digital computer, ENIAC, consumed 130,000 watts of power and occupied 1500 square feet. The invention of transistors changed all of that. In the 1950s, transistors replaced vacuum tubes in the design of computers. Then in 1959, the first IC (integrated circuit) was invented. This set into motion what many people believe is the second industrial revolution. In the 1960s the use of IC chips in the design of CPU boards became common. It was not until the 1970s that the entire CPU was put on a single IC chip. The first working CPU on a chip was invented by Intel in 1971. This CPU was called a *microprocessor*. The first microprocessor, the 4004, had a 4-bit data bus and was made of 2300 transistors. It was designed primarily for the hand-held calculator but soon came to be used in applications such as traffic-light controllers. The advances in IC fabrication made during the 1970s made it possible to design microprocessors with an 8-bit data bus and a 16-bit address bus. By the late 1970s, the Intel 8080/85 was one of the most widely used microprocessors, appearing in everything from microwave ovens to homemade computers. Meanwhile, many other companies joined in the race for faster and better microprocessors. Notable among them was Motorola with its 6800 and 68000 microprocessors. Apple's Macintosh computers use the 68000 series microprocessors.

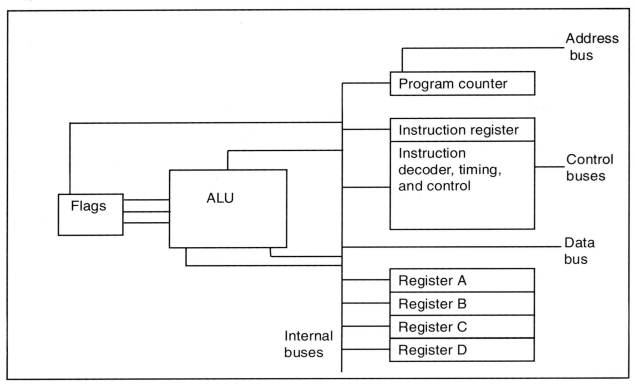

Figure 0-5. Internal block diagram of a CPU

CISC vs. RISC

Until the early 1980s, all CPUs, whether single-chip or whole-board, followed the *CISC* (complex instruction set computer) design philosophy. CISC refers to CPUs with hundreds of instructions designed for every possible situation. To design CPUs with so many instructions consumed not only hundreds of thousands of transistors, but also made the design very complicated, time-consuming, and expensive. In the early 1980s, a new CPU design philosophy called *RISC* (reduced instruction set computer) was developed. The proponents of RISC argued that no one was using all the instructions etched into the brain of CISC-type CPUs. Why not streamline the instructions by simplifying and reducing them from hundreds to around 40 or so and use all the transistors that are saved to enhance the power of the CPU? Although the RISC concept had been explored by computer scientists at IBM as early as the 1970s, the first working single-chip RISC microprocessor was implemented by a group of researchers at the University of California at Berkeley in 1980. Today the RISC design philosophy is no longer an experiment limited to research laboratories. Since the late 1980s, many companies designing new CPUs (either single-chip or whole-board) have used the RISC philosophy. It appears that eventually the only CISC microprocessors remaining in use will be members of the 80x86 family (8086, 8088, 80286, 80386, 80486, 80586, etc.) and the 680x0 family (68000, 68010, 68020, 68030, 68040, 68050, etc.). The 80x86 will be kept alive by the huge base of IBM PC, PS, and compatible computers, and the Apple Macintosh is prolonging the life of 680x0 microprocessors.

Review Questions

1. What is a microprocessor?
2. Describe briefly how advances in technology have affected the size, cost, and availability of computer systems.
3. Explain the major difference between CISC and RISC computers.

SUMMARY

The binary number system represents all numbers with a combination of the two binary digits, 0 and 1. The use of binary systems is necessary in digital computers because only two states can be represented: on or off. Any binary number can be coded directly into its hexadecimal equivalent for the convenience of humans. Converting from binary/hex to decimal, and vice versa, is a straightforward process that becomes easy with practice. The ASCII code is a binary code used to represent alphanumeric data internally in the computer. It is frequently used in peripheral devices for input and/or output.

The major components of any computer system are the CPU, memory, and I/O devices. "Memory" refers to temporary or permanent storage of data. In most systems, memory can be accessed as bytes or words. The terms *kilobyte, megabyte, gigabyte,* and *terabyte* are used to refer to large numbers of bytes. There are two main types of memory in computer systems: RAM and ROM. RAM (random access memory) is used for temporary storage of programs and data. ROM (read-only memory) is used for permanent storage of program and data that the computer system must have in order to function. All components of the computer system are under the control of the CPU. Peripheral devices such as I/O (input/output) devices allow the CPU to communicate with humans or other computer systems. There are three types of buses in computers: address, control, and data. Control buses are used by the CPU to direct other devices. The address bus is used by the CPU to locate a device or a memory location. Data buses are used to send information back and forth between the CPU and other devices.

As changes in technology were incorporated into the design of computers, their cost and size were reduced dramatically. The earliest computers were as large as an average home and were available only to a select group of scientists. The invention of and subsequent advances in transistor design have made the computer commonly available. As the limits of hardware innovation have been approached, computer designers are looking at new design techniques, such as RISC architecture, to enhance computer performance.

PROBLEMS

1. Convert the following decimal numbers to binary.
   (a) 12   (b) 123   (c) 63   (d) 128   (e) 1000
2. Convert the following binary numbers to decimal.
   (a) 100100   (b) 1000001   (c) 11101   (d) 1010   (e) 00100010
3. Convert the values in Problem 2 to hexadecimal.
4. Convert the following hex numbers to binary and decimal.
   (a) 2B9H   (b) F44H   (c) 912H   (d) 2BH   (e) FFFFH
5. Convert the values in Problem 1 to hex.
6. Find the 2's complement of the following binary numbers.
   (a) 1001010   (b) 111001   (c) 10000010   (d) 111110001
7. Add the following hex values.
   (a) 2CH+3FH   (b) F34H+5D6H   (c) 20000H+12FFH   (d) FFFFH+2222H
8. Perform hex subtraction for the following.
   (a) 24FH–129H (b) FE9H–5CCH   (c) 2FFFFH–FFFFFH (d) 9FF25H–4DD99H
9. Show the ASCII codes for numbers 0,1,2,3,...,9 in both hex and binary.
10. Show the ASCII code (in hex) for the following string:
    "U.S.A. is a country" CR,LF
    "in North America" CR,LF
    CR is carriage return
    LF is line feed

---

11. Answer the following:
    (a) How many nibbles are 16 bits?
    (b) How many bytes are 32 bits?
    (c) If a word is defined as 16 bits, how many words is a 64-bit data item?
    (d) What is the exact value (in decimal) of 1 meg?
    (e) How many K is 1 meg?
    (f) What is the exact value (in decimal) of giga?
    (g) How many K is 1 giga?
    (h) How many meg is 1 giga?
    (i) If a given computer has a total of 8 megabytes of memory, how many bytes (in decimal) is this? How many kilobytes is this?
12. A given mass storage device such as a hard disk can store 2 gigabytes of information. Assuming that each page of text has 25 rows and each row has 80 columns of ASCII characters (each character = 1 byte), approximately how many pages of information can this disk store?
13. In a given byte-addressable computer, memory locations 10000H to 9FFFFH are available for user programs. The first location is 10000H and the last location is 9FFFFH. Calculate the following:
    (a) The total number of bytes available (in decimal)
    (b) The total number of kilobytes (in decimal)
14. A given computer has a 32-bit data bus. What is the largest number that can be carried into the CPU at a time?
15. Below are listed several computers with their data bus widths. For each computer, list the maximum value that can be brought into the CPU at a time (in both hex and decimal).
    (a) Apple 2 with an 8-bit data bus
    (b) IBM PS/2 with a 16-bit data bus
    (c) IBM PS/2 model 80 with a 32-bit data bus
    (d) CRAY supercomputer with a 64-bit data bus
16. Find the total amount of memory, in the units requested, for each of the following CPUs, given the size of the address buses.
    (a) 16-bit address bus (in K)
    (b) 24-bit address bus (in meg)
    (c) 32-bit address bus (in megabytes and gigabytes)
    (d) 48-bit address bus (in megabytes, gigabytes and terabytes)
17. Regarding the data bus and address bus, which is unidirectional and which is bi-directional?
18. Which register of the CPU holds the address of the instruction to be fetched?
19. Which section of the CPU is responsible for performing addition?
20. Which type of CPU (CISC or RISC) has the greater variety of instructions?

ANSWERS TO REVIEW QUESTIONS

Section 0.1: Numbering and Coding Systems
1. Computers use the binary system because each bit can have one of two voltage levels: on and off.
2. $34_{10} = 100010_2 = 22_{16}$ 3. $110101_2 = 35_{16} = 53_{10}$
4. 1110001   5. 010100
6. 461   7. 275
8. 38 30 78 38 36 20 43 50 55 73

Section 0.2: Inside the Computer
1. 24,576
2. random access memory; it is used for temporary storage of programs that the CPU is running, such as the operating system, word processing programs, etc.
3. read only memory; it is used for permanent programs such as those which control the keyboard, etc.
4. the contents of RAM are lost when the computer is powered off
5. the CPU, memory, and I/O devices
6. central processing unit; it can be considered the "brain" of the computer, it executes the programs and controls all other devices in the computer
7. the address bus carries the location (address) needed by the CPU; the data bus carries information in and out of the CPU; the control bus is used by the CPU to send signals controlling I/O devices
8. (a) bidirectional   (b) unidirectional

9. 64K, or 65,536 bytes
10. arithmetic/logic unit; it performs all arithmetic and logic operations
11. for temporary storage of information
12. it holds the address of the next instruction to be executed
13. it tells the CPU what steps to perform for each instruction

Section 0.3: Brief History of the CPU
1. a CPU on a single chip
2. The transition from vacuum tubes to transistors to ICs reduced the size and cost of computers and therefore made them more widely available.
3. CISC computers use many instructions whereas RISC computers use a small set of instructions.

CHAPTER 1

THE 80x86 MICROPROCESSOR

OBJECTIVES

Upon completion of this chapter, you will be able to:

» Describe the Intel family of microprocessors from the 8085 to the 80486 in terms of bus size, physical memory, and special features

» Explain the function of the EU (execution unit) and BIU (bus interface unit)

» Describe pipelining and how it enables the CPU to work faster

» List the registers of the 8086

» Code simple MOV and ADD instructions and describe the effect of these instructions on their operands

» State the purpose of the code segment, data segment, stack segment, and extra segment

» Explain the difference between a logical address and a physical address

» Describe the "little endian" storage convention of 80x86 microprocessors

» State the purpose of the stack

» Explain the function of PUSH and POP instructions

» List the bits of the flag register and briefly state the purpose of each bit

» Demonstrate the effect of ADD instructions on the flag register

» List the addressing modes of the 8086 and recognize examples of each mode

This chapter begins with a history of the evolution of Intel's family of microprocessors. The second section is an overview of the internal workings of 80x86 microprocessors. An introduction to 80x86 Assembly language programming is given in the third section. The fourth and fifth sections cover segments of Assembly language programs and how physical addresses are generated. Finally, the last section describes in detail the addressing modes of the 80x86.

SECTION 1.1: BRIEF HISTORY OF THE 80x86 FAMILY

In this section we trace the evolution of Intel's family of microprocessors from the late 1970s, when the personal computer had not yet found widespread acceptance, to the powerful microcomputers widely in use today.

Evolution from 8080/8085 to 8086

In 1978, Intel Corporation introduced a 16-bit microprocessor called the 8086. This processor was a major improvement over the previous generation 8080/8085 series Intel microprocessors in several ways. First, the 8086's capacity of 1 megabyte of memory exceeded the 8080/8085's capability of handling a maximum of 64K bytes of memory. Second, the 8080/8085 was an 8-bit system, meaning that the microprocessor could work on only 8 bits of data at a time. Data larger than 8 bits had to be broken into 8-bit pieces to be processed by the CPU. In contrast, the 8086 is a 16-bit microprocessor. Third, the 8086 was a pipelined processor, as opposed to the nonpipelined 8080/8085. In a system with pipelining, the data and address buses are busy transferring data while the CPU is processing information, thereby increasing the effective processing power of the microprocessor. Although pipelining was a common feature of mini- and mainframe computers, Intel was a pioneer in putting pipelining on a single-chip microprocessor. Pipelining is discussed further in Section 1.2.

Evolution from 8086 to 8088

The 8086 is a microprocessor with a 16-bit data bus internally and externally, meaning that all registers are 16 bits wide and there is a 16-bit data bus to transfer data in and out of the CPU. Although the introduction of the 8086 marked a great advancement over the previous generation of microprocessors, there was still some resistance in using the 16-bit external data bus since at that time all peripherals were designed around an 8-bit microprocessor. In addition, a printed circuit board with a 16-bit data bus was much more expensive. Therefore, Intel came out with the 8088 version. It is identical to the 8086 as far as programming is concerned, but externally it has an 8-bit data bus instead of a 16-bit bus. It has the same memory capacity, 1 megabyte.

Success of the 8088

In 1981, Intel's fortune changed forever when IBM picked up the 8088 as their microprocessor of choice in designing the IBM PC. The 8088-based IBM PC was an enormous success, largely because IBM and Microsoft (the developer of the MS-DOS operating system) made it an *open system*, meaning that all documentation and specifications of the hardware and software of the PC were made public. This made it possible for many other vendors to clone the hardware successfully and thus spawned a major growth in both hardware and software designs based on the IBM PC. This is in contrast with the Apple computer, which was a closed system, blocking any attempt at cloning by other manufacturers, both domestically and overseas.

Other microprocessors: the 80286, 80386, and 80486

With a major victory behind Intel and a need from PC users for a more powerful microprocessor, Intel introduced the 80286 in 1982. Its features included 16-bit internal and external data buses; 24 address lines, which give 16 megabytes of memory (2^{24} = 16 megabytes); and most significantly, *virtual memory.* The 80286 can operate in one of two modes: real mode or protected mode. *Real mode* is simply a faster 8088/8086 with the same maximum of 1 megabyte of memory. *Protected mode* allows for 16M of memory but is also capable of protecting the operating system and programs from accidental or deliberate destruction by a user -- a feature that is absent in the single-user 8088/8086. Virtual memory is a way of fooling the microprocessor into thinking that it has access to an almost unlimited amount of memory by swapping data between disk storage and RAM. IBM picked up the 80286 for the design of the IBM PC AT, and the clone makers followed IBM's lead.

With users demanding even more powerful systems, in 1985 Intel introduced the 80386 (sometimes called 80386DX), internally and externally a 32-bit microprocessor with a 32-bit address bus. It is capable of handling physical memory of up to 4 gigabytes (2^{32}). Virtual memory was increased to 64 terabytes (2^{46}). All microprocessors discussed so far were general-purpose microprocessors and could not handle mathematical calculations rapidly. For this reason, Intel introduced numeric data processing chips, called math coprocessors, such as the 8087, 80287, and 80387. Later Intel introduced the 386SX, which is internally identical to the 80386 but has a 16-bit external data bus and a 24-bit address bus which gives a capacity of 16 megabytes (2^{24}) of memory. This makes the 386SX system much cheaper. With the introduction of the 80486 in 1989, Intel put a greatly enhanced version of the 80386 and the math coprocessor on a single chip plus additional features such as *cache memory.* Cache memory is static RAM with a very fast access time. Table 1-1 summarizes the evolution of Intel's microprocessors. It must be noted that all programs written for the 8086/88 will run on 286, 386, and 486 computers.

Table 1-1: Evolution of Intel's Microprocessors

Product	8080	8085	8086	8088	80286	80386	80486
Year introduced	1974	1976	1978	1979	1982	1985	1989
Clock rate (MHz)	2 - 3	3 - 8	5 - 10	5 - 8	6 - 16	16 - 33	25 - 50
No. transistors	4500	6500	29,000	29,000	130,000	275,000	1.2 million
Physical memory	64K	64K	1M	1M	16M	4G	4G
Internal data bus	8	8	16	16	16	32	32
External data bus	8	8	16	8	16	32	32
Address bus	16	16	20	20	24	32	32
Data type (bits)	8	8	8, 16	8, 16	8, 16	8, 16, 32	8, 16, 32

Notes:
1. The 80386SX architecture is the same as the 80386 except that the external data bus is 16 bits in the SX as opposed to 32 bits, and the address bus is 24 bits instead of 32; therefore, physical memory is 16MB.
2. Clock rates range from the rates when the product was introduced to current rates; some rates have risen during this time.

Review Questions

1. Name three features of the 8086 that were improvements over the 8080/8085.
2. What is the major difference between 8088 and 8086 microprocessors?
3. Give the size of the address bus and physical memory capacity of the following:
    (a) 8086   (b) 80286   (c) 80386
4. The 80286 is a _____-bit microprocessor, whereas the 80386 is a _____-bit microprocessor.
5. State the major difference between the 80386 and the 80386SX.
6. List additional features introduced with the 80286 that were not present in the 8086.
7. List additional features of the 80486 that were not present in the 80386.

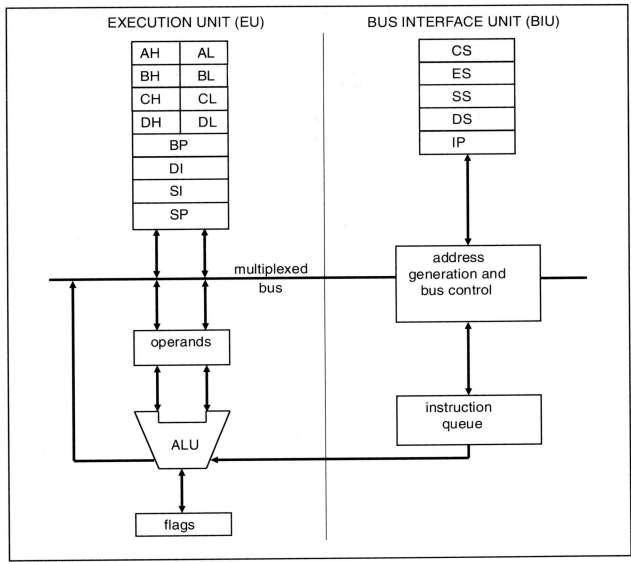

Figure 1-1. Internal Block Diagram of the 8088/86 CPU
(Reprinted by permission of Intel Corporation, Copyright Intel Corp. 1989)

SECTION 1.2: INSIDE THE 8088/8086

In this section we explore concepts important to the internal operation of the 8088/86, such as pipelining and registers.

Pipelining

There are two ways to make the CPU process information faster: increase the working frequency or change the internal architecture of the CPU. The first option is technology dependent, meaning that the designer must use whatever technology is available at the time, with consideration for cost. The technology and materials used in making ICs (*integrated circuits*) determine the working frequency, power consumption, and the number of transistors packed into a single-chip microprocessor. A detailed discussion of IC technology is beyond the scope of this book. It is sufficient for the purpose at hand to say that designers can make the CPU work faster by increasing the frequency under which it runs if technology and cost allow. The second option for improving the processing power of the CPU has to do with the internal working of the CPU. In the 8085 microprocessor, the CPU could either fetch or execute at a given time. In other words, the CPU had to fetch an instruction from memory, then execute it and then fetch again, execute it, and so on. The idea of *pipelining* in its simplest form is to allow the CPU to fetch and execute at the same time (see Figure 1-2). It is important to point out that Figure 1-2 is not meant to imply that the amount of time for fetch and execute are equal.

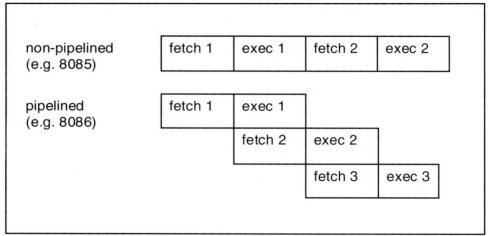

Figure 1-2. Pipelined vs. Nonpipelined Execution

Intel implemented the concept of pipelining in the 8088/86 by splitting the internal structure of the microprocessor into two sections: the *execution unit* (EU) and the *bus interface unit* (BIU). These two sections work simultaneously. The BIU accesses memory and peripherals while the EU executes instructions previously fetched. This works only if the BIU keeps ahead of the EU; thus the BIU of the 8088/86 has a buffer, or queue (see Figure 1-1). The buffer is 4 bytes long in the 8088 and 6 bytes in the 8086. If any instruction takes too long to execute, the queue is filled to its maximum capacity and the buses will sit idle. The BIU fetches a new instruction whenever the queue has room for 2 bytes in the 6-byte 8086 queue, and for 1 byte in the 4-byte 8088 queue. In some circumstances, the microprocessor must flush out the queue. For example, when a jump instruction is executed, the BIU starts to fetch information from the new location in memory and information in the queue that was fetched previously is discarded. In this situation the EU must wait until the BIU fetches the new instruction. This is referred to in computer science terminology as a *branch penalty*. In a pipelined CPU, this means that too much jumping around reduces the efficiency of a program. Pipelining in the 8088/86 has two stages: fetch and execute, but in more powerful computers pipelining can have many stages. The concept of pipelining combined with an increased number of data bus pins has, in recent years, led to the design of very powerful microprocessors.

Registers

In the CPU, registers are used to store information temporarily. That information could be one or two bytes of data to be processed or the address of data. The registers of the 8088/86 fall into the six categories outlined in Table 1-2. The general-purpose registers in 8088/86 microprocessors can be accessed as either 16-bit or 8-bit registers. All other registers can be accessed only as the full 16 bits. In the 8088/86, data types are either 8 or 16 bits. To access 12-bit data, for example, a 16-bit register must be used with the highest 4 bits set to 0. The bits of a register are numbered in descending order, as shown below.

AX	
16-bit register	
AH	AL
8-bit reg.	8-bit reg.

8-bit register:

| D7 | D6 | D5 | D4 | D3 | D2 | D1 | D0 |

16-bit register:

| D15 | D14 | D13 | D12 | D11 | D10 | D9 | D8 | D7 | D6 | D5 | D4 | D3 | D2 | D1 | D0 |

Different registers in the 8088/86 are used for different functions, and since some instructions use only specific registers to perform their tasks, the use of registers will be described in the context of instructions and their application in a given program. The first letter of each general register indicates its use. AX is used for the accumulator, BX as a base addressing register, CX is used as a counter in loop operations, and DX is used to point to data in I/O operations.

Table 1-2: Registers of the 8086/286 by Category

Category	Bits	Register Names
General	16	AX, BX, CX, DX
	8	AH, AL, BH, BL, CH, CL, DH, DL
Pointer	16	SP (stack pointer), BP (base pointer)
Index	16	SI (source index), DI (destination index)
Segment	16	CS (code segment), DS (data segment), SS (stack segment), ES (extra segment)
Instruction	16	IP (instruction pointer)
Flag	16	FR (flag register)

Note:
The general registers can be accessed as the full 16 bits (such as AX), or as the high byte only (AH) or low byte only (AL).

Review Questions

1. Explain the functions of the EU and the BIU.
2. What is pipelining, and how does it make the CPU execute faster?
3. Registers of the 8086 are either _____ bits or _____ bits in length.
4. List the 16-bit registers of the 8086 .

SECTION 1.3: INTRODUCTION TO ASSEMBLY PROGRAMMING

While the CPU can work only in binary, it can do so at very high speeds. However, it is quite tedious and slow for humans to deal with 0s and 1s in order to program the computer. A program that consists of 0s and 1s is called *machine language,* and in the early days of the computer, programmers actually coded programs in machine language. Although the hexadecimal system was used as a more efficient way to represent binary numbers, the process of working in machine code was still cumbersome for humans. Eventually, *Assembly languages* were developed which provided mnemonics for the machine code instructions, plus other features which made programming faster and less prone to error. The term *mnemonic* is frequently used in computer science and engineering literature to refer to codes and abbreviations that are relatively easy to remember. Assembly language programs must be translated into machine code by a program called an *assembler.* Assembly language is referred to as a *low-level language* because it deals directly with the internal structure of the CPU. To program in Assembly language, the programmer must know the number of registers and their size, as well as other details of the CPU.

Today, one can use many different programming languages, such as BASIC, Pascal, C, and numerous others. These languages are called *high-level languages* because the programmer does not have to be concerned with the internal details of the CPU. Whereas an assembler is used to translate an Assembly language program into machine code (sometimes called *object code*), high-level languages are translated into machine code by a program called a *compiler*. For instance, to write a program in C, one must use a C compiler to translate the program into machine language.

There are numerous assemblers available for translating 80x86 Assembly language programs into machine code. One of the most commonly used assemblers, MASM by Microsoft, is introduced in Chapter 2. The present chapter is designed to correspond to Appendix A: DEBUG programming. The program in this chapter can be entered and run with the use of the DEBUG program. If you are not familiar with DEBUG, refer to Appendix A for a tutorial introduction. The DEBUG utility is provided with the DOS operating system and therefore is widely accessible.

Assembly language programming

An Assembly language program consists of, among other things, a series of lines of Assembly language instructions. An Assembly language instruction consists of a mnemonic, optionally followed by one or two operands. The operands are the data items being manipulated, and the mnemonics are the commands to the CPU, telling it what to do with those items. We introduce Assembly language programming with two widely used instructions: the move and add instructions.

MOV instruction

Simply stated, the MOV instruction copies data from one location to another. It has the following format:

```
MOV    destination,source        ;copy source operand to destination
```

This instruction tells the CPU to move (in reality, copy) the source operand to the destination operand. For example, the instruction "MOV DX,CX" copies the contents of the register CX to register DX. After this instruction is executed, register DX will have the same value as register CX. The MOV instruction does not affect the source operand. The following program first loads CL with value 55H, then moves this value around to various registers inside the CPU.

```
MOV    CL,55H          ;move 55H into register CL
MOV    DL,CL           ;copy the contents of CL into DL (now DL=CL=55H)
MOV    AH,DL           ;copy the contents of DL into AH (now AH=DL=55H)
MOV    AL,AH           ;copy the contents of AH into AL (now AL=AH=55H)
MOV    BH,CL           ;copy the contents of CL into BH (now BH=CL=55H)
MOV    CH,BH           ;copy the contents of BH into CH (now CH=BH=55H)
```

The use of 16-bit registers is demonstrated below.

```
MOV    CX,468FH        ;move 468FH into CX (now CH=46,CL=8F)
MOV    AX,CX           ;copy contents of CX to AX (now AX=CX=468FH)
MOV    DX,AX           ;copy contents of AX to DX (now DX=AX=468FH)
MOV    BX,DX           ;copy contents of DX to BX (now BX=DX=468FH)
MOV    DI,BX           ;now DI=BX=468FH
MOV    SI,DI           ;now SI=DI=468FH
MOV    DS,SI           ;now DS=SI=468FH
MOV    BP,DI           ;now BP=DI=468FH
```

In the 8086 CPU, data can be moved among all the registers shown in Table 1-2 (except the flag register) as long as the source and destination registers match in size. Code such as "MOV AL,DX" will cause an error, since one cannot move the contents of a 16-bit register into an 8-bit register. The exception of the flag register means that there is no such instruction as "MOV FR,AX". Loading the flag register is done through other means, discussed in later chapters.

If data can be moved among all registers including the segment registers, can data be moved directly into all registers? The answer is no. Data can be moved directly into nonsegment registers only, using the MOV instruction. For example, look at the following instructions to see which are legal and which are illegal.

```
MOV    AX,58FCH      ;move 58FCH into AX    (LEGAL)
MOV    DX,6678H      ;move 6678H into DX    (LEGAL)
MOV    SI,924BH      ;move 924B  into SI    (LEGAL)
MOV    BP,2459H      ;move 2459H into BP    (LEGAL)
MOV    DS,2341H      ;move 2341H into DS    (ILLEGAL)
MOV    CX,8876H      ;move 8876H into CX    (LEGAL)
MOV    CS,3F47H      ;move 3F47H into CS    (ILLEGAL)
MOV    BH,99H        ;move 99H into BH      (LEGAL)
```

From the discussion above, note the following three points:

1. Values cannot be loaded directly into any segment register (CS, DS, ES, or SS). To load a value into a segment register, first load it to a nonsegment register and then move it to the segment register, as shown next.

```
MOV    AX,2345H      ;load 2345H into AX
MOV    DS,AX         ;then load the value of AX into DS

MOV    DI,1400H      ;load 1400H into DI
MOV    ES,DI         ;then move it into ES, now ES=DI=1400
```

2. If a value less than FFH is moved into a 16-bit register, the rest of the bits are assumed to be all zeros. For example, in "MOV BX,5" the result will be BX = 0005; that is, BH = 00 and BL = 05.

3. Moving a value that is too large into a register will cause an error.

```
MOV    BL,7F2H       ;ILLEGAL: 7F2H is larger than 8 bits
MOV    AX,2FE456H    ;ILLEGAL: the value is larger than AX
```

ADD instruction

The ADD instruction has the following format:

```
ADD    destination,source      ;ADD the source operand to the destination
```

The ADD instruction tells the CPU to add the source and the destination operands and put the result in the destination. To add two numbers such as 25H and 34H, each can be moved to a register and then added together:

```
MOV    AL,25H        ;move 25 into AL
MOV    BL,34H        ;move 34 into BL
ADD    AL,BL         ;AL = AL + BL
```

Executing the program above results in AL = 59H (25H + 34H = 59H) and BL = 34H. Notice that the contents of BL do not change. The program above can be written in many ways, depending on the registers used. Another way might be:

```
MOV    DH,25H          ;move 25 into DH
MOV    CL,34H          ;move 34 into CL
ADD    DH,CL           ;add CL to DH: DH = DH + CL
```

The program above results in DH = 59H and CL = 34H. There are always many ways to write the same program. One question that might come to mind after looking at the program above is whether it is necessary to move both data items into registers before adding them together. The answer is no, it is not necessary. Look at the following variation of the same program:

```
MOV    DH,25H          ;load one operand into DH
ADD    DH,34H          ;add the second operand to DH
```

In the case above, while one register contained one value, the second value followed the instruction as an operand. This is called an *immediate operand*. The examples shown so far for the ADD and MOV instructions show that the source operand can be either a register or immediate data. In the examples above, the destination operand has always been a register. The format for Assembly language instructions, descriptions of their use, and a listing of legal operand types are provided in Appendix B.

The largest number that an 8-bit register can hold is FFH. To use numbers larger than FFH (255 decimal), 16-bit registers such as AX, BX, CX, or DX must be used. For example, to add two numbers such as 34EH and 6A5H, the following program can be used:

```
MOV    AX,34EH         ;move 34EH into AX
MOV    DX,6A5H         ;move 6A5H into DX
ADD    DX,AX           ;add AX to DX: DX = DX + AX
```

Running the program above gives DX = 9F3H (34E + 6A5 = 9F3) and AX = 34E. Again, any 16-bit nonsegment registers could have been used to perform the action above:

```
MOV    CX,34EH         ;load 34EH into CX
ADD    CX,6A5H         ;add 6A5H to CX (now CX=9F3H)
```

The general-purpose registers are typically used in arithmetic operations. Register AX is sometimes referred to as the accumulator.

Review Questions

1. Write the Assembly language instruction to move value 1234H into register BX.
2. Write the Assembly language instructions to add the values 16H and ABH. Place the result in register AX.
3. No value can be moved directly into which registers?
4. What is the largest hex value that can be moved into a 16-bit register? Into an 8-bit register? What are the decimal equivalents of these hex values?

SECTION 1.4: INTRODUCTION TO PROGRAM SEGMENTS

A typical Assembly language program consists of at least three segments: a code segment, a data segment, and a stack segment. The *code segment* contains the Assembly language instructions that perform the tasks that the program was designed to accomplish. The *data segment* is used to store information (data) that needs to to be processed by the instructions in the code segment. The *stack* is used to store information temporarily. In this section we describe the code and data segments of a program in the context of some examples and discuss the way data is stored in memory. The stack segment is covered in Section 1.5.

Origin and definition of the segment

A segment is an area of memory that includes up to
on an address evenly divisible by 16 (such an address ends
size of 64K bytes came about because the 8085 microproc
maximum of 64K bytes of physical memory since it had only
lines (2^{16} = 64K). This limitation was carried into the des
ensure compatibility. Whereas in the 8085 there was only
for all code, data, and stack information, in the 8088/86 there
of memory assigned to each category. Within an Assembly la
categories are called the code segment, data segment, and s
reason, the 8088/86 can only handle a maximum of 64K bytes of code and 64K
bytes of data and 64K bytes of stack at any given time, although it has a range of 1
megabyte of memory because of its 20 address pins (2^{20} = 1 megabyte). How to
move this window of 64K bytes to cover all 1 megabyte of memory is discussed
below, after we discuss logical address and physical address.

Logical address and physical address

In Intel literature concerning the 8086, there are three types of addresses
mentioned frequently: the physical address, the offset address, and the logical
address. The *physical address* is the 20-bit address that is actually put on the address
pins of the 8086 microprocessor and decoded by the memory interfacing circuitry.
This address can have a range of 00000H to FFFFFH for the 8086 and real-mode
286, 386, and 486 CPUs. This is an actual physical location in RAM or ROM within
the 1 megabyte memory range. The *offset address* is a location within a 64K-byte
segment range. Therefore, an offset address can range from 0000H to FFFFH. The
logical address consists of a segment value and an offset address. The differences
among these addresses and the process of converting from one to another is best
understood in the context of some examples, as shown next.

Code segment

To execute a program, the 8086
fetches the instructions (opcodes and operands) from the code segment. The logical address of an instruction always

CS					IP			
2	5	0	0	:	9	5	F	3

consists of a CS (code segment) and an IP (instruction pointer), shown in CS:IP
format. The physical address for the location of the instruction is generated by
shifting the CS left one hex digit and then adding it to the IP. IP contains the offset
address. The resulting 20-bit address is called the physical address since it is put
on the external physical address bus pins to be decoded by the memory decoding
circuitry. To clarify this important concept, assume values in CS and IP as shown
in the diagram. The offset address is contained in IP, in this case it is 95F3H. The
logical address is CS:IP, or 2500:95F3H. The physical address will be 25000 + 95F3
= 2E5F3H. The physical address of an instruction can be calculated as follows:

1. Start with CS.

2	5	0	0

2. Shift left CS.

2	5	0	0	0

3. Add IP.

2	E	5	F	3

The microprocessor will retrieve the instruction from memory locations starting at 2E5F3. Since IP can have a minimum value of 0000H and a maximum of FFFFH, the logical address range in this example is 2500:0000 to 2500:FFFF. This means that the lowest memory location of the code segment above will be 25000H (25000 + 0000) and the highest memory location will be 34FFFH (25000 + FFFF). What happens if the desired instructions are located beyond these two limits? The answer is that the value of CS must be changed to access those instructions.

Example 1-1

If CS = 24F6H and IP = 634AH, show:
(a) The logical address
(b) The offset address
 and calculate:
(c) The physical address
(d) The lower range
(e) The upper range of the code segment

Solution:
(a) 24F6:634A   (b) 634A
(c) 2B2AA (24F60 + 634A)   (d) 24F60 (24F60 + 0000)
(e) 34F5F (24F60 + FFFF)

Logical address vs. physical address in the code segment

In the code segment, CS and IP hold the logical address of the instructions to be executed. The following Assembly language instructions have been assembled (translated into machine code) and stored in memory. The three columns show the logical address of CS:IP, the machine code stored at that address and the corresponding Assembly language code. This information can easily be generated by the DEBUG program using the Unassemble command.

Logical address CS:IP	Machine language opcode and operand	Assembly language mnemonics and operand
1132:0100	B057	MOV AL,57
1132:0102	B686	MOV DH,86
1132:0104	B272	MOV DL,72
1132:0106	89D1	MOV CX,DX
1132:0108	88C7	MOV BH,AL
1132:010A	B39F	MOV BL,9F
1132:010C	B420	MOV AH,20
1132:010E	01D0	ADD AX,DX
1132:0110	01D9	ADD CX,BX
1132:0112	05351F	ADD AX,1F35

The program above shows that the byte at address 1132:0100 contains B0, which is the opcode for moving a value into register AL, and address 1132:0101 contains the operand (in this case 57) to be moved to AL. Therefore, the instruction "MOV AL,57" has a machine code of B057, where B0 is the opcode and 57 is the operand. Similarly, the machine code B686 is located in memory locations 1132:0102 and 1132:0103 and represents the opcode and the operand for the instruction "MOV DH,86". The physical address is an actual location within RAM (or even ROM). The following are the physical addresses and the contents of each location for the program above. Remember that it is the physical address that is put on the address bus by the 8086 CPU to be decoded by the memory circuitry:

Logical address	Physical address	Machine code contents
1132:0100	11420	B0
1132:0101	11421	57
1132:0102	11422	B6
1132:0103	11423	86
1132:0104	11424	B2
1132:0105	11425	72
1132:0106	11426	89
1132:0107	11427	D1
1132:0108	11428	88
1132:0109	11429	C7
1132:010A	1142A	B3
1132:010B	1142B	9F
1132:010C	1142C	B4
1132:010D	1142D	20
1132:010E	1142E	01
1132:010F	1142F	D0
1132:0110	11430	01
1132:0111	11431	D9
1132:0112	11432	05
1132:0113	11433	35
1132:0114	11434	1F

Data segment

Assume that a program is being written to add 5 bytes of data, such as 25H, 12H, 15H, 1FH, and 2BH, where each byte represents a person's daily overtime pay. One way to add them is as follows:

```
MOV   AL,00H       ;initialize AL
ADD   AL,25H       ;add 25H to AL
ADD   AL,12H       ;add 12H to AL
ADD   AL,15H       ;add 15H to AL
ADD   AL,1FH       ;add 1FH to AL
ADD   AL,2BH       ;add 2BH to AL
```

In the program above, the data and code are mixed together in the instructions. The problem with writing the program this way is that if the data changes, the code must be searched for every place the data is included, and the data retyped. For this reason, the idea arose to set aside an area of memory strictly for data. In 80x86 microprocessors, the area of memory set aside for data is called the data segment. Just as the code segment is associated with CS and IP as its segment register and offset, the data segment uses register DS and an offset value.

The following demonstrates how data can be stored in the data segment and the program rewritten so that it can be used for any set of data. Assume that the offset for the data segment begins at 200H. The data is placed in memory locations:

```
DS:0200 = 25
DS:0201 = 12
DS:0202 = 15
DS:0203 = 1F
DS:0204 = 2B
```

and the program can be rewritten as follows:

```
MOV   AL,0         ;clear AL
ADD   AL,[0200]    ;add the contents of DS:200 to AL
ADD   AL,[0201]    ;add the contents of DS:201 to AL
ADD   AL,[0202]    ;add the contents of DS:202 to AL
ADD   AL,[0203]    ;add the contents of DS:203 to AL
ADD   AL,[0204]    ;add the contents of DS:204 to AL
```

Notice that the offset address is enclosed in brackets. The brackets indicate that the operand represents the address of the data and not the data itself. If the brackets were not included, as in "MOV AL,0200", the CPU would attempt to move 200 into AL instead of the contents of offset address 200. Keep in mind that there is one important difference in the format of code for MASM and DEBUG in that DEBUG assumes that all numbers are in hex (no "H" suffix is required), whereas MASM assumes that they are in decimal and the "H" must be included for hex data.

This program will run with any set of data. Changing the data has no effect on the code. Although this program is an improvement over the preceding one, it can be improved even further. If the data had to be stored at a different offset address, say 450H, the program would have to be rewritten. One way to solve this problem would be to use a register to hold the offset address, and before each ADD, to increment the register to access the next byte. Next a decision must be made as to which register to use. The 8086/88 allows only the use of registers BX, SI, and DI as offset registers for the data segment. In other words, while CS uses only the IP register as an offset, DS uses only BX, DI, and SI to hold the offset address of the data. The term *pointer* is often used for a register holding an offset address. In the following example, BX is used as a pointer:

```
MOV    AL,0           ;initialize AL
MOV    BX,0200H       ;BX points to the offset addr of first byte
ADD    AL,[BX]        ;add the first byte to AL
INC    BX             ;increment BX to point to the next byte
ADD    AL,[BX]        ;add the next byte to AL
INC    BX             ;increment the pointer
ADD    AL,[BX]        ;add the next byte to AL
INC    BX             ;increment the pointer
ADD    AL,[BX]        ;add the last byte to AL
```

The "INC" instruction adds 1 to (increments) its operand. "INC BX" achieves the same result as "ADD BX,1". For the program above, if the offset address where data is located is changed, only one instruction will need to be modified and the rest of the program will be unaffected. Examining the program above shows that there is a pattern of two instructions being repeated. This leads to the idea of using a loop to repeat certain instructions. Implementing a loop requires familiarity with the flag register, discussed later in this chapter.

Logical address and physical address in the data segment

The physical address for data is calculated using the same rules as for the code segment. That is, the physical address of data is calculated by shifting DS left one hex digit and then adding the offset value, as shown in the following examples:

Example 1-2

Assume that DS is 5000 and the offset is 1950. Calculate the physical address of the byte.

Solution: DS   :   offset

| 5 | 0 | 0 | 0 | : | 1 | 9 | 5 | 0 |

The physical address will be 50000 + 1950 = 51950.

1. Start with DS. | 5 | 0 | 0 | 0 |

2. Shift DS left. | 5 | 0 | 0 | 0 | 0 |

3. Add the offset. | 5 | 1 | 9 | 5 | 0 |

Example 1-3

If DS = 7FA2H and the offset is 438EH,
(a) Calculate the physical address.   (b) Calculate the lower range.
(c) Calculate the upper range of the data segment.   (d) Show the logical address.

Solution:
(a) 83DAE (7FA20 + 438E)   (b) 7FA20 (7FA20 + 0000)
(c) 8FA1F (7FA20 + FFFF)   (d) 7FA2:438E

Example 1-4

Assume that the DS register is 578C. To access a given byte of data at physical memory location 67F66, does the data segment cover the range where the data is located? If not, what changes need to be made?

Solution:
No, since the range is 578C0 to 678BF, location 67F66 is not included in this range. To access that byte, DS must be changed so that its range will include that byte.

Little endian convention

Previous examples used 8-bit or 1-byte data. In this case the bytes are stored one after another in memory. What happens when 16-bit data is used? For example:

```
MOV    AX,35F3H      ;load 35F3H into AX
MOV    [1500],AX     ;copy the contents of AX to offset 1500H
```

In cases like this, the low byte goes to the low memory location and the high byte goes to the high memory address. In the example above, memory location DS:1500 contains F3H and memory location DS:1501 contains 35H.

```
DS:1500 = F3          DS:1501 = 35
```

This convention is called little endian versus big endian. The origin of the terms *big endian* and *little endian* is from a *Gulliver's Travels* story about how an egg should be opened: from the little end or the big end. In the big endian method, the high byte goes to the low address, whereas in the little endian method, the high byte goes to the high address and the low byte to the low address. All Intel microprocessors and many minicomputers, notably Digital VAX, use the little endian convention. Motorola microprocessors (used in the Macintosh), along with some mainframes, use big endian. This difference might seem as trivial as whether

---

Example 1-5

Assume memory locations with the following contents: DS:6826 = 48 and DS:6827 = 22. Show the contents of register BX in the instruction "MOV BX,[6826]".

Solution:
According to the little endian convention used in all 80x86 microprocessors, register BL should contain the value from the low offset address 6826 and register BH the value from offset address 6827, giving BL = 48H and BH = 22H.

DS:6826 = 48
DS:6827 = 22

BH	BL
22	48

---

to break an egg from the big end or little end, but it is a nuisance in converting software from one camp to be run on a computer of the other camp.

Extra segment (ES)

ES is a segment register used as an extra data segment. Although in many normal programs this segment is not used, its use is absolutely essential for string operations and is discussed in detail in Chapter 6.

Memory map of the IBM PC

For a program to be executed on the PC, DOS must first load it into RAM. Where in RAM will it be loaded? To answer that question, we must first explain some very important concepts concerning memory in the PC. The 20-bit address of the 8088/86 allows a total of 1 megabyte (1024K bytes) of memory space with the address range 00000 - FFFFF. During the design phase of the first IBM PC, engineers had to decide on the allocation of the 1-megabyte memory space to various sections of the PC. This memory allocation is called a *memory map*. The memory map of the IBM PC is shown in Figure 1-3. Of this 1 megabyte, 640K bytes from address 00000 - 9FFFFH were set aside for RAM. The 128K bytes from A0000H - BFFFFH were allocated for video memory. The remaining 256K bytes from C0000H -FFFFFH were set aside for ROM.

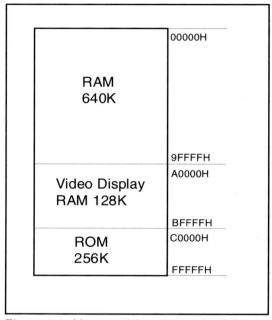

Figure 1-3. Memory Allocation in the PC

More about RAM

In the early 1980s, most PCs came with only 64K to 256K bytes of RAM memory, which was considered more than adequate at the time. Users had to buy memory expansion boards to expand memory up to 640K if they needed additional memory. The need for expansion depends on the DOS version being used and the memory needs of the application software being run. The DOS operating system first allocates the available RAM on the PC for its own use and then lets the rest be used for applications such as word processors. The complicated task of managing RAM memory is left to DOS since the amount of memory used by DOS varies among its various versions and since different computers have different amounts of RAM, plus the fact that the memory needs of application packages vary. For this reason we do not assign any values for the CS, DS, and SS registers since such an assignment means specifying an exact physical address in the range 00000 - 9FFFFH, and this is beyond the knowledge of the user. Another reason is that assigning a physical address might work on a given PC but it might not work on a PC with a different DOS version and RAM size. In other words, the program would not be portable to another PC. Therefore, memory management is one of the most important functions of the DOS operating system and should be left to DOS. This is very important to remember because in many examples in this book we have values for the segment registers CS, DS, and SS which will be different from the values that readers will get on their PCs. Therefore, do not try to assign the value to the segment registers to comply with the values in this book.

Video RAM

From A0000H to BFFFFH is set aside for video. The amount used and the location varies depending on the video board installed on the PC. Table E-2 of Appendix E lists the starting addresses for video boards.

More about ROM

From C0000H to FFFFFH is set aside for ROM. Not all the memory space in this range is used by the PC's ROM. Of this 256K bytes, only the 64K bytes from location F0000H - FFFFFH are used by BIOS (basic input/output system) ROM. Some of the remaining space is used by various adapter cards (such as cards for hard disks), and the rest are free. In recent years, newer versions of DOS have gained some very powerful memory management capabilities and can put to good use all the unused memory space beyond 640. The 640K-byte memory space from 00000 to 9FFFFH is referred to as *conventional memory*, while the 384K bytes from A0000H to FFFFFH are called the UMB (*upper memory block*) in DOS 5 literature. A complete discussion of the various memory terminology and configurations such as expanded and extended memory appears in Volume 2 of this series.

Function of BIOS ROM

Since the CPU can only execute programs that are stored in memory, there must be some permanent (nonvolatile) memory to hold the programs telling the CPU what to do when the power is turned on. This collection of programs held by ROM is referred to as BIOS in the PC literature. "BIOS", which stands for *basic input output system*, contains programs to test RAM and other components connected to the CPU. It also contains programs that allow DOS to communicate with peripheral devices such as the keyboard, video, printer, and disk. It is the function of BIOS to test all the devices connected to the PC when the computer is turned on, and to report any errors. For example, if the keyboard is disconnected from the PC before the computer is turned on, BIOS will report an error on the screen, indicating that condition. It is only after testing and setting up the peripherals that BIOS will load DOS from disk into RAM and hand over control of the PC to DOS. Although there are occasions when either DOS or applications programs need to use programs in BIOS ROM (as will be seen in Chapter 4), DOS always controls the PC once it is loaded.

Review Questions

1. A segment is an area of memory that includes up to _____ bytes.
2. How large is a segment in the 8086? Can the physical address 346E0 be the starting address for a segment? Why or why not?
3. State the difference between the physical and logical addresses.
4. A physical address is a _____ -bit address; an offset address is a _____ -bit address.
5. Which register is used as the offset register with segment register CS?
6. If BX = 1234H and the instruction "MOV [2400],BX" were executed, what would be the contents of memory locations at offsets 2400 and 2401?

SECTION 1.5: MORE ABOUT SEGMENTS IN THE 80x86

In this section we examine the concept of the stack, its use in 80x86 microprocessors, and its implementation in the stack segment. Then more advanced concepts relating to segments are discussed, such as overlapping segments.

What is a stack, and why is it needed?

The *stack* is a section of read/write memory (RAM) used by the CPU to store information temporarily. The CPU needs this storage area since there are only a limited number of registers. There must be some place for the CPU to store information safely and temporarily. Now one might ask why not design a CPU with more registers? The reason is that in the design of the CPU, every transistor is precious and not enough of them are available to build hundreds of registers. In addition, how many registers should a CPU have to satisfy every possible program and application? All applications and programming techniques are not the same. In a similar manner, it would be too costly in terms of real estate and construction costs to build a 50-room house to hold everything one might possibly buy throughout his or her lifetime. Instead, one builds or rents a shed for storage.

Having looked at the advantages of having a stack, what are the disadvantages? The main disadvantage of the stack is its access time. Since the stack is in RAM, it takes much longer to access compared to the access time of registers. After all, the registers are inside the CPU and RAM is outside. This is the reason that some very powerful (and consequently, expensive) computers do not have a stack; the CPU has a large number of registers to work with.

How stacks are accessed

If the stack is a section of RAM, there must be registers inside the CPU to point to it. The two main registers used to access the stack are the SS (stack segment) register and the SP (stack pointer) register. These registers must be loaded before any instructions accessing the stack are used. Every register inside the 80x86 (except segment registers and SP) can be stored into the stack and brought back into the CPU from the stack memory. The storing of a CPU register in the stack is called a *push,* and loading the contents of the stack into the CPU register is called a *pop.* In other words, a register is pushed onto the stack to store it and popped off the stack to retrieve it. The job of the SP is very critical when push and pop are performed. In the 80x86, the stack pointer register (SP) points at the current memory location used for the top of the stack and as data is pushed onto the stack it is decremented. It is incremented as data is popped off the stack into the CPU. When an instruction pushes or pops a general-purpose register, it must be the entire 16-bit register. In other words, one must code "PUSH AX"; there are no instructions such as "PUSH AL" or "PUSH AH". The reason that the SP is decremented after the push is to make sure that the stack is growing downward from upper addresses to lower addresses. This is the opposite of the IP (instruction pointer). As was seen in the preceding section, the IP points to the next instruction to be executed and is incremented as each instruction is executed. To ensure that the code section and stack section of the program never write over each other, they are located at opposite ends of the RAM memory set aside for the program and they grow toward each other but must not meet. If they meet, the program will crash. To see how the stack grows, look at the following examples.

Pushing onto the stack

Notice in Example 1-6 that as each PUSH is executed, the contents of the register are saved on the stack and SP is decremented by 2. For every byte of data saved on the stack, SP is decremented once, and since push is saving the contents of a 16-bit register, it is decremented twice. Notice also how the data is stored on the stack. In the 80x86, the lower byte is always stored in the memory location with the lower address. That is the reason that 24H, the contents of AH, is saved in memory location with address 1235 and AL in location 1234.

Popping the stack

Popping the contents of the stack back into the 80x86 CPU is the opposite process of pushing. With every pop, the top 2 bytes of the stack are copied to the register specified by the instruction and the stack pointer is incremented twice. Although the data actually remains in memory, it is not accessible since the stack pointer is beyond that point. Example 1-7 demonstrates the POP instruction.

Example 1-6

Assuming that SP = 1236, AX = 24B6, DI = 85C2, and DX = 5F93, show the contents of the stack as each of the following instructions is executed:

```
PUSH  AX
PUSH  DI
PUSH  DX
```

Solution:

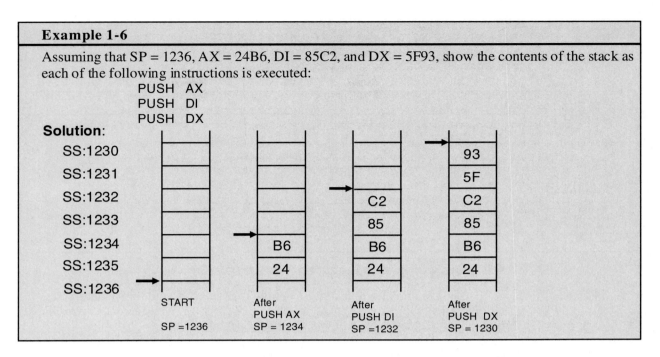

Example 1-7

Assuming that the stack is as shown below, and SP = 18FA, show the contents of the stack and registers as each of the following instructions is executed:

```
POP  CX
POP  DX
POP  BX
```

Solution:

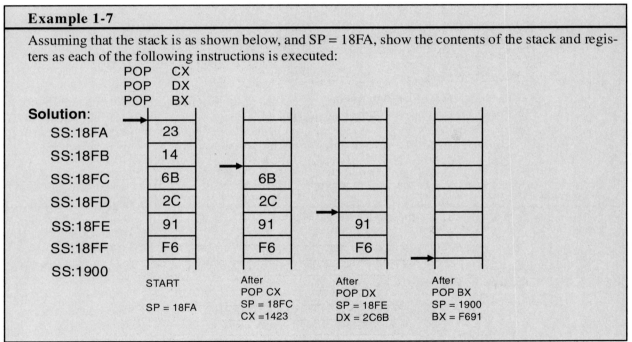

Logical address vs. physical address for the stack

Now one might ask, what is the exact physical location of the stack? That depends on the value of the stack segment (SS) register and SP, the stack pointer. To compute physical addresses for the stack, the same principle is applied as was used for the code and data segments. The method is to shift left SS and then add offset SP, the stack pointer register. This is demonstrated in Example 1-8.

What values are assigned to the SP and SS, and who assigns them? It is the job of the DOS operating system to assign the values for the SP and SS since memory management is the responsibility of the operating system. Before leaving the discussion of the stack, two points must be made. First, in the 80x86 literature, the top of the stack is the last stack location occupied. This is different from other

---

CPUs. Second, BP is another register that can be used as an offset into the stack, but it has very special applications and is widely used to access parameters passed between Assembly language programs and high-level language programs such as C. This is discussed in Chapter 7.

Example 1-8

If SS = 3500H and the SP is FFFEH,
(a) Calculate the physical address of the stack.   (b) Calculate the lower range.
(c) Calculate the upper range of the stack segment.   (d) Show the logical address of the stack.

Solution:
(a) 44FFE (35000 + FFFE)   (b) 35000 (35000 + 0000)
(c) 44FFF (35000 + FFFF)   (d) 3500:FFFE

A few more words about segments in the 80x86

Can a single physical address belong to many different logical addresses? Yes, look at the case of a physical address value of 15020H. There are many possible logical addresses that represent this single physical address:

Logical address (hex)	Physical address (hex)
1000:5020	15020
1500:0020	15020
1502:0000	15020
1400:1020	15020
1302:2000	15020

This shows the dynamic behavior of the segment and offset concept in the 8086 CPU. One last point that must be clarified is the case when adding the offset to the shifted segment register results in an address beyond the maximum allowed range of FFFFFH. In that situation, wrap-around will occur. This is shown in the following example.

Example 1-9

What is the range of physical addresses if CS = FF59?

Solution:
The low range is FF590 (FF590 + 0000). The range goes to FFFFF and wraps around, from 00000 to 0F58F (FF590 + FFFF = 0F58F), which is illustrated below.

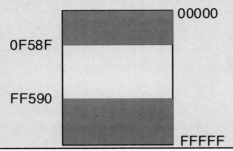

Overlapping

In calculating the physical address, it is possible that two segments can overlap, which is desirable in some circumstances. For example, overlapping is used in COM files, as will be seen in Chapter 2. Figure 1-4 illustrates overlapping and nonoverlapping segments.

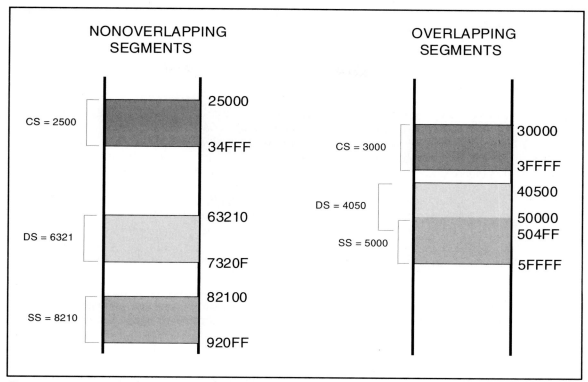

Figure 1-4. Nonoverlapping vs. Overlapping Segments

Flag register

The flag register is a 16-bit register sometimes referred to as the *status register*. Although the register is 16 bits wide, only some of the bits are used. The rest are either undefined or reserved by Intel. Six of the flags are called conditional flags, meaning that they indicate some condition that resulted after an instruction was executed. These six are CF, PF, AF, ZF, SF, and OF. The three remaining flags are sometimes called control flags since they are used to control the operation of instructions before they are executed. A diagram of the flag register is shown in Figure 1-5.

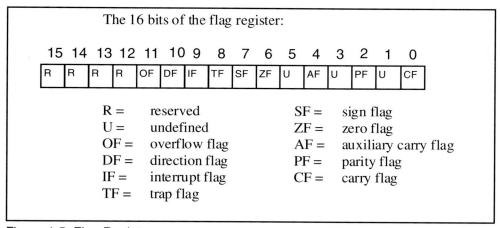

Figure 1-5. Flag Register
(Reprinted by permission of Intel Corporation, Copyright Intel Corp. 1989)

Bits of the flag register

Below are listed the bits of the flag register that are used in 80x86 Assembly language programming. A brief explanation of each bit is given. How these flag bits are used will be seen in programming examples throughout the textbook.

CF, the Carry Flag . This flag is set whenever there is a carry out, either from d7 after an 8-bit operation, or from d15 after a 16-bit data operation.

PF, the Parity Flag. After certain operations, the parity of the result's low-order byte is checked. If the byte has an even number of 1s, the parity flag is set to 1; otherwise, it is cleared.

AF, Auxiliary Carry Flag . If there is a carry from d3 to d4 of an operation, this bit is set; otherwise, it is cleared (set equal to zero). This flag is used by the instructions that perform BCD (binary coded decimal) arithmetic.

ZF, the Zero Flag. The zero flag is set to 1 if the result of an arithmetic or logical operation is zero; otherwise, it is cleared.

SF, the Sign Flag. Binary representation of signed numbers uses the most significant bit as the sign bit. After arithmetic or logic operations, the status of this sign bit is copied into the SF, thereby indicating the sign of the result.

TF, the Trap Flag. When this flag is set it allows the program to single-step, meaning to execute one instruction at a time. Single-stepping is used for debugging purposes.

IF, Interrupt Enable Flag. This bit is set or cleared to enable or disable only the external maskable interrupt requests.

DF, the Direction Flag. This bit is used to control the direction of string operations, which are described in Chapter 6.

OF, the Overflow Flag. This flag is set whenever the result of a signed number operation is too large, causing the high-order bit to overflow into the sign bit. In general, the carry flag is used to detect errors in unsigned arithmetic operations. The overflow flag is only used to detect errors in signed arithmetic operations.

Flag register and ADD instruction

In this section we examine the impact of the ADD instruction on the flag register as an example of the use of the flag bits. The flag bits affected by the ADD instruction are CF (carry flag), PF (parity flag), AF (auxiliary carry flag), ZF (zero flag), SF (sign flag), and OF (overflow flag). The overflow flag will be covered in Chapter 6, since it relates only to signed number arithmetic. To understand how each of these flag bits is affected, look at Examples 1-10 and 1-11.

Example 1-10

Show how the flag register is affected by the addition of 38H and 2FH.

Solution:

```
        MOV   BH,38H      ;BH= 38H
        ADD   BH,2FH      ;add 2F to BH, now BH=67H

            38            0011   1000
      +     2F            0010   1111
            67            0110   0111
```

CF = 0 since there is no carry beyond d7
PF = 0 since there is an odd number of 1s in the result
AF = 1 since there is a carry from d3 to d4
ZF = 0 since the result is not zero
SF = 0 since d7 of the result is zero

Example 1-11

Show how the flag register is affected by

```
        MOV     AL,9CH          ;AL=9CH
        MOV     DH,64H          ;DH=64H
        ADD     AL,DH           ;now AL=0
```

Solution:

```
        9C              1001    1100
   +    64              0110    0100
        00              0000    0000
```

CF=1 since there is a carry beyond d7
PF=1 since there is an even number of 1s in the result
AF=1 since there is a carry from d3 to d4
ZF=1 since the result is zero
SF=0 since d7 of the result is zero

The same concepts apply for 16-bit addition, as shown in Examples 1-12 and 1-13. It is important to notice the differences between 8-bit and 16-bit operations in terms of their impact on the flag bits. The parity bit only counts the lower 8-bits of the result and is set accordingly. Also notice the CF bit. The carry flag is set if there is a carry beyond bit d15 instead of bit d7.

Example 1-12

Show how the flag register is affected by
```
        MOV     AX,34F5H        ;AX= 34F5H
        ADD     AX,95EBH        ;now AX= CAE0H
```
Solution:

```
        34F5            0011    0100    1111    0101
   +    95EB            1001    0101    1110    1011
        CAE0            1100    1010    1110    0000
```

CF = 0 since there is no carry beyond d15
PF = 0 since there is an odd number of 1s in the lower byte
AF = 1 since there is a carry from d3 to d4
ZF = 0 since the result is not zero
SF = 1 since d15 of the result is one

Example 1-13

Show how the flag register is affected by
```
        MOV     BX,AAAAH        ;BX= AAAAH
        ADD     BX,5556H        ;now BX= 0000H
```
Solution:

```
        AAAA            1010    1010    1010    1010
   +    5556            0101    0101    0101    0110
        0000            0000    0000    0000    0000
```

CF = 1 since there is a carry beyond d15
PF = 1 since there is an even number of 1s in the lower byte
AF = 1 since there is a carry from d3 to d4
ZF = 1 since the result is zero
SF = 0 since d15 of the result is zero

Notice the zero flag (ZF) status after the execution of the ADD instruction. Since the result of the entire 16-bit operation is zero (meaning the contents of BX), ZF is set to high. Do all instructions affect the flag bits? The answer is no, some instructions such as data transfers (MOV) affect no flags. As an exercise, run these examples on DEBUG to see the effect of various instructions on the flag register.

Example 1-14

Show how the flag register is affected by

```
MOV   AX,94C2H      ;AX=94C2H
MOV   BX,323EH      ;BX=323EH
ADD   AX,BX         ;now AX=C700H
MOV   DX,AX         ;now DX=C700H
MOV   CX,DX         ;now CX=C700H
```

Solution:

```
      94C2        1001   0100   1100   0010
  +   323E        0011   0010   0011   1110
      C700        1100   0111   0000   0000
```

After the ADD operation, the following are the flag bits:
CF = 0 since there is no carry beyond d15
PF = 1 since there is an even number of 1s in the lower byte
AF = 1 since there is a carry from d3 to d4
ZF = 0 since the result is not zero
SF = 1 since d15 of the result is 1

Running the instructions above in DEBUG will verify that MOV instructions have no effect on the flag. How these flag bits are used in programming is discussed in future chapters in the context of many applications. In Appendix B we give additional information about the effect of various instructions on the flags.

Use of the zero flag for looping

One of the most widely used applications of the flag register is the use of the zero flag to implement program loops. The term *loop* refers to a set of instructions that is repeated a number of times. For example, to add 5 bytes of data, a counter can be used to keep track of how many times the loop needs to be repeated. Each time the addition is performed the counter is decremented and the the zero flag is checked. When the counter becomes zero, the zero flag is set (ZF = 1) and the loop is stopped. The following shows the implementation of the looping concept in the program, which adds 5 bytes of data. Register CX is used to hold the counter and BX is the offset pointer (SI or DI could have been used instead). AL is initialized before the start of the loop. In each iteration, ZF is checked by the JNZ instruction. JNZ stands for "Jump Not Zero" meaning that if ZF = 0, jump to a new address. If ZF = 1, the jump is not performed and the instruction below the jump will be executed. Notice that the JNZ instruction must come immediately after the instruction that decrements CX since JNZ needs to check the affect of "DEC CX" on the zero flag. If any instruction were placed between them, that instruction might affect the zero flag.

```
          MOV   CX,05        ;CX holds the loop count
          MOV   BX,0200H     ;BX holds the offset data address
          MOV   AL,00        ;initialize AL
ADD_LP:   ADD   AL,[BX]      ;add the next byte to AL
          INC   BX           ;increment the data pointer
          DEC   CX           ;decrement the loop counter
          JNZ   ADD_LP       ;jump to next iteration if counter not zero
```

Review Questions

1. Which registers are used to access the stack?
2. With each PUSH instruction, the stack pointer register SP is (circle one) incremented/decremented by 2.
3. With each POP instruction, SP is (circle one) incremented/decremented by 2.
4. List three possible logical addresses corresponding to physical address 143F0.
5. The ADD instruction can affect which bits of the flag register?
6. The carry flag will be set to 1 in an 8-bit ADD if there is a carry out from bit ___.
7. CF will be set to 1 in a 16-bit ADD if there is a carry out from bit ____.

SECTION 1.6: 80x86 ADDRESSING MODES

The CPU can access operands (data) in various ways, called addressing modes. The number of addressing modes is determined when the microprocessor is designed and cannot be changed. The 80x86 provides a total of seven distinct addressing modes:

(1) register
(2) immediate
(3) direct
(4) register indirect
(5) based relative
(6) indexed relative
(7) based indexed relative

Each addressing mode is explained below, and application examples are given in later chapters as the reader understands Assembly language programming in greater detail. Since the reader is now familiar with ADD and MOV instructions, these are used below to explain addressing modes.

Register addressing mode

The register addressing mode involves the use of registers to hold the data to be manipulated. Memory is not accessed when this addressing mode is executed; therefore, it is relatively fast. Examples of register addressing mode follow:

```
MOV   BX,DX          ;copy the contents of DX into BX
MOV   ES,AX          ;copy the contents of AX into ES
ADD   AL,BH          ;add the contents of BH to contents of AL
```

It should be noted that the source and destination registers must match in size. In other words coding "MOV CL,AX" will give an error, since the source is a 16-bit register and the destination is an 8-bit register.

Immediate addressing mode

In the immediate addressing mode, the source operand is a constant. In immediate addressing mode, as the name implies, when the instruction is assembled, the operand comes immediately after the opcode. For this reason, this addressing mode executes quickly. However, in programming it has limited use. Immediate addressing mode can be used to load information into any of the registers except the segment registers and flag registers. Examples:

```
MOV   AX,2550H       ;move 2550H into AX
MOV   CX,625         ;load the decimal value 625 into CX
MOV   BL,40H         ;load 40H into BL
```

To move information to the segment registers, the data must first be moved to a general-purpose register and then to the segment register. Example:

```
MOV    AX,2550H
MOV    DS,AX
```

In other words, the following would produce an error:

```
MOV DS,0123H          ;illegal!!
```

In the first two addressing modes, the operands are either inside the microprocessor or tagged along with the instruction. In most programs, the data to be processed is often in some memory location outside the CPU. There are many ways of accessing the data in the data segment. The following describes those different methods.

Direct addressing mode

In the direct addressing mode the data is in some memory location(s) and the address of the data in memory comes immediately after the instruction. Note that in immediate addressing, the operand itself is provided with the instruction, whereas in direct addressing mode, the address of the operand is provided with the instruction. This address is the offset address and one can calculate the physical address by shifting left the DS register and adding it to the offset as follows:

```
MOV    DL,[2400]        ;move contents of DS:2400H into DL
```

In this case the physical address is calculated by combining the contents of offset location 2400 with DS, the data segment register. Notice the bracket around the address. In the absence of this bracket it will give an error since it is interpreted to move the value 2400 (16-bit data) into register DL, an 8-bit register.

Example 1-15

Find the physical address of the memory location and its contents after the execution of the following, assuming that DS = 1512H.
```
MOV        AL,99H
MOV        [3518],AL
```

Solution:
First AL is initialized to 99H, then in line two, the contents of AL are moved to logical address DS:3518 which is 1512:3518. Shifting DS left and adding it to the offset gives the physical address of 18638H (15120H + 3518H = 18638H). That means after the execution of the second instruction, the memory location with address 18638H will contain the value 99H.

Register indirect addressing mode

In the register indirect addressing mode, the address of the memory location where the operand resides is held by a register. The registers used for this purpose are SI, DI, and BX. If these three registers are used as pointers, that is, if they hold the offset of the memory location, they must be combined with DS in order to generate the 20-bit physical address. For example:

```
MOV    AL,[BX]          ;moves into AL the contents of the memory location
                        ;pointed to by DS:BX.
```

Notice that BX is in brackets. In the absence of brackets, it is interpreted as an instruction moving the contents of register BX to AL (which gives an error because source and destination do not match) instead of the contents of the memory location whose offset address is in BX. The physical address is calculated by shifting DS left one hex position and adding BX to it. The same rules apply when using register SI or DI.

```
MOV    CL,[SI]          ;move contents of DS:SI into CL
MOV    [DI],AH          ;move contents of AH into DS:DI
```

In the examples above, the data moved is byte sized. The following example shows 16-bit operands.

Example 1-16

Assume that DS = 1120, SI = 2498, and AX = 17FE. Show the contents of memory locations after the execution of

MOV [SI],AX

Solution:

The contents of AX are moved into memory locations with logical address DS:SI and DS:SI + 1; therefore, the physical address starts at DS (shifted left) + SI = 13698. According to the little endian convention, low address 13698H contains FE, the low byte, and high address 13699H will contain 17, the high byte.

Based relative addressing mode

In the based relative addressing mode, base registers BX and BP, as well as a displacement value, are used to calculate what is called the effective address. The default segments used for the calculation of the physical address (PA) are DS for BX and SS for BP. For example:

```
MOV    CX,[BX]+10       ;move DS:BX+10 and DS:BX+10+1 into CX
                        ;PA = DS (shifted left) + BX + 10
```

Alternative codings are "MOV CX,[BX+10]" or "MOV CX,10[BX]". Again the low address contents will go into CL and the high address contents into CH. In the case of the BP register,

```
MOV    AL,[BP]+5        ;PA = SS (shifted left) + BP + 5
```

Again, alternative codings are "MOV AL,[BP+5]" or "MOV AL,5[BP]". A brief mention should be made of the terminology *effective address* used in Intel literature. In "MOV AL,[BP]+5", BP+5 is called the effective address since the fifth byte from the beginning of the offset BP is moved to register AL. Similarly in "MOV CX,[BX]+10", BX+10 is called the effective address.

Indexed relative addressing mode

The indexed relative addressing mode works the same as the based relative addressing mode, except that registers DI and SI hold the offset address. Examples:

```
MOV    DX,[SI]+5        ;PA = DS (shifted left) + SI + 5
MOV    CL,[DI]+20       ;PA = DS (shifted left) + DI + 20
```

Example 1-17

Assume that DS = 4500, SS = 2000, BX = 2100, SI = 1486, DI = 8500, BP = 7814, and AX = 2512. Show the exact physical memory location where AX is stored in each of the following. All values are in hex.

(a) MOV [BX]+20,AX   (b) MOV [SI]+10,AX
(c) MOV [DI]+4,AX   (d) MOV [BP]+12,AX

Solution:
In each case PA = segment register (shifted left) + offset register + displacement.

(a) DS:BX+20   location 47120 = (12) and 47121 = (25)
(b) DS:SI+10   location 46496 = (12) and 46497 = (25)
(c) DS:DI+4   location 4D504 = (12) and 4D505 = (25)
(d) SS:BP+12   location 27826 = (12) and 27827 = (25)

Based indexed addressing mode

By combining based and indexed addressing modes, a new addressing mode is derived called the based indexed addressing mode. In this mode, one base register and one index register are used. Examples:

```
MOV    CL,[BX][DI]+8          ;PA = DS (shifted left) + BX + DI + 8
MOV    CH,[BX][SI]+20         ;PA = DS (shifted left) + BX + SI + 20
MOV    AH,[BP][DI]+12         ;PA = SS (shifted left) + BP + DI + 12
MOV    AH,[BP][SI]+29         ;PA = SS (shifted left) + BP + SI + 29
```

The coding of the instructions above can vary; for example, the last example could have been written

```
MOV    AH,[BP+SI+29]
or
MOV    AH,[SI+BP+29] ;the register order does not matter.
```

Note that "MOV AX,[SI][DI]+displacement" is illegal.

In many of the examples above, the MOV instruction was used for the sake of clarity, even though one can use any instruction as long as that instruction supports the addressing mode. For example, the instruction "ADD DL,[BX]" would add the contents of the memory location pointed at by DS:BX to the contents of register DL.

Table 1-3: Offset Registers for Various Segments

Segment register:	CS	DS	ES	SS
Offset register(s):	IP	SI, DI, BX	SI, DI, BX	SP, BP

Segment overrides

Table 1-3 provides a summary of the offset registers that can be used with the four segment registers of the 80x86. The 80x86 CPU allows the program to override the default segment and use any segment register. To do that, specify the segment in the code. For example, in "MOV AL,[BX]", the physical address of the operand to be moved into AL is DS:BX, as was shown earlier since DS is the default segment for pointer BX. To override that default, specify the desired segment in the instruction as "MOV AL,ES:[BX]". Now the address of the operand being moved to AL is ES:BX instead of DS:BX. Extensive use of all these addressing modes is shown in future chapters in the context of program examples. Table 1-4 shows more examples of segment overrides shown next to the default address in the absence of the override. Table 1-5 summarizes addressing modes of the 8086/88.

Table 1-4: Sample Segment Overrides

Instruction	Segment Used	Default Segment
MOV AX,CS:[BP]	CS:BP	SS:BP
MOV DX,SS:[SI]	SS:SI	DS:SI
MOV AX,DS:[BP]	DS:BP	SS:BP
MOV CX,ES:[BX]+12	ES:BX+12	DS:BX+12
MOV SS:[BX][DI]+32,AX	SS:BX+DI+32	DS:BX+DI+32

Table 1-5: Summary of 80x86 Addressing Modes

Addressing Mode	Operand	Default Segment
Register	reg	none
Immediate	data	none
Direct	[offset]	DS
Register indirect	[BX]	DS
	[SI]	DS
	[DI]	DS
Based relative	[BX]+disp	DS
	[BP]+disp	SS
Indexed relative	[DI]+disp	DS
	[SI]+disp	DS
Based indexed relative	[BX][SI]+disp	DS
	[BX][DI]+disp	DS
	[BP][SI]+ disp	SS
	[BP][DI]+ disp	SS

SUMMARY

Intel's 80x86 family of microprocessors are used in all IBM PC, PS, and compatible computers. The 8088 was the microprocessor used by IBM in the first PCs, which revolutionized the computing industry in the early 1980s. Each generation of Intel microprocessor brought improvements in speed and processing power.

A typical Assembly language program consists of at least three segments. The code segment contains the Assembly language instructions to be executed. The data segment is used to store data needed by the program. The stack segment is used for temporary storage of data. Memory within each segment is accessed by combining a segment register and an offset register. The flag register is used to indicate certain conditions after the execution of an instruction such as carry, overflow, or zero result.

Assembly language instructions can use one of seven addressing modes. An addressing mode is simply a method by which the programmer tells the CPU where to find the operand for that instruction.

PROBLEMS

1. Which microprocessor, the 8088 or the 8086, was released first?
2. If the 80286 and 80386SX both have 16-bit external data buses, what is the difference between them?
3. What does "16-bit" or "32-bit" microprocessor mean? Does it refer to the internal or external data path?
4. Do programs written for the 88/86 run on 80286-, 80386-, and 80486-based CPUs?
5. What does the term *upward compatibility* mean?
6. Name a major difference between the 8088 and 8086.
7. Which has the larger queue, the 8088 or 8086?
8. State another way to increase the processing power of the CPU other than increasing the frequency.
9. What do "BIU" and "EU" stand for, and what are their functions?
10. Name the general-purpose registers of the 8088/86.
    (a) 8-bit   (b) 16-bit
11. Which of the following registers cannot be split into high and low bytes?
    (a) CS   (b) AX   (c) DS
    (d) SS   (e) BX   (f) DX
    (g) CX   (h) SI   (i) DI
12. Which of the following instructions cannot be coded in 8088/86 Assembly language? Give the reason why not, if any. To verify your answer, code each in DEBUG. Assume that all numbers are in hex.
    (a) MOV AX,27   (b) MOV AL,97F   (c) MOV DS,9BF2
    (d) MOV CX,397   (e) MOV SI,9516   (f) MOV CS,3490
    (g) MOV DS,BX   (h) MOV BX,CS   (i) MOV CH,AX
    (j) MOV AX,23FB9   (k) MOV CS,BH   (l) MOV AX,DL
13. Name the segment registers and their functions in the 8088/86.
14. If CS = 3499H and IP = 2500H, find:
    (a) The logical address
    (b) The physical address
    (c) The lower and upper ranges of the code segment
15. Repeat Problem 14 with CS = 1296H and IP = 100H.
16. If DS = 3499H and the offset = 3FB9H, find:
    (a) The physical address
    (b) The logical address of the data being fetched
    (c) The lower and upper range addresses of the data segment
17. Repeat Problem 16 using DS = 1298H and the offset = 7CC8H.
18. Assume that the physical address for a location is 0046CH. Suggest a possible logical address.
19. If an instruction that needs to be fetched is in physical memory location 389F2 and CS = 2700, does the code segment range include it or not? If not, what value should be assigned to CS if the IP must be = 1282?
20. Using DEBUG, assemble and unassemble the following program and provide the logical address, physical address, and the content of each address location. The CS value is decided by DOS, but use IP = 170H.
    MOV AL,76H
    MOV BH,8FH
    ADD BH,AL
    ADD BH,7BH
    MOV BL,BH
    ADD BL,AL

21. Repeat Problem 20 for the following programs from page 29.

```
MOV AL,0                ;clear AL
ADD AL,[0200]           ;add the contents of DS:200 to AL
ADD AL,[0201]           ;add the contents of DS:201 to AL
ADD AL,[0202]           ;add the contents of DS:202 to AL
ADD AL,[0203]           ;add the contents of DS:203 to AL
ADD AL,[0204]           ;add the contents of DS:204 to AL
```

22. The stack is:
    (a) A section of ROM
    (b) A section of RAM used for temporary storage
    (c) A 16-bit register inside the CPU
    (d) Some memory inside the CPU
23. In problem 22, choose the correct answer for the stack pointer.
24. When data is pushed onto the stack, the stack pointer is _____, but when data is popped off the stack, the stack pointer is _____.
25. Choose the correct answer:
    (a) The stack segment and code segment start at the same point of read/write memory and grow upward.
    (b) The stack segment and code segment start at opposite points of read/write memory and grow toward each other.
    (c) There will be no problem if the stack and code segments meet each other.
26. What is the main disadvantage of the stack as temporary storage compared to having a large number of registers inside the CPU?
27. If SS = 2000 and SP = 4578, find:
    (a) The physical address
    (b) The logical address
    (c) The lower range of the stack segment
    (d) The upper range of the stack segment
28. If SP = 24FC, what is the offset address of the first location of the stack that is available to push data into?
29. Assume that SP = FF2EH, AX = 3291H, BX = F43CH, and CX = 09. Find the content of the stack and stack pointer after the execution of each of the following instructions.

```
PUSH AX
PUSH BX
PUSH CX
```

30. In order for each register to get back their original values in Problem 29, show the sequence of instruction needs to be executed. Show the content of SP at each point.
31. The following registers are used as offsets. Assuming that the default segment is used to get the logical address, give the segment register associated with each offset.
    (a) BP   (b) DI   (c) IP
    (d) SI   (e) SP   (f) BX
32. Show the override segment register and the default segment register used (if there were no override) in each of the following cases.
    (a) MOV SS:[BX],AX   (b) MOV SS:[DI],BX
    (c) MOV DX,DS:[BP+6]
33. Find the status of the CF, PF, AF, ZF, and SF for the following operations.
    (a)MOV BL,9FH   (b) MOV AL,23H   (c) MOV DX,10FFH
       ADD BL,61H   ADD AL,97H   ADD DX,1
34. Assume that the registers have the following values (all in hex) and that CS = 1000, DS = 2000, SS = 3000, SI = 4000, DI = 5000, BX = 6080, BP = 7000, AX = 25FF, CX = 8791, and DX = 1299. Calculate the physical address of the memory where the operand is stored and the contents of the memory locations in each of the following addressing examples.
    (a) MOV [SI],AL   (b) MOV [SI+BX+8],AH
    (c) MOV [BX],AX   (d) MOV [DI+6],BX
    (e) MOV [DI][BX]+28,CX   (f) MOV [BP][SI]+10,DX

(g) MOV [3600],AX   (h) MOV [BX]+30,DX
(i) MOV [BP]+200,AX   (j) MOV [BP+SI+100],BX
(k) MOV [SI]+50,AH   (l) MOV [DI+BP+100],AX.

35. Give the addressing mode for each of the following:
    (a) MOV AX,DS   (b) MOV BX,5678H
    (c) MOV CX,[3000]   (d) MOV AL,CH
    (e) MOV [DI],BX   (f) MOV AL,[BX]
    (g) MOV DX,[BP+DI+4]   (h) MOV CX,DS
    (i) MOV [BP+6],AL   (j) MOV AH,[BX+SI+50]
    (k) MOV BL,[SI]+10   (l) MOV [BP][SI]+12,AX

36. Show the contents of the memory locations after the execution of each instruction.
    (a) MOV BX,129FH   (b) MOV DX,8C63H
        MOV [1450],BX   MOV [2348],DX
        DS:1450 ....   DS:2348 ....
        DS:1451 ....   DS:2349 ....

ANSWERS TO REVIEW QUESTIONS

Section 1.1: Brief History of the 80x86 Family
1. (1) increased memory capacity from 64K to 1 megabyte; (2) the 8086 is a 16-bit microprocessor instead of an 8-bit microprocessor; (3) the 8086 was a pipelined processor
2. the 8088 has an 8-bit external data bus whereas the 8086 has a 16-bit data bus
3. (a) 20-bit, 1 megabyte   (b) 24-bit, 16 megabytes   (c) 32-bit, 4 gigabytes
4. 16, 32
5. the 80386 has 32-bit address and data buses, whereas the 80386SX has a 24-bit address bus and a 16-bit external data bus
6. virtual memory, protected mode
7. math coprocessor on the CPU chip, cache memory and controller

Section 1.2: Inside the 8088/8086
1. the execution unit executes instructions; the bus interface unit fetches instructions
2. pipelining divides the microprocessor into two sections: the execution unit and the bus interface unit; this allows the CPU to perform these two functions simultaneously; that is, the BIU can fetch instructions while the EU executes the instructions previously fetched
3. 8, 16
4. AX, BX, CX, DX, SP, BP, SI, DI, CS, DS, SS, ES, IP, FR

Section 1.3: Introduction to Assembly Programming
1. MOV BX,1234H
2. MOV AX,16H
   ADD AX,ABH
3. the segment registers CS, DS, ES, and SS
4. FFFFH = 65535_{10}, FFH = 255_{10}

Section 1.4: Introduction to Program Segments
1. 64K
2. a segment contains 64K bytes; yes because 346E0H is evenly divisible by 16
3. the physical address is the 20-bit address that is put on the address bus to locate a byte; the logical address is the address in the form xxxx:yyyy, where xxxx is the segment address and yyyy is the offset into the segment
4. 20, 16
5. IP
6. 2400 would contain 34 and 2401 would contain 12

Section 1.5: More about Segments in the 80x86
1. SS is the segment register; SP and BP are used as pointers into the stack
2. decremented
3. incremented
4. 143F:0000, 1000:43F0, 1410:02F0
5. CF, PF, AF, ZF, SF, and OF
6. 7
7. 15

CHAPTER 2

ASSEMBLY LANGUAGE PROGRAMMING

OBJECTIVES

Upon completion of this chapter, you will be able to:

» Explain the difference between Assembly language instructions and pseudo-instructions

» Identify the segments of an Assembly language program

» Code simple Assembly language instructions

» Assemble, link, and run a simple Assembly language program

» Code control transfer instructions such as conditional and unconditional jumps and call instructions

» Code Assembly language data directives for binary, hex, decimal, or ASCII data

» Write an Assembly language program using either the full segment definition or the simplified segment definition

» Explain the difference between COM and EXE files and list the advantages of each

This chapter is an introduction to Assembly language programming with the 80x86. First the basic form of a program is explained, followed by the steps required to edit, assemble, link, and run a program. Next, control transfer instructions such as jump and call are discussed and then data types and data directives in 80x86 Assembly language are explained. Then the simplified segment definition is discussed. Finally, the differences between ".exe" and ".com" files are explained. The programs in this chapter and following ones can be assembled and run on any IBM PC, PS and compatible computer with an 8088, 8086, 80286, 80386, 80386SX, or 80486 microprocessor.

SECTION 2.1: DIRECTIVES AND A SAMPLE PROGRAM

In this section we explain the components of a simple Assembly language program to be assembled by the assembler. A given Assembly language program (see Figure 2-1) is a series of statements, or lines, which are either Assembly language instructions such as ADD and MOV, or statements called directives. Directives (also called pseudo-instructions) give directions to the assembler about how it should translate the Assembly language instructions into machine code. An Assembly language instruction consists of four fields:

[label:]   mnemonic   [operands]   [;comment]

Brackets indicate that the field is optional. Brackets should not be typed in.

1. The label field allows the program to refer to a line of code by name. The label field cannot exceed 31 characters. Labels for directives do not need to end with a colon. A label must end with a colon when it refers to an opcode generating instruction; the colon indicates to the assembler that this refers to code within this code segment. Appendix C Section 2 gives more information about labels.

2,3. The Assembly language mnemonic (instruction) and operand(s) fields together perform the real work of the program and accomplish the tasks for which the program was written. In Assembly language statements such as

        ADD   AL,BL
        MOV   AX,6764

ADD and MOV are the mnemonic opcodes and "AL,BL" and "AX,6764" are the operands. Instead of a mnemonic and operand, these two fields could contain assembler pseudo-instructions, or directives. They are used by the assembler to organize the program as well as other output files. Directives do not generate any machine code and are used only by the assembler as opposed to instructions, which are translated into machine code for the CPU to execute. In Figure 2-1 the commands SEGMENT, DB, ENDS, ASSUME, END, and ENDP are examples of directives.

4. The comment field begins with a ";". Comments may be at the end of a line or on a line by themselves. The assembler ignores comments, but they are indispensable to programmers. Although comments are optional, it is recommended that they be used to describe the program, to make it easier for someone to read and understand.

Segments of a program

Although one can write an Assembly language program that uses only one segment, normally a program consists of at least three segments discussed in Chapter 1: the stack segment, the data segment, and the code segment. The "SEGMENT" and "ENDS" directives indicate to the assembler the beginning and ending of a segment and have the following format:

```
label   SEGMENT     [options]
        ;place the statements belonging to this segment here
label   ENDS
```

The label, or name, must follow naming conventions (see the end of Section 2.4) and must be unique. The [options] field gives important information to the assembler for organizing the segment, but is not required. The ENDS label must be the same label as in the SEGMENT directive. Assembly language statements are grouped into segments in order to be recognized by the assembler and consequently by the CPU. The stack segment defines storage for the stack, the data segment defines the data that the program will use, and the code segment contains the Assembly language instructions. In Chapter 1 we gave an overview of how these segments were stored in memory. In the following pages we describe the stack, data, and code segments as they are defined in Assembly language programming.

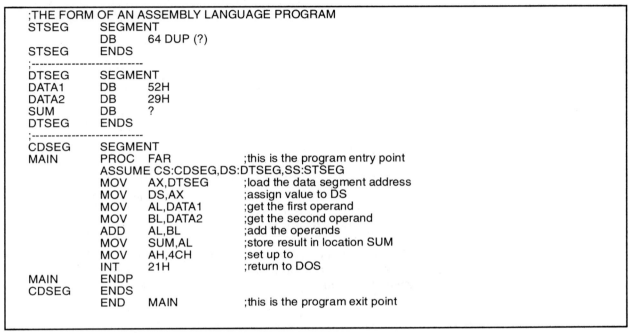

```
;THE FORM OF AN ASSEMBLY LANGUAGE PROGRAM
STSEG       SEGMENT
            DB      64 DUP (?)
STSEG       ENDS
;---------------------------
DTSEG       SEGMENT
DATA1       DB      52H
DATA2       DB      29H
SUM         DB      ?
DTSEG       ENDS
;---------------------------
CDSEG       SEGMENT
MAIN        PROC    FAR             ;this is the program entry point
            ASSUME CS:CDSEG,DS:DTSEG,SS:STSEG
            MOV     AX,DTSEG        ;load the data segment address
            MOV     DS,AX           ;assign value to DS
            MOV     AL,DATA1        ;get the first operand
            MOV     BL,DATA2        ;get the second operand
            ADD     AL,BL           ;add the operands
            MOV     SUM,AL          ;store result in location SUM
            MOV     AH,4CH          ;set up to
            INT     21H             ;return to DOS
MAIN        ENDP
CDSEG       ENDS
            END     MAIN            ;this is the program exit point
```

Figure 2-1. Simple Assembly Language Program

Stack segment definition

The stack segment shown below contains one line: "DB 64 DUP (?)". This directive reserves 64 bytes of memory for the stack. The directives DB and DUP are described later in greater detail.

```
STSEG       SEGMENT         ;the "SEGMENT" directive begins the segment
            DB 64 DUP (?)   ;this segment contains only one line
STSEG       ENDS            ;the "ENDS" segment ends the segment
```

Data segment definition

The data segment in the program of Figure 2-1 defines three data items: DATA1, DATA2, and SUM. Each is defined as DB (define byte). The DB directive is used by the assembler to allocate memory in byte-sized chunks. Memory can be allocated in different sizes, such as 2 bytes, which has the directive DW (define word). More of these pseudo-instructions are discussed in detail in Section 2.5. The data items defined in the data segment will be accessed in the code segment by their labels. DATA1 and DATA2 are given initial values in the data section. SUM is not given an initial value, but storage is set aside for later use by the program.

Code segment definition

The last section of the program in Figure 2-1 is the code segment. The first line of the segment after the SEGMENT directive is the PROC directive. A *procedure* is a group of instructions designed to accomplish a specific function. A code segment may consist of only one procedure, but usually is organized into several small procedures in order to make the program more structured. Every procedure must have a name defined by the PROC directive, followed by the assembly language instructions and closed by the ENDP directive. The PROC and ENDP statements must have the same label. The PROC directive may have the option FAR or NEAR. The operating system that controls the computer must be directed to the beginning of the program in order to execute it. DOS requires that the entry point to the user program be a FAR procedure. From then on, either FAR or NEAR can be used. The differences between a FAR and a NEAR procedure, as well as where and why each is used, are explained later in this chapter. For now, just remember that in order to run a program, FAR must be used at the program entry point.

In Figure 2-1, immediately after the PROC directive is the ASSUME directive, which associates segment registers with specific segments by assuming that the segment register is equal to the segment labels used in the program. If an extra segment had been used, ES would also be included in the ASSUME statement. The ASSUME statement is needed because a given Assembly language program can have several code segments, one or two or three or more data segments and more than one stack segment, but only one of each can be addressed by the CPU at a given time since there is only one of each of the segment registers available inside the CPU. Therefore, ASSUME tells the assembler which of the segments defined by the SEGMENT directives should be used. It also helps the assembler to calculate the offset addresses from the beginning of that segment. For example, in "MOV AL,[BX]" the BX register is the offset of the data segment. Clearly, the assembler must know which data segment should be used if there is more than one data segment in the program. This is precisely the purpose of the ASSUME directive.

A good question to ask at this point is: If ASSUME is only for the assembler, what value is actually assigned to the CS, DS, and SS registers for execution of the program? The DOS operating system must pass control to the program so that it may execute, but before it does that it assigns values for the segment registers. The operating system must do this because it knows how much memory is installed in the computer, how much of it is used by the system, and how much is available. In the IBM PC, the operating system first finds out how many kilobytes of RAM memory are installed, allocates some for its own use, and then allows the user program to use the portions that it needs. Various DOS versions require different amounts of memory, and since the user program must be able to run across different versions, one cannot tell DOS to give the program a specific area of memory, say from 25FFF to 289E2. Therefore, it is the job of DOS to assign exact values for the segment registers. Upon taking control from DOS, of the three segment registers, only CS and SS have the proper values. The DS value (and ES, if used) must be initialized by the program. This is done as follows:

```
MOV AX,DTSEG        ;DTSEG is the label for the data segment
MOV DS,AX
```

Remember from Chapter 1 that no segment register can be loaded directly. That is the reason the two lines of code above are needed. You cannot code "MOV DS,DTSEG".

After these housekeeping chores, the Assembly language program instructions can be written to perform the desired tasks. In Figure 2-1, the program loads AL and BL with DATA1 and DATA2, respectively, ADDs them together, and stores the result in SUM.

```
MOV    AL,DATA1
MOV    BL,DATA2
ADD    AL,BL
MOV    SUM,AL
```

Everything above and below the foregoing four lines in the code segment can be thought of as the shell of an Assembly language program. When writing your first few programs, it is handy to keep a copy of this shell on your disk and simply fill it in with the instructions and data for your program. Figure 2-2 shows a sample shell of an Assembly language program. The two last instructions in the shell are

```
MOV    AH,4CH
INT    21H
```

Their purpose is to return control to the operating system. The last three lines end the procedure, the segment, and the program, respectively. Note that the label for ENDP (MAIN) matches the label for PROC and that ENDS matches the SEGMENT. The END pseudo-instruction ends the entire program by indicating to DOS that the entry point MAIN has ended. For this reason the labels for the entry point and END must match.

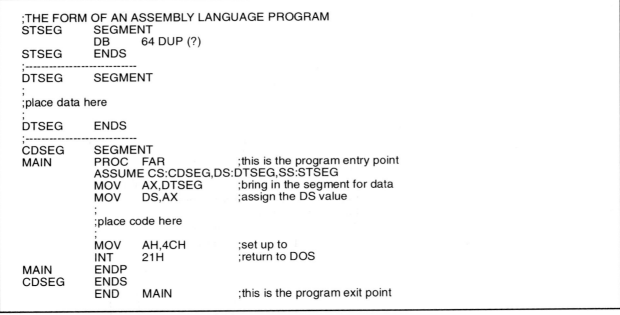

```
;THE FORM OF AN ASSEMBLY LANGUAGE PROGRAM
STSEG        SEGMENT
             DB      64 DUP (?)
STSEG        ENDS
;-------------------------
DTSEG        SEGMENT
;
;place data here
;
DTSEG        ENDS
;-------------------------
CDSEG        SEGMENT
MAIN         PROC    FAR              ;this is the program entry point
             ASSUME CS:CDSEG,DS:DTSEG,SS:STSEG
             MOV     AX,DTSEG         ;bring in the segment for data
             MOV     DS,AX            ;assign the DS value
             ;
             ;place code here
             ;
             MOV     AH,4CH           ;set up to
             INT     21H              ;return to DOS
MAIN         ENDP
CDSEG        ENDS
             END     MAIN             ;this is the program exit point
```

Figure 2-2. Shell of an Assembly Language Program

Review Questions

1. What is the purpose of pseudo-instructions?
2. _____ are translated by the assembler into machine code, whereas _____ are not.
3. Write an Assembly language program with the following characteristics:
   (a) A code segment named COD_SG
   (b) A data segment named DAT_SG
   (c) A stack segment named STK_SG
   (d) A data item named HIGH_DAT, which contains 95
   (e) Instructions that move HIGH_DAT to registers AH, BH, and DL
   (f) The program entry point will be named START
4. Find five errors in the following:

```
STAKSG          SEGMENT
                DB        100 DUP (?)
STA_SG          ENDS
DTSEG           SEGMENT
DATA1           DB        ?
DTSEG           END
CDSEG           SEGMENT
MAIN            PROC      FAR
                MOV       AX,DATSEG
                MOV       DS,AX
                MOV       AL,34H
                ADD       AL,4FH
                MOV       DATA1,AL
START           ENDP
CDSEG           ENDS
                END
```

SECTION 2.2: ASSEMBLE, LINK, AND RUN A PROGRAM

Now that the basic form of an Assembly language program has been given, the next question is: How is it created and assembled? The three steps to create an executable Assembly language program are outlined as follows:

Step	Input	Program	Output
1. Edit the program	keyboard	editor	myfile.asm
2. Assemble the program	myfile.asm	MASM	myfile.obj
3. Link the program	myfile.obj	LINK	myfile.exe

The MASM and LINK programs are the assembler and linker programs for Microsoft's MASM assembler. If you are using another assembler, such as Borland's TASM, consult the manual for the procedure to assemble and link a program. Many excellent editors or word processors are available that can be used to create and/or edit the program. The editor must produce an ASCII file. Although filenames follow the usual DOS conventions, the source file must end in ".asm" for the Assembler used in this book. This ".asm" source file is assembled by an assembler. Although the assembler used in this book is the MASM (Microsoft assembler), one can use assemblers by other companies. The assembler will produce an object file and a list file, along with other files that may be useful to the programmer. The extension for the object file must be ".obj". This object file is input to the LINK program, which pro-

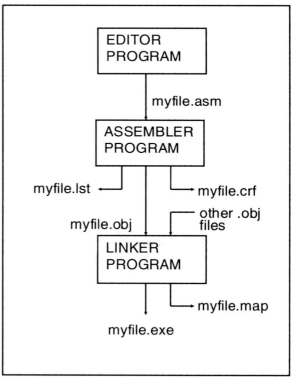

Figure 2-3. Steps to Produce an Executable Program

duces the executable program that ends in ".exe". The ".exe" file can be executed by the microprocessor. Before feeding the ".obj" file into LINK, all syntax errors produced by the assembler must be corrected. Of course, fixing these errors will not guarantee that the program will work as intended since the program may contain conceptual errors. Figure 2-3 shows the steps in producing an executable file.

Figure 2-4 shows how an executable program is created by following the steps outlined above, and then run under DEBUG. The portions in italics indicate what the user would type in to perform these steps. The bold portions represent the computer response. Figure 2-4 assumes that the MASM, LINK, and DEBUG programs are on drive A and the Assembly language program is on drive B. The drives used will vary depending on how the system is set up.

```
A>MASM B:MYFILE.ASM <CR>

Microsoft (R) Macro Assembler  Version  5.10
Copyright (C) Microsoft Corp 1981, 1988.  All rights reserved.

Object filename [B:MYFILE.OBJ]: B:<CR>
Source listing  [NUL.LST]:B:MYFILE.LST  <CR>
Cross-reference [NUL.CRF]: <CR>

    47962 + 413345 Bytes symbol space free

    0 Warning Errors
    0 Severe  Errors

A>LINK B:MYFILE.OBJ <CR>

Microsoft (R) Overlay Linker  Version 3.64
Copyright (C) Microsoft Corp 1983-1988.  All rights reserved.

Run File [B:MYFILE.EXE]:B:<CR>
List File [NUL.MAP]: <CR>
Libraries [.LIB]:<CR>
LINK : warning L4021: no stack segment

 A>DEBUG B:MYFILE.EXE <CR>
 -U CS:0 1 <CR>
 1064:0000 B86610        MOV     AX,1066
 -D 1066:0 F <CR>
 1066:0000 52 29 00 00 00 00 00 00-00 00 00 00 00 00 00 00  R).............
 -G <CR>
 Program terminated normally
 -D 1066:0 F <CR>
 1066:0000 52 29 7B 00 00 00 00 00-00 00 00 00 00 00 00 00  R){............
 -Q <CR>
 A>
```

Figure 2-4. Creating and Running the .exe File

.asm and .obj files

The ".asm" file (the source file) is the file created with a word processor or line editor. The MASM assembler converts the .asm file's Assembly language instructions into machine language (the ".obj" object file). In addition to creating the object program, MASM also creates the ".lst" list file.

.lst file

The ".lst" file, which is optional, is very useful to the programmer because it lists all the opcodes and offset addresses as well as errors that MASM detected. MASM assumes that the list file is not wanted (NUL.LST indicates no list). To get a list file, type in a filename after the prompt. This file can be displayed on the monitor or sent to the printer. The programmer uses it to help debug the program.

It is only after fixing all the errors indicated in the ".lst" file that the ".obj" file can be input to the LINK program to create the executable program. Before moving to that subject, a few points about the print list should be made. To list the ".lst" file to the screen, at the DOS prompt ">", type in

C>type B:myfile.lst <return>

The disadvantage of this is that it will scroll up the screen faster than it can be read. Control-S and control-Q can be used to stop and start the screen scrolling if your reflexes are fast enough. If you are using one of the later versions of DOS, you can use the "more" command to print one screen at a time to the monitor:

C>type B:myfile.lst | more <return>

Another way to look at the list file is to send it to the printer by typing in these two DOS commands:

C>mode lpt1:132,80 <return>
C>copy B:myfile.lst prn <return>

The mode command sets the printer mode to print 80 lines per page and 132 columns per page. The mode command should be in the DOS directory but works only for Epson or Epson-compatible printers. The mode command is not really necessary; it will just make the printout look better in that the lines will not wrap around. The second command copies the list file to the printer.

There are two assembler directives that can be used to make the ".lst" file more readable: PAGE and TITLE.

PAGE and TITLE directives

The format of the PAGE directive is

PAGE [lines],[columns]

and its function is to tell the printer how the list should be printed. In the default mode, meaning that the PAGE directive is coded with no numbers coming after it, the output will have 66 lines per page with a maximum of 80 characters per line. In this book, programs will normally change that to 60 and 132 as follows:

PAGE 60,132

The range for number of lines is 10 to 255 and for columns is 60 to 132. When the list is printed and it is more than one page, the assembler can be instructed to print the title of the program on top of each page. What comes after the TITLE pseudo-instruction is up to the programmer, but it is common practice to put the name of the program as stored on the disk right after the TITLE pseudo-instruction and then a brief description of the function of the program. Whatever is placed after the TITLE pseudo-instruction cannot be more than 60 ASCII characters (letters, numbers, spaces, punctuation, etc.).

.crf file

MASM produces another optional file, the cross-reference, which has the extension ".crf". It provides an alphabetical list of all symbols and labels used in the program as well as the program line numbers in which they are referenced. This can be a great help in large programs with many data segments and code segments. This file can be converted to an ASCII file by the CREF program supplied by MASM. The following converts the ".crf" file to ASCII file "CREF.ASC".

C>cref prog1.crf cref.asc <return>

LINKing the program

The assembler (MASM) creates the opcodes, operands, and offset addresses under the ".obj" file. It is the LINK program that produces the ready-to-run version of a program that has the ".exe" (EXEcutable) extension. The LINK program sets up the file so that it can be loaded by DOS and executed.

In Figure 2-4 we used DEBUG to execute the program in Figure 2-1 and analyze the result. In the program in Figure 2-1, three data items are defined in the data segment. Before running the program, one could look at the data in the data segment by dumping the contents of DS:offset as shown in Figure 2-4. Now what is the value for the DS register? This can vary from PC to PC and from DOS to DOS. For this reason it is important to look at the value in "MOV AX,xxxx" as was shown and use that number. The result of the program can be verified after it is run as shown in Figure 2-4. When the program is working successfully, it can be run at the DOS level. To execute myfile.exe, simply type in

B>myfile <return>

However, since this program produced no output, there would be no way to verify the results. When the program name is typed in at the DOS level, as shown above, DOS loads the program in memory. This is sometimes referred to as *mapping*, which means that the program is mapped into the physical memory of the PC. Before leaving this section it is necessary to point out the function of the ".map" file generated by the LINK program.

.map file

When there are many segments for code or data, there is a need to see where each is located and how many bytes are used by each. This is provided by the map file. This file, which is optional, gives the name of each segment, where it starts, where it stops, and its size in bytes. In Chapter 7 the importance of the map will be seen when many separate subroutines (modules) are assembled separately and then linked together.

Review Questions

1. (a) The input file to the MASM assembler program has the extension _____.
   (b) The input file to the LINK program has the extension _____.
2. Select all the file types from the second column that are the output of the program in the first column.

_____ Editor	(a) .obj	(b) .asm
_____ Assembler	(c) .exe	(d) .lst
_____ Linker	(e) .crf	(f) .map

SECTION 2.3: MORE SAMPLE PROGRAMS

Now that some familiarity with Assembly language programming in the IBM PC has been achieved, in this section we look at more example programs in order to allow the reader to master the basic features of Assembly programming. The following pages show Program 2-1 and the list file generated when the program was assembled. After the program was assembled and linked, DEBUG was used to dump the code segment to see what value is assigned to the DS register. Precisely where DOS loads a program into RAM depends on many factors, including the amount of RAM on the system, and the version of DOS used. Therefore, remember that the value you get could be different for "MOV AX,xxxx" as well as for CS in the program examples. Do not attempt to modify the segment register contents to conform to those in the examples, or your system may crash!

Write, run, and analyze a program that adds 5 bytes of data and saves the result. The data should be the following hex numbers: 25, 12, 15, 1F, and 2B.

```
        PAGE    60,132
        TITLE   PROG2-1 (EXE)  PURPOSE: ADDS 5 BYTES OF DATA
STSEG   SEGMENT
        DB      32 DUP (?)
STSEG   ENDS
;-------------------------
DTSEG   SEGMENT
DATA_IN DB      25H,12H,15H,1FH,2BH
SUM     DB      ?
DTSEG   ENDS
;-------------------------
CDSEG   SEGMENT
MAIN    PROC    FAR
        ASSUME CS:CDSEG,DS:DTSEG,SS:STSEG
        MOV     AX,DTSEG
        MOV     DS,AX
        MOV     CX,05               ;set up loop counter CX=5
        MOV     BX,OFFSET DATA_IN   ;set up data pointer BX
        MOV     AL,0                ;initialize AL
AGAIN:  ADD     AL,[BX]             ;add next data item to AL
        INC     BX                  ;make BX point to next data item
        DEC     CX                  ;decrement loop counter
        JNZ     AGAIN               ;jump if loop counter not zero
        MOV     SUM,AL              ;load result into sum
        MOV     AH,4CH              ;set up return
        INT     21H                 ;return to DOS
MAIN    ENDP
CDSEG   ENDS
        END     MAIN
```

After the program was assembled and linked, it was run using DEBUG:

```
C>debug prog2-1.exe
-u cs:0 19
1067:0000 B86610       MOV   AX,1066
1067:0003 8ED8         MOV   DS,AX
1067:0005 B90500       MOV   CX,0005
1067:0008 BB0000       MOV   BX,0000
1067:000D 0207         ADD   AL,[BX]
1067:000F 43           INC   BX
1067:0010 49           DEC   CX
1067:0011 75FA         JNZ   000D
1067:0013 A20500       MOV   [0005],AL
1067:0016 B44C         MOV   AH,4C
1067:0018 CD21         INT   21
-d 1066:0 f
1066:0000  25 12 15 1F 2B 00 00 00-00 00 00 00 00 00 00 00  %...+..........
-g

Program terminated normally
-d 1066:0 f
1066:0000  25 12 15 1F 2B 96 00 00-00 00 00 00 00 00 00 00  %...+..........
-q
C>
```

Program 2-1

Analysis of Program 2-1

The DEBUG program is explained thoroughly in Appendix A. The commands used in running Program 2-1 were (1) u, to unassemble the code from cs:0 for 19 bytes; (2) d, to dump the contents of memory from 1066:0 for the next F bytes; and (3) g, to go, that is, run the program.

```
Microsoft (R) Macro Assembler Version 5.10          4/28/92 09:25:49
PROG2-1 (EXE)  PURPOSE: ADDS 5 BYTES OF DATA          Page   1-1


                              PAGE   60,132
                              TITLE   PROG2-1 (EXE)   PURPOSE: ADDS 5  BYTES OF DATA
0000                          STSEG  SEGMENT
0000  0020[                            DB      32 DUP (?)
 ??                   ]
0020                          STSEG  ENDS
                              ;--------------------------
0000                          DTSEG   SEGMENT
0000  25 12 15 1F 2B          DATA_IN DB      25H,12H,15H,1FH,2BH
0005  00                      SUM     DB      ?
0006                          DTSEG   ENDS
                              ;--------------------------
0000                          CDSEG  SEGMENT
0000                          MAIN    PROC   FAR
                                      ASSUME CS:CDSEG,DS:DTSEG,SS:STSEG
0000  B8 ---- R                       MOV     AX,DTSEG
0003  8E D8                           MOV     DS,AX
0005  B9 0005                         MOV     CX,05            ;set up loop counter CX=5
0008  BB 0000 R                       MOV     BX,OFFSET DATA_IN ;set up data pointer BX
000B  B0 00                           MOV     AL,0             ;initialize AL
000D  02 07            AGAIN:         ADD     AL,[BX]          ;add next data item to AL
000F  43                              INC     BX               ;make BX point to next data item
0010  49                              DEC     CX               ;decrement loop counter
0011  75 FA                           JNZ     AGAIN            ;jump if loop counter not zero
0013  A2 0005 R                       MOV     SUM,AL           ;load result into sum
0016  B4 4C                           MOV     AH,4CH           ;set up return
0018  CD 21                           INT     21H              ;return to DOS
001A                          MAIN    ENDP
001A                          CDSEG  ENDS
                                      END     MAIN
```

```
Microsoft (R) Macro Assembler Version 5.10                          4/28/92
09:25:49 PROG2-1 (EXE)  PURPOSE: ADDS 5 BYTES OF DATA          Symbols-1

Segments and Groups:

           N a m e              Length   Align   Combine Class

CDSEG . . . . . . . . . . . .   001A     PARA    NONE
DTSEG . . . . . . . . . . . .   0006     PARA    NONE
STSEG . . . . . . . . . . . .   0020     PARA    NONE

Symbols:

           N a m e              Type      Value   Attr

AGAIN . . . . . . . . . . . .   L NEAR  000D    CDSEG
DATA_IN. . . . . . . . . . . .  L BYTE  0000    DTSEG
MAIN . . . . . . . . . . . .    F PROC 0000     CDSEG        Length = 001A
SUM . . . . . . . . . . . .     L BYTE  0005    DTSEG


@CPU. . . . . . . . . . . . . . TEXT  0101h
@FILENAME . . . . . . . . .     TEXT  PROG2-1
@VERSION . . . . . . . . . . .  TEXT  510

  30 Source  Lines    30 Total  Lines    12 Symbols
47900 + 403391 Bytes symbol space free

  0 Warning Errors    0 Severe  Errors
```

List File for Program 2-1

Notice in Program 2-1 that when the program was run in DEBUG, the contents of the data segment memory were dumped before and after execution of the program to verify that the program worked as planned. Normally, it is not necessary to unassemble as much code, but it was done here because in later sections of the chapter we examine the jump instruction in this program. Also notice that the first 5 bytes dumped above are the data items defined in the data segment of the program, the sixth item is the sum of those five items, so it appears that the program worked correctly (25H + 12H + 15H + 1FH + 2BH = 96H). Program 2-1 is explained below, instruction by instruction.

"MOV CX,05" will load the value 05 into the CX register. This register is used by the program as a counter for iteration (looping).

"MOV BX,OFFSET DATA_IN" will load into BX the offset address assigned to DATA. The assembler starts at offset 0000 and uses memory for the data and then assigns the next available offset memory for SUM (in this case, 0005).

"ADD AL,[BX]" adds the contents of the memory location pointed at by the register BX to AL. Note that [BX] is a pointer to a memory location.

"INC BX" simply increments the pointer by adding 1 to register BX. This will cause BX to point to the next data item, that is, the next byte.

"DEC CX" will decrement (subtract 1 from) the CX counter and will set the zero flag high if CX becomes zero.

"JNZ AGAIN" will jump back to the label AGAIN as long as the zero flag is indicating that CX is not zero. "JNZ AGAIN" will not jump (that is, execution will resume with the next instruction after the JNZ instruction) only after the zero flag has been set high by the "DEC CX" instruction (that is, CX becomes zero). When CX becomes zero, this means that the loop is completed and all five numbers have been added to AL.

Various approaches to Program 2-1

There are many ways in which any program may be written. The method shown for Program 2-1 defined one field of data and used pointer [BX] to access data elements. In the method used below, a name is assigned to each data item that will be accessed in the program. Variations of Program 2-1 are shown below to clarify the use of addressing modes in the context of a real program and also to show that the 80x86 can use any general-purpose register to do arithmetic and logic operations. In earlier-generation CPUs, the accumulator had to be the destination of all arithmetic and logic operations, but in the 80x86 this is not the case. Since the purpose of these examples is to show different ways of accessing operands, it is left to the reader to run and analyze the programs.

```
;from the data segment:
DATA1        DB      25H
DATA2        DB      12H
DATA3        DB      15H
DATA4        DB      1FH
DATA5        DB      2BH
SUM          DB      ?
;from the code segment:
             MOV     AL,DATA1        ;MOVE DATA1 INTO AL
             ADD     AL,DATA2        ;ADD DATA2 TO AL
             ADD     AL,DATA3
             ADD     AL,DATA4
             ADD     AL,DATA5
             MOV     SUM,AL          ;SAVE AL IN SUM
```

There is quite a difference between these two methods of writing the same program. While in the first one, the register indirect addressing mode was used to access the data, in the second method the direct addressing mode was used. In the example above, each byte of data could have been moved into a different register and then added together, one at time:

```
MOV     AL,DATA1
MOV     AH,DATA2
MOV     BL,DATA3
MOV     BH,DATA4
MOV     DH,DATA5
ADD     DH,AL                    ;Add to  DH the contents of AL
ADD     DH,AH                    ;etc.
ADD     DH,BL
ADD     DH,BH
MOV     SUM,DH                   ;save DH in SUM
```

Write and run a program that adds four words of data and saves the result. The values will be 234DH, 1DE6H, 3BC7H, and 566AH. Use DEBUG to verify the sum is D364.

```
TITLE       PROG2-2  (EXE) PURPOSE: ADDS 4 WORDS OF DATA
PAGE        60,132
STSEG       SEGMENT
            DB      32 DUP (?)
STSEG       ENDS
;---------------------------
DTSEG       SEGMENT
DATA_IN     DW      234DH,1DE6H,3BC7H,566AH
            ORG     10H
SUM         DW      ?
DTSEG       ENDS
;---------------------------
CDSEG       SEGMENT
MAIN        PROC    FAR
            ASSUME CS:CDSEG,DS:DTSEG,SS:STSEG
            MOV     AX,DTSEG
            MOV     DS,AX
            MOV     CX,04            ;set up loop counter CX=4
            MOV     DI,OFFSET DATA_IN ;set up data pointer DI
            MOV     BX,00            ;initialize BX
ADD_LP:     ADD     BX,[DI]          ;add contents pointed at by [DI] to BX
            INC     DI               ;increment DI twice
            INC     DI               ;to point to next word
            DEC     CX               ;decrement loop counter
            JNZ     ADD_LP           ;jump if loop counter not zero
            MOV     SI,OFFSET SUM    ;load pointer for sum
            MOV     [SI],BX          ;store in data segment
            MOV     AH,4CH           ;set up return
            INT     21H              ;return to DOS
MAIN        ENDP
CDSEG       ENDS
            END     MAIN
```

After the program was assembled and linked, it was run using DEBUG:

```
A>debug B:prog2-2.exe
-u cs:0 1
1068:0000  B86610          MOV     AX,1066
-D 1066:0 1F
1066:0000  4D 23 E6 1D C7 3B 6A 56-00 00 00 00 00 00 00 00   M#f.G;jV........
1066:0010  00 00 00 00 00 00 00 00-00 00 00 00 00 00 00 00   ................
-G

Program terminated normally
-D 1066:0 1F
1066:0000  4D 23 E6 1D C7 3B 6A 56-00 00 00 00 00 00 00 00   M#f.G;jV........
1066:0010  64 D3 00 00 00 00 00 00-00 00 00 00 00 00 00 00   dS..............
-Q
A>
```

Program 2-2

Analysis of Program 2-2

First notice that the 16-bit data (a word) is stored with the low-order byte first. For example, "234D" as defined in the data segment is stored as "4D23" meaning that the lower address, 0000, has the least significant byte, 4D, and the higher address 0001 has the most significant byte, 23. This is shown in the DEBUG display of the data segment. Similarly, the sum, D364, is stored as 64D3. As discussed in Chapter 1, this method of low byte to low address and high byte to high address operand assignment is referred to as "little endian".

Second, note that the address pointer is incremented twice, since the operand being accessed is a word (two bytes). The program could have used "ADD DI,2" instead of using "INC DI" twice. When storing the result of word addition, "MOV DI,OFFSET SUM" was used to load the pointer (in this case 0010, as defined by ORG 0010H) for the memory allocated for the label SUM, and then "MOV [DI],BX" was used to move the contents of register BX to memory locations with offsets 0010 and 0011. Again, as was done previously, it could have been coded simply as "MOV SUM,BX", using the direct addressing mode.

Program 2-2 uses the ORG directive. In previous programs where ORG was not used, the assembler would start at offset 0000 and use memory for each data item. The ORG directive can be used to set the offset addresses for data items. Although the programmer cannot assign exact physical addresses, one is allowed to assign offset addresses. The ORG directive in Program 2-2 caused SUM to be stored at DS:0010, as can be seen by looking at the DEBUG display of the data segment.

Analysis of Program 2-3

The DEBUG example shows the data segment being dumped before the program was run and after to verify that the data was copied and that the program ran successfully. Notice that C4 was coded in the data segments as 0C4. This is required by the assembler to indicate that C is a hex number and not a letter. This is required if the first digit is a hex digit A - F.

This program uses two registers, SI and DI, as pointers to the data items being manipulated. The first is used as a pointer to the data item to be copied and the second as a pointer to the location the data item is to be copied to. With each iteration of the loop, both data pointers are incremented to point to the next byte.

Stack segment definition revisited

One of the primary functions of the DOS operating system is to determine the total amount of RAM installed on the PC and then manage it properly. DOS uses the portion it needs for the operating system and allocates the rest. Since memory requirements vary for different DOS versions, a program cannot dictate the exact physical memory location for the stack or any segment. Since memory management is the responsibility of DOS, it will map Assembly programs into the memory of the PC with the help of LINK.

When assembling and linking programs in previous examples, the "warning: no stack segment" message was generated. Why does this message appear? After all, the program did define the segment. Since it was not a fatal error, it did not interfere with running the programs. The reason the message appeared is that despite the fact that the stack was defined, it was not linked with the stack of the system. Although in the DOS environment, a program can have multiple code segments and data segments, it is strongly recommended that it have only one stack segment, to prevent RAM fragmentation by the stack. Further, the stack segment must be named in a way that it can be recognized by the linking process. It is the function of LINK to combine all different code and data segments to create a single executable program with a single stack, which is the stack of the system. In order to tell LINK that it should combine the user program's defined stack segment with the system stack (which will get rid of the warning message), the stack must be defined in the following manner:

```
name SEGMENT STACK 'stack'
```

This will instruct DOS to combine the stack defined in the program with the stack of the system. Various options for the SEGMENT directive are discussed in Chapter 7 and many of these concepts are explained there.

Write and run a program that transfers 6 bytes of data from memory locations with offset of 0010H to memory locations with offset of 0028H.

```
TITLE       PROG2-3 (EXE)  PURPOSE: TRANSFERS 6 BYTES OF DATA
PAGE        60,132
STSEG       SEGMENT
            DB      32 DUP (?)
STSEG       ENDS
;---------------------------
DTSEG       SEGMENT
            ORG     10H
DATA_IN     DB      25H,4FH,85H,1FH,2BH,0C4H
            ORG     28H
COPY        DB      6 DUP(?)
DTSEG       ENDS
;---------------------------
CDSEG       SEGMENT
MAIN        PROC    FAR
            ASSUME CS:CDSEG,DS:DTSEG,SS:STSEG
            MOV     AX,DTSEG
            MOV     DS,AX
            MOV     SI,OFFSET DATA_IN      ;SI points to data to be copied
            MOV     DI,OFFSET COPY         ;DI points to copy of data
            MOV     CX,06H                 ;loop counter = 6
MOV_LOOP:   MOV     AL,[SI]                ;move the next byte from DATA area to AL
            MOV     [DI],AL                ;move the next byte to COPY area
            INC     SI                     ;increment DATA pointer
            INC     DI                     ;increment COPY pointer
            DEC     CX                     ;decrement LOOP counter
            JNZ     MOV_LOOP               ;jump if loop counter not zero
            MOV     AH,4CH                 ;set up to return
            INT     21H                    ;return to DOS
MAIN        ENDP
CDSEG       ENDS
            END     MAIN
```

After the program was assembled and linked, it was run using DEBUG:

```
C>debug prog2-3.exe
-u cs:0 1
1069:0000  B86610        MOV    AX,1066
-d 1066:0 2f
1066:0000 00 00 00 00 00 00 00 00-00 00 00 00 00 00 00 00  ................
1066:0010 25 4F 85 1F 2B C4 00 00-00 00 00 00 00 00 00 00  %O..+D..........
1066:0020 00 00 00 00 00 00 00 00-00 00 00 00 00 00 00 00  ................
-g

Program terminated normally
-d 1066:0 2f
1066:0000 00 00 00 00 00 00 00 00-00 00 00 00 00 00 00 00  ................
1066:0010 25 4F 85 1F 2B C4 00 00-00 00 00 00 00 00 00 00  %O..+D..........
1066:0020 00 00 00 00 00 00 00 00-25 4F 85 1F 2B C4 00 00  %O..+D..........
-q
C>
```

Program 2-3

Review Questions

1. What is the purpose of the INC instruction?
2. What is the purpose of the DEC instruction?
3. In Program 2-1, why does label AGAIN have a colon after it, whereas label MAIN does not?
4. State the difference between the following two instructions:
   MOV   BX,DATA1
   MOV   BX,OFFSET DATA1
5. State the difference between the following two instructions:
   ADD   AX,BX
   ADD   AX,[BX]

SECTION 2.4: CONTROL TRANSFER INSTRUCTIONS

In the sequence of instructions to be executed, it is often necessary to transfer program control to a different location. There are many instructions in the 80x86 to achieve this. This section covers the control transfer instructions available in the 8086 Assembly language. Before that, however, it is necessary to explain the concept of FAR and NEAR as it applies to jump and call instructions.

FAR and NEAR

If control is transferred to a memory location within the current code segment, it is NEAR. This is sometimes called *intrasegment* (within segment). If control is transferred outside the current code segment, it is a FAR or intersegment (between segments) jump. Since the CS:IP registers always point to the address of the next instruction to be executed, they must be updated when a control transfer instruction is executed. In a NEAR jump, the IP is updated and CS remains the same, since control is still inside the current code segment. In a FAR jump, because control is passing outside the current code segment, both CS and IP have to be updated to the new values. In other words, in any control transfer instruction such as jump or call, the IP must be changed, but only in the FAR case is the CS changed, too.

Conditional jumps

Conditional jumps, summarized in Table 2-1, have mnemonics such as JNZ (jump not zero) and JC (jump if carry). In the conditional jump, control is transferred to a new location if a certain condition is met. The flag register is the one that indicates the current condition. For example, with "JNZ label", the processor looks at the zero flag to see if it is raised. If not, the CPU starts to fetch and execute instructions from the address of the label. If $ZF = 1$, it will not jump but will execute the next instruction below the JNZ.

Short jumps

All conditional jumps are short jumps. In a short jump, the address of the target must be within -128 to $+127$ bytes of the IP. In other words, the conditional jump is a two-byte instruction: one byte is the opcode of the J condition and the second byte is a value between 00 and FF. An offset range of 00 to FF gives 256 possible addresses; these are split between backward jumps (to -128) and forward jumps (to $+127$).

In a jump backward, the second byte is the 2's complement of the displacement value. To calculate the target address, the second byte is added to the IP of the instruction after the jump. To understand this, look at the unassembled code of Program 2-1 for the instruction JNZ AGAIN, repeated below.

```
1067:0000 B86610        MOV    AX,1066
1067:0003 8ED8          MOV    DS,AX
1067:0005 B90500        MOV    CX,0005
1067:0008 BB0000        MOV    BX,0000
1067:000D 0207          ADD    AL,[BX]
1067:000F 43            INC    BX
1067:0010 49            DEC    CX
1067:0011 75FA          JNZ    000D
1067:0013 A20500        MOV    [0005],AL
1067:0016 B44C          MOV    AH,4C
1067:0018 CD21          INT    21
```

The instruction "JNZ AGAIN" was assembled as "JNZ 000D", and 000D is the address of the instruction with the label AGAIN. The instruction "JNZ 000D" has the opcode 75 and the target address FA, which is located at offset addresses 0011 and 0012. This is followed by "MOV SUM,AL" which is located beginning at offset address 0013. The IP value of MOV, 0013, is added to FA to calculate the address of label AGAIN (0013 + FA = 000D) and the carry is dropped. In reality, FA is the 2's complement of −6, meaning that the address of the target is −6 bytes from the IP of the next instruction.

Table 2-1: 8086 Conditional JMP Instructions

Mnemonic	Condition Tested	"Jump IF ..."
JA/JNBE	(CF or ZF) = 0	above/not below nor equal
JAE/JNB	CF = 0	above or equal/not below
JB/JNAE	CF = 1	below/not above nor equal
JBE/JNA	(CF or ZF) = 1	below or equal/not above
JC	CF = 1	carry
JE/JZ	ZF = 1	equal/zero
JG/JNLE	((SF xor OF) or ZF) = 0	greater/not less nor equal
JGE/JNL	(SF xor OF) = 0	greater or equal/not less
JL/JNGE	(SF xor OF) = 1	less/not greater nor equal
JLE/JNG	((SF xor OF) or ZF) = 1	less or equal/not greater
JNC	CF = 0	not carry
JNE/JNZ	ZF = 0	not equal/not zero
JNO	OF = 0	not overflow
JNP/JPO	PF = 0	not parity/parity odd
JNS	SF = 0	not sign
JO	OF = 1	overflow
JP/JPE	PF = 1	parity/parity equal
JS	SF = 1	sign

Note:
"Above" and "below" refer to the relationship of two unsigned values; "greater" and "less" refer to the relationship of two signed values.

Reprinted by permission of Intel Corporation, Copyright Intel Corp. 1989.

Similarly, the target address for a forward jump is calculated by adding the IP of the following instruction to the operand. In that case the displacement value is positive, as shown next. Below is a portion of a list file, showing the opcodes for several conditional jumps.

```
0005    8A 47 02    AGAIN: MOV    AL,[BX]+2
0008    3C 61              CMP    AL,61H
000A    72 06              JB     NEXT
000C    3C 7A              CMP    AL,7AH
000E    77 02              JA     NEXT
0010    24 DF              AND    AL,ODFH
0012    88 04       NEXT:  MOV    [SI],AL
```

In the program above, "JB NEXT" has the opcode 72 and the target address 06 and is located at IP = 000A and 000B. The jump will be 6 bytes from the next instruction which is IP = 000C. Adding gives us 000CH + 0006H = 0012H, which is the exact address of the NEXT label. Look also at "JA NEXT", which has 77 and 02 for the opcode and displacement, respectively. The IP of the following instruction, 0010, is added to 02 to get 0012, the address of the target location.

It must be emphasized that regardless of whether the jump is forward or backward, for conditional jumps the address of the target address can never be more than −128 to + 127 bytes away from the IP associated with the instruction following the jump (− for the backward jump and + for the forward jump). If any attempt is made to violate this rule, the assembler will generate a "relative jump out of range" message. These conditional jumps are sometimes referred to as SHORT jumps.

Unconditional jumps

"JMP label" is an unconditional jump in which control is transferred unconditionally to target location label. The unconditional jump can take the following forms:

1. SHORT JUMP, which is specified by format "JMP SHORT label". This is a jump in which the address of the target location is within −128 to +127 bytes of memory relative to the address of the current IP. In this case, the opcode is EB and the operand is 1 byte in the range 00 to FF. The operand byte is added to the current IP to calculate the target address. If the jump is backward, the operand is in 2's complement. This is exactly like the J condition case. Coding the directive "short" makes the jump more efficient in that it will be assembled into a 2-byte instruction instead of a 3-byte instruction.

2. NEAR JUMP, which is the default, has the format "JMP label". This is a near jump (within the current code segment) and has the opcode E9. The target address can be any of the addressing modes of direct, register, register indirect, or memory indirect:

   (a) Direct JUMP is exactly like the short jump explained earlier, except that the target address can be anywhere in the segment within the range +32767 to −32768 of the current IP.

   (b) Register indirect JUMP; the target address is in a register. For example, in "JMP BX", IP takes the value BX.

   (c) Memory indirect JMP; the target address is the contents of two memory locations pointed at by the register. Example: "JMP [DI]" will replace the IP with the contents of memory locations pointed at by DI and DI+1.

3. FAR JUMP which has the format "JMP FAR PTR label". This is a jump out of the current code segment, meaning that not only the IP but also the CS is replaced with new values.

CALL statements

Another control transfer instruction is the CALL instruction, which is used to call a procedure. CALLs to procedures are used to perform tasks that need to be performed frequently. This makes a program more structured. The target address could be in the current segment, in which case it will be a NEAR call or outside the current CS segment, which is a FAR call. To make sure that after execution of the called subroutine the microprocessor knows where to come back, the microprocessor automatically saves the address of the instruction following the call on the stack. It must be noted that in the NEAR call only the IP is saved on the stack, and in a FAR call both CS and IP are saved. When a subroutine is called, control is transferred to that subroutine and the processor saves the IP (and CS in the case of a FAR call) and begins to fetch instructions from the new location. After finishing execution of the subroutine, for control to be transferred back to the caller, the last instruction in the called subroutine must be RET (return). In the same way that the assembler generates different opcode for FAR and NEAR calls, the opcode for the RET instruction in case of NEAR and FAR is different, as well. For NEAR calls, the IP is restored; for FAR calls, both CS and IP are restored. This will ensure that control is given back to the caller. As an example, assume that SP = FFFEH and the following code is a portion of the program unassembled in DEBUG:

```
12B0:0200 BB1295          MOV   BX,9512
12B0:0203 E8FA00          CALL  0300
12B0:0206 B82F14          MOV   AX,142F
```

Since the CALL instruction is a NEAR call, meaning that it is in the same code segment (different IP, same CS), only IP is saved on the stack. In this case, the IP address of the instruction after the call is saved on the stack as shown in Figure 2-5. That IP will be 0206, which belongs to the "MOV AX,142F" instruction.

The last instruction of the called subroutine must be a RET instruction which directs the CPU to POP the top 2 bytes of the stack into the IP and resume executing at offset address 0206. For this reason, the number of PUSH and POP instructions (which alter the SP) must match. In other words, for every PUSH there must be a POP.

```
12B0:0300 53           PUSH  BX
12B0:0301 ...          ......   ..
...........    ...     ......   ..
12B0:0309 5B           POP   BX
12B0:030A C3           RET
```

Assembly language subroutines

In Assembly language programming it is common to have one main program and many subroutines to be called from the main program. This allows you to make each subroutine into a separate module. Each module can be tested separately and then brought together, as will be shown in Chapter 7. The main program is the entry point from DOS and is FAR, as explained earlier, but the subroutines called within the main program can be FAR or NEAR. Remember that NEAR routines are in the same code segment, while FAR routines are outside the current code segment. If there is no specific mention of FAR after the directive PROC, it defaults to NEAR, as shown in Figure 2-6. From now on, all code segments will be written in that format.

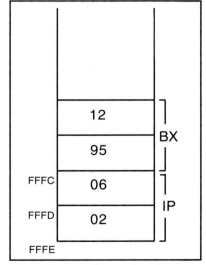

Figure 2-5. IP in the Stack

Rules for names in Assembly Language

By choosing label names that are meaningful, a programmer can make a program much easier to read and maintain. There are several rules that names must follow. First, each label name must be unique. The names used for labels in

Assembly language programming consist of alphabetic letters in both upper and lower case, the digits 0 through 9, and the special characters question mark (?), period (.), at (@), underline (_), and dollar sign ($). The first character of the name must be an alphabetic character or special character. It cannot be a digit. The period can only be used as the first character, but this is not recommended since later versions of MASM have several reserved words that begin with a period. Names may be up to 31 characters long. A list of reserved words is given at the end of Appendix C.

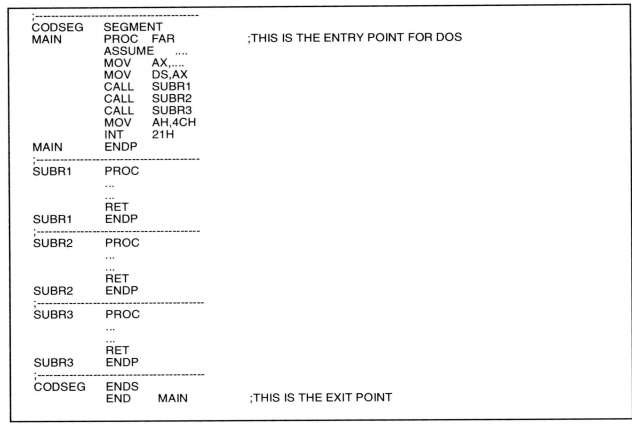

```
;------------------------------------
CODSEG      SEGMENT
MAIN        PROC    FAR             ;THIS IS THE ENTRY POINT FOR DOS
            ASSUME  ....
            MOV     AX,....
            MOV     DS,AX
            CALL    SUBR1
            CALL    SUBR2
            CALL    SUBR3
            MOV     AH,4CH
            INT     21H
MAIN        ENDP
;------------------------------------
SUBR1       PROC
            ...
            ...
            RET
SUBR1       ENDP
;------------------------------------
SUBR2       PROC
            ...
            ...
            RET
SUBR2       ENDP
;------------------------------------
SUBR3       PROC
            ...
            ...
            RET
SUBR3       ENDP
;------------------------------------
CODSEG      ENDS
            END     MAIN            ;THIS IS THE EXIT POINT
```

Figure 2-6. Shell of Assembly Language Subroutines

Review Questions

1. If control is transferred outside the current code segment, is it NEAR or FAR?
2. If a conditional jump is not taken, what is the next instruction to be executed?
3. In calculating the target address to jump to, a displacement is added to the contents of register _____.
4. What is the advantage in coding the operator "SHORT" in an unconditional jump?
5. A _____ jump is within −128 to +127 bytes of the current IP. A _____ jump is within the current code segment, whereas a _____ jump is outside the current code segment.
6. How does the CPU know where to return to after executing a RET?
7. Describe briefly the function of the RET instruction.
8. State why the following label names are invalid.
   (a) GET.DATA
   (b) 1_NUM
   (c) TEST-DATA
   (d) RET

SECTION 2.5: DATA TYPES AND DATA DEFINITION

The assembler supports all the various data types of the 80x86 microprocessor by providing data directives that define the data types and set aside memory for them. In this section we study these directives and how they are used to represent different data types of the 80x86. The application of these directives becomes clearer in the context of examples in subsequent chapters.

80x86 data types

The 8088/86 microprocessor supports many data types, but none are longer than 16 bits wide since the size of the registers is 16 bits. It is the job of the programmer to break down data larger than 16 bits (0000 to FFFFH, or 0 to 65535 in decimal) to be processed by the CPU. Many of these programs are shown in Chapter 3. The data types used by the 8088/86 can be 8-bit or 16-bit, positive or negative. If a number is less than 8 bits wide, it still must be coded as an 8-bit register with the higher digits as zero. Similarly, if the number is less than 16 bits wide it must use all 16 bits, with the rest being 0s. For example, the number 5 is only 3 bits wide (101) in binary, but the 8088/86 will accept it as 05 or "0000 0101" in binary. The number 514 is "10 0000 0010" in binary, but the 8088/86 will accept it as "0000 0010 0000 0010" in binary. The discussion of signed numbers is postponed until later chapters since their representation and application are unique.

Assembler data directives

All the assemblers designed for the 80x86 (8088, 8086, 80188, 80186, 80286, 80386, 80386SX, and 80486) microprocessors have standardized the directives for data representation. The following are some of the data directives used by the 80x86 microprocessor and supported by all software and hardware vendors of IBM PCs and compatibles.

ORG (origin)

ORG is used to indicate the beginning of the offset address. The number that comes after ORG can be either in hex or in decimal. If the number is not followed by H, it is decimal and the assembler will convert it to hex. Although the ORG directive is used extensively in this book in the data segment to separate fields of data to make it more readable for the student, it can also be used for the offset of the code segment (IP).

DB (define byte)

The DB directive is one of the most widely used data directives in the assembler. It allows allocation of memory in byte-sized chunks. This is indeed the smallest allocation unit permitted. DB can be used to define numbers in decimal, binary, hex, and ASCII. For decimal, the D after the decimal number is optional, but using B (binary) and H (hexadecimal) for the others is required. Regardless of which one is used, the assembler will convert them into hex. To indicate ASCII, simply place it in single quotation marks ('like this'). The assembler will assign the ASCII code for the numbers or characters automatically. DB is the only directive that can be used to define ASCII strings larger than two characters; therefore, it should be used for all ASCII data definitions. Following are some DB examples:

```
DATA1     DB   25            ;DECIMAL
DATA2     DB   10001001B     ;BINARY
DATA3     DB   12H           ;HEX
          ORG  0010H
DATA4     DB   '2591'        ;ASCII NUMBERS
          ORG  0018H
DATA5     DB   ?             ;SET ASIDE A BYTE
```

```
                            ORG  0020H
          DATA6             DB   'My name is Joe'  ;ASCII CHARACTERS
```

```
0000 19                     DATA1  DB   25          ;DECIMAL
0001 89                     DATA2  DB   10001001B   ;BINARY
0002 12                     DATA3  DB   12H         ;HEX
0010                               ORG  0010H
0010 32 35 39 31            DATA4  DB   '2591'      ;ASCII NUMBERS
0018                               ORG  0018H
0018 00                     DATA5  DB   ?           ;SET ASIDE A BYTE
0020                               ORG  0020H
0020 4D 79 20 6E 61 6D      DATA6  DB   'My name is Joe'    ;ASCII CHARACTERS
     65 20 69 73 20 4A
     6F 65
```

List File for DB Examples

Either single or double quotes can be used around ASCII strings. This can be useful for strings which should contain a single quote such as "O'Leary".

DUP (duplicate)

DUP is used to duplicate a given number of characters. This can avoid a lot of typing. For example, contrast the following two methods of filling six memory locations with FFH:

```
                  ORG  0030H
DATA7             DB   0FFH,0FFH,0FFH,0FFH,0FFH,0FFH  ;FILL 6 BYTES WITH FF
                  ORG  38H
DATA8             DB   6 DUP(0FFH)    ;FILL 6 BYTES WITH FF

; the following reserves 32 bytes of memory with no initial value given
                  ORG  40H
DATA9             DB   32 DUP (?)     ;SET ASIDE 32 BYTES
;DUP can be used inside another DUP
; the following fills 10 bytes with 99
DATA10            DB   5 DUP (2 DUP (99)) ;FILL 10 BYTES WITH 99
```

```
0030                                   ORG  0030H
0030 FF FF FF FF FF FF      DATA7  DB  0FFH,0FFH,0FFH,0FFH,0FFH,0FFH ;FILL 6 BYTES WITH FF
0038                                   ORG  38H
0038 0006[                  DATA8  DB     6 DUP(0FFH)    ;FILL 6 BYTES WITH FF
        FF
              ]
0040                                   ORG  40H
0040 0020[                  DATA9  DB     32 DUP (?)        ;SET ASIDE 32 BYTES
     ??
              ]
0060                                   ORG  60H
0060 0005[                  DATA10 DB     5 DUP (2 DUP (99)) ;FILL 10 BYTES WITH 99
        0002[
           63
              ]
        ]
```

List File for DUP Examples

DW (define word)

DW is used to allocate memory 2 bytes (one word) at a time. DW is used widely in the 8088/8086 and 80286 microprocessors since the registers are 16 bits wide. The following are some examples of DW:

```
                    ORG  70H
DATA11              DW   954                        ;DECIMAL
DATA12              DW   100101010100B             ;BINARY
DATA13              DW   253FH                      ;HEX
                    ORG  78H
DATA14              DW   9,2,7,0CH,00100000B,5,'HI'  ;MISCELLANEOUS DATA
DATA15              DW   8 DUP (?)                  ;SET ASIDE 8 WORDS
```

```
0070                          ORG  70H
0070 03BA                     DATA11 DW  954                        ;DECIMAL
0072 0954                     DATA12 DW  100101010100B             ;BINARY
0074 253F                     DATA13 DW  253FH                      ;HEX
0078                          ORG  78H
0078 0009 0002 0007 000C      DATA14 DW  9,2,7,0CH,00100000B,5,'HI'  ;MISCELLANEOUS DATA
     0020 0005 4849
0086 0008[                    DATA15 DW  8 DUP (?)                  ;SET ASIDE 8 WORDS
        ????                         ]
```

List File for DW Examples

EQU (equate)

This is used to define a constant without occupying a memory location. EQU does not set aside storage for a data item but associates a constant value with a data label so that when the label appears in the program, its constant value will be substituted for the label. EQU can also be used outside the data segment, even in the middle of a code segment. Using EQU for the counter constant in the immediate addressing mode:

```
COUNT          EQU    25
```

When executing the instructions "MOV CX,COUNT", the register CX will be loaded with the value 25. This is in contrast to using DB:

```
COUNT          DB     25
```

When executing the same instruction "MOV CX,COUNT" it will be in the direct addressing mode. Now what is the real advantage of EQU? First, note that EQU can also be used in the data segment:

```
COUNT          EQU    25
COUNTER1       DB     COUNT
COUNTER2       DB     COUNT
```

Assume that there is a constant (a fixed value) used in many different places in the data and code segments. By the use of EQU, one can change it once and the assembler will change all of them, rather than making the programmer try to find every location and correct it.

DD (define doubleword)

The DD directive is used to allocate memory locations that are 4 bytes (two words) in size. Again, the data can be in decimal, binary, or hex. In any case the data is converted to hex and placed in memory locations according to the rule of low byte to low address and high byte to high address. DD examples are:

SECTION 2.5: DATA TYPES AND DATA DEFINITION   **71**

```
                         ORG  00A0H
            DATA16       DD   1023                        ;DECIMAL
            DATA17       DD   10001001011001011100B       ;BINARY
            DATA18       DD   5C2A57F2H                   ;HEX
            DATA19       DD   23H,34789H,65533
```

```
00A0                                ORG  00A0H
00A0 000003FF              DATA16   DD   1023                        ;DECIMAL
00A4 0008965C              DATA17   DD   10001001011001011100B       ;BINARY
00A8 5C2A57F2              DATA18   DD   5C2A57F2H                   ;HEX
00AC 00000023 00034789     DATA19   DD   23H,34789H,65533
     0000FFFD
```

List File for DD Examples

DQ (define quadword)

DQ is used to allocate memory 8 bytes (four words) in size. This can be used to represent any variable up to 64 bits wide:

```
                         ORG  00C0H
            DATA20       DQ   4523C2H       ;HEX
            DATA21       DQ   'HI'          ;ASCII CHARACTERS
            DATA22       DQ   ?             ;NOTHING
```

```
00C0                                ORG  00C0H
00C0 C223450000000000      DATA20   DQ   4523C2H       ;HEX
00C8 4948000000000000      DATA21   DQ   'HI'          ;ASCII CHARACTERS
00D0 0000000000000000      DATA22   DQ   ?             ;NOTHING
```

List File for DQ Examples

DT (define ten bytes)

DT is used for memory allocation of packed BCD numbers. The application of DT will be seen in the multibyte addition of BCD numbers in Chapter 3. For now, observe how they are located in memory. Notice that the "H" after the data is not needed. This allocates 10 bytes, but a maximum of 18 digits can be entered.

```
                         ORG  00E0H
            DATA23       DT   867943569829     ;BCD
            DATA24       DT   ?                ;NOTHING
```

```
00E0                         ORG   00E0H
00E0 299856437986000000     DATA23   DT   867943569829    ;BCD
     00
00EA 000000000000000000     DATA24   DT   ?               ;NOTHING
     00
```

List File for DT Examples

DT can also be used to allocate 10-byte integers by using the "D" option:

```
            DEC          DT   65535d       ;the assembler will convert the decimal
                                           ;number to hex and store it
```

Figure 2-7 shows the memory dump of the data section, including all the examples in this section. It is essential to understand the way operands are stored in memory. Looking at the memory dump shows that all of the data directives use the little endian format for storing data, meaning that the least significant byte is located in the memory location of the lower address and the most significant byte resides in the memory of the higher address. For example, look at the case of "DATA20 DQ 4523C2", residing in memory starting at offset 00C0H. C2, the least significant byte, is in location 00C0, with 23 in 00C1, and 45, the most significant byte, in 00C2. It must also be noted that for ASCII data, only the DB directive can be used to define data of any length, and the use of DD, DQ, or DT directives for ASCII strings of more than 2 bytes gives an assembly error. When DB is used for ASCII numbers, notice how it places them backwards in memory. For example, see "DATA4 DB '2591'" at origin 10H: 32, ASCII for 2, is in memory location 10H; 35, ASCII for 5, is in 11H; and so on.

```
-D 1066:0 100
1066:0000  19 89 12 00 00 00 00 00-00 00 00 00 00 00 00 00  ................
1066:0010  32 35 39 31 00 00 00 00-00 00 00 00 00 00 00 00  2591............
1066:0020  4D 79 20 6E 61 6D 65 20-69 73 20 4A 6F 65 00 00  My name is Joe..
1066:0030  FF FF FF FF FF FF 00 00-FF FF FF FF FF FF 00 00  ................
1066:0040  00 00 00 00 00 00 00 00-00 00 00 00 00 00 00 00  ................
1066:0050  00 00 00 00 00 00 00 00-00 00 00 00 00 00 00 00  ................
1066:0060  63 63 63 63 63 63 63 63-63 63 00 00 00 00 00 00  cccccccccc......
1066:0070  BA 03 54 09 3F 25 00 00-09 00 02 00 07 00 0C 00  ..T.?%..........
1066:0080  20 00 05 00 4F 48 00 00-00 00 00 00 00 00 00 00  ...OH...........
1066:0090  00 00 00 00 00 00 00 00-00 00 00 00 00 00 00 00  ................
1066:00A0  FF 03 00 00 5C 96 08 00-F2 57 2A 5C 23 00 00 00  ....\...rW*\#...
1066:00B0  89 47 03 00 FD FF 00 00-00 00 00 00 00 00 00 00  B#E......IH.....
1066:00C0  C2 23 45 00 00 00 00 00-49 48 00 00 00 00 00 00  ................
1066:00D0  00 00 00 00 00 00 00 00-00 00 00 00 00 00 00 00  ................
1066:00E0  29 98 56 43 79 86 00 00-00 00 00 00 00 00 00 00  9.VCy6..........
```

Figure 2-7. DEBUG Dump of Data Segment

Review Questions

1. The _____ directive is always used for ASCII strings longer than 2 bytes.
2. How many bytes are defined by the following?
   DATA_1   DB   6 DUP (4 DUP (0FFH))
3. Do the following two data segment definitions result in the same storage in bytes at offset 10H and 11H? If not, explain why.

DTSEG	SEGMENT			DTSEG	SEGMENT
	ORG 10H				ORG 10H
DATA_1	DB 72H			DATA_1	DW 7204H
DATA_2	DB 04H			DTSEG	ENDS
DTSEG	ENDS				

4. The DD directive is used to allocate memory locations that are _____ bytes in length. The DQ directive is used to allocate memory locations that are _____ bytes in length.
5. State briefly the purpose of the ORG directive.
6. What is the advantage in using the EQU directive to define a constant value?
7. How many bytes are set aside by each of the following directives?
   (a) ASC_DATA DB '1234'   (b) HEX_DATA DW 1234H
8. Does the little endian storage convention apply to the storage of ASCII data?

SECTION 2.6: SIMPLIFIED SEGMENT DEFINITION

The way that segments have been defined in the programs above is the traditional definition referred to as *full segment definition*. In recent years a new method of segment definition has been introduced, called *simplified segment definition*, or simplified format. This simplified format is supported by Microsoft's MASM 5.0 and higher, Borland's TASM version 1 and higher, and many other compatible assemblers. Although the simplified segment definition is much easier to understand and use, especially for beginners, it is essential to master full segment definition since many older programs use it.

Memory model

Before using the simplified segment definition, the memory model for the program must be chosen. Among the options for the memory model are SMALL, MEDIUM, COMPACT, and LARGE.

SMALL MODEL: This is one of the most widely used memory models for Assembly language programs and is sufficient for the programs in this book. SMALL model uses a maximum of 64K bytes of memory for code and another 64K bytes for data.

MEDIUM MODEL: In this model, the data must also fit into 64K bytes, but the code can exceed 64K bytes of memory.

COMPACT MODEL: This is the opposite of the MEDIUM model. While data can exceed 64K bytes of memory, code cannot.

LARGE MODEL: Combining the two preceding models gives the LARGE model. Although this model allows both data and code to exceed 64K bytes of memory, no single set of data (such as an array) should exceed 64K bytes.

HUGE MODEL: Both code and data can exceed 64K bytes of memory, and a single set of data, such as an array, can exceed 64K bytes as well.

There is another memory model, called **TINY**. This model is used with COM files, and the total memory for both code and data must fit into 64K bytes. This model cannot be used with the simplified segment definition.

Segment definition

As mentioned in Chapter 1, the 80x86 CPU has four segment registers: CS (code segment), DS (data segment), SS (stack segment), and ES (extra segment). Every line of an Assembly language program must correspond to one of these segments. The simplified segment definition format uses three simple directives: ".CODE", ".DATA", and ".STACK", which correspond to the CS, DS, and SS registers, respectively. Using this method makes the SEGMENT and ENDS directives unnecessary. Figure 2-8 shows the full segment definition and simplified format, side by side. This is followed by Programs 2-2 and 2-3, rewritten using the simplified segment definition.

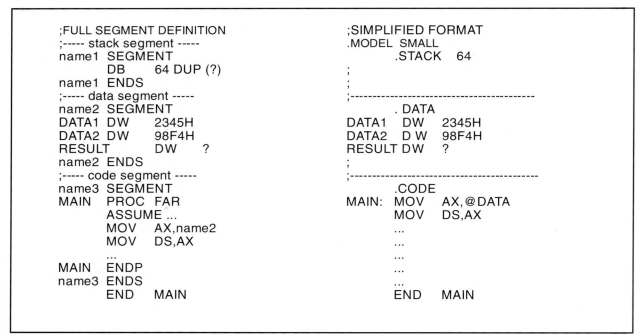

```
;FULL SEGMENT DEFINITION              ;SIMPLIFIED FORMAT
;----- stack segment -----            .MODEL  SMALL
name1  SEGMENT                              .STACK   64
       DB      64 DUP (?)             ;
name1  ENDS                           ;
;----- data segment -----             ;----------------------------------------
name2  SEGMENT                              . DATA
DATA1 DW    2345H                     DATA1   DW    2345H
DATA2 DW    98F4H                     DATA2   D W   98F4H
RESULT       DW    ?                   RESULT DW    ?
name2  ENDS                           ;
;----- code segment -----             ;----------------------------------------
name3  SEGMENT                              .CODE
MAIN   PROC  FAR                      MAIN:  MOV    AX,@DATA
       ASSUME ...                            MOV    DS,AX
       MOV   AX,name2                        ...
       MOV   DS,AX                           ...
       ...                                   ...
MAIN   ENDP                                  ...
name3  ENDS                                  ...
       END   MAIN                     END     MAIN
```

Figure 2-8. Full vs. Simplified Segment Definition

```
TITLE       PROG2-2 (EXE) Rewritten with simple segment definition
PAGE        60,132
            .MODEL SMALL
            .STACK 32
            .DATA
DATA1       DW      234DH,1DE6H,3BC7H,566AH
            ORG     10H
SUM         DW      ?
            .CODE
START:      MOV     AX,@DATA
            MOV     DS,AX
            MOV     CX,04               ;set up loop counter CX=4
            MOV     DI,OFFSET DATA1     ;set up data pointer DI
            SUB     BX,BX               ;initialize sum BX
ADD_LP:     ADD     BX,[DI]             ;add next word to BX
            INC     DI                  ;increment data pointer twice
            INC     DI                  ;  to point to next word
            DEC     CX                  ;decrement loop counter
            JNZ     ADD_LP              ;jump if loop counter not zero
            MOV     SI,OFFSET SUM       ;set up pointer for sum
            MOV     [SI],BX             ;store sum
            MOV     AH,4CH              ;set up to return
            INT     21H                 ;return to DOS
            END     START
```

Program 2-2, rewritten with simple segment definition

Program 2-3, rewritten below with simple segment definition, demonstrates that the order of the segments does not matter. The program above coded the segments in the order

```
.STACK
.DATA
.CODE
```

whereas the program below coded them in reverse order:

```
.CODE
.DATA
.STACK
```

```
TITLE       PROG2-3  (EXE) Rewritten with simple segment definition
PAGE        60,132
            .MODEL SMALL
            .CODE
MAIN:       MOV     AX,@DATA
            MOV     DS,AX
            MOV     SI,OFFSET DATA1     ;SI points to original DATA
            MOV     DI,OFFSET COPY      ;DI points to area DATA to be copied to
            MOV     CX,06H              ;CX is loop counter
MOV_LOOP:   MOV     AL,[SI]             ;move next byte from DATA to AL
            MOV     [DI],AL             ;move AL to copy area
            INC     SI                  ;increment DATA pointer
            INC     DI                  ;increment COPY pointer
            DEC     CX                  ;decrement LOOP counter
            JNZ     MOV_LOOP            ;jump if loop counter not zero
            MOV     AH,4CH              ;set up to return
            INT     21H                 ;return to DOS
            .DATA                       ;notice segments can be in any order
            ORG     10H
DATA1       DB      25H,4FH,85H,1FH,2BH,0C4H
            ORG     28H
COPY        DB      6 DUP (?)
            .STACK 32
            END     MAIN
```

Program 2-3, rewritten with simple segment definition

SECTION 2.7: EXE VS. COM FILES

All programs examples so far were designed to be assembled and linked into EXE files. This section looks at the COM file, which like the EXE file, contains the executable machine code and can be run at the DOS level. At the end of this section, the process of conversion from one file to other is shown.

Why COM files?

There are occasions where, due to a limited amount of memory, one needs to have very compact code. This is the time when the COM file is useful. The fact that the EXE file can be of any size is one of the main reasons that EXE files are used so widely. On the other hand, COM file are used because of their compactness since they cannot be greater than 64K bytes. The reason for the 64K-byte limit is that the COM file must fit into a single segment, and since in the 80x86 the size of a segment is 64K bytes, the COM file cannot be larger than 64K. To limit the size of the file to 64K bytes requires defining the data inside the code segment and also using an area (the end area) of the code segment for the stack. One of the distinguishing features of the COM file program is the fact that in contrast to the EXE file, it has no separate data segment definition. One can summarize the differences between COM and EXE files as shown in Table 2-2.

Table 2-2: EXE vs. COM File Format

EXE File	COM File
unlimited size	maximum size 64K bytes
stack segment is defined	no stack segment definition
data segment is defined	data segment defined in code segment
code, data can be defined at any offset address	code and data must begin at offset 0100H
larger file (takes more memory)	smaller file (takes less memory)

Another reason for the difference in the size of the EXE and COM file is the fact that the COM file does not have a header block. The header block, which occupies 512 bytes of memory, precedes every EXE file and contains information such as size, address location in memory, and stack address of the EXE module.

```
TITLE       PROG2-4 COM PROGRAM TO ADD TWO WORDS
PAGE        60,132
CODSG       SEGMENT
            ORG    100H
            ASSUME  CS:CODSG,DS:CODSG,ES:CODSG
;-----THIS IS THE CODE AREA
PROGCODE PROC   NEAR
            MOV    AX,DATA1        ;move the first word into AX
            ADD    DATA2           ;add the second word
            MOV    SUM,AX          ;move the sum
            MOV    AH,4CH          ;return to DOS
            INT    21H
PROGCODE ENDP
;-----THIS IS THE DATA AREA
DATA1       DW     2390
DATA2       DW     3456
SUM         DW     ?
;-----------------------------
CODSG       ENDS
            END    PROGCODE
```

Program 2-4

Program 2-4, written in COM format, adds two words of data and saves the result. This format is very similar to many programs written on the 8080/85 microprocessors, the generation before the 8088/86. This format of first having the code and then the data takes longer to assemble; therefore, it is strongly recommended to put the data first and then the code, but the program must bypass the data area by the use of a JUMP instruction, as shown next.

```
TITLE       PROG2-5 COM PROGRAM TO ADD TWO WORDS
PAGE        60,132
CODSG       SEGMENT
            ASSUME  CS:CODSG,DS:CODSG,ES:CODSG
            ORG     100H
START:      JMP     PROGCODE        ;go around the data area
;-----THIS IS THE DATA AREA
DATA1       DW      2390
DATA2       DW      3456
SUM         DW      ?
;-----THIS IS THE CODE AREA
PROGCODE: MOV       AX,DATA1        ;move the first word into AX
          ADD       AX,DATA2        ;add the second word
          MOV       SUM,AX          ;move the sum
          MOV       AH,4CH
          INT       21H             ;return to DOS
;---------------------------
CODSG       ENDS
            END     START
```

Program 2-5

Converting from EXE to COM

For the sake of memory efficiency, it is often desired to convert an EXE file into a COM. The source file must be changed to the COM format shown above, then assembled and linked as usual. Then it must be input to a utility program called EXE2BIN that comes with DOS. Its function is to convert the EXE file to a COM file. For example, to convert an EXE file called PROG1.EXE in drive B, assuming that EXE2BIN utility is in drive A, do the following:

A>EXE2BIN B:PROG1,B:PROG1.COM <return>

Notice that there is no extension of EXE for PROG1 since it is assumed that one is converting an EXE file. Keep in mind that for a program to be converted into a COM file, it must be in the format shown in Programs 2-4 and 2-5.

SUMMARY

An Assembly language program is composed of a series of statements that are either instructions or pseudo-instructions, also called directives. Instructions are translated by the assembler into machine code. Pseudo-instructions are not translated into machine code: They direct the assembler in how to translate the instructions into machine code. The statements of an Assembly language program are grouped into segments. The beginning and ending points of segments are defined by the SEGMENT and ENDS pseudo-instructions. Other pseudo-instructions, often called data directives, are used to define the data in the data segment. Data can be allocated in units ranging in size from byte, word, doubleword, and quadword to 10 bytes at a time. The data can be in binary, hex, decimal, or ASCII.

The flow of a program proceeds sequentially, from instruction to instruction, unless a control transfer instruction is executed. The various types of control transfer instructions in Assembly language include conditional and unconditional jumps, and call instructions.

PROBLEMS

1. Fill in the blanks in the following program. The labels are unorthodox, but this is just an exercise. The program does not really do anything.

```
CATSG          SEGMENT
               DB              64 DUP(?)
_____          ENDS
;-------------------------------
DOGSG          _____
MYDATA         DB              25H
_____          ENDS
;-------------------------------
MYSG           SEGMENT
START_HERE     PROC            FAR
               ASSUME          _____:MYSG,DS:DOGSG;SS:_____
               MOV             _____,DOGSG
               MOV             DS,_____
               CALL            JOE
               CALL            TOM
               MOV             AH,4CH
               INT             21H
_____        ENDP
;-----------------------------
_____        PROC            NEAR
               NOP
               NOP
               RET
JOE            ENDP
;-----------------------------
TOM            _____          NEAR
               NOP
               NOP
               RET

_____
_____          ENDS
               END             _____
```

2. List the steps in getting a ready-to-run program.
3. Which program produces the ".exe" file?
4. Which program produces the ".obj" file?
5. True or false: The ".lst" file is produced by the assembler regardless of whether or not the programmer wants it.
6. The source program file must have the ".asm" extension in some assemblers. such as MASM.   Is this true for the assembler you are using?
7. Circle one: The linking process comes (after, before) assembling.
8. In some applications it is common practice to save all registers at the beginning of a subroutine. Assume that SP = 1288H before a subroutine CALL. Show the contents of the stack pointer and the exact memory contents of the stack after PUSHF, for the following:

```
1132:0450      CALL    PROC1
1132:0453      INC     BX

PROC1          PROC
               PUSH    AX
               PUSH    BX
               PUSH    CX
               PUSH    DX
               PUSH    SI
               PUSH    DI
               PUSHF
               ....
               ....
PROC1          ENDP
```

9. To restore the original information inside the CPU at the end of a CALL to a subroutine, the sequence of POP instructions must follow a certain order. Write the sequence of POP instructions that will restore the information in Problem 8. At each point, show the contents of the SP.

10. When a CALL is executed, how does the CPU know where to return?

11. In a FAR CALL, _____ and _____ are saved on the stack, whereas in a NEAR CALL, _____ is saved on the stack.

12. Compare the number of bytes of stack taken due to NEAR and FAR CALLs.

13. Find the contents of the stack and stack pointer after execution of the CALL instruction shown next.

```
CS  : IP
2450:673A     CALL   SUM
2450:673D     DEC    AH
```

SUM is a near procedure. Assume that SS:1296 right before the execution of CALL.

14. The following is a section of BIOS of the IBM PC which is described in detail in Chapter 3. All the jumps below are short jumps, meaning that the labels are in the range -128 to +127.

```
IP    Code
E06C 733F                        JNC  ERROR1
...              ...             ...
...              ...             ...
E072 7139                        JNO  ERROR1
...              ...             ...
...              ...             ...
E08C 8ED8        C8:             MOV  DS,AX
...              ...             ...
...              ...             ...
E0A7 EBE3                        JMP  C8
...              ...             ...
...              ...             ...
E0AD F4          ERROR1:         HLT
```

Verify the address calculations of:
(a) JNC ERROR1
(b) JNO ERROR1
(c) JMP C8

15. Find the precise offset location of each ASCII character or data in the following:

```
        ORG     20H
DATA1   DB      '1-800-555-1234'
        ORG     40H
DATA2   DB      'Name: John Jones'
        ORG     60H
DATA3   DB      '5956342'
        ORG     70H
DATA4   DW      2560H,1000000000110B
DATA5   DW      49
        ORG     80H
DATA6   DD      25697F6EH
DATA7   DQ      9E7BA21C99F2H
        ORG     90H
DATA8   DT      439997924999828
DATA9   DB      6 DUP (0EEH)
```

16. The following program contains some errors. Fix the errors and make the program run correctly. Verify it through the DEBUG program. This program adds four words and saves the result.

```
TITLE   PROBLEM (EXE)  PROBLEM 16 PROGRAM
PAGE    60,132
STSEG   SEGMENT
        DB 32 DUP(?)
STSEG   END
;---------------------------
DTSEG           SEGMENT
DATA    DW      234DH,DE6H,3BC7H,566AH
        ORG     10H
SUM     DW      ?
DTSG    ENDS
;---------------------------
```

```
CDSEG  SEGMENT
START: PROC    FAR
               ASSUME CS:CDSEG,DS:DTSEG,SS:STSEG
       MOV     AX,DTSEG
       MOV     DS,AX
       MOV     CX,04            ;SET UP LOOP COUNTER CX=4
       MOV     BX,0             ;INITIALIZE BX TO ZERO
       MOV     DI,OFFSET DATA   ;SET UP DATA POINTER BX
LOOP1: ADD     BX,[DI]          ;ADD CONTENTS POINTED AT BY [DI] TO BX
       INC     DI               ;INCREMENT DI
       DEC     BX               ;DECREMENT LOOP COUNTER
       JNZ     LOOP1            ;JUMP IF LOOP COUNTER NOT ZERO
       MOV     SI,OFFSET RESULT ;LOAD POINTER FOR THE RESULT
       MOV     [SI],BX          ;STORE THE SUM
       MOV     AH,4CH
       INT     21H
CDSEG: ENDS
START  ENDP
       END     STRT
```

ANSWERS TO REVIEW QUESTIONS

Section 2.1: Directives and a Sample Program
1. Pseudo-instructions direct the assembler as to how to assemble the program.
2. Instructions, pseudo-instructions, or directives
3.
```
   STK_SG       SEGMENT
                DB 64 DUP (?)
   STK_SG       ENDS
   ;
   DAT_SG       SEGMENT
   HIGH_DAT     DB      95
   DAT_SG       ENDS
   ;
   COD_SG       SEGMENT
   START        PROC FAR
                ASSUME CS:COD_SG,DS:DAT_SG,SS:STK_SG
                MOV AX,DAT_SG
                MOV DS,AX
                MOV AH,HIGH_DAT
                MOV BH,AH
                MOV DL,BH
                MOV AH,4CH
                INT 21H
   START        ENDP
   COD_SG       ENDS
                END START
```
4. (1) stack segment labels do not match for SEGMENT and ENDS directives
    (2) ENDP label does not match label for PROC directive
    (3) data segment needs "ENDS" directive, not "END"
    (4) "MOV AX,DATSEG" should be "MOV AX,DTSEG"
    (5) END must have the entry point label "MAIN"

Section 2.2: Assemble, Link, and Run a Program
1. (a) MASM must have the ".asm" file as input
    (b) LINK must have the ".obj" file as input
2. Editor outputs : (b) .asm
    Assembler outputs: (a) .obj, (d) .lst, and (e) .crf files
    Linker outputs: (c) .exe and (f) .map files

Section 2.3: More Sample Programs
1. increments the operand, that is, it causes 1 to be added to the operand
2. decrements the operand, that is, it causes 1 to be subtracted from the operand
3. a colon is required after labels referring to instructions; colons are not placed after labels for directives
4. the first moves the contents of the word beginning at offset DATA1, the second moves the offset address of DATA1
5. the first adds the contents of BX to AX, the second adds the contents of the memory location at offset BX.

Section 2.4: Control Transfer Instructions
1. far
2. the instruction right below the jump
3. IP
4. the machine code for the instruction will take up 1 less byte
5. short, near, far
6. the contents of CS and IP were stored on the stack when the call is executed
7. it restores the contents of CS:IP and returns control to the instruction immediately following the CALL
8. (a) GET.DATA, invalid because "." is only allowed as the first character
   (b) 1_NUM, because the first character cannot be a number
   (c) TEST-DATA, because "-" is not allowed
   (d) RET, is a reserved word

Section 2.5: Data Types and Data Definition
1. DB
2. 24
3. no because of the little endian storage conventions, which will cause the word "7204H" to be stored with the lower byte (04) at offset 10H and the upper byte at offset 11H; DB allocates each byte as it is defined
4. 4, 8
5. it is used to assign the offset address
6. if the value is to be changed later, it can be changed in one place instead of at every occurrence
7. (a) 4   (b) 2
8. no

CHAPTER 3

ARITHMETIC AND LOGIC INSTRUCTIONS AND PROGRAMS

OBJECTIVES

» Upon completion of this chapter, you will be able to:

» Demonstrate how 8-bit and 16-bit unsigned numbers are added in the 80x86
» Convert data to any of the forms: ASCII, packed BCD, or unpacked BCD
» Explain the effect of unsigned arithmetic instructions on the flag register
» Code the following Assembly language unsigned arithmetic instructions:
»   Addition instructions ADD and ADC
»   Subtraction instructions SUB and SBB
»   Multiplication and division instructions MUL and DIV
» Code BCD and ASCII arithmetic instructions:
»   DAA, DAS, AAA, AAS, AAM, and AAD
» Code the following Assembly language logic instructions:
»   AND, OR, and XOR
»   logical shift instructions SHR and SHL
»   the compare instruction CMP
» Code BCD and ASCII arithmetic instructions
» Code bitwise rotation instructions ROR, ROL, RCR, and RCL
» Demonstrate an ability to use all of the instructions above in Assembly language programs

In this chapter, most of the arithmetic and logic instructions are discussed and program examples are given to illustrate the application of these instructions. Unsigned numbers are used in this discussion of arithmetic and logic instructions. Signed numbers are discussed separately in Chapter 6. Unsigned numbers are defined as data in which all the bits are used to represent data and no bits are set aside for the positive or negative sign. This means that the operand can be between 00 and FFH (0 to 255 decimal) for 8-bit data and between 0000 and FFFFH (0 to 65535 decimal) for 16-bit data.

SECTION 3.1: UNSIGNED ADDITION AND SUBTRACTION

Addition of unsigned numbers

The form of the ADD instruction is

```
ADD   destination,source  ;dest. operand = dest. operand + source operand
```

The instructions ADD and ADC are used to add two operands. The destination operand can be a register or in memory. The source operand can be a register, in memory, or immediate. Remember that memory-to-memory operations are never allowed in 80x86 Assembly language. The instruction could change any of ZF, SF, AF, CF, or PF bits of the flag register, depending on the operands involved. The effect of the ADD instruction on the overflow flag is discussed in Chapter 6 since it is used in signed number operations. Look at the following example:

Example 3-1

Show how the flag register is affected by

```
    MOV    AL,0F5H
    ADD    AL,0BH
```

Solution:

```
    F5H         1111 0101
  + 0BH       + 0000 1011
   100H         0000 0000
```

After the addition, the AL register (destination) contains 00 and the flags are as follows:
CF = 1 since there is a carry out from D7
SF = 0 the status of D7 of the result
PF = 1 the number of 1s is zero (zero is an even number)
AF = 1 there is a carry from D3 to D4
ZF = 1 the result of the action is zero (for the 8 bits)

In discussing addition, the following two cases will be examined:

(1) Addition of individual byte and word data
(2) Addition of multibyte data

CASE 1: Addition of individual byte and word data

In Chapter 2 there was a program that added 5 bytes of data. The total sum was purposely kept less than FFH, the maximum value an 8-bit register can hold. To calculate the total sum of any number of operands, the carry flag should be checked after the addition of each operand. Program 3-1a uses AH to accumulate carries as the operands are added to AL.

Write a program to calculate the total sum of 5 bytes of data. Each byte represents the daily wages of a worker. This person does not make more than $255 (FFH) a day. The decimal data is as follows: 125, 235, 197, 91, and 48.

```
TITLE      PROG3-1A (EXE)  ADDING 5 BYTES
PAGE       60,132
STSEG      SEGMENT
           DB      64 DUP (?)
STSEG      ENDS
;---------------------------
DTSEG      SEGMENT
COUNT      EQU     05
DATA       DB      125,235,197,91,48
           ORG     0008H
SUM        DW      ?
DTSEG      ENDS
;---------------------------
CDSEG      SEGMENT
MAIN       PROC    FAR
           ASSUME CS:CDSEG,DS:DTSEG,SS:STSEG
           MOV     AX,DTSEG
           MOV     DS,AX
           MOV     CX,COUNT        ;CX is the loop counter
           MOV     SI,OFFSET DATA;SI is the data pointer
           MOV     AX,00           ;AX will hold the sum
BACK:      ADD     AL,[SI]         ;add the next byte to AL
           JNC     OVER            ;If no carry, continue
           INC     AH              ;else accumulate carry in AH
OVER:      INC     SI              ;increment data pointer
           DEC     CX              ;decrement loop counter
           JNZ     BACK            ;if not finished, go add next byte
           MOV     SUM,AX          ;store sum
           MOV     AH,4CH
           INT     21H             ;go back to DOS
MAIN       ENDP
CDSEG      ENDS
           END     MAIN
```

Program 3-1a

Analysis of Program 3-1a

These numbers are converted to hex by the assembler as follows: $125 = 7DH$, $235 = 0EBH$, $197 = 0C5H$, $91 = 5BH$, $48 = 30H$. Three iterations of the loop are shown below. The tracing of the program is left to the reader as an exercise.

1. In the first iteration of the loop, 7DH is added to AL with $CF = 0$ and $AH = 00$. $CX = 04$ and $ZF = 0$.
2. In the second iteration of the loop, EBH is added to AL, which results in $AL = 68H$ and $CF = 1$. Since a carry occurred, AH is incremented. $CX = 03$ and $ZF = 0$.
3. In the third iteration, C5H is added to AL, which makes $AL = 2DH$. Again a carry occurred, so AH is incremented again. $CX = 02$ and $ZF = 0$.

This process continues until $CX = 00$ and the zero flag becomes 1, which will cause JNZ to fall through. Then the result will be saved in the word-sized memory set aside in the data segment. Although this program works correctly, due to pipelining it is strongly recommended that the following lines of the program be replaced:

```
Replace these lines              With these lines
BACK: ADD    AL,[SI]             BACK: ADD    AL,[SI]
      JNC    OVER                      ADC    AH,00  ;add 1 to AH if CF=1
      INC    AH                        INC    SI
OVER: INC    SI
```

The "ADC AH,00" instruction in reality means add $00 + AH + CF$ and place the result in AH. This is much more efficient since the instruction "JNC OVER" has to empty the queue of pipelined instructions and fetch the instructions from the OVER target every time the carry is zero ($CF = 0$).

The addition of many word operands works the same way. Register AX (or CX or DX or BX) could be used as the accumulator and BX (or any general-purpose 16-bit register) for keeping the carries. Program 3-1b is the same as Program 3-1a, rewritten for word addition.

Write a program to calculate the total sum of five words of data. Each data value represents the yearly wages of a worker. This person does not make more than $65,555 (FFFFH) a year. The decimal data is as follows: 27345, 28521, 29533, 30105, and 32375.

```
TITLE       PROG3-1B (EXE)  ADDING 5 WORDS
PAGE        60,132
STSEG       SEGMENT
            DB      64 DUP (?)
STSEG       ENDS
;--------------------------
DTSEG       SEGMENT
COUNT       EQU     05
DATA        DW      27345,28521,29533,30105,32375
            ORG     0010H
SUM         DW      2 DUP(?)
DTSEG       ENDS
;--------------------------
CDSEG       SEGMENT
MAIN        PROC    FAR
            ASSUME CS:CDSEG,DS:DTSEG,SS:STSEG
            MOV     AX,DTSEG
            MOV     DS,AX
            MOV     CX,COUNT        ;CX is the loop counter
            MOV     SI,OFFSET DATA;SI is the data pointer
            MOV     AX,00           ;AX will hold the sum
            MOV     BX,AX           ;BX will hold the carries
BACK:       ADD     AX,[SI]         ;add the next word to AX
            ADC     BX,0            ;add carry to BX
            INC     SI              ;increment data pointer twice
            INC     SI              ;  to point to next word
            DEC     CX              ;decrement loop counter
            JNZ     BACK            ;if not finished, continue adding
            MOV     SUM,AX          ;store the sum
            MOV     SUM+2,BX        ;store the carries
            MOV     AH,4CH
            INT     21H             ;go back to DOS
MAIN        ENDP
CDSEG       ENDS
            END     MAIN
```

Program 3-1b

CASE 2: Addition of multiword numbers

Assume a program is needed that will add the total U. S. budget for the last 100 years or the mass of all the planets in the solar system. In cases like this, the numbers being added could be up to 8 bytes wide or more. Since registers are only 16 bits wide (2 bytes), it is the job of the programmer to write the code to break down these large numbers into smaller chunks to be processed by the CPU. If a 16-bit register is used and the operand is 8 bytes wide, that would take a total of four iterations. However, if an 8-bit register is used, the same operands would require eight iterations. This obviously takes more time for the CPU. This is one reason to have wide registers in the design of the CPU. Large and powerful computers such as the CRAY have registers of 64 bits wide and larger.

Write a program that adds the following two multiword numbers and saves the result:
DATA1 = 548FB9963CE7H and DATA2 = 3FCD4FA23B8DH.

```
TITLE     PROG3-2 (EXE)  MULTIWORD ADDITION
PAGE      60,132
STSEG     SEGMENT
          DB      64 DUP (?)
STSEG     ENDS
;---------------------------
DTSEG     SEGMENT
DATA1     DQ      548FB9963CE7H
          ORG     0010H
DATA2     DQ      3FCD4FA23B8DH
          ORG     0020H
DATA3     DQ      ?
DTSEG     ENDS
;---------------------------
CDSEG     SEGMENT
MAIN      PROC   FAR
          ASSUME CS:CDSEG,DS:DTSEG,SS:STSEG
          MOV    AX,DTSEG
          MOV    DS,AX
          CLC                        ;clear carry before first addition
          MOV    SI,OFFSET DATA1     ;SI is pointer for operand1
          MOV    DI,OFFSET DATA2     ;DI is pointer for operand2
          MOV    BX,OFFSET DATA3     ;BX is pointer for the sum
          MOV    CX,04               ;CX is the loop counter
BACK:     MOV    AX,[SI]             ;move the first operand to AX
          ADC    AX,[DI]             ;add the second operand to AX
          MOV    [BX],AX             ;store the sum
          INC    SI                  ;point to next word of operand1
          INC    SI
          INC    DI                  ;point to next word of operand2
          INC    DI
          INC    BX                  ;point to next word of sum
          INC    BX
          LOOP   BACK                ;if not finished, continue adding
          MOV    AH,4CH
          INT    21H                 ;go back to DOS
MAIN      ENDP
CDSEG     ENDS
          END    MAIN
```

Program 3-2

Analysis of Program 3-2

In writing this program, the first thing to be decided was the directive used for coding the data in the data segment. DQ was chosen since it can represent data as large as 8 bytes wide. The question is: Which add instruction should be used? In the addition of multibyte (or multiword) numbers, the ADC instruction is always used since the carry must be added to the next-higher byte (or word) in the next iteration. Before executing ADC, the carry flag must be cleared (CF = 0) so that in the first iteration, the carry would not be added. Clearing the carry flag is achieved by the CLC (clear carry) instruction. Three pointers have been used: SI for DATA1, DI for DATA2, and BX for DATA3 where the result is saved. There is a new instruction in that program, "LOOP XXXX", which replaces the often used "DEC CX" and "JNZ XXXX". In other words:

```
LOOP   xxxx   ;is equivalent to the following two instructions

DEC    CX
JNZ    xxxx
```

When the "LOOP xxxx" is executed, CX is decremented automatically, and if CX is not 0, the microprocessor will jump to target address xxxx. If CX is 0, the next instruction (the one below "LOOP xxxx") is executed.

Subtraction of unsigned numbers

```
SUB  dest,source                    ;dest = dest – source
```

In subtraction, the 80x86 microprocessors (indeed, almost all modern CPUs) use the 2's complement method. Although every CPU contains adder circuitry, it would be too cumbersome (and take too many transistors) to design separate subtractor circuitry. For this reason, the 80x86 uses internal adder circuitry to perform the subtraction command. Assuming that the 80x86 is executing simple subtract instructions, one can summarize the steps of the hardware of the CPU in executing the SUB instruction for unsigned numbers, as follows.

1. Take the 2's complement of the subtrahend (source operand).
2. Add it to the minuend (destination operand).
3. Invert the carry.

These three steps are performed for every SUB instruction by the internal hardware of the 80x86 CPU regardless of the source and destination of the operands as long as the addressing mode is supported. It is after these three steps that the result is obtained and the flags are set. The next example illustrates the three steps.

Example 3-2

Show the steps involved in the following:
```
    MOV     AL,3FH           ;load AL=3FH
    MOV     BH,23H           ;load BH=23H
    SUB     AL,BH            ;subtract BH from AL.  Place result in AL.
```

Solution:

```
    AL      3F    0011 1111              0011 1111
  – BH     – 23  – 0010 0011            +1101 1101     (2's complement)
            1C                         1 0001 1100     CF=0 (step 3)
```

The flags would be set as follows: CF = 0, ZF = 0, AF = 0, PF = 0, and SF = 0. The programmer must look at the carry flag (not the sign flag) to determine if the result is positive or negative.

After the execution of SUB, if CF = 0, the result is positive; if CF = 1, the result is negative and the destination has the 2's complement of the result. Normally, the result is left in 2's complement, but the NOT and INC instructions can be used to change it. The NOT instruction performs the 1's complement of the operand; then the operand is incremented to get the 2's complement.

Example 3-3

Analyze the following program:
```
  ;from the data segment:
    DATA1   DB      4CH
    DATA2   DB      6EH
    DATA3   DB      ?
  ;from the code segment:
            MOV     DH,DATA1         ;load DH with DATA1 value (4CH)
            SUB     DH,DATA2         ;subtract DATA2 (6E) from DH (4CH)
            JNC     NEXT             ;if CF=0 jump to NEXT target
            NOT     DH               ;if CF=1 then take 1's complement
            INC     DH               ;and increment to get 2's complement
    NEXT:   MOV     DATA3,DH         ;save DH in DATA3
```

Solution:
Following the three steps for "SUB DH,DATA2":
```
    4C    0100 1100                 0100 1100
  – 6E    0110 1110    2's comp    +1001 0010
  – 22                              0 1101 1110     CF=1 (step 3) the result is negative
```

SBB (subtract with borrow)

This instruction is used for multibyte (multiword) numbers and will take care of the borrow of the lower operand. If the carry flag is 0, SBB works like SUB. If the carry flag is 1, SBB subtracts 1 from the result. Notice the "PTR" operand in Example 3-4. The PTR (pointer) data specifier directive is widely used to specify the size of the operand when it differs from the defined size. In Example 3-4, "WORD PTR" tells the assembler to use a word operand, even though the data is defined as a doubleword.

Example 3-4

Analyze the following program:

```
DATA_A      DD      62562FAH
DATA_B      DD      412963BH
RESULT      DD      ?
...         ...     ...
            MOV     AX,WORD PTR DATA_A          ;AX=62FA
            SUB     AX,WORD PTR DATA_B          ;SUB 963B from AX
            MOV     WORD PTR RESULT,AX          ;save the result
            MOV     AX,WORD PTR DATA_A +2       ;AX=0625
            SBB     AX,WORD PTR DATA_B +2       ;SUB 0412 with borrow
            MOV     WORD PTR RESULT+2,AX        ;save the result
```

Solution:

After the SUB, AX =963B − 62FA =CCBF and the carry flag is set. Since CF = 1, when SBB is executed, AX =625 − 412 − 1 =212. Therefore, the value stored in RESULT is 0212CCBF.

Review Questions

1. The ADD instruction that has the syntax "ADD destination, source" replaces the _____ operand with the sum of the two operands.
2. Why is the following ADD instruction illegal?
   ADD DATA_1,DATA_2
3. Rewrite the instruction above in a correct form.
4. The ADC instruction that has the syntax "ADC destination, source" replaces the _____ operand with the sum of _____.
5. The execution of part (a) below results in ZF = 1, whereas the execution of part (b) results in ZF = 0. Explain why.
   (a) MOV BL,04FH   (b) MOV BX,04FH
        ADD BL,0B1H   ADD BX,0B1H
6. The instruction "LOOP ADD_LOOP" is equivalent to what two instructions?
7. Show how the CPU would subtract 05H from 43H.
8. If CF = 1, AL = 95, and BL = 4F prior to the execution of "SBB AL,BL", what will be the contents of AL after the subtraction?

SECTION 3.2: UNSIGNED MULTIPLICATION AND DIVISION

One of the major changes from the 8080/85 microprocessor to the 8086 was inclusion of instructions for multiplication and division. In this section we cover each one with examples. This is multiplication and division of unsigned numbers. Signed numbers are treated in Chapter 6.

In multiplying or dividing two numbers in the 80x86 microprocessor, the use of registers AX, AL, AH, and DX is necessary since these functions assume the use of those registers.

Multiplication of unsigned numbers

In discussing multiplication, the following cases will be examined: (1) byte times byte, (2) word times word, and (3) byte times word.

---

byte × byte: In byte by byte multiplication, one of the operands must be in the AL register and the second operand can be either in a register or in memory as addressed by one of the addressing modes discussed in Chapter 1. After the multiplication, the result is in AX. See the following example:

```
RESULT  DW   ?                ;result is defined in the data segment
        ...
        MOV  AL,25H           ;a byte is moved to AL
        MOV  BL,65H           ;immediate data must be in a register
        MUL  BL               ;AL = 25 × 65H
        MOV  RESULT,AX        ;the result is saved
```

In the program above, 25H is multiplied by 65H and the result is saved in word-sized memory named RESULT. In that example, the register addressing mode was used. The next three examples show the register, direct, and register indirect addressing modes.

```
;from the data segment:
DATA1 DB      25H
DATA2 DB      65H
RESULT        DW   ?
;from the code segment:
        MOV  AL,DATA1
        MOV  BL,DATA2
        MUL  BL                      ;register addressing mode
        MOV  RESULT,AX
or
        MOV  AL,DATA1
        MUL  DATA2                   ;direct addressing mode
        MOV  RESULT,AX
or
        MOV  AL,DATA1
        MOV  SI,OFFSET DATA2
        MUL  BYTE PTR [SI]           ;register indirect addressing mode
        MOV  RESULT,AX
```

In the register addressing mode example, any 8-bit register could have been used in place of BL. Similarly, in the register indirect example, BX or DI could have been used as pointers. If the register indirect addressing mode is used, the operand size must be specified with the help of the PTR pseudo-instruction. In the absence of the "BYTE PTR" directive in the example above, the assembler could not figure out if it should use a byte or word operand pointed at by SI. This confusion would cause an error.

word × word: In word by word multiplication, one operand must be in AX and the second operand can be in a register or memory. After the multiplication, registers AX and DX will contain the result. Since word × word multiplication can produce a 32-bit result, AX will hold the lower word and DX the higher word. Example:

```
DATA3         DW   2378H
DATA4         DW   2F79H
RESULT1       DW   2 DUP(?)
        .......
        MOV  AX,DATA3               ;load first operand into AX
        MUL  DATA4                  ;multiply it by the second operand
        MOV  RESULT1,AX             ;store the lower word result
        MOV  RESULT1+2,DX           ;store the higher word result
```

word × byte: This is similar to word by word multiplication except that AL contains the byte operand and AH must be set to zero. Example:

```
;from the data segment:
DATA5       DB     6BH
DATA6       DW     12C3H
RESULT3     DW     2 DUP(?)

;from the code segment:
    ...     ...
    MOV     AL,DATA5            ;AL holds byte operand
    SUB     AH,AH               ;AH must be cleared
    MUL     DATA6               ;byte in AL multiplied by word operand
    MOV     BX,OFFSET RESULT3   ;BX points to storage for product
    MOV     [BX],AX             ;AX holds lower word
    MOV     [BX]+2,DX           ;DX holds higher word
```

Table 3-1 gives a summary of multiplication of unsigned numbers. Using the 80x86 microprocessor to perform multiplication of operands larger than 16-bit size takes some manipulation, although in such cases the 8087 coprocessor is normally used.

Table 3-1: Unsigned Multiplication Summary

Multiplication	Operand 1	Operand 2	Result
byte × byte	AL	register or memory	AX
word × word	AX	register or memory	DX AX
word × byte	AL = byte, AH = 0	register or memory	DX AX

Division of unsigned numbers

In the division of unsigned numbers, the following cases are discussed:

(1) Byte over byte
(2) Word over word
(3) Word over byte
(4) Doubleword over word

In divide, there could be cases where the CPU cannot perform the division. In these cases an interrupt is activated. In recent years this is referred to as an *exception.* In what situation can the microprocessor not handle the division and must call an interrupt? They are

(1) if the denominator is zero (dividing any number by 00), and
(2) if the quotient is too large for the assigned register.

In the IBM PC and compatibles, if either of these cases happens, the PC will display the "divide error" message.

byte/byte: In dividing a byte by a byte, the numerator must be in the AL register and AH must be set to zero. The denominator cannot be immediate but can be in a register or memory as supported by the addressing modes. After the DIV instruction is performed, the quotient is in AL and the remainder is in AH. The following shows the various addressing modes that the denominator can take.

```
DATA7       DB      95
DATA8       DB      10
QOUT1       DB      ?
REMAIN1     DB      ?

;using immediate addressing mode will give an error
            MOV     AL,DATA7        ;move data into AL
            SUB     AH,AH           ;clear AH
            DIV     10              ;immed. mode not allowed!!

;allowable modes include:

;using direct mode
            MOV     AL,DATA7        ;AL holds numerator
            SUB     AH,AH           ;AH must be cleared
            DIV     DATA8           ;divide AX by DATA8
            MOV     QOUT1,AL        ;quotient = AL = 09
            MOV     REMAIN1,AH      ;remainder = AH = 05

;using register addressing mode
            MOV     AL,DATA7        ;AL holds numerator
            SUB     AH,AH           ;AH must be cleared
            MOV     BH,DATA8        ;move denom. to register
            DIV     BH              ;divide AX by BH
            MOV     QOUT1,AL        ;quotient = AL = 09
            MOV     REMAIN1,AH      ;remainder = AH = 05

;using register indirect addressing mode
            MOV     AL,DATA7            ;AL holds numerator
            SUB     AH,AH               ;AH must be cleared
            MOV     BX,OFFSET DATA8     ;BX holds offset of DATA8
            DIV     BYTE PTR [BX]       ;divide AX by DATA8
            MOV     QOUT2,AX
            MOV     REMAIND2,DX
```

word/word: In this case the numerator is in AX and DX must be cleared. The denominator can be in a register or memory. After the DIV, AX will have the quotient and the remainder will be in DX.

```
            MOV     AX,10050        ;AX holds numerator
            SUB     DX,DX           ;DX must be cleared
            MOV     BX,100          ;BX used for denominator
            DIV     BX
            MOV     QOUT2,AX        ;quotient = AX = 64H = 100
            MOV     REMAIND2,DX     ;remainder = DX = 32H = 50
```

word/byte: Again, the numerator is in AX and the denominator can be in a register or memory. After the DIV instruction, AL will contain the quotient, and AH will contain the remainder. The maximum quotient is FFH. The following program divides AX = 2055 by CX=100. Then AL = 14H (20 decimal) is the quotient and AH = 37H (55 decimal) is the remainder.

```
            MOV     AX,2055         ;AX holds numerator
            MOV     CX,100          ;CX used for denominator
            DIV     CX
            MOV     QUO,AL          ;AL holds quotient
            MOV     REMI,AH         ;AH holds remainder
```

doubleword/word: The numerator is in AX and DX, with the most significant word in DX and the least significant word in AX. The denominator can be in a register or in memory. After the DIV instruction, the quotient will be in AX, the remainder in DX. The maximum quotient is FFFFH.

```
;from the data segment:
DATA1       DD      105432
DATA2       DW      10000
QUOT        DW      ?
REMAIN      DW      ?
;from the code segment:
            MOV     AX,WORD PTR DATA1       ;AX holds lower word
            MOV     DX,WORD PTR DATA1+2     ;DX higher word of numerator
            DIV     DATA2
            MOV     QUOT,AX                 ;AX holds quotient
            MOV     REMAIN,DX               ;DX holds remainder
```

In the program above, the contents of DX:AX are divided by a word-sized data value, 10000. Now one might ask: How does the CPU know that it must use the doubleword in DX:AX for the numerator? The 8086/88 automatically uses DX:AX as the numerator anytime the denominator is a word in size, as was seen earlier in the case of a word divided by a word. This explains why DX had to be cleared in that case. Notice in the example above that DATA1 is defined as DD but fetched into a word-size register with the help of WORD PTR. In the absence of WORD PTR, the assembler will generate an error. A summary of the results of division of unsigned numbers is given in Table 3-2.

Table 3-2: Unsigned Division Summary

Division	Numerator	Denominator	Quotient	Rem
byte/byte	AL = byte, AH = 0	register or memory	AL ^{1}	AH
word/word	AX = word, DX = 0	register or memory	AX ^{2}	DX
word/byte	AX = word	register or memory	AL ^{1}	AH
doubleword/word	DXAX = doubleword	register or memory	AX ^{2}	DX

Notes:
1. Divide error interrupt if AL > FFH.
2. Divide error interrupt if AX > FFFFH.

Review Questions

1. In unsigned multiplication of a byte in DATA1 with a byte in AL, the product will be placed in register(s) _____ .
2. In unsigned multiplication of AX with BX, the product is placed in register(s) _____.
3. In unsigned multiplication of CX with a byte in AL, the product is placed in register(s) _____.
4. In unsigned division of a byte in AL by a byte in DH, the quotient will be placed in _____ and the remainder in _____.
5. In unsigned division of a word in AX by a word in DATA1, the quotient will be placed in _____ and the remainder in _____.
6. In unsigned division of a word in AX by a byte in DATA2, the quotient will be placed in _____ and the remainder in _____.
7. In unsigned division of a doubleword in DXAX by a word in CX, the quotient will be placed in _____ and the remainder in _____.

SECTION 3.3: LOGIC INSTRUCTIONS AND SAMPLE PROGRAMS

In this section we discuss the logic instructions AND, OR, XOR, SHIFT, and COMPARE. Instructions are given in the context of examples.

AND

AND destination, source

This instruction will perform a logical AND on the operands and place the result in the destination. The destination operand can be a register or in memory. The source operand can be a register, in memory, or immediate.

X	Y	X AND Y
0	0	0
0	1	0
1	0	0
1	1	1

Example 3-5

Show the results of the following:

```
    MOV    BL,35H
    AND    BL,0FH          ;AND BL with 0FH.  Place the result in BL.
```

Solution:

```
    35H    0 0 1 1 0 1 0 1
    0FH    0 0 0 0 1 1 1 1
    05H    0 0 0 0 0 1 0 1    Flag settings will be:  SF = 0, ZF = 0, PF = 1, CF = OF = 0.
```

AND will automatically change the CF and OF to zero and PF, ZF and SF are set according to the result. The rest of the flags are either undecided or unaffected. As seen above, AND can be used to mask certain bits of the operand. It can also be used to test for a zero operand:

```
    AND    DH,DH
    JZ     XXXX
    ...
XXXX: ...
```

The above will AND DH with itself and set ZF = 1 if the result is zero, making the CPU fetch from the target address XXXX. Otherwise, the instruction below JZ is executed. AND can thus be used to test if a register contains zero.

OR

OR   destination,source

The destination and source operands are ORed and the result is placed in the destination. OR can be used to set certain bits of an operand to 1. The destination operand can be a register or in memory, the source operand can be a register, in memory, or immediate.

X	Y	X OR Y
0	0	0
0	1	1
1	0	1
1	1	1

The flags will be set the same as for the AND instruction. CF and OF will be reset to zero and SF, ZF, and PF will be set according to the result. All other flags are not affected.

The OR instruction can also be used to test for a zero operand. For example, "OR BL,0" will OR the register BL with 0 and make ZF = 1 if BL is zero. "OR BL,BL" will achieve the same result.

Example 3-6

Show the results of the following:

```
MOV AX,0504        ;AX = 0504
OR  AX,0DA68H      ;AX = DF6C
```

Solution:

0504H	0000 0101 0000 0100.	
DA68H	1101 1010 0110 1000	Flags will be: SF =1 , ZF = 0, PF = 1, CF = OF = 0.
DF6C	1101 1111 0110 1100	Notice that parity is checked for the lower 8 bits only.

XOR

XOR dest,src

The XOR instruction will eXclusive-OR the operands and place the result in the destination. XOR sets the result bits to 1 if they are not equal; otherwise, they are reset to 0. The flags are set the same as for the AND instruction. $CF = 0$ and $OF = 0$ are set internally and the rest are changed according to the result of the operation. The rules for the operands are the same as in the AND and OR instructions.

X	Y	X XOR Y
0	0	0
0	1	1
1	0	1
1	1	0

Example 3-7

Show the results of the following:

```
MOV    DH,54H
XOR    DH,78H
```

Solution:

54H	0 1 0 1 0 1 0 0	
78H	0 1 1 1 1 0 0 0	
2C	0 0 1 0 1 1 0 0	Flag settings will be: SF = 0, ZF = 0, PF = 0, CF = OF = 0.

Example 3-8

The XOR instruction can be used to clear the contents of a register by XORing it with itself. Show how "XOR AH,AH" clears AH, assuming that AH = 45H.

Solution:

45H	01000101	
45H	01000101	
00	00000000	Flag settings will be: SF = 0, ZF = 1, PF =1 , CF = OF = 0.

XOR can also be used to see if two registers have the same value. "XOR BX,CX" will make ZF = 1 if both registers have the same value, and if they do, the result (0000) is saved in BX, the destination.

Another widely used application of XOR is to toggle bits of an operand. For example, to toggle bit 2 of register AL:

```
XOR    AL,04H        ;XOR  AL with 0000 0100
```

This would cause bit 2 of AL to change to the opposite value; all other bits would remain unchanged.

SHIFT

There are two kinds of shift: logical and arithmetic. The logical shift is for unsigned operands, and the arithmetic shift is for signed operands. Logical shift will be discussed in this section and the discussion of arithmetic shift is postponed to Chapter 6. Using shift instructions shifts the contents of a register or memory location right or left. The number of times (or bits) that the operand is shifted can be specified directly if it is once only, or through the CL register if it is more than once.

SHR: This is the logical shift right. The operand is shifted right bit by bit, and for

$$0 \longrightarrow \boxed{MSB \longrightarrow LSB} \longrightarrow CF$$

every shift the LSB (least significant bit) will go to the carry flag (CF) and the MSB (most significant bit) is filled with 0. The following examples should help to clarify SHR.

Example 3-9

Show the result of SHR in the following:

```
    MOV    AL,9AH
    MOV    CL,3        ;set number of times to shift
    SHR    AL,CL
```

Solution:

```
    9AH = 10011010
                01001101      CF=0    (shifted once)
                00100110      CF=1    (shifted twice)
                00010011      CF=0    (shifted three times)
    After three times of shifting right, AL = 13H and CF = 0.
```

If the operand is to be shifted once only, this is specified in the SHR instruction itself rather than placing 1 in the CL. This saves coding of one instruction:

```
    MOV    BX,0FFFFH              ;BX=FFFFH
    SHR    BX,1                   ;shift right BX once only
```

After the shift above, BX = 7FFFH and CF = 1. Although SHR does affect the OF, SF, PF, and ZF flags, they are not important in this case. The operand to be shifted can be in a register or in memory, but immediate addressing mode is not allowed for shift instructions. For example, "SHR 25,CL" will cause the assembler to give an error.

Example 3-10

Show the results of SHR in the following:
```
    ;from the data segment:
    DATA1  DW      7777H
    ;from the code segment:
    TIMES  EQU     4
    MOV    CL,TIMES       ;CL=04
    SHR    DATA1,CL       ;shift DATA1 CL times
```

Solution:

After the four shifts, the word at memory location DATA1 will contain 0777. The four LSBs are lost through the carry, one by one, and 0s fill the four MSBs.

SHL: Shift left is also a logical shift. It is the reverse of SHR. After every shift, the LSB is filled with 0 and the MSB goes to CF. All the rules are the same as SHR.

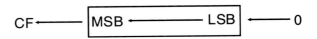

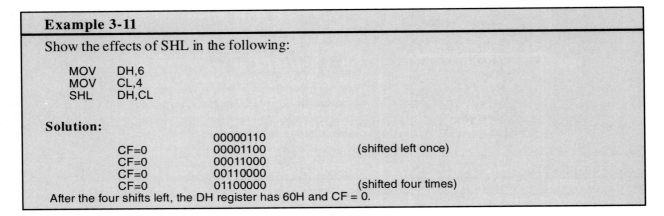

Example 3-11

Show the effects of SHL in the following:

```
    MOV   DH,6
    MOV   CL,4
    SHL   DH,CL
```

Solution:

```
                    00000110
        CF=0        00001100          (shifted left once)
        CF=0        00011000
        CF=0        00110000
        CF=0        01100000          (shifted four times)
```
After the four shifts left, the DH register has 60H and CF = 0.

Example 3-11 could have been coded as

```
    MOV   DH,6
    SHL   DH,1
    SHL   DH,1
    SHL   DH,1
    SHL   DH,1
```

COMPARE of unsigned numbers

```
    CMP   destination,source  ;compare dest and src
```

The CMP instruction compares two operands and changes the flags according to the result of the comparison. The operands themselves remain unchanged. The destination operand can be in a register or in memory and the source operand can be in a register, in memory, or immediate. Although all the CF, AF, SF, PF, ZF, and OF flags reflect the result of the comparison, only the CF and ZF are used, as outlined in Table 3-3.

Table 3-3: Flag Settings for Compare Instruction

Compare operands	CF	ZF
destination > source	0	0
destination = source	0	1
destination < source	1	0

The following demonstrates how the CMP instruction is used:

```
DATA1       DW    235FH

            ....
            MOV   AX,0CCCCH
            CMP   AX,DATA1    ;compare CCCC with 235F
            JNC   OVER        ;jump if CF=0
            SUB   AX,AX
OVER:       INC   DATA1
```

In the program above, AX is greater than the contents of memory location DATA1 (0CCCCH >235FH); therefore, CF = 0 and JNC (jump no carry) will go to target OVER. In contrast, look at the following:

```
            MOV     BX,7888H
            MOV     CX,9FFFH
            CMP     BX,CX           ;compare 7888 with 9FFF
            JNC     NEXT
            ADD     BX,4000H
NEXT:       ADD     CX,250H
```

In the above, BX is smaller than CX (7888H < 9FFFH), which sets CF = 1, making "JNC NEXT" fall through so that "ADD BX,4000H" is executed. In the example above, CX and BX still have their original values (CX = 9FFFH and BX = 7888H) after the execution of "CMP BX,CX". Notice that CF is always checked for cases of greater or smaller than, but for equal, ZF must be used. The next program sample has a variable named TEMP, which is being checked to see if it has reached 99:

```
TEMP        DB      ?
            ...
            MOV     AL,TEMP         ;move the TEMP variable into AL
            CMP     AL,99           ;compare AL with 99
            JZ      HOT_HOT         ;if ZF=1 (TEMP = 99) jump to HOT_HOT
            INC     BX              ;otherwise (ZF=0) increment BX
            ...
HOT_HOT:    HLT                     ;halt the system
```

The compare instruction is really a SUBtraction except that the values of the operands do not change. The flags are changed according to the execution of SUB. Although all the flags are affected, the only ones of interest are ZF and CF. It must be emphasized that in CMP instructions, the operands are unaffected regardless of the result of the comparison. Only the flags are affected. This is despite the fact that CMP uses the SUB operation to set or reset the flags. Program 3-3 uses the CMP instruction to search for the highest byte in a series of 5 bytes defined in the data segment. The instruction "CMP AL,[BX]" works as follows, where [BX] is the contents of the memory location pointed at by register BX.

If AL < [BX], then CF = 1 and [BX] becomes the basis of the new comparison.
If AL > [BX], then CF = 0 and AL is the larger of the two values and remains the basis of comparison.

Although JC (jump carry) and JNC (jump no carry) check the carry flag and can be used after a compare instruction, it is recommended that JA (jump above) and JB (jump below) be used for two reasons. One reason is that DEBUG will unassemble JC as JB, and JNC as JA, which may be confusing to beginning programmers. Another reason is that "jump above" and "jump below" are easier to understand than "jump carry" and "jump no carry", since it is more immediately apparent that one number is larger than another, than whether a carry would be generated if the two numbers were subtracted.

Program 3-3 uses the CMP instruction to search through 5 bytes of data to find the highest grade. The program uses register AL to hold the highest grade found so far. AL is given the initial value of 0. A loop is used to compare each of the 5 bytes with the value in AL. If AL contains a higher value, the loop continues to check the next byte. If AL is smaller than the byte being checked, the contents of AL are replaced by that byte, and the loop continues.

Assume that there is a class of five people with the following grades: 69, 87, 96, 45, and 75. Find the highest grade.

```
TITLE     PROG3-3  (EXE)  CMP EXAMPLE
PAGE      60,132
STSEG     SEGMENT
          DB      64 DUP (?)
STSEG     ENDS
;--------------------------
DTSEG     SEGMENT
GRADES    DB      69,87,96,45,75
          ORG     0008
HIGHEST   DB      ?
DTSEG     ENDS
;--------------------------
CDSEG     SEGMENT
MAIN      PROC    FAR
          ASSUME CS:CDSEG,DS:DTSEG,SS:STSEG
          MOV     AX,DTSEG
          MOV     DS,AX
          MOV     CX,5              ;set up loop counter
          MOV     BX,OFFSET GRADES  ;BX points to GRADE data
          SUB     AL,AL             ;AL holds highest grade found so far
AGAIN:    CMP     AL,[BX]           ;compare next grade to highest
          JA      NEXT              ;jump if AL still highest
          MOV     AL,[BX]           ;else AL holds new highest
NEXT:     INC     BX                ;point to next grade
          LOOP    AGAIN             ;continue search
          MOV     HIGHEST,AL        ;store highest grade
          MOV     AH,4CH
          INT     21H               ;go back to dos
MAIN      ENDP
CDSEG     ENDS
          END     MAIN
```

Program 3-3

Program 3-4 uses the CMP instruction to determine if an ASCII character is uppercase or lowercase. Note that small and capital letters in ASCII have the following values:

Letter	Hex	Binary	Letter	Hex	Binary
A	41	01000001	a	61	01100001
B	42	01000010	b	62	01100010
C	43	01000011	c	63	01100011
...	...	...	...	...	...
Y	59	01011001	y	79	01111001
Z	5A	01011010	z	7A	01111010

As can be seen, there is a relationship between the pattern of lowercase and uppercase letters, as shown below for A and a:

```
A       0100 0001      41H
a       0110 0001      61H
```

The only bit that changes is d5. To change from lowercase to uppercase, d5 must be masked. The program shown next first detects if the letter is in lowercase, and if it is, it is ANDed with 1101 1111B = DFH. Otherwise, it is simply left alone. To determine if it is a lowercase letter, it is compared with 61H and 7AH, to see if it is in the range a to z. Anything above or below this range should be left alone.

```
TITLE      PROG3-4  (EXE)  LOWERCASE TO UPPERCASE CONVERSION
PAGE       60,132
STSEG      SEGMENT
           DB      64 DUP (?)
STSEG      ENDS
;---------------------------
DTSEG      SEGMENT
DATA1      DB      'mY NAME is jOe'
           ORG     0020H
DATA2      DB      14 DUP(?)
DTSEG      ENDS
;---------------------------
CDSEG      SEGMENT
MAIN       PROC    FAR
           ASSUME CS:CDSEG,DS:DTSEG,SS:STSEG
           MOV     AX,DTSEG
           MOV     DS,AX
           MOV     SI,OFFSET DATA1      ;SI points to original data
           MOV     BX,OFFSET DATA2      ;BX points to uppercase data
           MOV     CX,14               ;CX is loop counter
BACK:      MOV     AL,[SI]             ;get next character
           CMP     AL,61H              ;if less than 'a'
           JB      OVER                ;then no need to convert
           CMP     AL,7AH              ;if greater than 'z'
           JA      OVER                ;then no need to convert
           AND     AL,11011111B        ;mask d5 to convert to uppercase
OVER:      MOV     [BX],AL             ;store uppercase character
           INC     SI                  ;increment pointer to original
           INC     BX                  ;increment pointer to uppercase data
           LOOP    BACK                ;continue looping if CX > 0
           MOV     AH,4CH
           INT     21H                 ;go back to dos
MAIN       ENDP
CDSEG      ENDS
           END     MAIN
```

Program 3-4

In Program 3-4, 20H could have been subtracted from the lowercase letters instead of ANDing with 1101 1111B. That is what IBM does, as shown next.

IBM BIOS method of converting from lowercase to uppercase

```
                2357    ;----- CONVERT ANY LOWER CASE TO UPPER CASE
                2358
EBFB            2359    K60:                                ;LOWER TO UPPER
EBFB 3C61       2360         CMP     AL,'a'                 ;FIND OUT IF ALPHABETIC
EBFD 7206       2361         JB      K61                    ;NOT_CAPS_STATE
EBFF 3C7A       2362         CMP     AL,'z'
EC01 7702       2363         JA      K61                    ;NOT_CAPS_STATE
EC03 2C20       2364         SUB     AL,'a'-'A'             ;CONVERT TO UPPER CASE
EC05            2365    K61:
EC05 8B1E1C00   2366         MOV     BX,BUFFER_TAIL         ;GET THE END POINTER
                                                            ;TO THE BUFFER
```

(Reprinted by permission from "IBM Technical Reference" c. 1984 by International Business Machines Corporation)

Review Questions

1. Use operands 4FCAH and C237H to perform:
   (a) AND   (b) OR   (c) XOR
2. ANDing a word operand with FFFFH will result in what value for the word operand? To set all bits of an operand to 0, it should be ANDed with _____.
3. To set all bits of an operand to 1, it could be ORed with _____.
4. XORing an operand with itself results in what value for the operand? ○
5. Show the steps if value A0F2H were shifted left three times. Then show the steps if A0F2H were shifted right three times.
6. The CMP instructions works by performing a ___*SUB*___ operation on the operands and sets the flags accordingly.
7. True or false. The CMP instruction alters the contents of its operands. *F*

SECTION 3.3: LOGIC INSTRUCTIONS AND SAMPLE PROGRAMS   **99**

BIOS examples of logic instructions

In this section we examine some real-life examples from IBM PC BIOS programs. The purpose is see the instructions discussed so far in the context of real-life applications.

When the computer is turned on, the CPU starts to execute the programs stored in BIOS in order to set the computer up for DOS. If anything has happened to the BIOS programs, the computer can do nothing. The first subroutine of BIOS is to test the CPU. This involves checking the flag register bit by bit as well as checking all other registers. The BIOS program for testing the flags and registers is given followed by their explanation:

```
              306              ASSUME CS:CODE,DS:NOTHING,ES:NOTHING,SS:NOTHING
E05B          307              ORG     0E05BH
E05B                           ...     ...
E05B          309       START:
E05B FA       310              CLI                        ; DISABLE INTERRUPTS
E05C B4D5     311              MOV     AH,0D5H            ; SET SF, CF, ZF, AND AF FLAGS ON
E05E 9E       312              SAHF
E05F 734C     313              JNC     ERRO1              ; GO TO ERR ROUTINE IF CF NOT SET
E061 754A     314              JNZ     ERRO1              ; GO TO ERR ROUTINE IF ZF NOT SET
E063 7B48     315              JNP     ERRO1              ; GO TO ERR ROUTINE IF PF NOT SET
E065 7946     316              JNS     ERRO1              ; GO TO ERR ROUTINE IF SF NOT SET
E067 9F       317              LAHF                       ; LOAD FLAG IMAGE TO AH
E068 B105     318              MOV     CL,5               ; LOAD CNT REG WITH SHIFT CNT
E06A D2EC     319              SHR     AH,CL              ; SHIFT AF INTO CARRY BIT POS
E06C 733F     320              JNC     ERRO1              ; GO TO ERR ROUTINE IF AF NOT SET
E06E B040     321              MOV     AL,40H             ; SET THE OF FLAG ON
E070 D0E0     322              SHL     AL,1               ; SETUP FOR TESTING
E072 7139     323              JNO     ERRO1              ; GO TO ERR ROUTINE IF OF NOT SET
E074 32E4     324              XOR     AH,AH              ; SET AH = 0
E076 9E       325              SAHF                       ; CLEAR SF, CF, ZF, AND PF
E077 7634     326              JBE     ERRO1              ; GO TO ERR ROUTINE IF CF ON
              327                                         ; OR GO TO ERR ROUTINE IF ZF ON
E079 7832     328              JS      ERRO1              ; GO TO ERR ROUTINE IF SF ON
E07B 7A30     329              JP      ERRO1              ; GO TO ERR ROUTINE IF PF ON
E07D 9F       330              LAHF                       ; LOAD FLAG IMAGE TO AH
E07E B105     331              MOV     CL,5               ; LOAD CNT REG WITH SHIFT CNT
E080 D2EC     332              SHR     AH,CL              ; SHIFT 'AF' INTO CARRY BIT POS
E082 7229     333              JC      ERRO1              ; GO TO ERR ROUTINE IF ON
E084 D0E4     334              SHL     AH,1               ; CHECK THAT 'OF' IS CLEAR
E086 7025     335              JO      ERRO1              ; GO TO ERR ROUTINE IF ON
              336
              337       ;----- READ/WRITE THE 8088 GENERAL AND SEGMENTATION REGISTERS
              338       ;           WITH ALL ONE'S AND ZEROES'S.
              339
E088 B8FFFF   340              MOV     AX,0FFFFH          ; SET UP ONE'S PATTERN IN AX
E08B F9       341              STC
E08C          342       C8:
E08C 8ED8     343              MOV     DS,AX              ; WRITE PATTERN TO ALL REGS
E08E 8CDB     344              MOV     BX,DS
E090 8EC3     345              MOV     ES,BX
E092 8CC1     346              MOV     CX,ES
E094 8ED1     347              MOV     SS,CX
E096 8CD2     348              MOV     DX,SS
E098 8BE2     349              MOV     SP,DX
E09A 8BEC     350              MOV     BP,SP
E09C 8BF5     351              MOV     SI,BP
E09E 8BFE     352              MOV     DI,SI
E0A0 7307     353              JNC     C9                 ; TST1A
E0A2 33C7     354              XOR     AX,DI              ; PATTERN MAKE IT THRU ALL REGS
E0A4 7507     355              JNZ     ERRO1              ; NO - GO TO ERR ROUTINE
E0A6 F8       356              CLC
E0A7 EBE3     357              JMP     C8
E0A9          358       C9:
E0A9 0BC7     359              OR      AX,DI              ; ZERO PATTERN MAKE IT THRU?
E0AB 7401     360              JZ      C10                ; YES - GO TO NEXT TEST
E0AD F4       361       ERRO1: HLT                        ; HALT SYSTEM
```

(Reprinted by permission from "IBM Technical Reference" c. 1984 by International Business Machines Corporation)

Line-by-line explanation:

Line	Explanation
310	CLI ensures that no interrupt will occur while the test is being conducted.
311	MOV AH,0D5H:

```
flag    S Z - AC - P - C
D5H     1 1 0  1  0 1 0 1
```

312	SAHF (store AH into lower byte of the flag register) is one way to move data to flags. Another is to use the stack

```
        MOV    AX,00D5H
        PUSH   AX
        POPF
```

However, there is no RAM available yet to use for the stack because the CPU is tested before memory is tested.

Line	Explanation
313 - 316	Will make the CPU jump to HLT if any flag does not work.
317	LAHF (load AH with the lower byte of flag register) is the opposite of SAHF.
318	Loads CL for five shifts.
319	"SHR AH,CL". By shifting AH five times, AF (auxiliary carry) will be in the CF position.
320	If no AF, there is an error. Lines 317 to 320 are needed because there is no jump condition instruction for AF.
321 - 323	Checks the OF flag. This is discussed in Chapter 6 when signed numbers are discussed.
324 - 335	Checks the same flags for zero. Remember that JNZ is the same as JBE.
340	Loads AX with FFFFH.
341	STC (set the carry) makes CF = 1.
343 - 352	Moves the AX value (FFFFH) into every register and ends up with DI = FFFFH if the registers are good.
353	Since CF=1 (remember STC) it falls through.
354	Exclusive-ORing AX and DI with both having the same FFFFH value makes AX = 0000 and ZF = 1 if the registers are good (see lines 343 - 352). If ZF = 0, one of the registers must have corrupted the data FFFF, therefore the CPU is bad.
355	If ZF = 0, there is an error.
356	CLC clears the carry flag. This is the opposite of STC.
357	Jumps to C8 and repeats the same process, this time with value 0000. The contents of AX are moved around to every register until DI = 0000, and at 353 the JNC C9 will jump since CF = 0 by the CLC instruction before it went to the loop.
359	At C9, AX and DI are ORed. If 0000, the contents of AX are copied successfully to all registers, DI will be 0000; therefore, ORing will raise the ZF, making ZF = 1.
360	If ZF = 1, the CPU is good and the system can perform the next test. Otherwise, ZF = 0, meaning that the CPU is bad and the system should be halted.

SECTION 3.4: BCD AND ASCII OPERANDS AND INSTRUCTIONS

In 80x86 microprocessors, there are many instructions that handle ASCII and BCD numbers. This section covers these instructions with examples.

BCD number system

BCD stands for binary coded decimal. BCD is needed because human beings use the digits 0 to 9 for numbers. Binary representation of 0 to 9 is called BCD (see Figure 3-1). In computer literature one encounters two terms for BCD numbers:
(1) unpacked BCD   (2) packed BCD

Digit	BCD
0	0000
1	0001
2	0010
3	0011
4	0100
5	0101
6	0110
7	0111
8	1000
9	1001

Figure 3-1. BCD Code

Unpacked BCD

In unpacked BCD, the lower 4 bits of the number represent the BCD number and the rest of the bits are 0. Example: "0000 1001" and "0000 0101" are unpacked BCD for 9 and 5, respectively. In the case of unpacked BCD it takes 1 byte of memory location or a register of 8 bits to contain it.

Packed BCD

In the case of packed BCD, a single byte has two BCD numbers in it, one in the lower 4 bits and one in the upper 4 bits. For example, "0101 1001" is packed BCD for 59. It takes only 1 byte of memory to store the packed BCD operands. This is one reason to use packed BCD since it is twice as efficient in storing data.

ASCII numbers

In ASCII keyboards, when key "0" is activated, for example, "011 0000" (30H) is provided to the computer. In the same way, 31H (011 0001) is provided for key "1", and so on, as shown in the following list.

Key	ASCII (hex)	Binary	BCD (unpacked)
0	30	011 0000	0000 0000
1	31	011 0001	0000 0001
2	32	011 0010	0000 0010
3	33	011 0011	0000 0011
4	34	011 0100	0000 0100
5	35	011 0101	0000 0101
6	36	011 0110	0000 0110
7	37	011 0111	0000 0111
8	38	011 1000	0000 1000
9	39	011 1001	0000 1001

It must be noted that although ASCII is standard in the United States (and many other countries), BCD numbers have universal application. Now since the keyboard and printers and monitors are all ASCII, how does data get converted from ASCII to BCD, and vice versa? These are the subjects covered next.

ASCII to BCD conversion

To process data in BCD, first the ASCII data provided by the keyboard must be converted to BCD. Whether it should be converted to packed or unpacked BCD depends on the instructions to be used. There are instructions which require that data be in unpacked BCD and there are others that must have packed BCD data to work properly. Each is covered separately.

ASCII to unpacked BCD conversion

To convert ASCII data to BCD, the programmer must get rid of the tagged "011" in the higher 4 bits of the ASCII. To do that, each ASCII number is ANDed with "0000 1111" (0FH), as shown in the next example. This example is written below in three different ways using different addressing modes. The following three programs show three different methods for converting the 10 ASCII digits to unpacked BCD. All use the same data segment:

```
ASC        DB          '9562481273'
           ORG         0010H
UNPACK     DB          10 DUP(?)
```

In Program 3-5a, notice that although the data was defined as DB, a byte definition directive, it was accessed in word-sized chunks. This is a workable approach; however, using the PTR directive as shown in Program 3-5b makes the code more readable for programmers.

```
           MOV   CX,5
           MOV   BX,OFFSET ASC        ;BX points to ASCII data
           MOV   DI,OFFSET UNPACK     ;DI points to unpacked BCD data
AGAIN:     MOV   AX,[BX]              ;move next 2 ASCII numbers to AX
           AND   AX,0F0FH             ;remove ASCII 3s
           MOV   [DI],AX              ;store unpacked BCD
           ADD   DI,2                 ;point to next unpacked BCD data
           ADD   BX,2                 ;point to next ASCII data
           LOOP  AGAIN
```

Program 3-5a

```
           MOV   CX,5                 ;CX is loop counter
           MOV   BX,OFFSET ASC        ;BX points to ASCII data
           MOV   DI,OFFSET UNPACK     ;DI points to unpacked BCD data
AGAIN:     MOV   AX,WORD PTR [BX]     ;move next 2 ASCII numbers to AX
           AND   AX,0F0FH             ;remove ASCII 3s
           MOV   WORD PTR [DI],AX     ;store unpacked BCD
           ADD   DI,2                 ;point to next unpacked BCD data
           ADD   BX,2                 ;point to next ASCII data
           LOOP  AGAIN
```

Program 3-5b

In both of the solutions so far, registers BX and DI were used as pointers for an array of data. An array is simply a set of data located in consecutive memory locations. Now one might ask: What happens if there are four, five, or six arrays? How can they all be accessed with only three registers as pointers: BX, DI, and SI? Program 3-5c shows how this can be done with a single register used as a pointer to access two arrays. However, to do that, the arrays must be of the same size and defined similarly.

```
           MOV   CX,10                ;load the counter
           SUB   BX,BX                ;clear BX
AGAIN:     MOV   AL,ASC[BX]           ;move to AL content of mem [BX+ASC]
           AND   AL,0FH               ;mask the upper nibble
           MOV   UNPACK[BX],AL        ;move to mem [BX+UNPACK] the AL
           INC   BX                   ;make the pointer to point at next byte
           LOOP  AGAIN                ;loop until it is finished
```

Program 3-5c

Program 3-5c uses the based addressing mode since BX+ASC is used as a pointer. ASC is the displacement added to BX. Either DI or SI could have been used for this purpose. For word-sized operands, "WORD PTR" would be used since the data is defined as DB. This is shown below.

```
           MOV   AX,WORD PTR ASC[BX]
           AND   AX,0F0FH
           MOV   WORD PTR UNPACKED[BX],AX
```

ASCII to packed BCD conversion

To convert ASCII to packed BCD, it is first converted to unpacked BCD (to get rid of the 3) and then combined to make packed BCD. For example, for 9 and 5 the keyboard gives 39 and 35, respectively. The goal is to produce 95H or "1001 0101", which is called packed BCD, as discussed earlier. This process is illustrated in detail below.

Key	ASCII	Unpacked BCD	Packed BCD
4	34	00000100	
7	37	00000111	01000111 or 47H

SECTION 3.4: BCD AND ASCII OPERANDS AND INSTRUCTIONS

```
              ORG    0010H
VAL_ASC       DB     '47'
VAL_BCD       DB     ?
;reminder: the DB will put 34 in 0010H location and 37 in 0011H.
              MOV    AX,WORD PTR VAL_ASC      ;AH=37,AL=34
              AND    AX,0F0FH                 ;mask 3 to get unpacked BCD
              XCHG   AH,AL                    ;swap AH and AL. :
              MOV    CL,4                     ;CL=04 to shift 4 times
              SHL    AH,CL                    ;shift left AH to get AH=40H
              OR     AL,AH                    ;OR them to get packed BCD
              MOV    VAL_BCD,AL               ;save the result
```

After this conversion, the packed BCD numbers are processed and the result will be in packed BCD format. As will be seen later in this section, there are special instructions, such as DAA and DAS, which require that the data be in packed BCD form and give the result in packed BCD. For the result to be displayed on the monitor or be printed by the printer, it must be in ASCII format. Conversion from packed BCD to ASCII is discussed next.

Packed BCD to ASCII conversion

To convert packed BCD to ASCII, it must first be converted to unpacked and then the unpacked BCD is tagged with 011 0000 (30H). The following shows the process of converting from packed BCD to ASCII.

Packed BCD	Unpacked BCD	ASCII
29H	02H & 09H	32H & 39H
0010 1001	0000 0010 & 0000 1001	011 0010 & 011 1001

```
VAL1_BCD      DB     29H
VAL3-ASC      DW     ?

              ...
              MOV    AL,VAL1_BCD
              MOV    AH,AL           ;copy AL to AH. now AH=29,AL=29H
              AND    AX,0F00FH       ;mask 9 from AH and 2 from AL
              MOV    CL,4            ;CL=04 for shift
              SHR    AH,CL           ;shift right AH to get unpacked BCD
              OR     AX,3030H        ;combine with 30 to get ASCII
              XCHG   AH,AL           ;swap for ASCII storage convention
              MOV    VAL3_ASC,AX     ;store the ASCII
```

BCD addition and subtraction

After learning how to convert ASCII to BCD, the application of BCD numbers is the next step. There are two instructions that deal specifically with BCD numbers: DAA and DAS. Each is discussed separately.

BCD addition and correction

There is a problem with adding BCD numbers which must be corrected. The problem is that after adding packed BCD numbers, the result is no longer BCD. Look at this example:

```
      MOV AL,17H
      ADD AL,28H
```

Adding them gives 0011 1111B (3FH), which is not BCD! A BCD number can only have digits from 0000 to 1001 (or 0 to 9). In other words, adding two BCD numbers must give a BCD result. The result above should have been $17 + 28 = 45$ (0100 0101). To correct this problem, the programmer must add 6 (0110) to the low digit: 3F + 06 = 45H. The same problem could have happened in the upper digit (for example, in 52H + 87H = D9H). Again to solve this problem, 6 must be added to the upper digit (D9H +60H =139H), to ensure that the result is BCD (52 + 87 = 139). This problem is so pervasive that all single-chip CISC microprocessors such as Intel 80x86 and Motorola 680x0 have an instruction to deal with it. The RISC processors have eliminated this instruction.

DAA

The DAA (decimal adjust for addition) instruction in 80x86 microprocessors is provided exactly for the purpose of correcting the problem associated with BCD addition. DAA will add 6 to the lower nibble or higher nibble if needed; otherwise, it will leave the result alone. The following example will clarify these points:

```
DATA1   DB      47H
DATA2   DB      25H
DATA3   DB      ?

        MOV     AL,DATA1        ;AL holds first BCD operand
        MOV     BL,DATA2        ;BL holds second BCD operand
        ADD     AL,BL           ;BCD addition
        DAA                     ;adjust for BCD addition
        MOV     DATA3,AL        ;store result in correct BCD form
```

After the program is executed, the DATA3 field will contain 72H (47 + 25 = 72). Note that DAA works only on AL. In other words, while the source can be an operand of any addressing mode, the destination must be AL in order for DAA to work. It needs to be emphasized that DAA must be used after the addition of BCD operands and that BCD operands can never have any digit greater than 9. In other words, no A - F digit is allowed. It is also important to note that DAA works only after an ADD instruction; it will not work after the INC instruction.

Summary of DAA action

1. If after an ADD or ADC instruction, the lower nibble (4 bits) is greater than 9, or if AF = 1, add 0110 to the lower 4 bits.
2. If the upper nibble is greater than 9, or if CF = 1, add 0110 to the upper nibble.

In reality there is no other use for the AF (auxiliary flag) except for BCD addition and correction. For example, adding 29H and 18H will result in 41H, which is incorrect as far as BCD is concerned.

```
    Hex             BCD
    29              0010 1001
+   18          +   0001 1000
    41              0100 0001   AF = 1
+    6          +        0110   because AF = 1 DAA will add 6 to the lower nibble
    47              0100 0111   The final result is BCD.
```

Program 3-6 demonstrates the use of DAA after addition of multibyte packed BCD numbers.

BCD subtraction and correction

The problem associated with the addition of packed BCD numbers also shows up in subtraction. Again, there is an instruction (DAS) specifically designed to solve the problem. Therefore, when subtracting packed BCD (single-byte or multibyte) operands, the DAS instruction is put after the SUB or SBB instruction. AL must be used as the destination register to make DAS work.

Two sets of ASCII data have come in from the keyboard. Write and run a program to :
1. Convert from ASCII to packed BCD.
2. Add the multibyte packed BCD and save it.
3. Convert the packed BCD result into ASCII.

```
TITLE       PROG3-6  (EXE)  ASCII TO BCD CONVERSION AND ADDITION
PAGE        60,132
STSEG       SEGMENT
            DB        64 DUP(?)
STSEG       ENDS
;---------------------------
DTSEG             SEGMENT
DATA1_ASC         DB        '0649147816'
                  ORG       0010H
DATA2_ASC         DB        '0072687188'
                  ORG       0020H
DATA3_BCD         DB        5 DUP (?)
                  ORG       0028H
DATA4_BCD         DB        5 DUP (?)
                  ORG       0030H
DATA5_ADD         DB        5 DUP (?)
                  ORG       0040H
DATA6_ASC         DB        10 DUP (?)
DTSEG             ENDS
;---------------------------
CDSEG       SEGMENT
MAIN        PROC  FAR
            ASSUME CS:CDSEG,DS:DTSEG,SS:STSEG
            MOV     AX,DTSEG
            MOV     DS,AX
            MOV     BX,OFFSET DATA1_ASC        ;BX points to first ASCII data
            MOV     DI,OFFSET DATA3_BCD        ;DI points to first BCD data
            MOV     CX,10                      ;CX holds number bytes to convert
            CALL    CONV_BCD                   ;convert ASCII to BCD
            MOV     BX,OFFSET DATA2_ASC        ;BX points to second ASCII data
            MOV     DI,OFFSET DATA4_BCD        ;DI points to second BCD data
            MOV     CX,10                      ;CX holds number bytes to convert
            CALL    CONV_BCD                   ;convert ASCII to BCD
            CALL    BCD_ADD                    ;add the BCD operands
            MOV     SI,OFFSET DATA5_ADD        ;SI points to BCD result
            MOV     DI,OFFSET DATA6_ASC        ;DI points to ASCII result
            MOV     CX,05                      ;CX holds count for convert
            CALL    CONV_ASC                   ;convert result to ASCII
            MOV     AH,4CH
            INT     21H                        ;go back to DOS
MAIN        ENDP
;---------------------------
;THIS SUBROUTINE CONVERTS ASCII TO PACKED BCD
CONV_BCD  PROC
AGAIN:      MOV     AX,[BX] ;BX=pointer for ASCII data
            XCHG    AH,AL
            AND     AX,0F0FH        ;mask ASCII 3s
            PUSH    CX              ;save the counter
            MOV     CL,4            ;shift AH left 4 bits
            SHL     AH,CL           ;  to get ready for packing
            OR      AL,AH           ;combine to make packed BCD
            MOV     [DI],AL         ;DI=pointer for BCD data
            ADD     BX,2            ;point to next 2 ASCII bytes
            INC     DI              ;point to next BCD data
            POP     CX              ;restore loop counter
            LOOP    AGAIN
            RET
CONV_BCD  ENDP
;---------------------------
```

Program 3-6 *(continued on the following page)*

```
          ;THIS SUBROUTINE ADDS TWO MULTIBYTE PACKED BCD OPERANDS
BCD_ADD   PROC
          MOV     BX,OFFSET DATA3_BCD  ;BX=pointer for operand 1
          MOV     DI,OFFSET DATA4_BCD  ;DI=pointer for operand 2
          MOV     SI,OFFSET DATA5_ADD  ;SI=pointer for sum
          MOV     CX,05
          CLC
BACK:     MOV     AL,[BX]+4            ;get next byte of operand 1
          ADC     AL,[DI]+4           ;add next byte of operand 2
          DAA                         ;correct for BCD addition
          MOV     [SI] +4,AL          ;save sum
          DEC     BX                  ;point to next byte of operand 1
          DEC     DI                  ;point to next byte of operand 2
          DEC     SI                  ;point to next byte of sum
          LOOP    BACK
          RET
BCD_ADD   ENDP
;----------------------------
          ;THIS SUBROUTINE CONVERTS FROM PACKED BCD TO ASCII
CONV_ASC  PROC
AGAIN2:   MOV     AL,[SI]             ;SI=pointer for BCD data
          MOV     AH,AL               ;duplicate to unpack
          AND     AX,0F00FH           ;unpack
          PUSH    CX                  ;save counter
          MOV     CL,04               ;shift right 4 bits to unpack
          SHR     AH,CL               ;   the upper nibble
          OR      AX,3030H            ;make it ASCII
          XCHG    AH,AL               ;swap for ASCII storage convention
          MOV     [DI],AX             ;store ASCII data
          INC     SI                  ;point to next BCD data
          ADD     DI,2                ;point to next ASCII data
          POP     CX                  ;restore loop counter
          LOOP    AGAIN2
          RET
CONV_ASC  ENDP
CDSEG     ENDS
          END     MAIN
```

Program 3-6 *(continued from preceding page)*

Summary of DAS action

1. If after a SUB or SBB instruction, the lower nibble is greater than 9, or if AF = 1, subtract 0110 from the lower 4 bits.
2. If the upper nibble is greater than 9, or CF = 1, subtract 0110 from the upper nibble.

Due to the widespread use of BCD numbers, a specific data directive, DT, has been created. DT can be used to represent BCD numbers from 0 to 10^{20} - 1 (that is, twenty 9s). Assume that the following operands represent the budget, the expenses, and the balance, which is the budget minus the expenses.

```
BUDGET      DT      87965141012
EXPENSES    DT      31610640392
BALANCE     DT      ?                              ;balance = budget - expenses

            MOV     CX,10                          ;counter=10
            MOV     BX,00                          ;pointer=0
            CLC                                    ;clear carry for the 1st iteration
BACK:       MOV     AL,BYTE PTR BUDGET[BX]         ;get a byte of the BUDGET
            SBB     AL,BYTE PTR EXPENSES[BX]       ;subtract a byte from it
            DAS                                    ;correct the result for BCD
            MOV     BYTE PTR BALANCE[BX],AL        ;save it in BALANCE
            INC     BX                             ;increment for the next byte
            LOOP    BACK                           ;continue until CX=0
```

Notice in the code section above that (1) no H (hex) indicator is needed for BCD numbers when using the DT directive, and (2) the use of the based relative addressing mode (BX + displacement) allows access to all three arrays with a single register BX.

In Program 3-7 the DB directive is used to define ASCII values. This makes the LSD (least significant digit) to be located at the highest memory location of the array. In VALUE1, 37, the ASCII for 7 is in memory location 0009; therefore, BX must be pointed to that and then decremented. Program 3-7 is repeated at the end of this chapter, rewritten with the simple segment definition.

```
         Write a program that adds two multidigit ASCII numbers. The result should be in ASCII.

         TITLE      PROG3-7 (EXE)  ADDING ASCII NUMBERS
         PAGE       60,132
         STSEG      SEGMENT
                    DB       64 DUP (?)
         STSEG      ENDS
         ;----------------------------
         DTSEG      SEGMENT
         VALUE1     DB       '0659478127'
                    ORG      0010H
         VALUE2     DB       '0779563678'
                    ORG      0020H
         RESULT1    DB       10 DUP (?)
                    ORG      0030H
         RESULT2    DB       10 DUP (?)
         DTSEG      ENDS
         ;----------------------------
         CDSEG      SEGMENT
         MAIN       PROC    FAR
                    ASSUME CS:CDSEG,DS:DTSEG,SS:STSEG
                    MOV      AX,DTSEG
                    MOV      DS,AX
                    CALL     ASC_ADD           ;call ASCII addition subroutine
                    CALL     CONVERT           ;call convert to ascii subroutine
                    MOV      AH,4CH
                    INT      21H               ;go back to DOS
         MAIN       ENDP
         ;----------------------------
         ;THIS SUBROUTINE ADDS THE ASCII NUMBERS AND MAKES THE RESULT UNPACKED.
         ASC_ADD PROC
                    CLC                        ;clear the carry
                    MOV      CX,10             ;set up loop counter
                    MOV      BX,9              ;point to LSD
         BACK:      MOV      AL,VALUE1[BX]     ;move next byte of operand 1
                    ADC      AL,VALUE2[BX]     ;add next byte of operand 2
                    AAA                        ;adjust to make it unpacked BCD
                    MOV      RESULT1[BX],AL    ;store BCD sum
                    DEC      BX                ;point to next byte
                    LOOP     BACK
                    RET
         ASC_ADD ENDP
         ;----------------------------
         ;THIS SUBROUTINE CONVERTS UNPACKED BCD TO ASCII
         CONVERT PROC
                    MOV      BX,OFFSET RESULT1  ;BX points to unpacked BCD data
                    MOV      SI,OFFSET RESULT2  ;SI points to ASCII data
                    MOV      CX,05             ;CX is loop counter
         BACK2:     MOV      AX,WORD PTR [BX]  ;get next 2 ASCII bytes
                    OR       AX,3030H          ;insert ASCII 3s
                    MOV      WORD PTR [SI],AX  ;store ASCII
                    ADD      BX,2              ;increment BCD pointer
                    ADD      SI,2              ;increment ASCII pointer
                    LOOP     BACK2
                    RET
         CONVERT ENDP
         CDSEG      ENDS
                    END      MAIN
```

Program 3-7

ASCII addition and subtraction

In the case of ASCII numbers, they can be used as operands in add and subtract instructions the way they are, without masking the tagged 011. AAA and AAS instructions are designed specifically for that. Look at the following cases:

```
MOV   AL,'5'          ;AL=35
ADD   AL,'2'          ;add to AL 32 the ASCII for 2
AAA                   ;changes 67H to 07H
OR    AL,30           ;OR  AL with 30H to get ASCII
```

In the program above:
```
  0011  0101
  0011  0010
  0110  0111
```

If the addition results in a value of more than 9, AAA will correct it and pass the extra bit to carry and add 1 to AH.

```
SUB   AH,AH           ;AH=00
MOV   AL,'7'          ;AL=37H
MOV   BL,'5'          ;BL=35H
ADD   AL,BL           ;37H+35H=6CH therefore AL=6C.
AAA                   ;changes 6CH to 02 in AL and AH=CF=1
OR    AX,3030H        ;AX=3132 which is the ASCII for 12H.
```

Two facts must be noted. First, AAA and AAS work only on the AL register, and second, the data added can be unpacked BCD rather than ASCII, and AAA and AAS will work fine. The following shows how AAS works on subtraction of unpacked BCD to correct the result into unpacked BCD:

```
MOV   AX,105H         ;AX=0105H unpacked BCD for 15
MOV   CL,06           ;CL=06H
SUB   AL,CL           ;5 - 6 = -1 (FFH)
AAS                   ;FFH in AL is adjusted to 09, and
                      ;AH is decremented, leaving AX = 0009
```

Unpacked BCD multiplication and division

There are two instructions designed specifically for multiplication and division of unpacked BCD operands. They convert the result of the multiplication and division to unpacked BCD.

AAM

The Intel manual says that this mnemonic stands for "ASCII adjust multiplication," but it really is unpacked multiplication correction. If two unpacked BCD numbers are multiplied, the result can be converted back to BCD by AAM.

```
MOV   AL,'7'          ;AL=37H
AND   AL,0FH          ;AL=07 unpacked BCD
MOV   DL,'6'          ;DL=36H
AND   DL,0FH          ;DL=06 unpacked BCD
MUL   DL             ;AX=ALxDL. =07x06=002AH=42
AAM                   ;AX=0402 (7x6=42 unpacked BCD)
OR    AX,3030H        ;AX=3432 result in ASCII
```

The multiplication above is byte by byte and the result is HEX. Using AAM converts it to unpacked BCD to prepare it for tagging with 30H to make it ASCII.

AAD

Again, the Intel manual says that AAD represents "ASCII adjust for division," but that can be misleading since the data must be unpacked BCD for this instruction to work. Before dividing the unpacked BCD by another unpacked BCD, AAD is used to convert it to HEX. By doing that the quotient and remainder are both in unpacked BCD.

```
MOV   AX,3539H    ;AX=3539.  ASCII for 59
AND   AX,0F0FH    ;AH=05,AL=09 unpacked BCD data
AAD               ;AX=003BH hex equivalent of 59
MOV   BH,08H      ;divide by 08
DIV   BH          ;3B / 08 gives AL=07 ,AH=03
OR    AX,3030H    ;AL=37H (quotient) AH=33H (rem)
```

As can be seen in the example above, dividing 59 by 8 gives a quotient of 7 and a remainder of 3. With the help of AAD, the result is converted to unpacked BCD, so it can be tagged with 30H to get the ASCII result. It must be noted that both AAM and AAD work only on AX.

Review Questions

1. For the following decimal numbers, give the packed BCD and unpacked BCD representations.
   (a) 15   (b) 99
2. Match the following instruction mnemonic with its function.
   _____ DAA   (a) ASCII addition
   _____ DAS   (b) ASCII subtraction
   _____ AAS   (c) BCD subtraction
   _____ AAA   (d) BCD addition

SECTION 3.5: ROTATE INSTRUCTIONS

In many applications there is need to perform a bitwise rotation of an operand. The rotation instructions ROR, ROL and RCR, RCL are designed specifically for that purpose. They allow a program to rotate an operand right or left. In this section we explore the rotate instructions, which frequently have highly specialized applications. In rotate instructions, the operand can be in a register or memory. If the number of times an operand is to be rotated is more than 1, this is indicated by CL. This is similar to the shift instructions. There are two type of rotations. One is a simple rotation of the bits of the operand, and the other is a rotation through the carry. Each is explained below.

Rotating the bits of an operand right and left

ROR   rotate right

In rotate right, as bits are shifted from left to right they exit from the right end (LSB)

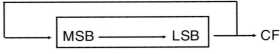

and enter the left end (MSB). In addition, as each bit exits the LSB, a copy of it is given to the carry flag. In other words, in ROR the LSB is moved to the MSB and is also copied to CF, as shown in the diagram. If the operand is to be rotated once, the 1 is coded, but if it is to be rotated more than once, register CL is used to hold the number of times it is to be rotated.

```
        MOV    AL,36H        ;AL=0011 0110
        ROR    AL,1          ;AL=0001 1011  CF=0
        ROR    AL,1          ;AL=1000 1101  CF=1
        ROR    AL,1          ;AL=1100 0110  CF=1
or
        MOV    AL,36H        ;AL=0011 0110
        MOV    CL,3          ;CL=3 number of times to rotate
        ROR    AL,CL         ;AL=1100 0110 CF=1
```

```
;the operand can be a word:
        MOV    BX,0C7E5H     ;BX=1100 0111 1110 0101
        MOV    CL,6          ;CL=6 number of times to rotate
        ROR    BX,CL         ;BX=1001 0111 0001 1111 CF=1
```

ROL rotate left

In rotate left, as bits are shifted from right to left they exit the left end (MSB) and enter the right end (LSB). In addition, every bit that leaves the MSB is copied to the carry flag. In other words, in ROL the MSB is moved to the LSB and is also copied to CF, as shown in the diagram. If the operand is to be rotated once, the 1 is coded. Otherwise, the number of times it is to be rotated is in CL.

```
        MOV    BH,72H        ;BH=0111 0010
        ROL    BH,1          ;BH=1110 0100  CF=0
        ROL    BH,1          ;BH=1100 1001  CF=1
        ROL    BH,1          ;BH=1001 0011  CF=1
        ROL    BH,1          ;BH=0010 0111  CF=1
or
        MOV    BH,72H        ;BH=0111 0010
        MOV    CL,4          ;CL=4 number of times to rotate
        ROL    BH,CL         ;BH=0010 0111  CF=1
```

```
The operand can be a word:
        MOV    DX,672AH      ;DX=0110 0111 0010 1010
        MOV    CL,3          ;CL=3 number of times to rotate
        ROL    DX,CL         ;DX=0011 1001 0101 0011 CF=1
```

Program 3-8 shows an application of the rotation instruction.

```
    Write a program that finds the number of 1s in a byte.

From the data segment:
DATA1    DB      97H
COUNT    DB      ?
From the code segment:
        SUB     BL,BL          ;clear BL to keep the number of 1s
        MOV     DL,8           ;rotate total of 8 times
        MOV     AL,DATA1
AGAIN:  ROL     AL,1           ;rotate it once
        JNC     NEXT           ;check for 1
        INC     BL             ;if CF=1 then add one to count
NEXT:   DEC     DL             ;go through this 8 times
        JNZ     AGAIN          ;if not finished go back
        MOV     COUNT,BL       ;save the number of 1s
```

Program 3-8

SECTION 3.5: ROTATE INSTRUCTIONS   **111**

The maximum count in Program 3-8 will be 8 since the program is counting the number of 1s in a byte of data. If the operand is a 16-bit word, the number of 1s can go as high as 16. Program 3-9 is Program 3-8, rewritten for a word-sized operand. It also provides the count in BCD format instead of hex.

```
         Write a program to count the number of 1s in a word.  Provide the count in BCD.

DATAW1   DW     97F4H
COUNT2   DB     ?
         ...
         SUB    AL,AL          ;clear AL to keep the number of 1s in BCD
         MOV    DL,16          ;rotate total of 16 times
         MOV    BX,DATAW1      ;move the operand to BX
AGAIN:   ROL    BX,1           ;rotate it once
         JNC    NEXT           ;check for 1.  If CF=0 then jump
         ADD    AL,1           ;if CF=1 then add one to count
         DAA                   ;adjust the count for BCD
NEXT:    DEC    DL             ;go through this 16 times
         JNZ    AGAIN          ;if not finished go back
         MOV    COUNT2,AL      ;save the number of 1s in COUNT2
```

Program 3-9

Reminder: AL is used to make a BCD counter because the DAA instruction works only on AL.

Rotation through the carry

RCR rotate right through carry

In RCR, as bits are shifted from left to right, they exit the right end (LSB) to the carry flag, and the carry flag

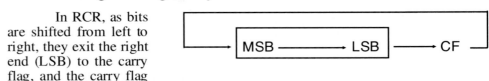

enters the left end (MSB). In other words, in RCR the LSB is moved to CF and CF is moved to the MSB. In reality, CF acts as if it is part of the operand. This is shown in the diagram. If the operand is to be rotated once, the 1 is coded, but if it is to be rotated more than once, the register CL holds the number of times.

```
         CLC                   ;make CF=0
         MOV    AL,26H         ;AL=0010 0110
         RCR    AL,1           ;AL=0001 0011 CF=0
         RCR    AL,1           ;AL=0000 1001 CF=1
         RCR    AL,1           ;AL=1000 0100 CF=1
or:
         CLC                   ;make CF=0
         MOV    AL,26H         ;AL=0010 0110
         MOV    CL,3           ;CL=3 number of times to rotate
         RCR    AL,CL          ;AL=1000 0100 CF=1

;the operand can be a word
         STC                   ;make CF=1
         MOV    BX,37F1H       ;BX=0011 0111 1111 0001
         MOV    CL,5           ;CL=5 number of times to rotate
         RCR    BX,CL          ;BX=0001 1001 1011 1111 CF=0
```

RCL rotate left through carry

In RCL, as bits are shifted from right to left they exit the left end (MSB) and enter the carry flag, and the

CHAPTER 3: ARITHMETIC AND LOGIC INSTRUCTIONS

carry flag enters the right end (LSB). In other words, in RCL the MSB is moved to CF and CF is moved to the LSB. In reality, CF acts as if it is part of the operand. This is shown in the diagram. If the operand is to be rotated once, the 1 is coded, but if it is to be rotated more than once, register CL holds the number of times.

```
            STC                     ;make CF=1
            MOV     BL,15H          ;BL=0001 0101
            RCL     BL,1            ;0010 1011 CF=0
            RCL     BL,1            ;0101 0110 CF=0
or:
            STC                     ;make CF=1
            MOV     BL,15H          ;BL=0001 0101
            MOV     CL,2            ;CL=2 number of times for rotation
            RCL     BL,CL           ;BL=0101 0110 CF=0

;the operand can be a word:
            CLC                     ;make CF=0
            MOV     AX,191CH        ;AX=0001 1001 0001 1100
            MOV     CL,5            ;CL=5 number of times to rotate
            RCL     AX,CL           ;AX=0010 0011 1000 0001 CF=1
```

Review Questions

1. What is the value of BL after the following?
   ```
   MOV   BL,25H
   MOV   CL,4
   ROR   BL,CL
   ```
2. What are the values of DX and CF after the following?
   ```
   MOV   DX,3FA2H
   MOV   CL,7
   ROL   DX,CL
   ```
3. What is the value of BH after the following?
   ```
   SUB   BH,BH
   STC
   RCR   BH,1
   STC
   RCR   BH,1
   ```
4. What is the value of BX after the following?
   ```
   MOV    BX,FFFFH
   MOV    CL,5
   CLC
   RCL    BX,CL
   ```
5. Why does "ROR BX,4" give an error in the 8086? How would you change the code to make it work?

SUMMARY

The 8- or 16-bit data items in 80x86 computers can be treated as either signed or unsigned data. Unsigned data uses the entire 8 or 16 bits for data representation. Signed data uses the MSB as a sign bit and the remaining bits for data representation. This chapter covered the arithmetic and logic instructions that are used for unsigned data. The instructions ADD and SUB perform addition and subtraction on unsigned data. Instructions ADC and SBB do the same, but also take the carry flag into consideration. Instructions MUL and DIV perform multiplication and division on unsigned data. Logic instructions AND, OR, XOR, and CMP perform logic operations on all the bits of their operands and were therefore included in this chapter. Shift and rotate instructions for unsigned data include SHR, SHL, ROR, ROL, RCL, and RCR. ASCII and BCD data operations for addition and subtraction were also covered.

Write a program that adds two multidigit ASCII numbers. The result should be in ASCII.

```
TITLE       PROG3-7 (EXE)  ADDING ASCII NUMBERS
;rewritten with simplified segment definition
PAGE        60,132
            .MODEL SMALL
            .STACK 64
;---------------------------
            .DATA
VALUE1  DB      '0659478127'
        ORG     0010H
VALUE2  DB      '0779563678'
        ORG     0020H
RESULT1 DB      10 DUP (?)
        ORG     0030H
RESULT2 DB      10 DUP (?)
;---------------------------
            .CODE
MAIN:   MOV     AX,@DATA
        MOV     DS,AX
        CALL    ASC_ADD         ;call ASCII addition subroutine
        CALL    CONVERT         ;call convert to ascii subroutine
        MOV     AH,4CH
        INT     21H             ;go back to DOS
;---------------------------
;THIS SUBROUTINE ADDS THE ASCII NUMBERS AND MAKES THE RESULT UNPACKED.
ASC_ADD PROC
        CLC                     ;clear the carry
        MOV     CX,10           ;set up loop counter
        MOV     BX,9            ;point to LSD
BACK:   MOV     AL,VALUE1[BX]   ;move next byte of operand 1
        ADC     AL,VALUE2[BX]   ;add next byte of operand 2
        AAA                     ;adjust to make it ASCII
        MOV     RESULT1[BX],AL  ;store ASCII sum
        DEC     BX              ;point to next byte
        LOOP    BACK
        RET
ASC_ADD ENDP
;---------------------------
;THIS SUBROUTINE CONVERTS UNPACKED BCD TO ASCII
CONVERT PROC
        MOV     BX,OFFSET RESULT1   ;BX points to BCD data
        MOV     SI,OFFSET RESULT2   ;SI points to ASCII data
        MOV     CX,05               ;CX is loop counter
BACK2:  MOV     AX,WORD PTR [BX]    ;get next 2 ASCII bytes
        OR      AX,3030H            ;insert ASCII 3s
        MOV     WORD PTR [SI],AX    ;store ASCII
        ADD     BX,2                ;increment BCD pointer
        ADD     SI,2                ;increment ASCII pointer
        LOOP    BACK2
        RET
CONVERT ENDP
        END     MAIN
```

Program 3-7, rewritten with simplified segment definition

PROBLEMS

1. Find CF, ZF, and AF for each of the following. Also indicate the result of the addition and where the result is saved.

(a) MOV BH,3FH
    ADD BH,45H

(b) MOV DX,4599H
    MOV CX,3458H
    ADD CX,DX

(c) MOV AX,255
    STC
    ADC AX,00

(d) MOV BX,0FF01H
    ADD BL,BH

(e) MOV CX,0FFFFH
    STC
    ADC CX,00

(f) MOV AH,0FEH
    STC
    ADC AH,00

2. Write, run, and analyze a program that calculates the total sum paid to a salesperson for eight months. The following are the monthly paychecks for those months: $2300, $4300, $1200, $3700, $1298, $4323, $5673, $986.

3. Rewrite Program 3-2 (in Section 3.1) using byte addition.

4. Write a program that subtracts two multibytes and saves the result. Subtraction should be done a byte at a time. Use the data in Program 3-2.

5. State the three steps involved in a SUB action and show the steps for the following data.
   (a) 23H-12H   (b) 43H-51H   (c) 99-99

6. Write, run, and analyze the result of a program that performs the following:
   (1)(a) byte1 × byte2   (b) byte1 × word1   (c) word1 × word2
   (2) (a) byte1 / byte2   (b) word1 / word2   (c) doubleword/byte1
   Assume byte1=230, byte2=100, word1=9998, word2=300 and doubleword =100000.

7. Assume that the following registers contain these HEX contents: $AX = F000$, $BX = 3456$, and $DX = E390$. Perform the following operations. Indicate the result and the register where it is stored. Give also ZF and CF in each case.
   Note: the operations are independent of each other.

   (a) AND DX,AX   (b) OR DH,BL
   (c) XOR AL,76H   (d) AND DX,DX
   (e) XOR AX,AX   (f) OR BX,DX
   (g) AND AH,OFF   (h) OR AX,9999H
   (i) XOR DX,0EEEEH   (j) XOR BX,BX
   (k) MOV CL,04   (l) SHR DX,1
        SHL AL,CL
   (m) MOV CL,3   (n) MOV CL,5
        SHR DL,CL   SHL BX,CL
   (o) MOV CL,6
        SHL DX,CL

8. Indicate the status of ZF and CF after CMP is executed in each of the following cases.

   (a) MOV BX,2500   (b) MOV AL,0FFH   (c) MOV DL,34
        CMP BX,1400   CMP AL,6FH   CMP DL,88
   (d) SUB AX,AX   (e) XOR DX,DX   (f) SUB CX,CX
        CMP AX,0000   CMP DX,0FFFFH   DEC CX
                                                         CMP CX,0FFFFH

   (g) MOV BX,2378H   (h) MOV AL,0AAH
        MOV DX,4000H   AND AL,55H
        CMP DX,BX   CMP AL,00

9. Indicate whether or not the jump happens in each case.

   (a) MOV CL,5   (b) MOV BH,65H   (c) MOV AH,55H
        SUB AL,AL   MOV AL,48H   SUB DL,DL
        SHL AL,CL   OR AL,BH   OR DL,AH
        JNC TARGET   SHL AL,1   MOV CL,AH
                            JC TARGET   AND CL,0FH
                                                SHR DL,CL
                                              JNC TARGET

10. Rewrite Program 3-3 to find the lowest grade in that class.

11. Rewrite Program 3-4 to convert all uppercase letters to lowercase.

12. In the IBM BIOS program for testing flags and registers, verify every jump (conditional and unconditional) address calculation. Reminder, as mentioned in Chapter 2, in forward jumps the target address is calculated by adding the displacement value to IP of the instruction after the jump and by subtracting in backward jumps.

13. In Program 3-6 rewrite BCD_ADD to do subtraction of the multibyte BCD.

14. Rewrite Program 3-7 to do subtraction. Use the following data.
    DATA1   DB   '0999999999'
    DATA2   DB   '0077777775'
    Subtract DATA2 from DATA1.

PROBLEMS

15. Using the DT directive, write a program to add two 10-byte BCD numbers.
16. We would like to make a counter that counts up from 0 to 99 in BCD. What instruction would you place in the dotted area?

```
SUB  AL,AL
ADD  AL,1
....    ....
```

17. Write Problem 16 to do a down counting (from 99 to 0).
18. An instructor named Mr. Mo Allem has the following grading policy: "The curving of the grades is achieved by adding to every grade the difference between 99 and the highest grade in the class". If the following are the grades of various students in the class, write a program that calculates the grades after they have been curved: 81, 65, 77, 82, 73, 55, 88, 78, 51, 91, 86, 76.
(Your program should work for any set of grades.)
19. If we try to divide 1,000,000 by 2:
(a) What kind of problem is associated with this operation in 8086/286 CPUs?
(b) How does the CPU let us know that there is a problem?
20. Which of the following groups of code perform the same operation as LOOP XXX?

```
(a) DEC CL      (b) DEC CH      (c) DEC BX      (d) DEC CX
    JNZ XXX         JNZ XXX         JNZ             JNZ XXX
```

21. Write a progam that finds the number of zeros in a 16-bit word.
22. In Program 3-2, which demonstrated multiword addition, pointers were updated by two INC instructions instead of "ADD SI,2". Why?

ANSWERS TO REVIEW QUESTIONS

Section 3.1: Unsigned Addition and Subtraction
1. destination
2. in 80x86 Assembly language, there are no memory to memory operations
3. MOV AX,DATA_2
   ADD   DATA_1,AX
4. destination, source + destination + CF
5. in (a), the byte addition results in a carry to CF, in (b), the word addition results in a carry to the high byte BH
6. DEC CX
   JNZ ADD_LOOP
7.   43H   0100 0011   0100 0011
   - 05H   0000 0101   2's complement=+1111 1011
     3EH   0011 1110
   CF=1; therefore, the result is negative
8. AL = 95 - 4F - 1 = 45

Section 3.2: Unsigned Multiplication and Division
1. AX   2. DX and AX
3. AX   4. AL, AH
5. AX, DX   6. AL, AH
7. AX, DX

Section 3.3: Logic Instructions and Sample Programs
1. (a) 4202   (b) CFFF   (c) 8DFD
2. the operand will remain unchanged; all zeros
3. all ones
4. all zeros

5. A0F2 =   1010 0000 1111 0010
   shift left: 0100 0001 1110 0100 CF =1
   shift again: 1000 0011 1100 1000 CF =0
   shift again: 0000 0111 1001 0000 CF =1
   A0F2 shifted left three times = 0790.
   A0F2 =   1010 0000 1111 0010
   shift right: 0101 0000 0111 1001 CF = 0
   shift again: 0010 1000 0011 1100 CF = 1
   shift again: 0001 0100 0001 1110 CF = 0
   A0F2 shifted right three times = 141E
6. SUB   7. false

Section 3.4: BCD and ASCII Operands and their Instructions
1. (a) 15 = 0001 0101 packed BCD = 0000 0001 0000 0101 unpacked BCD
    (b) 99 = 1001 1001 packed BCD = 0000 1001 0000 1001 unpacked BCD
2. DAA   BCD addition
    DAS   BCD subtraction
    AAS   ASCII subtraction
    AAA   ASCII addition

Section 3.5: Rotate Instructions
1. BL = 52H, CF = 0
2. DX = D11FH, CF = 1
3. BH = C0H
4. BX = FFEFH
5. the source operand cannot be immediate; to fix it:
    MOV CL,4
    ROR BX,CL

CHAPTER 4

BIOS INT 10H AND DOS INT 21H PROGRAMMING

OBJECTIVES

Upon completion of this chapter, you will be able to:

» Use INT 10H function calls to:
»   Clear the screen
»   Set the cursor position
»   Write characters to the screen in text mode
»   Draw lines on the screen in graphics mode
»   Change the video mode
» Use INT 21H function calls to:
»   Input characters from the keyboard
»   Output characters to the screen
»   Input or output strings
» Use the LABEL directive to set up structured data items

There are some extremely useful subroutines within BIOS and DOS that are available to the user through the INT (interrupt) instruction. In this chapter, some of them are studied to see how they are used in the context of applications. First, a few words about the interrupt itself. The INT instruction is somewhat like a FAR call. When it is invoked, it saves CS:IP and the flags on the stack and goes to the subroutine associated with that interrupt. The INT instruction has the following format:

```
INT xx          ;the interrupt number xx can be 00 - FFH
```

Since interrupts are numbered 00 to FF, this gives a total of 256 interrupts in 80x86 microprocessors. Of these 256 interrupts, two of them are the most widely used: INT 10H and INT 21H. Each one can perform many functions. A list of these functions is provided in Appendices D and E. Before the service of INT 10H or INT 21H is requested, certain registers must have specific values in them, depending on the function being requested. Various functions of INT 21H and INT 10H are selected by the value put in the AH register, as shown in Appendices D and E. Interrupt instructions are discussed in detailed in Appendix B.

SECTION 4.1: BIOS INT 10H PROGRAMMING

INT 10H subroutines are burned into the ROM BIOS of the 80x86-based IBM PC and compatibles and are used to communicate with the computer's screen video. Much of the manipulation of screen text or graphics is done through INT 10H. There are many functions associated with INT 10H. Among them are changing the color of characters or the background color, clearing the screen, and changing the location of the cursor. These options are chosen by putting a specific value in register AH. In this section we show how to use INT 10H to clear the screen, change the cursor position, change the screen color, and draw lines on the screen.

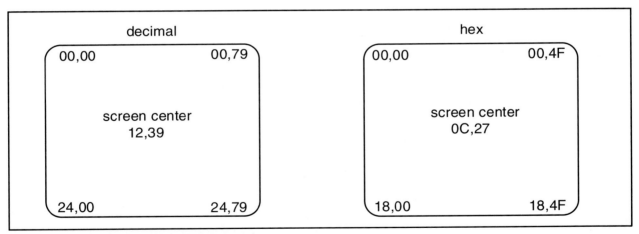

Figure 4-1. Cursor Locations (row,column)

Monitor screen in text mode

The monitor screen in the IBM PC is divided into 80 columns and 25 rows in normal text mode (see Figure 4-1). This is the case for all monitors regardless of whether they are color or monochrome, as long as they are in text mode. When the computer is turned on, the monitor is set to the default text mode. The mode can be changed, depending on the type of the monitor. Monitor types include MDA, CGA, EGA, and VGA. The text screen is 80 characters wide by 25 characters long.

Since both a row and a column number are associated with each location on the screen, one can move the cursor to any location on the screen simply by changing the row and column values. The 80 columns are numbered from 0 to 79 and the 25 rows are numbered 0 to 24. The top left corner has been assigned 00,00 (row = 00, column = 00). Therefore, the top right corner will be 00,79 (row = 00, column = 79). Similarly, the bottom left corner is 24,00 (row = 24, column = 00) and the bottom right corner of the monitor is 24,79 (row = 24, column = 79). Figure 4-1 shows each location of the screen in both decimal and hex.

Clearing the screen using INT 10H function 06H

It is often desired to clear the screen before displaying data. To use INT 10H to clear the screen, the following registers must contain certain values before INT 10H is called: AH = 06, AL = 00, BH = 07, CX = 0000, DH = 24, and DL = 79. The code will look like this:

```
MOV   AH,06        ;AH=06 to select scroll function
MOV   AL,00        ;AL=00 the entire page
MOV   BH,07        ;BH=07 for normal attribute
MOV   CH,00        ;CH=00 row value of start point
MOV   CL,00        ;CL=00 column value of start point
MOV   DH,24        ;DH=24 row value of ending point
MOV   DL,79        ;DL=79 column value of ending point
INT   10H          ;invoke the interrupt
```

Remember that DEBUG assumes immediate operands to be in hex; therefore, DX would be entered as 184F. However, MASM assumes immediate operands to be in decimal. In that case DH = 24 and DL = 79.

In the program above, one of many options of INT 10H was chosen by putting 06 into AH. Option AH = 06, called the *scroll* function, will cause the screen to scroll upward. The CH and CL registers hold the starting row and column, respectively, and DH and DL hold the ending row and column. To clear the entire screen, one must use the top left cursor position of 00,00 for the start point and bottom right position of 24,79 for the end point.

Option AH = 06 of INT 10H is in reality the "scroll window up" function; therefore, one could use that to make a window of any size by choosing appropriate values for the start and end rows and columns. However, to clear the screen, the top left and bottom right values are used for start and stop points in order to scroll up the entire screen. It is much more efficient coding to clear the screen by combining some of the lines above as follows:

```
MOV   AX,0600H     ;scroll entire screen
MOV   BH,07        ;normal attribute
MOV   CX,0000      ;start at 00,00
MOV   DX,184FH     ;end at 24,79 (hex = 18,4F)
INT   10H          ;invoke the interrupt
```

INT 10H function 02: setting the cursor to a specific location

INT 10H function AH = 02 will change the position of the cursor to any location. The desired position of the cursor is identified by the row and column values in DX, where DH = row and DL = column. Video RAM can have more than one page of text, but only one of them can be viewed at a time. When AH = 02, to set the cursor position, page zero is chosen by making BH = 00.

It must be pointed out that after INT 10H (or INT 21H) has executed, the registers that have not been used by the interrupt remain unchanged. In other words, these registers have the same values after execution of the interrupt as before the interrupt was invoked.

Example 4-1

Write the code to set the cursor position to row = 15 = 0FH and column = 25 = 19H.

Solution:

```
MOV   AH,02          ;set cursor option
MOV   BH,00          ;page 0
MOV   DL,25          ;column position
MOV   DH,15          ;row position
INT   10H            ;invoke interrupt 10H
```

Example 4-2

Write a program that (1) clears the screen and (2) sets the cursor at the center of the screen.

Solution:

The center of the screen is the point at which the middle row and middle column meet. Row 12 is at the middle of rows 0 to 24 and column 39 (or 40) is at the middle of columns 0 to 79. Therefore, by setting row = DH = 12 and column = DL = 39, the cursor is set to the screen center.

```
;clearing the screen
MOV   AX,0600H       ;scroll the entire page
MOV   BH,07          ;normal attribute
MOV   CX,0000        ;row and column of top left
MOV   DX,184FH       ;row and column of bottom right
INT   10H            ;invoke the video BIOS service

;setting the cursor to the center of screen
MOV   AH,02          ;set cursor option
MOV   BH,00          ;page 0
MOV   DL,39          ;center column position
MOV   DH,12          ;center row position
INT   10H            ;invoke interrupt 10H.
```

INT 10H function 03: get current cursor position

In text mode, one is able to determine where the cursor is located at any time by executing the following:

```
MOV   AH,03          ;option 03 of BIOS INT 10H
MOV   BH,00          ;page 00
INT   10H            ;interrupt 10H routine
```

After execution of the program above, registers DH and DL will have the current row and column positions, and CX provides information about the shape of the cursor. The reason that page 00 was chosen is that the video memory could contain more than one page of data, depending on the video board installed on the PC. In text mode, page 00 is chosen for the currently viewed page.

Changing the video mode

First it must be noted that regardless of what type of adapter is used (MDA, CGA, EGA, MCGA, or VGA), all are upwardly compatible. For example, the VGA emulates all the functions of MCGA, EGA, CGA, and MDA. Similarly, the EGA emulates the functions of CGA and MDA, and so on. Therefore, there must be a way to change the video mode to a desired mode. To do that, one can use INT 10H with AH = 00 and AL = video mode. A list of video modes is given in Appendix E, Table E-2.

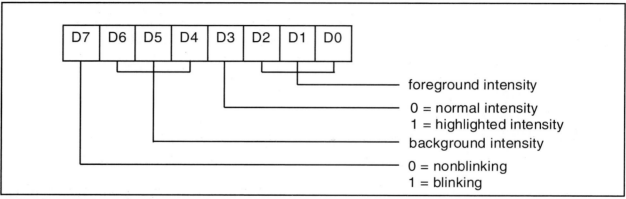

Figure 4-2. Attribute Byte for Monochrome Monitors

Attribute byte in monochrome monitors

There is an attribute associated with each character on the screen. The attribute provides information to the video circuitry, such as color and intensity of the character (foreground) and the background. The attribute byte for each character on the monochrome monitor is limited. Figure 4-2 shows bit definitions of the monochrome byte attribute.

Foreground refers to the actual character displayed. Normal, highlighted intensity and blinking are for the foreground only. The following are some possible variations of the attributes above.

Binary	Hex	Result
0000 0000	00	white on white (no display)
0000 0111	07	white on black normal
0000 1111	0F	white on black highlight
1000 0111	87	white on black blinking
0111 0111	77	black on black (no display)
0111 0000	70	black on white
1111 0000	F0	black on white blinking

For example, "00000111" would give the normal screen mode where the background is black, the foreground is normal intensity, nonblinking. "00001111" would give the same mode with the foreground highlighted. "01110000" would give a reverse video screen mode with the foreground black and the background normal intensity. See Example 4-3.

Attribute byte in CGA text mode

Since all color monitors and their video circuitry are upwardly compatible, in examples concerning color, in this chapter we use CGA mode, the common denominator for all color monitors. The bit definition of the attribute byte in CGA text mode is as shown in Figure 4-3. From the bit definition it can be seen that the background can take eight different colors by combining the prime colors red, blue, and green.

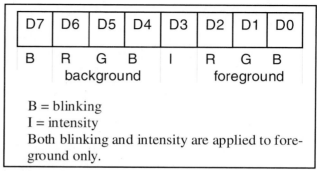

Figure 4-3. CGA Attribute Byte

The foreground can be any of 16 different colors by combining red, blue, green, and intensity. Table 4-1 lists the possible colors. As examples of some possible variations look at following cases:

Binary	Hex	Color effect
0000 0000	00	Black on black
0000 0001	01	Blue on black
0001 0010	12	Green on blue
0001 0100	14	Red on blue
0001 1111	1F	High-intensity white on blue

Example 4-3

Write a program using INT 10H to:
(a) Change the video mode.
(b) Display letter "D" in 200H locations with attributes black on white blinking (blinking letters "D" are black and the screen background is white).
(c) Then use DEBUG to run and verify the program.

Solution:

(a) INT 10H function AH = 00 is used with AL = video mode to change the video mode. Use AL = 07 for monochrome (MDA), EGA, or VGA; otherwise, use any of the 80x25 text modes, or use AL = 03 for CGA, which all color monitors emulate.

```
MOV    AH,00          ;SET MODE OPTION
MOV    AL,07          ;7 FOR MONOCHROME OR 03 FOR CGA TEXT
INT    10H            ;MODE OF 80X25 FOR ANY COLOR MONITOR
```

(b) With INT 10H function AH=09, one can display a character a certain number of times with specific attributes.

```
MOV    AH,09          ;DISPLAY OPTION
MOV    BH,00          ;PAGE 0
MOV    AL,44H         ;THE ASCII FOR LETTER "D"
MOV    CX,200H        ;REPEAT IT 200H TIMES
MOV    BL,0F0H        ;BLACK ON WHITE BLINKING
INT    10H
```

(c) Reminder: DEBUG assumes that all the numbers are in hex.

```
C>debug
-A
1131:0100 MOV AH,00
1131:0102 MOV AL,07          ;USE 03 IF MONITOR IS COLOR
1131:0104 INT 10
1131:0106 MOV AH,09
1131:0108 MOV BH,00
1131:010A MOV AL,44
1131:010C MOV CX,200
1131:010F MOV BL,F0
1131:0111 INT 10
1131:0113 INT 3
1131:0114
-
```

Now see the result by typing in the command -G. Make sure that IP = 100 before running it.

As an exercise, change the BL register to other attribute values given earlier. For example, BL = 07 white on black, or BL = 87H white on black blinking.

Example 4-4

Write a program that puts 20H (ASCII space) on the entire screen. Use high-intensity white on a blue background attribute for any characters to be displayed.

Solution:

```
MOV   AH,00          ;SET MODE OPTION
MOV   AL,03          ;CGA COLOR TEXT MODE OF 80X25
INT   10H
MOV   AH,09          ;DISPLAY OPTION
MOV   BH,00          ;PAGE 0
MOV   AL,20H         ;ASCII FOR SPACE
MOV   CX,800H        ;REPEAT IT 800H TIMES
MOV   BL,1FH         ;HIGH INTENSITY WHITE ON BLUE
INT   10H
```

Graphics: pixel resolution and color

In the text mode, the screen is viewed as a matrix of rows and columns of characters. In graphics mode, the screen is viewed as a matrix of horizontal and vertical pixels. The number of pixels varies among monitors and depends on monitor resolution and the video board. In this section we show how to access and program pixels on the screen. Before embarking on pixel programming, the relationship between pixel resolution, the number of colors available, and the amount of video memory in a given video board must be clarified. There are two facts associated with every pixel on the screen, (1) the locations of the pixel, and (2) its attributes: color and intensity. These two facts must be stored in the video RAM. Therefore, the higher the number of pixels and colors, the larger the amount memory that is needed to store them. In other words, the memory requirement goes up as the resolution and the number of colors on the monitor go up. The CGA board can have a maximum of 16K bytes video memory due to its inherent design structure. The 16K bytes memory can be used in three different ways.

Table 4-1: The 16 Possible Colors

I	R	G	B	Color
0	0	0	0	black
0	0	0	1	blue
0	0	1	0	green
0	0	1	1	cyan
0	1	0	0	red
0	1	0	1	magenta
0	1	1	0	brown
0	1	1	1	white
1	0	0	0	gray
1	0	0	1	light blue
1	0	1	0	light green
1	0	1	1	light cyan
1	1	0	0	light red
1	1	0	1	light magenta
1	1	1	0	yellow
1	1	1	1	high intensity white

1. Text mode of 80×25 characters; This takes a total of 2K bytes ($80 \times 25 = 2000$) for the characters plus 2K bytes of memory for their attributes, since each character has one attribute byte. That means that each screen (frame) takes 4K bytes, and that results in CGA supporting a total of four pages of data, where each page represents one full screen. In this mode, 16 colors are supported. To select this mode, use AL = 03 for mode selection in INT 10H option AH = 00.
2. Graphics mode of 320×200 (medium resolution); In this mode there are a total of 64,000 pixels (320 columns $\times$ 200 rows = 64,000). Dividing the total video RAM memory of 128K bits ($16K \times 8$ bits = 128K bits) by the 64,000 pixels gives 2 bits

for the color of each pixel. These 2 bits give four possibilities. Therefore, the 320 $\times$ 200 resolution CGA can support no more than 4 colors. To select this mode, use AL = 04.

3. Graphics resolution of 640 $\times$ 200 (high resolution); In this mode there are a total of 128,000 pixels (200 $\times$ 640 = 128,000). Dividing the 16K bytes of memory by this gives 1 bit (128,000/128,000 = 1) for color. The bit can be on (white) or off (black). Therefore, the 640 $\times$ 200 high-resolution CGA can support only black and white. To select this mode, use AL = 06.

The 160 $\times$ 100 low-resolution mode used with color TV sets was bypassed in this discussion since no computer uses that anymore. From the discussion above one can conclude that with a fixed amount of video RAM, as the resolution increases the number of supported colors decreases. That is the reason that to create more colors in VGA boards, one must increase the memory on the video board since there must be a storage place to store the extra colors. Many VGA boards do provide the capacity to expand the video RAM up to 1 megabyte, or more.

INT 10H and pixel programming

To address a single pixel on the screen, use INT 10H with AH = 0CH. The X and Y coordinates of the pixel must be known. The values for X (column) and Y (row) vary, depending on the resolution of the monitor. The registers holding these values are CX = the column point (the X coordinate) and DX = row point (Y coordinate). If the display mode supports more than one page, BH = page number; otherwise, it is ignored. To turn the pixel on or off, AL = 1 or AL = 0 for black and white. The value of AL can be modified for various colors.

Drawing horizontal or vertical lines in graphics mode

To draw a horizontal line, choose values for the row and column to point to the beginning of the line and then continue to increment the column until it reaches the end of the line, as shown in Example 4-5.

Example 4-5

Write a program to:
  (a) Clear the screen
  (b) Set the mode to CGA of 640 $\times$ 200 resolution
  (c) Draw a horizontal line starting at column = 100, row = 50, and ending at column 200, row 50.

Solution:

```
        MOV    AX,0600H      ;SCROLL THE SCREEN
        MOV    BH,07         ;NORMAL ATTRIBUTE
        MOV    CX,0000       ;FROM ROW=00,COLUMN=00
        MOV    DX,184FH      ;TO ROW=18H,COLUMN=4FH
        INT    10H           ;INVOKE INTERRUPT TO CLEAR SCREEN
        MOV    AH,00         ;SET MODE
        MOV    AL,06         ;MODE = 06 (CGA HIGH RESOLUTION)
        INT    10H           ;INVOKE INTERRUPT TO CHANGE MODE
        MOV    CX,100        ;START LINE AT COLUMN =100 AND
        MOV    DX,50         ;ROW = 50
BACK:   MOV    AH,0CH        ;AH=0CH TO DRAW A LINE
        MOV    AL,01         ;PIXELS = WHITE
        INT    10H           ;INVOKE INTERRUPT TO DRAW LINE
        INC    CX            ;INCREMENT HORIZONTAL POSITION
        CMP    CX,200        ;DRAW LINE UNTIL COLUMN = 200
        JNZ    BACK
```

As an exercise, put INT 3 at the end of the program above and run it in DEBUG to get a feeling of the concept. To draw a vertical line, simply increment the vertical value held by DX register and keep CX constant. The linear equation $y = mx + b$ can be used to draw any line.

SECTION 4.1: BIOS INT 10H PROGRAMMING **125**

Changing the background color

CGA graphics medium resolution provides 16 colors. Option AH = 0BH can be used to change the background color as shown in Example 4-6. Running that program in DEBUG causes the entire screen to change to blue, and when INT 3 is invoked, all the registers are displayed in very large letters. The cursor gets lost as well, since the screen is in graphics mode. To get out of that mode, simply type Q, followed by the return key to get out of DEBUG and back to DOS. Then use the DOS command "MODE CO80" (the letters CO followed by the number 80) to get back the original screen mode.

Example 4-6

Write and run a program in DEBUG to:
(a) Change the video mode to 320 × 200 graphics with four colors (mode AL = 4)
(b) Make the entire screen blue

Solution:
```
;a
    MOV    AH,00          ;SET MODE
    MOV    AL,4           ;CGA STANDARD 300X 200 WITH 4 COLOR
    INT    10H
;b
    MOV    AH,0B          ;SET COLOR
    MOV    BH,0           ;SET BACKGROUND COLOR
    MOV    BL,1           ;BLUE (SEE TABLE 4-2)
    INT    10H
    INT    3              ;STOP
```

Review Questions

1. Interrupt 10H function calls perform what services?
2. The monitor in text mode has _____ columns and _____ rows. The top left position is (__,__) and the bottom right position is (__,__).
3. Fill in the blanks in the following program, which clears the screen. Write comments on each line stating the purpose of each line of code.
```
        MOV    AH,___
        MOV    AL,___
        MOV    BH,___
        MOV    CH,___
        MOV    CL,___
        MOV    DH,___
        MOV    DL,___
        INT    10H
```
4. INT 10 function AH = 03 was used. Afterward, DH = 05 and DL = 34. What does this indicate?
5. What is the purpose of the attribute byte for monochrome monitors?
6. In text mode, there is one attribute byte associated with each _____ on the screen.
7. Write the attribute byte to display background green, foreground white blinking.
8. State the purpose of the following program, which is for a monochrome monitor.

```
        MOV    AH,02
        MOV    BH,00
        MOV    DX,0000
        INT    10H
        MOV    AH,09
        MOV    BH,00
        MOV    AL,2AH
        MOV    CX,80
        MOV    BL,0F0H
        INT    10H
```

SECTION 4.2: DOS INTERRUPT 21H

INT 21H is provided by DOS in contrast to INT 10H, which is BIOS-ROM based. When MS-DOS (or its IBM version PC-DOS) is loaded into the computer, INT 21H can be invoked to perform some extremely useful functions. These functions are commonly referred to as DOS INT 21H function calls. A partial list of these options is provided in Appendix D. In this section we use only the options dealing with inputting information from the keyboard and displaying it on the screen. In previous chapters, a fixed set of data was defined in the data segment and the results were viewed in a memory dump. Starting with this chapter, data will come from the keyboard and after it is processed, the results will be displayed on the screen. This is a much more dynamic way of processing information and is the main reason for placing this chapter at this point of the book. Although data is input and output through the keyboard and monitor, there is still a need to dump memory to verify the data when troubleshooting programs.

INT 21H option 09: outputting a string of data to the monitor

INT 21H can be used to send a set of ASCII data to the monitor. To do that, the following registers must be set: AH = 09 and DX = the offset address of the ASCII data to be displayed. Then INT 21H is invoked. The address in the DX register is an offset address and DS is assumed to be the data segment. INT 21H option 09 will display the ASCII data string pointed at by DX until it encounters the dollar sign "$". In the absence of encountering a dollar sign, DOS function call 09 will continue to display any garbage that it can find in subsequent memory locations until it finds "$". For example, to display the message "The earth is but one country", the following is from the data segment and code segment.

```
DATA_ASC    DB      'The earth is but one country','$'

            MOV     AH,09               ;Option 09 to display string of data
            MOV     DX,OFFSET DATA_ASC  ;DX= offset address of data
            INT     21H                 ;invoke the interrupt
```

INT 21H option 02: outputting a single character to the monitor

There are occasions when it is necessary to output to the monitor only a single character. To do that, 02 is put in AH, and DL is loaded with the character to be displayed and then INT 21H is invoked. The following displays letter "J".

```
            MOV     AH,02               ;option 02 displays one character
            MOV     DL,'J'              ;DL holds the character to be displayed
            INT     21H                 ;invoke the interrupt
```

This option can also be used to display '$' on the monitor since the string display option (option 09) will not display '$'.

INT 21H option 01: inputting a single character, with echo

This functions waits until a character is input from the keyboard, then echoes it to the monitor. After the interrupt, the input character will be in AL.

```
            MOV     AH,01               ;option 01 inputs one character
            INT     21H                 ;after this interrupt, AL = input character
```

Program 4-1 combines INT 10H and INT 21H. The program does the following: (1) clears the screen, (2) sets the cursor to the center of the screen, and (3) starting at that point of the screen, displays the message "This is a test of the display routine".

```
TITLE      PROG4-1     SIMPLE DISPLAY PROGRAM
PAGE       60,132
STSEG      SEGMENT
           DB      64 DUP (?)
STSEG      ENDS
;---------------------------
DTSEG      SEGMENT
MESSAGE DB         'This is a test of the display routine','$'
DTSEG      ENDS
;---------------------------
CDSEG      SEGMENT
MAIN       PROC   FAR
           ASSUME CS:CDSEG,DS:DTSEG,SS:STSEG
           MOV    AX,DTSEG
           MOV    DS,AX
           CALL   CLEAR              ;CLEAR THE SCREEN
           CALL   CURSOR             ;SET CURSOR POSITION
           CALL   DISPLAY            ;DISPLAY MESSAGE
           MOV    AH,4CH
           INT    21H                ;GO BACK TO DOS
MAIN       ENDP
;---------------------------
;THIS SUBROUTINE CLEARS THE SCREEN
CLEAR      PROC
           MOV    AX,0600H           ;SCROLL SCREEN FUNCTION
           MOV    BH,07              ;NORMAL ATTRIBUTE
           MOV    CX,0000            ;SCROLL FROM ROW=00,COL=00
           MOV    DX,184FH           ;TO ROW=18H,COL=4FH
           INT    10H                ;INVOKE INTERRUPT TO CLEAR SCREEN
           RET
CLEAR      ENDP
;---------------------------
;THIS SUBROUTINE SETS THE CURSOR AT THE CENTER OF THE SCREEN
CURSOR  PROC
           MOV    AH,02              ;SET CURSOR FUNCTION
           MOV    BH,00              ;PAGE 00
           MOV    DH,12              ;CENTER ROW
           MOV    DL,39              ;CENTER COLUMN
           INT    10H                ;INVOKE INTERRUPT TO SET CURSOR POSITION
           RET
CURSOR  ENDP
;---------------------------
;THIS SUBROUTINE DISPLAYS A STRING ON THE SCREEN
DISPLAY PROC
           MOV    AH,09              ;DISPLAY FUNCTION
           MOV    DX,OFFSET MESSAGE  ;DX POINTS TO OUTPUT BUFFER
           INT    21H                ;INVOKE INTERRUPT TO DISPLAY STRING
           RET
DISPLAY ENDP
CDSEG      ENDS
           END    MAIN
```

Program 4-1

INT 21H option 0AH: inputting a string of data from the keyboard

Option 0AH of INT 21H provides a means by which one can get data from
the keyboard and store it in a predefined area of memory in the data segment. To
do that, registers are set as follows: AH = 0AH and DX = offset address at which
the string of data is stored. This is commonly referred to as a *buffer* area. DOS
requires that a buffer area be defined in the data segment and the first byte specifies
the size of the buffer. DOS will put the number of characters that came in through
the keyboard in the second byte and the keyed-in data is placed in the buffer starting
at the third byte. For example, the following program will accept up to six
characters from the keyboard, including the return (carriage return) key. Six
locations were reserved for the buffer and filled with FFH. The following shows
portions of the data segment and code segment.

```
                ORG  0010H
DATA1           DB   6,?,6 DUP (FF)          ;0010H=06, 0012H to 0017H = FF

                MOV  AH,0AH                   ;string input option of INT 21H
                MOV  DX,OFFSET DATA1          ;load the offset address of buffer
                INT  21H                      ;invoke interrupt 21H
```

The following shows the memory contents of offset 0010H:

0010	0011	0012	0013	0014	0015	0016	0017
06	00	FF	FF	FF	FF	FF	FF

When this program is executed, the computer waits for the information to come in from the keyboard. When the data comes in, the IBM PC will not exit the INT 21H routine until it encounters the return key. Assuming the data that was entered through the keyboard was "USA" <RETURN>, the contents of memory locations starting at offset 0010H would look like this:

0010	0011	0012	0013	0014	0015	0016	0017
06	03	55	53	41	0D	FF	FF
		U	S	A	CR		

The following is a step-by-step analysis:

0010H=06   DOS requires the size of the buffer in the first location
0011H=03   the keyboard was activated three times (excluding the RETURN key) to key in the letters U, S, and A.
0012H=55H   this is ASCII hex value for letter U
0013H=53H   this is ASCII hex value for letter S
0014H=41H   this is ASCII hex value for letter A
0015H=0DH   this is ASCII hex value for CR (carriage return)

One might ask where the value 03 in 0011H came from. DOS puts that value there to indicate that three characters were entered. How can this character count byte be accessed? See the following:

```
                MOV  AH,0AH
                MOV  DX,OFFSET DATA1
                INT  21H

;After data has been keyed-in, next fetch the count value
                MOV  BX,OFFSET DATA1
                SUB  CH,CH                    ;CH=00
                MOV  CL,[BX]+1                 ;move count to CL
```

To locate the CR value 0DH in the string and replace it, say with 00, simply code the following line next:

```
                MOV  SI,CX
                MOV  BYTE PTR[BX+SI]+2,00
```

The actual keyed-in data is located beginning at location [BX]+2.

Inputting more than the buffer size

Now what happens if more than six characters (five the maximum length + the CR = 6) are keyed in? Entering a message like "USA a country in north America" <RETURN> will cause the computer to sound the speaker and the contents of the buffer will look like this:

```
0010    0011    0012    0013    0014    0015    0016    0017
06      05      55      53      41      20      61      0D
                U       S       A       SP      a       CR
```

Location 0015 has ASCII 20H for space and 0016 has ASCII 61H for "a" and finally, the 0D for RETURN key at 0017. The actual length is 05 at memory offset 0011H. Another question is: What happens if only the CR key is activated and no other character is entered? For example, in the following,

```
                ORG    20H
DATA4 DB        10,?,10 DUP (FF)
```

which puts 0AH in memory 0020H, the 0021H is for the count and the 0022H is the first location which will have the data that was entered. So if only the return key is activated, 0022H has 0DH, the hex code for CR.

```
0020 0021 0022 0023 0024 0025 0026 0027 0028 0029 002A 002B 002C ...
0A   00   0D   FF   FF   FF   FF   FF   FF   FF   FF   FF   FF   ...
```

The actual number of characters entered is 0 at location 0021. Remember that CR is not included in the count. It must be noted that as data is entered it is displayed on the screen. This is called *echo*. So the 0AH option of INT 21H accepts the string of data from the keyboard and echoes (displays) it on the screen as it is keyed in.

Program 4-2 performs the following,
(1) clears the screen,
(2) sets the cursor at the beginning of the third line from the top of the screen,
(3) accepts the message "IBM perSonal COmputer" from the keyboard,
(4) converts any lowercase letter of that message to uppercase, and finally
(5) displays the converted results on the next line.

```
TITLE       PROG4-2
PAGE        60,132
STSEG       SEGMENT
            DB      64 DUP (?)
STSEG       ENDS
;---------------------------
DTSEG       SEGMENT
BUFFER      DB      22,?,22 DUP (?)        ;BUFFER FOR KEYED-IN DATA
            ORG     18H
DATAREA     DB      CR,LF,22 DUP (?),'$'   ;AREA TO PLACE DATA AFTER CONVERSION
DTSEG       ENDS
CR          EQU     0DH
LF          EQU     0AH
;---------------------------
CDSEG       SEGMENT
MAIN        PROC    FAR
            ASSUME CS:CDSEG,DS:DTSEG,SS:STSEG
            MOV     AX,DTSEG
            MOV     DS,AX
            CALL    CLEAR                  ;CLEAR THE SCREEN
            CALL    CURSOR                 ;SET CURSOR POSITION
            CALL    GETDATA                ;INPUT A STRING INTO BUFFER
            CALL    CONVERT                ;CONVERT STRING TO UPPER CASE
            CALL    DISPLAY                ;DISPLAY STRING DATAREA
            MOV     AH,4CH
            INT     21H                    ;GO BACK TO DOS
MAIN        ENDP
;---------------------------
```

Program 4-2 *(continued on next page)*

```
;THIS SUBROUTINE CLEARS THE SCREEN
CLEAR     PROC
          MOV    AX,0600H              ;SCROLL SCREEN FUNCTION
          MOV    BH,07                 ;NORMAL ATTRIBUTE
          MOV    CX,0000               ;SCROLL FROM ROW=00,COL=00
          MOV    DX,184FH              ;TO ROW=18H,4FH
          INT    10H                   ;INVOKE INTERRUPT TO CLEAR SCREEN
          RET
CLEAR     ENDP
;---------------------------
;THIS SUBROUTINE SETS THE CURSOR TO THE BEGINNING OF THE 3RD LINE
CURSOR  PROC
          MOV    AH,02                 ;SET CURSOR FUNCTION
          MOV    BH,00                 ;PAGE 0
          MOV    DL,01                 ;COLUMN 1
          MOV    DH,03                 ;ROW 3
          INT    10H                   ;INVOKE INTERRUPT TO SET CURSOR
          RET
CURSOR  ENDP
;---------------------------
;THIS SUBROUTINE DISPLAYS A STRING ON THE SCREEN
DISPLAY  PROC
          MOV    AH,09                 ;DISPLAY STRING FUNCTION
          MOV    DX,OFFSET DATAREA     ;DX POINTS TO BUFFER
          INT    21H                   ;INVOKE INTERRUPT TO DISPLAY STRING
          RET
DISPLAY   ENDP
;---------------------------
;THIS SUBROUTINE PUTS DATA FROM THE KEYBOARD INTO A BUFFER
GETDATA PROC
          MOV    AH,0AH                ;INPUT STRING FUNCTION
          MOV    DX,OFFSET BUFFER      ;DX POINTS TO BUFFER
          INT    21H                   ;INVOKE INTERRUPT TO INPUT STRING
          RET
GETDATA ENDP
;---------------------------
;THIS SUBROUTINE CONVERTS ANY SMALL LETTER TO ITS CAPITAL
CONVERT PROC
          MOV    BX,OFFSET BUFFER
          MOV    CL,[BX]+1             ;GET THE CHAR COUNT
          SUB    CH,CH                 ;CX = TOTAL CHARACTER COUNT
          MOV    DI,CX                 ;INDEXING INTO BUFFER
          MOV    BYTE PTR[BX+DI]+2,20H ;REPLACE CR WITH SPACE
          MOV    SI,OFFSET DATAREA+12  ;STRING ADDRESS
AGAIN:    MOV    AL,[BX]+2             ;GET THE KEYED-IN DATA
          CMP    AL,61H                ;CHECK FOR 'a'
          JB     NEXT                  ;IF BELOW, GO TO NEXT
          CMP    AL,7AH                ;CHECK FOR 'z'
          JA     NEXT                  ;IF ABOVE GO TO NEXT
          AND    AL,11011111B          ;CONVERT TO CAPITAL
NEXT:     MOV    [SI],AL               ;PLACE IN DATA AREA
          INC    SI                    ;INCREMENT POINTERS
          INC    BX
          LOOP   AGAIN                 ;LOOP IF COUNTER NOT ZERO
          RET
CONVERT ENDP
CDSEG     ENDS
          END    MAIN
```

Program 4-2 *(continued from preceding page)*

Use of carriage return and line feed

In Program 4-2, the EQU statement was used to equate CR (carriage return) with its ASCII value of 0DH, and LF (line feed) with its ASCII value of 0AH. This makes the program much more readable. Since the result of the conversion was to be displayed in the next line, the string was preceded by CR and LF. In the absence of CR the string would be displayed wherever the cursor happened to be. In the case of CR and no LF, the string would be displayed on the same line after it had been returned to the beginning of the line by the CR and consequently, would write over some of the characters on that line.

Program 4-3 prompts for the user to type in a name. The name can have a maximum of eight letters. After the name is typed in, the program gets the length of the name and prints it to the screen.

Program 4-4 demonstrates many of the functions described in this chapter.

```
TITLE      PROG4-3          READS IN LAST NAME AND DISPLAYS LENGTH
PAGE       60,132
STSEG      SEGMENT
           DB 64 DUP (?)
STSEG      ENDS
;---------------------------
DTSEG      SEGMENT
MESSAGE1   DB  'What is your last name?','$'
           ORG  20H
BUFFER1    DB   9,?,9 DUP (0)
           ORG  30H
MESSAGE2   DB   CR,LF,'The number of letters in your name is: ','$'
DTSEG      ENDS
ROW        EQU     08
COLUMN     EQU     05
CR         EQU     0DH              ;EQUATE CR WITH ASCII CODE FOR CARRIAGE RETURN
LF         EQU     0AH              ;EQUATE LF WITH ASCII CODE FOR LINE FEED
;---------------------------
CDSEG      SEGMENT
MAIN       PROC    FAR
           ASSUME CS:CDSEG,DS:DTSEG,SS:STSEG
           MOV     AX,DTSEG
           MOV     DS,AX
           CALL    CLEAR
           CALL    CURSOR
           MOV     AH,09            ;DISPLAY THE PROMPT
           MOV     DX,OFFSET MESSAGE1
           INT     21H
           MOV     AH,0AH           ;GET LAST NAME FROM KEYBOARD
           MOV     DX,OFFSET BUFFER1
           INT     21H
           MOV     BX,OFFSET BUFFER1 ;FIND OUT NUMBER OF LETTERS IN NAME
           MOV     CL,[BX+1]        ;GET NUMBER OF LETTERS
           OR      CL,30H           ;MAKE IT ASCII
           MOV     MESSAGE2+40,CL   ;PLACE AT END OF STRING
           MOV     AH,09            ;DISPLAY SECOND MESSAGE
           MOV     DX,OFFSET MESSAGE2
           INT     21H
           MOV     AH,4CH
           INT     21H              ;GO BACK TO DOS
MAIN       ENDP
;---------------------------
CLEAR      PROC                     ;CLEAR THE SCREEN
           MOV     AX,0600H
           MOV     BH,07
           MOV     CX,0000
           MOV     DX,184FH
           INT     10H
           RET
CLEAR      ENDP
;---------------------------
CURSOR     PROC                     ;SET CURSOR POSITION
           MOV     AH,02
           MOV     BH,00
           MOV     DL,COLUMN
           MOV     DH,ROW
           INT     10H
           RET
CURSOR     ENDP
CDSEG      ENDS
           END     MAIN
```

Program 4-3

INT 21H option 07: keyboard input without echo

There are situations that require the user to enter a single character but that character should not be displayed on the screen; in other words, it should not echo. Option 07 of INT 21H provides that service.

```
MOV   AH,07   ;keyboard input without echo
INT   21H
```

After execution of the code above, the PC waits until a single character is entered and then provides the character in the AL register.

Using the LABEL directive to define a string buffer

A more systematic way of defining the buffer area for the string input is to use the LABEL directive. The LABEL directive can be used in the data segment to assign multiple names to a given data. When it is used in data segment it looks like this:

```
name   LABEL attribute
```

The attribute can be either BYTE, WORD, DWORD, FWORD, QWORD, or TBYTE. Simply put, the LABEL directive is used to assign the same offset address to two names. For example, in the following,

```
JOE   LABEL BYTE
TOM   DB      20 DUP(0)
```

the offset address assigned to JOE is the same offset address for TOM since the LABEL directive does not occupy any memory space (see Appendix C for many examples of the use of the LABEL directive). Next it will be shown how to use this directive to define a buffer area for the string keyboard input:

```
DATA_BUF     LABEL BYTE
MAX_SIZE     DB      10
BUF_COUNT    DB      ?
BUF_AREA     DB      10 DUP(20H)
```

Now in the code segment, it is easy to access any of the foregoing parameters by name as follows:

```
MOV   AH,0AH                   ;load string into buffer
MOV   DX,OFFSET DATA_BUF
INT   21H
MOV   CL,BUF_COUNT       ;load the actual length of string
MOV   SI,OFFSET BUF_AREA;SI=address of first byte of string
```

This is much more structured and easier to follow. By using this method, it is easy to refer to any parameter by its name. For example, using the LABEL directive, one can rewrite the CONVERT subroutine in Program 4-2 as follows:

In that data segment the BUFFER is redefined as

```
BUFFER       LABEL BYTE
BUFSIZE      DB      22
BUFCOUNT     DB      ?
REALDATA     DB      22 DUP(' ')
```

and in the code segment, in place of the CONVERT procedure:

```
CONVERT    PROC
           MOV    CL,BUFCOUNT          ;load the counter
           SUB    CH,CH               ;CX=counter
           MOV    DI,CX               ;index into data field
           MOV    BX,OFFSET REALDATA;actual data address in buffer
           MOV    BYTE PTR[BX+DI],20H ;replace the CR with space
           MOV    SI,OFFSET DATAREA   ;SI=address of converted data
AGAIN:     MOV    AL,[BX]             ;move the char into AL
           CMP    AL,61H              ;check if is below 'a'
           JB     NEXT                ;if yes then go to next
           CMP    AL,7AH              ;check for above 'z'
           JA     NEXT                ;if yes then go to next
           AND    AL,11011111B        ;if not then mask it to capital
NEXT:      MOV    [SI],AL             ;move the character
           INC    SI                  ;increment the pointer
           INC    BX                  ;increment the pointer
           LOOP   AGAIN               ;repeat if CX not zero yet
           RET                        ;return to main procedure
CONVERT    ENDP
```

Review Questions

1. INT ____ function calls reside in ROM BIOS, whereas INT ___ function calls are provided by DOS.
2. What is the difference between the following two programs?
   ```
   MOV AH,09                          MOV AH,0AH
   MOV DX,OFFSET BUFFER               MOV DX,OFFSET BUFFER
   INT 21H                            INT 21H
   ```
3. INT 21H function 09 will display a string of data beginning at the location specified in register DX. How does the system know where the end of the string is?
4. Fill in the blanks to display the following string using INT 21H.
   ```
   MESSAGE1    DB     'What is your last name?$'
               MOV  AH,_____
               MOV  DX,_____
               INT    21H
   ```
5. The following prompt needs to be displayed. What will happen if this string is output using INT 21H function 09?
   ```
   PROMPT1       DB     'Enter (round to nearest $) your annual salary'
   ```
6. Use the EQU directive to equate name "BELL" with the ASCII code for sounding the bell.
7. Write a program to sound the bell.
8. Code the data definition directives for a buffer area where INT 21H Option 0AH will input a social security number.

SUMMARY

INT 10H function calls provide the capability to manipulate text and graphics on the screen. These interrupts reside in ROM BIOS because speed is an important factor in these often used routines. The function calls described in this chapter include calls to clear or scroll the screen, change the video mode, and write text or graphics to the screen. In text mode, the programmer works with a matrix of 80×25 characters. In pixel mode, the programmer works with a matrix of pixels, the number varying with the video mode used.

INT 21H function calls are provided by DOS to perform many useful functions. The function calls described in this chapter include calls to input or output characters or strings to the monitor.

Write a program to perform the following:
1) clear the screen
2) set the cursor at row 5 and column 1 of the screen,
3) prompt "There is a message for you from Mr. Jones. To read it enter Y ". If the user enters 'Y' or 'y' then the message "Hi! I must leave town tomorrow, therefore I will not be able to see you" will appear on the screen. If the user enters any other key, then the prompt "no more messages for you" should appear on the next line.

```
        TITLE    PROGRAM 4-4
        PAGE 60,132
        STSEG    SEGMENT
                 DB 64 DUP (?)
        STSEG    ENDS
        ;---------------------------
        DTSEG    SEGMENT
        PROMPT1  DB       'There is a message for you from Mr. Jones. '
                 DB                'To read it enter Y','$'
        MESSAGE  DB       CR,LF,'Hi!  I must leave town tomorrow, '
                 DB                'therefore I will not be able to see you','$'
        PROMPT2  DB       CR,LF,'No more messages for you','$'
        DTSEG    ENDS
        CR       EQU      0DH
        LF       EQU      0AH
        ;---------------------------
        CDSEG    SEGMENT
        MAIN     PROC     FAR
                 ASSUME CS:CDSEG,DS:DTSEG,SS:STSEG
                 MOV      AX,DTSEG
                 MOV      DS,AX
                 CALL     CLEAR           ;CLEAR THE SCREEN
                 CALL     CURSOR          ;SET CURSOR POSITION
                 MOV      AH,09           ;DISPLAY THE PROMPT
                 MOV      DX,OFFSET PROMPT1
                 INT      21H
                 MOV      AH,07           ;GET ONE CHAR, NO ECHO
                 INT      21H
                 CMP      AL,'Y'          ;IF 'Y', CONTINUE
                 JZ       OVER
                 CMP      AL,'y'
                 JZ       OVER
                 MOV      AH,09           ;DISPLAY SECOND PROMPT IF NOT Y
                 MOV      DX,OFFSET PROMPT2
                 INT      21H
                 JMP      EXIT
        OVER:    MOV      AH,09           ;DISPLAY THE MESSAGE
                 MOV      DX,OFFSET MESSAGE
                 INT      21H
        EXIT:    MOV      AH,4CH
                 INT      21H             ;GO BACK TO DOS
        MAIN     ENDP
        ;---------------------------
        CLEAR    PROC                     ;CLEARS THE SCREEN
                 MOV      AX,0600H
                 MOV      BH,07
                 MOV      CX,0000
                 MOV      DX,184FH
                 INT      10H
                 RET
        CLEAR    ENDP
        ;---------------------------
        CURSOR   PROC                     ;SET CURSOR POSITION
                 MOV      AH,02
                 MOV      BH,00
                 MOV      DL,05           ;COLUMN 5
                 MOV      DH,08           ;ROW 8
                 INT      10H
                 RET
        CURSOR   ENDP
        CDSEG    ENDS
                 END      MAIN
```

Program 4-4

SUMMARY

This is the same as Program 4-4, rewritten with simplified segment defintion.

The program performs the following:
(1) Clear the screen.
(2) Set the cursor at row 5 and column 1 of the screen.
(3) Prompt "There is a message for you from Mr. Jones. To read it enter Y ". If the user enters 'Y' or 'y' then the message "Hi! I must leave town tomorrow, therefore I will not be able to see you" will appear on the screen. If the user enters any other key, the prompt "no more messages for you" should appear on the next line.

```
TITLE     PROGRAM 4-4
;rewritten with simplified segment defintion
PAGE 60,132
            .MODEL SMALL
            .STACK 64
;---------------------------
            .DATA
PROMPT1  DB        'There is a message for you from Mr. Jones. '
         DB        'To read it enter Y','$'
MESSAGE  DB        CR,LF,'Hi!  I must leave town tomorrow, '
         DB        'therefore I will not be able to see you','$'
PROMPT2  DB        CR,LF,'No more messages for you','$'
CR       EQU       0DH
LF       EQU       0AH
;---------------------------
            .CODE
MAIN     PROC
         MOV       AX,@DATA
         MOV       DS,AX
         CALL      CLEAR          ;CLEAR THE SCREEN
         CALL      CURSOR         ;SET CURSOR POSITION
         MOV       AH,09          ;DISPLAY THE PROMPT
         MOV       DX,OFFSET PROMPT1
         INT       21H
         MOV       AH,07          ;GET ONE CHAR, NO ECHO
         INT       21H
         CMP       AL,'Y'         ;IF 'Y', CONTINUE
         JZ        OVER
         CMP       AL,'y'
         JZ        OVER
         MOV       AH,09          ;DISPLAY SECOND PROMPT IF NOT Y
         MOV       DX,OFFSET PROMPT2
         INT       21H
         JMP       EXIT
OVER:    MOV       AH,09          ;DISPLAY THE MESSAGE
         MOV       DX,OFFSET MESSAGE
         INT       21H
EXIT:    MOV       AH,4CH
         INT       21H            ;GO BACK TO DOS
MAIN     ENDP
;---------------------------
CLEAR    PROC                     ;CLEARS THE SCREEN
         MOV       AX,0600H
         MOV       BH,07
         MOV       CX,0000
         MOV       DX,184FH
         INT       10H
         RET
CLEAR    ENDP
;---------------------------
CURSOR   PROC                     ;SET CURSOR POSITION
         MOV       AH,02
         MOV       BH,00
         MOV       DL,05          ;COLUMN 5
         MOV       DH,08          ;ROW 8
         INT       10H
         RET
CURSOR   ENDP
         END       MAIN
```

Program 4-4, rewritten with simplified segment definition

PROBLEMS

1. Write a program that:
    (a) Clears the screen
    (b) Sets the cursor position at row = 5 and column = 12
2. What is the function of the following program?

    ```
    MOV  AH,02
    MOV  BH,00
    MOV  DL,20
    MOV  DH,10
    INT  10H
    ```
3. The following program is meant to set the cursor at position row = 14 and col = 20. Fix the error and run to verify your solution.

    ```
    MOV  AH,02
    MOV  BH,00
    MOV  DH,14H
    MOV  DL,20H
    INT  10H
    ```
4. Write a program that first sets the cursor at position row = 12 and col = 15, then use the following program to get the current cursor position.

    ```
    MOV  AH,03
    MOV  BH,00
    INT  10H
    ```

    The current cursor position is register DX with DH = row and DL = col. Is the current cursor position provided by DH and DL in decimal or hex? Verify your answer.
5. In clearing the screen, does the sequence of the code prior to the instruction INT 10H matter? What about in setting the cursor position? Verify your answer by juggling around the instructions and then execute it.
6. It is intended to clear the screen using the following program, but there are some errors. Fix the errors and run the program to verify it.

    ```
    MOV  AX,0600H
    MOV  BH,07
    MOV  CX,0000
    MOV  DX,184F
    INT  10H
    ```
7. Write a program that:
    (a) Clears the screen
    (b) Sets the cursor at row = 8 and column = 14
    (c) Displays the string "IBM Personal Computer"
8. Run the following program and dump the memory to verify the contents of memory locations 0020H - 002FH if "IBM PC with 8088 CPU" is keyed in.

    ```
    ORG  220H
    BUFFER       DB    15,16 DUP(FF)
    ```

    and for the code :

    ```
    MOV  AH,0AH
    MOV  DX,OFFSET BUFFER
    INT  21H
    ```
9. Write a program that:
    (a) Clears the screen
    (b) Puts the cursor on position row = 15 and column = 20
    (c) Displays the prompt "What is your name?"
    (d) Gets the response from the keyboard and displays it at row = 17 and column = 20.
10. Write a program that sets the mode to medium resolution, then draws a vertical line in the middle of the screen. Then draw a horizontal line across the middle of the screen.

---

11. Write a program to input a social security number in the form 123-45-6789 and transfer it to another area with the dashes removed, as in 123456789. Use the following data definition.

```
SS_AREA      LABEL BYTE
SS_SIZE      DB    12
SS_ACTUAL    DB    ?
SS_DASHED    DB    12 DUP (?)
SS_NUM       DB    9 DUP (?)
```

12. Write a program (use the simplified segment definition) to input two seven-digit numbers in response to the prompts "Enter the first number" and "Enter the second number". Add them together (using AAA, covered in Chapter 3) and display the sum with the message "The total sum is: ".

ANSWERS TO REVIEW QUESTIONS

Section 4.1: BIOS INT 10H Programming
1. perform screen i/o
2. 80, 25; 00,00 and 24,79
3.
```
MOV AH,06    ;SELECT CLEAR SCREEN FUNCTION
MOV AL,00    ;AH=0 TO SCROLL ENTIRE PAGE
MOV BH,07    ;BH=07 FOR NORMAL ATTRIBUTE
MOV CH,00    ;START AT ROW 00
MOV CL,00    ;START AT COLUMN 00
MOV DH,24    ;END AT ROW 24
MOV DL,79    ;END AT ROW 79
INT 10H      ;INVOKE THE INTERRUPT
```
4. indicates that the cursor is at row 5, column 34
5. it provides information about the foreground and background intensity, whether the foreground is blinking and/or highlighted
6. character
7. 10100111
8. the first time INT 10H is invoked, it sets the cursor to position 00,00; the second time it is invoked, it displays the character '*' 80 times with attributes of white on black, blinking.

Section 4.2: DOS Interrupt 21H
1. 10H, 21H
2. the leftmost code inputs a string from the keyboard into a buffer; the code on the right outputs a string from a buffer to the monitor
3. the end of the string is the dollar sign '$'
4. 0AH, OFFSET MESSAGE1
5. When the '$' within the string is encountered, the computer will stop displaying the string.
6. BELL   EQU   07H
7. Using the EQU in Answer 6, the code segment would include the following:
```
             MOV    AH,02
             MOV    DL,BELL
             INT    21H
```
8.
```
SS_AREA      LABEL  BYTE
SS_SIZE      DB     12
SS_ACTUAL    DB     ?
SS_NUM       DB     12 DUP (?)
```

CHAPTER 5

MACROS

OBJECTIVES

Upon completion of this chapter, you will be able to:

» List the advantages of using macros
» Define macros by coding macro definition directives MACRO and ENDM
» Code Assembly language instructions to invoke macros
» Explain how macros are expanded by the assembler
» Use .XALL, .SALL, and .LALL directives to control macro expansion within the list file
» Use the LOCAL directive to define local variables within macros
» Use the INCLUDE directive to include macros from another file in a program

In this chapter we explore the concept of the macro and its use in Assembly language programming. The format and usage of macros are defined and many examples of their application are explored.

SECTION 5.1: WHAT IS A MACRO AND HOW IS IT USED?

There are applications in Assembly language programming where a group of instructions performs a task that is used repeatedly. For example, INT 21H function 09H for displaying a string of data and function 0AH for keying in data are used repeatedly in the same program as was seen in Chapter 4. So it does not make sense to rewrite them every time they are needed. Therefore, to reduce the time that it takes to write these codes, and reduce the possibility of errors, the concept of macros was born. Macros allow the programmer to write the task (set of codes to perform a specific job) once only and to invoke it whenever it is needed wherever it is needed.

MACRO definition

Every macro definition must have three parts, as follows:

```
name         MACRO          dummy1,dummy2,...,dummyN
             ......
             ......
             ENDM
```

The MACRO directive indicates the beginning of the macro definition and the ENDM directive signals the end. What goes in between the MACRO and ENDM directives is called the body of the macro. The name must be unique and must follow Assembly language naming conventions. The dummies are names, or parameters, or even registers that are mentioned in the body of the macro. After the macro has been written, it can be invoked (or called) by its name, and appropriate values are substituted for dummy parameters. Displaying a string of data using function 09 of INT 21H is a widely used service. The following is a macro for that service:

```
STRING       MACRO          DATA1
             MOV    AH,09
             MOV    DX,OFFSET DATA1
             INT    21H
             ENDM
```

The above is the macro *definition*. Note that dummy argument DATA1 is mentioned in the body of macro. In the following example, assume that a prompt has already been defined in the data segment as shown below. In the code segment, the macro can be invoked by its name with the user's actual data:

```
MESSAGE1     DB     'What is your name?','$'
             ...
             STRING MESSAGE1
```

The instruction "STRING MESSAGE" *invokes* the macro. The assembler *expands* the macro by providing the following code in the .LST file:

```
1      MOV    AH,09
1      MOV    DX,OFFSET MESSAGE1
1      INT    21H
```

The (1) indicates that the code is from the macro. In earlier versions of MASM, a plus sign (+) indicated lines from macros.

Comments in a macro

Now the question is: Can macros contain comments? The answer is yes, but there is a way to suppress comments and make the assembler show only the lines that generate opcodes. There are basically two types of comments in the macro: listable and nonlistable. If comments are preceded by a single semicolon (;) as is done in Assembly language programming, they will show up in the ".lst" file, but if comments are preceded by a double semicolon (;;) they will not appear in the ".lst" file when the program is assembled. There are also three directives designed to make programs that use macros more readable, meaning that they only effect the ".lst" file and have no affect on the ".obj" or ".exe" files. They are as follows:

.LALL (List ALL) will list all the instructions and comments that are preceded by a single semicolon in the ".lst" file. The comments preceded by a double semicolon cannot be listed in the ".lst" file in any way.

.SALL (Suppress ALL) is used to make the list file shorter and easier to read. It suppresses the listing of the macro body and the comments. This is especially useful if the macro is invoked many times within the same program and there is no need to see it listed every time. It must be emphasized that the use of .SALL will not eliminate any opcode from the object file. It only affects the listing in the ".lst" file.

.XALL (eXecutable ALL), which is the default listing directive, is used to list only the part of the macro that generates opcodes.

Example 5-1

Write macro definitions for setting the cursor position, displaying a string, and clearing the screen.

Solution:

```
CURSOR  MACRO  ROW,COLUMN
;THIS MACRO SETS THE CURSOR LOCATION TO ROW,COLUMN
;;USING BIOS INT 10H FUNCTION 02
        MOV   AH,02          ;SET CURSOR FUNCTION
        MOV   BH,00          ;PAGE 00
        MOV   DH,ROW         ;ROW POSITION
        MOV   DL,COLUMN      ;COLUMN POSITION
        INT   10H            ;INVOKE THE INTERRUPT
        ENDM

DISPLAY  MACRO  STRING
;THIS MACRO DISPLAYS A STRING OF DATA
;;DX = ADDRESS OF STRING.  USES FUNCTION 09 INT 21H.
        MOV   AH,09                 ;DISPLAY STRING FUNCTION
        MOV   DX,OFFSET STRING      ;DX = OFFSET ADDRESS OF DATA
        INT   21H                   ;INVOKE THE INTERRUPT
        ENDM

CLEARSCR  MACRO
;THIS MACRO CLEARS THE SCREEN
;;USING OPTION 06 OF INT 10H
        MOV   AX,0600H       ;SCROLL SCREEN FUNCTION
        MOV   BH,07          ;NORMAL ATTRIBUTE
        MOV   CX,0           ;FROM ROW=00,COLUMN=00
        MOV   DX,184FH       ;TO ROW=18H,COLUMN=4FH
        INT   10H            ;INVOKE THE INTERRUPT
        ENDM
```

Remember that the comments marked with ";;" will not be listed in the list file as seen in the list file for Program 5-1.

Using the macro definition in Example 5-1, write a program that clears the screen and then at each of the following screen locations displays the indicated message:

at row 2 and column 4 "My name"   at row 12 and column 44 "what is"
at row 7 and column 24 "is Joe"   at row 19 and column 64 "your name?"

```
                TITLE       PROG5-1
                PAGE        60,132
                ;---------------------------
                CLEARSCR        MACRO
                ;THIS MACRO CLEARS THE SCREEN
                ;;USING OPTION 06 OF INT 10H
                        MOV     AX,0600H        ;SCROLL SCREEN FUNCTION
                        MOV     BH,07           ;NORMAL ATTRIBUTE
                        MOV     CX,0            ;FROM ROW=00,COLUMN=00
                        MOV     DX,184FH        ;TO ROW=18H,COLUMN=4FH
                        INT     10H             ;INVOKE THE INTERRUPT
                        ENDM
                ;---------------------------
                DISPLAY         MACRO   STRING
                ;THIS MACRO DISPLAYS A STRING OF DATA
                ;;DX = ADDRESS OF STRING.  USES FUNCTION 09 INT 21H.
                        MOV     AH,09                   ;DISPLAY STRING FUNCTION
                        MOV     DX,OFFSET STRING        ;DX = OFFSET ADDRESS OF DATA
                        INT     21H                     ;INVOKE THE INTERRUPT
                        ENDM
                ;---------------------------
                CURSOR          MACRO   ROW,COLUMN
                ;THIS MACRO SETS THE CURSOR LOCATION TO ROW,COLUMN
                ;;USING BIOS INT 10H FUNCTION 02
                        MOV     AH,02           ;SET CURSOR FUNCTION
                        MOV     BH,00           ;PAGE 00
                        MOV     DH,ROW          ;ROW POSITION
                        MOV     DL,COLUMN       ;COLUMN POSITION
                        INT     10H             ;INVOKE THE INTERRUPT
                        ENDM
                ;---------------------------
                STSEG   SEGMENT
                        DB      64 DUP (?)
                STSEG   ENDS
                ;---------------------------
                DTSEG       SEGMENT
                MESSAGE1  DB      'My name ','$'
                MESSAGE2  DB      'is Joe','$'
                MESSAGE3  DB      'What is ','$'
                MESSAGE4  DB      'your name?','$'
                DTSEG       ENDS
                ;---------------------------
                CDSEG   SEGMENT
                MAIN    PROC    FAR
                        ASSUME CS:CDSEG,DS:DTSEG,SS:STSEG
                        MOV     AX,DTSEG
                        MOV     DS,AX
                        .LALL                   ;LIST ALL
                        CLEARSCR                ;INVOKE CLEAR SCREEN MACRO
                        CURSOR  2,4             ;SET CURSOR TO ROW2,COL 2
                        DISPLAY MESSAGE1        ;INVOKE DISPLAY MACRO
                        .XALL                   ;LIST ALL EXECUTABLE
                        CURSOR  7,24            ;SET CURSOR TO ROW 7,COL 24
                        DISPLAY MESSAGE2        ;INVOKE DISPLAY MACRO
                        .SALL                   ;SUPPRESS ALL
                        CURSOR  12,44           ;SET CURSOR TO ROW 12,COL 44
                        DISPLAY MESSAGE3        ;INVOKE DISPLAY MACRO
                        CURSOR  19,64           ;SET CURSOR TO ROW 19,COL 64
                        DISPLAY MESSAGE4        ;INVOKE DISPLAY MACRO
                        MOV     AH,4CH
                        INT     21H             ;GO BACK TO DOS
                MAIN    ENDP
                CDSEG   ENDS
                        END     MAIN
```

Program 5-1

Analysis of Program 5-1

Compare the ".asm" and ".lst" files to see the use of .LALL, .XALL and .SALL. The .LALL directive was used for each macro and then .XALL was used for two of them. From then on, all were suppressed.

```
Microsoft (R) Macro Assembler  Version 5.10        1/13/92  00:17:15
PROG5-1                                                      Page    1-1


                         TITLE    PROG5-1
                         PAGE    60,132
                         ;----------------------------
                         CLEARSCR        MACRO
                         ;THIS MACRO CLEARS THE SCREEN
                         ;;USING OPTION 06 OF INT 10H
                                 MOV      AX,0600H      ;SCROLL SCREEN FUNCTION
                                 MOV      BH,07         ;NORMAL ATTRIBUTE
                                 MOV      CX,0          ;FROM ROW=00,COLUMN=00
                                 MOV      DX,184FH      ;TO ROW=18H,COLUMN=4FH
                                 INT      10H           ;INVOKE THE INTERRUPT
                                 ENDM
                         ;----------------------------
                         DISPLAY         MACRO  STRING
                         ;THIS MACRO DISPLAYS A STRING OF DATA
                         ;;DX = ADDRESS OF STRING.  USES FUNCTION 09 INT 21H.
                                 MOV      AH,09              ;DISPLAY STRING FUNCTION
                                 MOV      DX,OFFSET STRING   ;DX = OFFSET ADDRESS OF DATA
                                 INT      21H                ;INVOKE THE INTERRUPT
                                 ENDM
                         ;----------------------------
                         CURSOR          MACRO  ROW,COLUMN
                         ;THIS MACRO SETS THE CURSOR LOCATION TO ROW,COLUMN
                         ;;USING BIOS INT 10H FUNCTION 02
                                 MOV      AH,02         ;SET CURSOR FUNCTION
                                 MOV      BH,00         ;PAGE 00
                                 MOV      DH,ROW        ;ROW POSITION
                                 MOV      DL,COLUMN     ;COLUMN POSITION
                                 INT      10H           ;INVOKE THE INTERRUPT
                                 ENDM
                         ;----------------------------
0000                     STSEG  SEGMENT
0000   0040 [                   DB       64 DUP(?)
       ??
          ]

0040                            STSEG  ENDS
                         ;----------------------------
0000                     DTSEG          SEGMENT
0000   4D 79 20 6E 61 6D MESSAGE1 DB       'My name ','$'
       65 20 24
0008   69 73 20 4A 6F 65 MESSAGE2 DB       'is Joe','$'
000E   57 68 61 74 20 69 MESSAGE3 DB       'What is ','$'
       73 20 24
0016   79 6F 75 72 20 6E MESSAGE4 DB       'your name?','$'
       61 6D 65 3F 24
0020                     DTSEG          ENDS
                         ;----------------------------
0000                     CDSEG  SEGMENT
0000                     MAIN   PROC   FAR
                                ASSUME CS:CDSEG,DS:DTSEG,SS:STSEG
0000  B8 ---- R                 MOV      AX,DTSEG
0003  8E D8                     MOV      DS,AX
                                .LALL                       ;LIST ALL
                                CLEARSCR                    ;INVOKE CLEAR SCREEN MACRO
```

List File for Program 5-1 *(continued on next page)*

```
Microsoft (R) Macro Assembler  Version 5.10          1/13/92  00:17:15
PROG5-1                                                         Page    1-2

                        1 ;THIS MACRO CLEARS THE SCREEN
                        1 ;
0005 B8 0600            1              MOV  AX,0600H       ;SCROLL SCREEN FUNCTION
0008 B7 07              1              MOV  BH,07          ;NORMAL ATTRIBUTE
000A B9 0000            1              MOV  CX,0           ;FROM ROW=00,COLUMN=00
000D BA 184F            1              MOV  DX,184FH       ;TO ROW=18H,COLUMN=4FH
0010 CD 10              1              INT  10H            ;INVOKE THE INTERRUPT
                                      CURSOR  2,4;CURSOR MACRO WILL SET CURSOR TO 2, 2
                        1 ;THIS MACRO SETS THE CURSOR LOCATION
                        1 ;
0012 B4 02              1              MOV  AH,02          ;SET CURSOR FUNCTION
0014 B7 00              1              MOV  BH,00          ;PAGE 00
0016 B6 02              1              MOV  DH,2           ;ROW POSITION
0018 B2 04              1              MOV  DL,4           ;COLUMN POSITION
001A CD 10              1              INT  10H            ;INVOKE THE INTERRUPT
                                      DISPLAY MESSAGE1  ;INVOKE DISPLAY MACRO
                        1 ;THIS MACRO DISPLAYS A STRING OF DATA
                        1 ;
001C B4 09              1              MOV  AH,09  ;DISPLAY STRING FUNCTION
001E BA 0000 R          1              MOV  DX,OFFSET MESSAGE1 ;DX = OFFSET ADDRESS OF DATA
0021 CD 21              1              INT  21H            ;INVOKE THE INTERRUPT
                                      .XALL               ;LIST ALL EXECUTABLE
                                      CURSOR 7,24         ;SET CURSOR TO ROW=7,COL= 24
0023 B4 02              1              MOV  AH,02          ;SET CURSOR FUNCTION
0025 B7 00              1              MOV  BH,00          ;PAGE 00
0027 B6 07              1              MOV  DH,7           ;ROW POSITION
0029 B2 18              1              MOV  DL,24          ;COLUMN POSITION
002B CD 10              1              INT  10H            ;INVOKE THE INTERRUPT
                                      DISPLAY MESSAGE2  ;INVOKE DISPLAY MACRO
002D B4 09              1              MOV  AH,09          ;DISPLAY STRING FUNCTION
002F BA 0008 R          1              MOV  DX,OFFSET MESSAGE2  ;DX = OFFSET ADDRESS OF DATA
0032 CD 21              1              INT  21H            ;INVOKE THE INTERRUPT
                                      .SALL               ;SUPPRESS ALL
                                      CURSOR  12,44       ;SET CURSOR TO ROW=12,COL=44
                                      DISPLAY MESSAGE3  ;INVOKE DISPLAY MACRO
                                      CURSOR  19,64       ;SET CURSOR TO ROW=19,COL=64
                                      DISPLAY MESSAGE4  ;INVOKE DISPLAY MACRO
0056 B4 4C                            MOV  AH,4CH
0058 CD 21                            INT  21H            ;GO BACK TO DOS
005A            MAIN     ENDP
005A            CDSEG    ENDS
                         END    MAIN
```

List File for Program 5-1 *(continued from preceding page)*

LOCAL directive and its use in macros

In the discussion of macros so far, examples have been chosen that do not
have a label or name in the body of the macro. This is because if a macro is
expanded more than once in a program and there is a label in the label field of the
body of the macro, these labels must be declared as LOCAL. Otherwise, an
assembler error would be generated when the same label was encountered in two
or more places. The following rules must be observed in the body of the macro:

1. All labels in the label field must be declared LOCAL.
2. The LOCAL directive must be right after the MACRO directive. In other words, it
   must be placed even before comments and the body of the macro; otherwise, the
   assembler gives an error.
3. The LOCAL directive can be used to declare all names and labels at once as follows:

                LOCAL name1,name2,name3

   or one at a time as:

                LOCAL name1
                LOCAL name2
                LOCAL name3

To clarify these points, look at Example 5-2.

Example 5-2

Write a macro that multiplies two words by repeated addition, then saves the result.

Solution:

The following macro can be expanded as often as desired in the same program since the label "back" has been declared as LOCAL.

```
MULTIPLY MACRO VALUE1, VALUE2, RESULT
   LOCAL  BACK
;   THIS MACRO COMPUTES RESULT = VALUE1 X VALUE2
;;  BY REPEATED ADDITION
;;VALUE1 AND VALUE2 ARE WORD OPERANDS; RESULT IS A DOUBLEWORD
          MOV     BX,VALUE1       ;BX=MULTIPLIER
          MOV     CX,VALUE2       ;CX=MULTIPLICAND
          SUB     AX,AX           ;CLEAR AX
          MOV     DX,AX           ;CLEAR DX
BACK:     ADD     AX,BX           ;ADD BX TO AX
          ADC     DX,00           ;ADD CARRIES IF THERE IS ONE
          LOOP    BACK            ;CONTINUE UNTIL CX=0
          MOV     RESULT,AX       ;SAVE THE LOW WORD
          MOV     RESULT+2,DX     ;SAVE THE HIGH WORD
          ENDM
```

```
Use the macro definition in Example 5-2 to write a program that multiplies the following:
    (1) 2000 x 500         (2) 2500 x 500          (3) 300 x 400

    TITLE    PROG5-2
    PAGE 60,132
    ;---------------------------
    MULTIPLY  MACRO VALUE1, VALUE2, RESULT
         LOCAL BACK
    ;THIS MACRO COMPUTES RESULT = VALUE1 X VALUE2
    ;;BY REPEATED ADDITION
    ;;VALUE1 AND VALUE2 ARE WORD OPERANDS; RESULT IS A DOUBLEWORD
              MOV     BX,VALUE1       ;BX=MULTIPLIER
              MOV     CX,VALUE2       ;CX=MULTIPLICAND
              SUB     AX,AX           ;CLEAR AX
              MOV     DX,AX           ;CLEAR DX
    BACK:     ADD     AX,BX           ;ADD BX TO AX
              ADC     DX,00           ;ADD CARRIES IF THERE IS ONE
              LOOP    BACK            ;CONTINUE UNTIL CX=0
              MOV     RESULT,AX       ;SAVE THE LOW WORD
              MOV     RESULT+2,DX     ;SAVE THE HIGH WORD
              ENDM
    ;---------------------------
    STSEG     SEGMENT
              DB      64 DUP (?)
    STSEG     ENDS
    ;---------------------------
    DTSEG     SEGMENT
    RESULT1 DW      2 DUP (0)
    RESULT2 DW      2 DUP (0)
    RESULT3 DW      2 DUP (0)
    DTSEG     ENDS
    ;---------------------------
    CDSEG     SEGMENT
    MAIN      PROC    FAR
              ASSUME CS:CDSEG,DS:DTSEG,SS:STSEG
              MOV     AX,DTSEG
              MOV     DS,AX
              MULTIPLY 2000,500,RESULT1
              MULTIPLY 2500,500,RESULT2
              MULTIPLY  300,400,RESULT3
              MOV     AH,4CH
              INT     21H                    ;GO BACK TO DOS
    MAIN      ENDP
    CDSEG     ENDS
              END     MAIN
```

Program 5-2

Notice in Example 5-2 that the "BACK" label is defined as LOCAL right after the MACRO directive. Defining this anywhere else causes an error. The use of a LOCAL directive allows the assembler to define the labels separately each time it encounters them.

```
Microsoft (R) Macro Assembler Version 5.10        1/13/92  00:33:14
PROG5-2                                                              Page    1-1

                              TITLE   PROG5-2
                              PAGE 60,132
                              ;----------------------------
                              MULTIPLY  MACRO  VALUE1, VALUE2, RESULT
                                      LOCAL BACK
                              ;THIS MACRO COMPUTES RESULT = VALUE1 X VALUE2
                              ;;BY REPEATED ADDITION
                              ;;VALUE1 AND VALUE2 ARE WORD OPERANDS; RESULT IS A DOUBLE
                                      MOV  BX,VALUE1         ;BX=MULTIPLIER
                                      MOV  CX,VALUE2         ;CX=MULTIPLICAND
                                      SUB  AX,AX             ;CLEAR AX
                                      MOV  DX,AX             ;CLEAR DX
                              BACK:   ADD  AX,BX             ;ADD BX TO AX
                                      ADC  DX,00             ;ADD CARRIES IF THERE IS ONE
                                      LOOP BACK              ;CONTINUE UNTIL CX=0
                                      MOV  RESULT,AX         ;SAVE THE LOW WORD
                                      MOV  RESULT+2,DX       ;SAVE THE HIGH WORD
                                      ENDM
                              ;----------------------------
0000                          STSEG  SEGMENT
0000  0040 [                         DB 64 DUP(?)
        ??
         ]

0040                          STSEG  ENDS
                              ;----------------------------
0000                          DTSEG   SEGMENT
0000  0002 [                  RESULT1  DW      2 DUP (0)
       0000
         ]

0004  0002 [                  RESULT2  DW      2 DUP (0)
       0000
         ]

0008  0002 [                  RESULT3  DW      2 DUP (0)
       0000
         ]

000C                          DTSEG   ENDS
                              ;----------------------------
0000                          CDSEG  SEGMENT
0000                          MAIN    PROC  FAR
                                      ASSUME CS:CDSEG,DS:DTSEG,SS:STSEG
0000  B8 ---- R                       MOV    AX,DTSEG
0003  8E D8                           MOV    DS,AX
                                      MULTIPLY 2000,500,RESULT1
0005  BB 07D0          1              MOV    BX,2000         ;BX=MULTIPLIER
0008  B9 01F4          1              MOV    CX,500          ;CX=MULTIPLICAND
000B  2B C0            1              SUB    AX,AX           ;CLEAR AX
000D  8B D0            1              MOV    DX,AX           ;CLEAR DX
000F  03 C3            1   ??0000:    ADD    AX,BX           ;ADD BX TO AX
0011  83 D2 00         1              ADC    DX,00           ;ADD CARRIES IF THERE IS ONE
0014  E2 F9            1              LOOP   ??0000          ;CONTINUE UNTIL CX=0
0016  A3 0000 R        1              MOV    RESULT1,AX      ;SAVE THE LOW WORD
0019  89 16 0002 R     1              MOV    RESULT1+2,DX    ;SAVE THE HIGH WORD
```

List File for Program 5-2 *(continued on next page)*

```
                                        MULTIPLY 2500,500,RESULT2
001D  BB 09C4      1             MOV    BX,2500          ;BX=MULTIPLIER
0020  B9 01F4      1             MOV    CX,500           ;CX=MULTIPLICAND
0023  2B C0        1             SUB    AX,AX            ;CLEAR AX
0025  8B D0        1             MOV    DX,AX            ;CLEAR DX
0027  03 C3        1??0001:      ADD    AX,BX            ;ADD BX TO AX
0029  83 D2 00     1             ADC    DX,00            ;ADD CARRIES IF THERE IS ONE
002C  E2 F9        1             LOOP   ??0001           ;CONTINUE UNTIL CX=0
002E  A3 0004 R    1             MOV    RESULT2,AX       ;SAVE THE LOW WORD
0031  89 16 0006 R 1             MOV    RESULT2+2,DX     ;SAVE THE HIGH WORD
                                        MULTIPLY 300,400,RESULT3
0035  BB 012C      1             MOV    BX,300           ;BX=MULTIPLIER
0038  B9 0190      1             MOV    CX,400           ;CS=MULTIPLICAND
003B  2B C0        1             SUB    AX,AX            ;CLEAR AX
003D  8B D0        1             MOV    DX,AX            ;CLEAR DX
003F  03 C3        1??0002:      ADD    AX,BX            ;ADD BX TO AX
0041  83 D2 00     1             ADC    DX,00            ;ADD CARRIES IF THERE IS ONE
0044  E2 F9        1             LOOP   ??0002           ;CONTINUE UNTIL CX=0
0046  A3 0008 R    1             MOV    RESULT3,AX       ;SAVE THE LOW WORD
0049  89 16 000A R 1             MOV    RESULT3+2,DX     ;SAVE THE HIGH WORD
004D  B4 4C                      MOV    AH,4CH
004F  CD 21                      INT    21H              ;GO BACK TO DOS
0051                      MAIN   ENDP
0051                      CDSEG  ENDS
                                 END    MAIN
```

List File for Program 5-2 *(continued from preceding page)*

Notice that when the macro is expanded for the first time, the list file has "??0000". For the second time it is "??0001", and for the third time "??0002" in place of the "BACK" label, indicating that the label "BACK" is local. To clarify this concept, try Example 5-2 without the LOCAL directive to see how the assembler will give an error.

INCLUDE directive

Assume that there are several macros that are used in every program. Must they be rewritten every time? The answer is no if the concept of the INCLUDE directive is known. The INCLUDE directive allows a programmer to write macros and save them in a file, and later bring them into any file. For example, assume that the following widely used macros were written and then saved under the filename "MYMACRO1.MAC".

The clear screen macro:

```
CLEARSCR     MACRO
             MOV    AX,0600H
             MOV    BH,07
             MOV    CX,0000
             MOV    DX,184FH
             INT    10H
             ENDM
```

and string display:

```
DISPLAY      MACRO          STRING
             MOV    AH,09
             MOV    DX,OFFSET STRING
             INT    21H
             ENDM
```

The next two macros save and restore the registers.

SECTION 5.1: WHAT IS A MACRO AND HOW IS IT USED?   **147**

```
REGSAVE        MACRO
               PUSH  AX
               PUSH  BX
               PUSH  CX
               PUSH  DX
               PUSH  DI
               PUSH  SI
               PUSH  BP
               PUSHF
               ENDM

REGRESTO       MACRO
               POPF
               POP   BP
               POP   SI
               POP   DI
               POP   DX
               POP   CX
               POP   BX
               POP   AX
               ENDM
```

Assuming that these macros are saved on a disk under the filename "MYMACRO1.MAC", the INCLUDE directive can be used to bring it to any ".asm" file and then the program can call upon any of them as many times as needed. When a file includes all macros, the macros are listed at the beginning of the ".lst" file and as they are expanded, they will be part of the program. To understand that, see the following program.

Program 5-3 includes macros to clear the screen, set the cursor, and display strings. These macros are all saved under the "MYMACRO2.MAC" filename. The ".asm" and ".lst" versions of the program that use the clear screen and display string macros only to display "This is a test of macro concepts" are shown on the following pages.

```
TITLE     PROG5-3
PAGE      60,132
          INCLUDE  MYMACRO2.MAC
;---------------------------
STSEG     SEGMENT
          DB       64 DUP (?)
STSEG     ENDS
;---------------------------
DTSEG     SEGMENT
MESSAGE1  DB       'This is a test of macro concepts','$'
DTSEG     ENDS
;---------------------------
CDSEG     SEGMENT
MAIN      PROC   FAR
          ASSUME CS:CDSEG,DS:DTSEG,SS:STSEG
          MOV    AX,DTSEG
          MOV    DS,AX
          CLEARSCR            ;INVOKE CLEAR SCREEN MACRO
          DISPLAY MESSAGE1    ;INVOKE DISPLAY MACRO
          MOV    AH,4CH
          INT    21H          ;GO BACK TO DOS
MAIN      ENDP
CDSEG     ENDS
          END    MAIN
```

Program 5-3

Below is the list file of Program 5-3. The letter "C" in front of the lines indicates that it is a copy from another file included in the present file.

```
Microsoft (R) Macro Assembler Version 5.10        1/13/92  00:41:49
PROG5-3                                                              Page    1-1


                            TITLE    PROG5-3
                            PAGE 60,132
                            INCLUDE  MYMACRO2.MAC
              C ;      MYMACRO2 (MAC)  FOR PROGRAM5-3
              C ;--------------------------
              C CURSOR  MACRO  ROW,COLUMN
              C ;THIS MACRO SETS THE CURSOR LOCATION AT ROW,COLUMN
              C ;;USING BIOS INT 10H FUNCTION 02
              C         MOV AH,02              ;SET CURSOR FUNCTION
              C         MOV BH,00              ;PAGE 00
              C         MOV DH,ROW             ;ROW POSITION
              C         MOV DL,COLUMN          ;COLUMN POSITION
              C         INT  10H               ;INVOKE THE INTERRUPT
              C         ENDM
              C ;--------------------------
              C DISPLAY  MACRO  STRING
              C ;THIS MACRO DISPLAYS A STRING OF DATA
              C ;;DX = ADDRESS OF STRING.  USES FUNCTION 09 INT 21H.
              C         MOV AH,09                ;DISPLAY STRING FUNCTION
              C         MOV DX,OFFSET STRING     ;DX = OFFSET ADDRESS OF DATA
              C         INT  21H                 ;INVOKE THE INTERRUPT
              C         ENDM
              C ;--------------------------
              C CLEARSCR MACRO
              C ;THIS MACRO CLEARS THE SCREEN
              C ;;USING OPTION 06 OF INT 10H
              C         MOV AX,0600H  ;SCROLL SCREEN FUNCTION
              C         MOV BH,07                ;NORMAL ATTRIBUTE
              C         MOV CX,0                 ;FROM ROW=00,COLUMN=00
              C         MOV DX,184FH             ;TO ROW=18H,COLUMN=4FH
              C         INT  10H                 ;INVOKE THE INTERRUPT
              C         ENDM
              C ;--------------------------
                            ;--------------------------
0000                        STSEG  SEGMENT
0000  0040 [                       DB      64 DUP (?)
         ??
           ]

0040                        STSEG  ENDS
                            ;--------------------------
0000                        DTSEG      SEGMENT
0000  54 68 69 73 20 69     MESSAGE1 DB     'This is a test of macro concepts','$'
      73 20 61 20 74 65
      73 74 20 6F 66 20
      6D 61 63 72 6F 20
      63 6F 6E 63 65 70
      74 73 24
0021                        DTSEG  ENDS
                            ;--------------------------
0000                        CDSEG SEGMENT
0000                            MAIN   PROC FAR
                                ASSUME CS:CDSEG,DS:DTSEG,SS:STSEG
0000  B8 ---- R                 MOV    AX,DTSEG
0003  8E D8                     MOV    DS,AX
                                CLEARSCR             ;INVOKE CLEAR SCREEN MACRO
0005  B8 0600        1          MOV  A X,0600H       ;SCROLL SCREEN FUNCTION
```

List File for Program 5-3 *(continued on next page)*

```
Microsoft (R) Macro Assembler Version 5.10          1/13/92  00:41:49
PROG5-3                                                            Page     1-2


0008  B7 07            1               MOV  BH,07              ;NORMAL ATTRIBUTE
000A  B9 0000          1               MOV  CX,0               ;FROM ROW=00,COLUMN=00
000D  BA 184F          1               MOV  DX,184FH           ;TO ROW=18H,COLUMN=4FH
0010  CD 10            1               INT  10H                ;INVOKE THE INTERRUPT
                                       DISPLAY  MESSAGE1       ;INVOKE DISPLAY MACRO
0012  B4 09            1               MOV  AH,09              ;DISPLAY STRING FUNCTION
0014  BA 0000 R        1               MOV  DX,OFFSET MESSAGE1 ;DX =OFFSET ADDRESS OF DATA
0017  CD 21            1               INT   21H               ;INVOKE THE INTERRUPT
0019  B4 4C                            MOV  AH,4CH
001B  CD 21                            INT   21H               ;GO BACK TO DOS
001D                          MAIN     ENDP
001D                          CDSEG  ENDS
                                       END  MAIN
```

List File for Program 5-3 *(continued from preceding page)*

SUMMARY

Macros are used by programmers to save time in coding and debugging. Whenever a set of instructions must be performed repeatedly, these become ideal candidates for a macro. Values can be passed to macros to be used by instructions within the macro. Programmers can place several often-used macros within a file which can be brought into one or more programs.

PROBLEMS

1. Every macro must start with directive _____ and end with directive _____.

2. Identify the name, body, and dummy argument in the following macro:
   ```
   WORK_HOUR MACRO   OVRTME_HR
               MOV      AL,40             ;WEEKLY HRS
               ADD      AL,OVRTME_HR      ;TOTAL HRS WORKED
               ENDM
   ```

3. Explain the difference between the .SALL, .LALL, and .XALL directives.

4. What is the total value in registers DX and AX after invoking the following macro?
   ```
   WAGES          MACRO          SALARY,OVERTIME,BONUSES
                  ;FINDING THE TOTAL WAGES
                  ;;ADDS SALARY + OVERTIME + BONUSES
                  SUB  AX,AX                ;CLEAR
                  MOV  DX,AX                ;AX AND DX
                  ADD  AX,SALARY
                  ADD  AX,OVERTIME
                  ADC  DX,0                 ;TAKE CARE OF CARRY
                  ADD  AX,BONUSES
                  ADC  DX,0
                  ENDM
   ```
   The macro is invoked as
   ```
   WAGES          60000,25000,3000
   ```

5. In Problem 4, in the body of the macro, dummies were used as they are listed from left to right. Can they be used in any order? Rewrite the body (leave the dummies alone) by adding OVERTIME first.

6. In Problem 4, state the comments that are listed if the macro is expanded as:
   ```
   .LALL
   WAGES          X,Y,Z
   ```

---

150   **CHAPTER 5: MACROS**

7. Macros can use registers as dummies. Show the ".lst" file and explain what the macro in Problem 4 does if it is invoked as follows:

```
          WAGES          BX,CX,SI
```

8. Fill in the blanks for the following macro to add an array of bytes. Some blanks might not need to be filled.

```
SUMMING    MACRO          COUNT,VALUES
           LOCAL  ......
           ;;this macro adds an array of byte size elements.
           ;;ax will hold the total sum
           MOV   CX,....         ;size of array
           MOV   SI,OFFSET .... .;load offset address of array
           SUB   AX,AX           ;clear ax
AGAIN:     ADD   AL,[SI]
           ADC   AH,0            ;add bytes and takes care of carries
           INC   SI              ;point to next byte
           LOOP  AGAIN                          ;continue until finished
           ENDM  .....
```

9. Invoke and run the macro above for the following data.
   In the data segment:

```
DATA1      DB   89,75,98,91,65
SUM1       DW   ?
DATA2      DB   86,69,99,14,93,99,54,39
SUM2       DW   ?
DATA3      DB   10 DUP (99)
SUM3       DW   ?
```

   (*Hint*: For the format, see Problem 10.)

10. Insert the listing directives in Problem 9 as follows and analyze the ".lst" file.
    From the code segment:

```
           ......
           .LALL
SUMMING    5,DATA1           ;adding and saving data1
           .XALL
SUMMING    ........          ;adding and saving data2
           .....
           .SALL             ;adding and saving data3
           .....
           .....
```

11. Rewrite Problem 8 to have a third dummy argument for SUM. Then rework Problem 9.

12. Rewrite Program 5-2 using the DD directive for RESULT1, RESULT2, and RESULT3.

CHAPTER 6

SIGNED NUMBERS, STRINGS, AND TABLES

OBJECTIVES

Upon completion of this chapter, you will be able to:

» Represent 8- or 16-bit signed numbers as used in computers
» Convert a number to its 2's complement
» Code signed arithmetic instructions for addition, subtraction, multiplication, and division: ADD, SUB, IMUL, and IDIV
» Demonstrate how arithmetic instructions affect the sign flag
» Explain the difference between a carry and an overflow in signed arithmetic
» Prevent overflow errors by sign-extending data
» Code signed shift instructions SAL and SAR
» Code logic instruction CMP for signed numbers and demonstrate understanding of the effect on the flag register
» Code conditional jump instructions after CMP of signed data
» Explain the function of registers SI and DI in string operations
» Describe the operation of the direction flag in string instructions
» Code instructions CLD and STD to control the direction flag
» Describe the operation of the REP prefixes
» Code string instructions:
» MOVSB and MOVSW for data transfer
» STOS, LODS to store and load the contents of AX
» CMPS to compare two strings of data
» SCAS to scan a string for data matching that in AX
» XLAT for table processing

In the first section of this chapter we focus on the concept of signed numbers in software engineering. Signed number operations are explained along with examples. In the second section we discuss string operations and table processing.

SECTION 6.1: SIGNED NUMBER ARITHMETIC OPERATIONS

All data items used so far have been unsigned numbers, meaning that the entire 8-bit or 16-bit operand was used for the magnitude. Many applications require signed data. In this section the concept of signed numbers is discussed along with related instructions.

Concept of signed numbers in computers

In everyday life, numbers are used that could be positive or negative. For example, a temperature of 5 degrees below zero can be represented as −5, and 20 degrees above zero as +20. Computers must be able to accommodate such numbers. To do that, computer scientists have devised the following arrangement for the representation of signed positive and negative numbers: The most significant bit (MSB) is set aside for the sign (+ or −) and the rest of the bits are used for the magnitude. The sign is represented by 0 for positive (+) numbers and 1 for negative (−) numbers. Signed byte and word representations are discussed below.

Signed byte operands

D7	D6	D5	D4	D3	D2	D1	D0
sign			magnitude				

In signed byte operands, D7 (MSB) is the sign and D0 to D6 are set aside for the magnitude of the number. If D7 = 0, the operand is positive, and if D7 = 1, it is negative.

Positive numbers

The range of positive numbers that can be represented by the format above is 0 to +127.

```
    0      0000 0000
   +1      0000 0001
   +5      0000 0101
   ..      .... ....
   ..      .... ....
 +127      0111 1111
```

If a positive number is larger than +127, a word-sized operand must be used. Word operands are discussed later.

Negative numbers

For negative numbers D7 is 1, but the magnitude is represented in 2's complement. Although the assembler does the conversion, it is still important to understand how the conversion works. To convert to negative number representation (2's complement), follow these steps:

1. Write the magnitude of the number in 8-bit binary (no sign).
2. Invert each bit.
3. Add 1 to it.

The following three examples demonstrate these three steps.

Example 6-1

Show how the computer would represent –5.

Solution:
1. `0000 0101`   5 in 8-bit binary
2. `1111 1010`   invert each bit
3. `1111 1011`   add 1   (hex = FBH)
This is the signed number representation in 2's complement for –5.

Example 6-2

Show –34H as it is represented internally.

Solution:
1. `0011 0100`
2. `1100 1011`
3. `1100 1100`   (which is CCH)

Example 6-3

Show the representation for -128_{10}.

Solution:
1. `1000 0000`
2. `0111 1111`
3. `1000 0000`   Notice that this is not negative zero (-0).

From the examples above it is clear that the range of byte-sized negative numbers is –1 to –128. The following lists byte-sized signed numbers ranges:

```
Decimal      Binary           Hex
-128         1000 0000        80
-127         1000 0001        81
-126         1000 0010        82
 . .         .... ....        . .
 -2          1111 1110        FE
 -1          1111 1111        FF
  0          0000 0000        00
 +1          0000 0001        01
 +2          0000 0010        02
 . .         .... ....        . .
+127         0111 1111        7F
```

Word-sized signed numbers

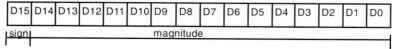

In 80x86 computers a word is 16 bits in length. Setting aside the MSB (D15) for the sign leaves a total of 15 bits (D14 - D0) for the magnitude. This gives a range of –32768 to +32767. If a number is larger than this, it must be treated as a multiword operand and be processed chunk by chunk the same way as unsigned numbers (as discussed in Chapter 3). The following shows the range of signed word operands. To convert a negative to its word operand representation, the three steps discussed in negative byte operands are used.

```
Decimal              Binary                      Hex
-32 768              1000 0000 0000 0000         8000
-32 767              1000 0000 0000 0001         8001
-32 766              1000 0000 0000 0010         8002
......               ...................         ....
......               ...................         ....
 -2                  1111 1111 1111 1110         FFFE
 -1                  1111 1111 1111 1111         FFFF
  0                  0000 0000 0000 0000         0000
 +1                  0000 0000 0000 0001         0001
 +2                  0000 0000 0000 0010         0002
...                  ...................         ....
...                  ...................         ....
+32 766              0111 1111 1111 1110         7FFE
+32 767              0111 1111 1111 1111         7FFF
```

Overflow problem in signed number operations

When using signed numbers, a serious problem arises that must be dealt with. This is the overflow problem. The CPU indicates the existence of the problem by raising the OF (overflow) flag, but it is up to the programmer to take care of it. The CPU understands only 0s and 1s and ignores the human convention of positive and negative numbers. Now what is an overflow? If the result of an operation on signed numbers is too large for the register, an overflow has occurred and the programmer must be notified. Look at the following example.

Example 6-4

Look at the following code and data segments:

```
DATA1     DB      +96
DATA2     DB      +70
          ...     ....
          MOV     AL,DATA1      ;AL=0110 0000 (AL=60H)
          MOV     BL,DATA2      ;BL=0100 0110 (BL=46H)
          ADD     AL,BL         ;AL=1010 0110 (AL=A6H= -90 invalid!)


+ 96      0110 0000
+ 70      0100 0110
+166      1010 0110  According to the CPU, this is -90, which is wrong. (OF = 1, SF = 1, CF = 0)
```

In the example above, +96 is added to +70 and the result according to CPU came out to be -90. Why? The reason is that the result was more than what AL could handle. Like all other 8-bit registers, AL could only contain up to +127. The designers of the CPU created the overflow flag specifically for the purpose of informing the programmer that the result of the signed number operation is erroneous.

When the overflow flag is set in 8-bit operations

In 8-bit signed number operations, OF is set to 1 if either of the following two occurs:

1. There is carry from D6 to D7 but no carry out of D7 (CF = 0).
2. There is a carry from D7 out (CF = 1) but no carry from D6 to D7.

In other words, the overflow flag is set to 1 if there is a carry from D6 to D7 or from D7 out, but not both. This means that if there is carry both from D6 to D7 and from D7 out, OF = 0. In Example 6-4, since there is only a carry from D6 to D7 and no carry from D7 out, OF = 1. The next three examples give further illustrations of the overflow flag in signed arithmetic.

Example 6-5

Observe the results of the following:

```
        MOV     DL,-128     ;DL=1000 0000 (DL=80H)
        MOV     CH,-2       ;CH=1111 1110 (CH=FEH)
        ADD     DL,CH       ;DL=0111 1110 (DL=7EH=+126 invalid!)
```

```
    -128    1000 0000
  + - 2    1111 1110
    -130    0111 1110    OF=1, SF=0 (positive), CF=1
```

According to the CPU, the result is +126, which is wrong. The error is indicted by the fact that OF=1

Example 6-6

Observe the results of the following:

```
        MOV     AL,-2       ;AL=1111 1110 (AL=FEH)
        MOV     CL,-5       ;CL=1111 1011 (CL=FBH)
        ADD     CL,AL       ;CL=1111 1001 (CL=F9H=-7 which is correct)
```

```
    -2     1111 1110
  + -5     1111 1011
    -7     1111 1001    OF = 0, CF = 0 ,SF = 1 (negative); the result is correct since OF = 0.
```

Example 6-7

Observe the results of the following:

```
        MOV     DH,+7       ;DH=0000 0111   (DH=07H)
        MOV     BH,+18      ;BH=0001 0010   (BH=12H)
        ADD     BH,DH       ;BH=0001 1001   (BH=19H=+25, correct)
```

```
    +7     0000 0111
  + +18    0001 0010
    +25    0001 1001        OF = 0, CF = 0 and SF = 0 (positive).
```

Overflow flag in 16-bit operations

In a 16-bit operation, OF is set to 1 in either of two cases:

1. There is carry from D14 to D15 but no carry out of D15 (CF = 0).
2. There is carry from D15 out (CF = 1) but no carry from D14 to D15.

Again the overflow flag is low (not set) if there is a carry from both D14 to D15 and from D15 out. The OF is set to 1 only when there is carry from D14 to D15 or from D15 out but not from both.

Example 6-8

Observe the results in the following:

```
        MOV     AX,6E2FH    ;  28,207
        MOV     CX,13D4H    ;+  5,076
        ADD     AX,CX       ;= 33,283 is the expected answer
```

```
    6E2F        0110 1110 0010 1111
  + 13D4        0001 0011 1101 0100
    8203        1000 0010 0000 0011  = -32,253  incorrect!    OF = 1, CF = 0, SF = 1
```

Example 6-9

Observe the results in the following:

```
MOV   DX,542FH     ;  21,551
MOV   BX,12E0H     ; + 4,832
ADD   DX,BX        ;=26,383
```

```
  543F          0101 0100 0010 1111
+ 12E0          0001 0010 1110 0000
  670F          0110 0111 0000 1111 = 26,383 (correct answer)   OF = 0, CF = 0, SF = 0
```

Avoiding erroneous results in signed number operations

To avoid the problems associated with signed number operations, one can *sign-extend* the operand. Sign extension copies the sign bit (D7) of the lower byte of a register into the upper bits of the register, or copies the sign bit of a 16-bit register into another register. CBW (convert signed byte to signed word) and CWD (convert signed word to signed double word) are used to perform sign extension. They work as follows:

CBW will copy D7 (the sign flag) to all bits of AH. This is demonstrated below. Notice that the operand is assumed to be AL and the previous contents of AH are destroyed.

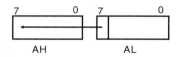

```
MOV   AL,+96       ;AL=0110 0000
CBW                ;now AH=0000 0000 and AL=0110 0000
```

or:

```
MOV   AL,–2        ;AL=1111 1110
CBW                ;AH=1111 1111 and AL=1111 1110
```

CWD sign extends AX. It copies D15 of AX to all bits of the DX register. This is used for signed word operands. This is illustrated below.

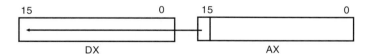

Look at the following example:
```
MOV   AX,+260      ;AX=0000 0001 0000 0100 or AX=0104H
CWD                ;DX=0000H and AX=0104H
```

Another example:
```
MOV   AX,–32766    ;AX=1000 0000 0000 0010B or AX=8002H
CWD                ;DX=FFFF and AX=8002
```

As can be seen in the examples above, CWD does not alter AX. The sign of AX is copied to the DX register. How can these instructions help correct the overflow error? To answer that question, Example 6-10 shows Example 6-4 rewritten to correct the overflow problem.

In Example 6-10, if the overflow flag is not raised (OF = 0), the result of the signed number is correct and JNO (jump if no overflow) will jump to OVER. However, if OF = 1, which means that the result is erroneous, each operand must be sign extended and then added. That is the function of the code below the JNO instruction. The program in Example 6-10 works for addition of any two signed bytes.

Example 6-10

Rewrite Example 6-4 to provide for handling the overflow problem.

Solution:

```
DATA1    DB     +96
DATA2    DB     +70
RESULT   DW     ?
         ......
         SUB    AH,AH         ;AH=0
         MOV    AL,DATA1      ;GET OPERAND 1
         MOV    BL,DATA2      ;GET OPERAND 2
         ADD    AL,BL         ;ADD THEM
         JNO    OVER          ;IF OF=0 THEN GO TO OVER
         MOV    AL,DATA2      ;OTHERWISE GET OPERAND 2 TO
         CBW                  ;SIGN EXTEND IT
         MOV    BX,AX         ;SAVE IT IN BX
         MOV    AL,DATA1      ;GET BACK OPERAND 1 TO
         CBW                  ;SIGN EXTEND IT
         ADD    AX,BX         ;ADD THEM AND
OVER:    MOV    RESULT,AX     ;SAVE IT
```

The following is an analysis of the values in Example 6-10. Each is sign extended and then added as follows:

```
S       AH              AL
0       000 0000        0110 0000       +96  after sign extension
0       000 0000        0100 0110       +70  after sign extension
0       000 0000        1010 0110       +166
```

As a rule, if the possibility of overflow exists, all byte-sized signed numbers should be sign extended into a word, and similarly, all word-sized signed operands should be sign extended before they are processed. This will be shown shortly in Program 6-1. Before discussing that, it is important to understand the division and multiplication of signed operands.

IDIV (Signed number division)

The Intel manual says that IDIV means "integer division"; it is used for signed number division. In actuality, all arithmetic instructions of the 8088/86 are for integer numbers regardless of whether the operands are signed or unsigned. To perform operations on real numbers, the 8087 coprocessor is used. Remember that real numbers are the ones with decimal points such as "3.56". Division of signed numbers is very similar to division of unsigned numbers discussed in Chapter 3. Table 6-1 summarizes signed number division. It is very similar to Table 3-2, which summarized unsigned number division.

Table 6-1: Signed Division Summary

Division	Numerator	Denominator	Quotient	Remainder
byte/byte	AL = byte CBW	register or memory	AL	AH
word/word	AX = word CWD	register or memory	AX	DX
word/byte	AX = word	register or memory	AL [1]	AH
doubleword/word	DXAX = doubleword	register or memory	AX [2]	DX

Notes:
1. Divide error interrupt if -127 > AL > +127.
2. Divide error interrupt if -32767 > AL > +32767.

Table 6-2: Signed Multiplication Summary

Multiplication	Operand 1	Operand 2	Result
byte $\times$ byte	AL	register or memory	AX [1]
word $\times$ word	AX	register or memory	DXAX [2]
word $\times$ byte	AL=byte CBW	register or memory	DXAX [2]

Notes:

1. CF = 1 and OF = 1 if AH has part of the result, but if the result is not large enough to need the AH, the sign bit is copied to the unused bits and the CPU makes CF = 0 and OF = 0 to indicate that.
2. CF = 1 and OF = 1 if DX has part of the result, but if the result is not large enough to need the DX, the sign bit is copied to the unused bits and the CPU makes CF = 0 and OF = 0 to indicate that.

   One can use J condition to find out which of the conditions above has occurred. The rest of the flags are undefined.

IMUL (Signed number multiplication)

This is signed number multiplication, and in its operation is similar to the unsigned multiplication described in Chapter 3. The only difference between them is that the operands in signed number operations can be positive or negative; therefore, the result must indicate the sign. Table 6-2 summarizes signed number multiplication; it is similar to Table 3-1.

```
TITLE      PROG 6-1               FIND THE AVERAGE TEMPERATURE
PAGE       60,132
;---------------------------
STSEG      SEGMENT
           DB 64 DUP (?)
STSEG      ENDS
;---------------------------
DTSEG           SEGMENT
SIGN_DAT        DB      +13,-10,+19,+14,-18,-9,+12,-9,+16
                ORG     0010H
AVERAGE         DW      ?
REMAINDER       DW      ?
DTSEG           ENDS
;---------------------------
CDSEG      SEGMENT
MAIN       PROC   FAR
           ASSUME CS:CDSEG,DS:DTSEG,SS:STSEG
           MOV    AX,DTSEG
           MOV    DS,AX
           MOV    CX,9                ;LOAD COUNTER
           SUB    BX,BX               ;CLEAR BX, USED AS ACCUMULATOR
           MOV    SI,OFFSET SIGN_DAT  ;SET UP POINTER
BACK:      MOV    AL,[SI]             ;MOVE BYTE INTO AL
           CBW                        ;SIGN EXTEND INTO AX
           ADD    BX,AX               ;ADD TO BX
           INC    SI                  ;INCREMENT POINTER
           LOOP   BACK                ;LOOP IF NOT FINISHED
           MOV    AL,9                ;MOVE COUNT TO AL
           CBW                        ;SIGN EXTEND INTO AX
           MOV    CX,AX               ;SAVE DENOMINATOR IN CX
           MOV    AX,BX               ;MOVE SUM TO AX
           CWD                        ;SIGN EXTEND THE SUM
           IDIV   CX                  ;FIND THE AVERAGE
           MOV    AVERAGE,AX          ;STORE THE AVERAGE (QUOTIENT)
           MOV    REMAINDER,DX        ;STORE THE REMAINDER
           MOV    AH,4CH
           INT    21H                 ;GO BACK TO DOS
MAIN       ENDP
CDSEG      ENDS
           END    MAIN
```

Program 6-1

An application of signed number arithmetic is given in Program 6-1. It computes the average of the following Celsius temperatures: +13, −10, +19, +14, −18, −9, +12, −19, and +16.

The program is written in such a way as to handle any overflow that may occur. In Program 6-1, each byte of data was sign extended and added to BX, computing the total sum, which is a signed word. Then the sum and the count were sign extended and by dividing the total sum by the count (number of bytes, which in this case is 9), the average was calculated.

The following is the ".lst" file of the program above. Notice the signed number format provided by the assembler.

```
Microsoft (R) Macro Assembler  Version 5.10              12/30/91  06:14:2
PROG6-1                                                              Page  1-1


                                TITLE    PROG6-1 FIND THE AVERAGE TEMPERATURE
                                PAGE 60,132
                                ;----------------------------
0000                            STSEG   SEGMENT
0000  0040 [                            DB 64 DUP (?)
       ??
       ]

0040                            STSEG  ENDS
                                ;----------------------------
0000                            DTSEG           SEGMENT
0000  0D F6 13 0E EE F7         SIGN_DAT        DB      +13,-10,+19,+14,-18,-9,+12,-9,+16
      0C F7 10
0010                                            ORG     0010H
0010  0000                      AVERAGE         DW      ?
0012  0000                      REMAINDER       DW      ?
0014                            DTSEG           ENDS
                                ;----------------------------
0000                            CDSEG SEGMENT
0000                            MAIN   PROC FAR
                                       ASSUME CS:CDSEG,DS:DTSEG,SS:STSEG
0000  B8 ---- R                        MOV     AX,DTSEG
0003  8E D8                            MOV     DS,AX
0005  B9 0009                          MOV     CX,9              ;LOAD COUNTER
0008  2B DB                            SUB     BX,BX             ;CLEAR BX, USED AS ACCUMULATOR
000A  BE 0000 R                        MOV     SI,OFFSET SIGN_DAT ;SET UP POINTER
000D  8A 04                    BACK:   MOV     AL,[SI]           ;MOVE BYTE INTO AL
000F  98                               CBW                       ;SIGN EXTEND INTO AX
0010  03 D8                            ADD     BX,AX             ;ADD TO BX
0012  46                               INC     SI                ;INCREMENT POINTER
0013  E2 F8                            LOOP    BACK              ;LOOP IF NOT FINISHED
0015  B0 09                            MOV     AL,9              ;MOVE COUNT TO AL
0017  98                               CBW                       ;SIGN EXTEND INTO AX
0018  8B C8                            MOV     CX,AX             ;SAVE DENOMINATOR IN CX
001A  8B C3                            MOV     AX,BX             ;MOVE SUM TO AX
001C  99                               CWD                       ;SIGN EXTEND THE SUM
001D  F7 F9                            IDIV    CX                ;FIND THE AVERAGE
001F  A3 0010 R                        MOV     AVERAGE,AX        ;STORE THE AVERAGE (QUOTIENT)
0022  89 16 0012 R                     MOV     REMAINDER,DX ;STORE THE REMAINDER
0026  B4 4C                            MOV     AH,4CH
0028  CD 21                            INT     21H               ;GO BACK TO DOS
002A                            MAIN   ENDP
002A                            CDSEG ENDS
                                       END     MAIN
```

List File for Program 6-1

Arithmetic shift

As discussed in Chapter 3, there are two types of shifts: logical and arithmetic. Logical shift, which is used for unsigned numbers, was discussed previously. The arithmetic shift is used for signed numbers. It is basically the same as the logical shift, except that the sign bit is copied to the shifted bits. SAR (shift arithmetic right) and SAL (shift arithmetic left) are two instructions for the arithmetic shift.

SAR (shift arithmetic right)

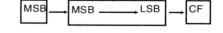

SAR   destination,count

As the bits of the destination are shifted to the right into CF, the empty bits are filled with the sign bit. As far as the signed number shift is concerned, this instruction will suffice, but it should be noted that the Intel manual gives the following instructions as well.

SAL (shift arithmetic left) and SHL (shift left)

These two instructions do exactly the same thing. It is basically the same instruction with two mnemonics. As far as signed numbers are concerned, there is no need for SAL. For a discussion of SHL (SAL), see Chapter 3. One can use the SAR instruction to divide a signed number by 2, as shown next:

```
MOV    AL,-10        ;AL=-10=F6H=1111 0110
SAR    AL,1          ;AL is shifted right arithmetic once
                     ;AL=1111 1011=FDH=-5
```

Example 6-11

Using DEBUG, evaluate the results of the following:

```
MOV      AX,-9
MOV      BL,2
IDIV     BL            ;divide -9 by 2     results in FCH
MOV      AX,-9
SAR      AX,1          ;divide -9 by 2 with arithmetic shift   results in FBH
```

Solution:

The DEBUG trace demonstrates that an IDIV of –9 by 2 gives FCH (–4), whereas SAR –9 gives FBH (–5). This is because SAR rounds negative numbers down but IDIV rounds up.

Signed number comparison

CMP   dest,source

Although the CMP (compare) instruction is the same for both signed and unsigned numbers, the J condition instruction used to make a decision for the signed numbers is different from the unsigned numbers. While in unsigned number comparisons CF and ZF are checked for conditions of larger, equal, and smaller (see Chapter 3), in signed number comparison, OF, ZF, and SF are checked:

```
destination > source        OF=SF or ZF=0
destination = source        ZF=1
destination < source        OF=negation of SF
```

The mnemonics used to detect the conditions above are as follows:

JG	Jump Greater	jump if OF=SF or ZF=0
JGE	Jump Greater or Equal	jump if OF=SF
JL	Jump Less	jump if OF=inverse of SF
JLE	Jump Less or Equal	jump if OF=inverse of SF or ZF=1
JE	Jump if Equal	jump of ZF = 1

Example 6-12 should help clarify how the condition flags are affected by the compare instruction. Program 6-2 is an example of the application of the signed number comparison. It uses the data in Program 6-1 and finds the lowest temperature.

The concept of signed number arithmetic is so important and widely used that even the RISC processors in their attempt to streamline the instruction set could not eliminate these instructions.

Example 6-12

Show the DEBUG trace of the following instructions comparing several signed numbers.

```
        MOV     AL,-5
        CMP     AL,-9
        CMP     AL,-2
        CMP     AL,-5
        CMP     AL,+7
```

Solution:

```
C>debug
-a 100
103D:0100 mov al,-5
103D:0102 cmp al,-9
103D:0104 cmp al,-2
103D:0106 cmp al,-5
103D:0108 cmp al,7
103D:010A int 3
103D:010B
-t=100,5

AX=00FB BX=0000 CX=0000 DX=0000 SP=CFDE BP=0000 SI=0000 DI=0000
DS=103D ES=103D SS=103D CS=103D IP=0102  NV UP DI PL NZ NA PO NC
103D:0102 3CF7        CMP    AL,F7

AX=00FB BX=0000 CX=0000 DX=0000 SP=CFDE BP=0000 SI=0000 DI=0000
DS=103D ES=103D SS=103D CS=103D IP=0104  NV UP DI PL NZ NA PO NC
103D:0104 3CFE        CMP    AL,FE

AX=00FB BX=0000 CX=0000 DX=0000 SP=CFDE BP=0000 SI=0000 DI=0000
DS=103D ES=103D SS=103D CS=103D IP=0106  NV UP DI NG NZ AC PO CY
103D:0106 3CFB        CMP    AL,FB

AX=00FB BX=0000 CX=0000 DX=0000 SP=CFDE BP=0000 SI=0000 DI=0000
DS=103D ES=103D SS=103D CS=103D IP=0108  NV UP DI PL ZR NA PE NC
103D:0108 3C07        CMP    AL,07

AX=00FB BX=0000 CX=0000 DX=0000 SP=CFDE BP=0000 SI=0000 DI=0000
DS=103D ES=103D SS=103D CS=103D IP=010A  NV UP DI NG NZ NA PO NC
103D:010A CC          INT    3


-q
```

```
TITLE       PROG6-2         ;FIND THE LOWEST TEMPERATURE
PAGE        60,132
;---------------------------
STSEG       SEGMENT
            DB      64 DUP (?)
STSEG       ENDS
;---------------------------
DTSEG       SEGMENT
SIGN_DAT            DB      +13,-10,+19,+14,-18,-9,+12,-9,+16
            ORG     0010H
LOWEST   DB      ?
DTSEG       ENDS
;---------------------------
CDSEG       SEGMENT
MAIN        PROC    FAR
            ASSUME CS:CDSEG,DS:DTSEG,SS:STSEG
            MOV     AX,DTSEG
            MOV     DS,AX
            MOV     CX,8                    ;LOAD COUNTER (NUMBER ITEMS - 1)
            MOV     SI,OFFSET SIGN_DAT      ;SET UP POINTER
            MOV     AL,[SI]                 ;AL HOLDS LOWEST VALUE FOUND SO FAR
BACK:       INC     SI                      ;INCREMENT POINTER
            CMP     AL,[SI]                 ;COMPARE NEXT BYTE TO LOWEST
            JLE     SEARCH                  ;IF AL IS LOWEST, CONTINUE SEARCH
            MOV     AL,[SI]                 ;OTHERWISE SAVE NEW LOWEST
SEARCH:  LOOP    BACK                    ;LOOP IF NOT FINISHED
            MOV     LOWEST,AL               ;SAVE LOWEST TEMPERATURE
            MOV     AH,4CH
            INT     21H                     ;GO BACK TO DOS
MAIN        ENDP
CDSEG       ENDS
            END     MAIN
```

Program 6-2

Review Questions

1. In an 8-bit operand, bit _____ is used for the sign bit, whereas in a 16-bit operand, bit _____ is used for the sign bit.
2. Covert 16H to its 2's complement representation.
3. The range of byte-sized signed operands is −_____ to +_____. The range of word-sized signed operands is −_____ to +_____.
4. Explain the difference between a carry and an overflow.
5. Explain the purpose of the CBW and CWD instructions. Demonstrate the effect of CBW on AL = F6H. Demonstrate the effect of CWD on AX = 124CH.
6. The instruction for signed multiplication is _____. The instruction for signed division is _____.
7. Explain the difference between the SHR (discussed in Chapter 3) and SAR instructions.
8. For each of the following instructions, indicate the flag condition necessary for each jump to occur:
   (a) JLE   (b) JG

SECTION 6.2: STRING AND TABLE OPERATIONS

There are a group of instructions referred to as *string* instructions in the 80x86 family of microprocessors. They are capable of performing operations on a series of operands located in consecutive memory locations. For example, while the CMP instruction can compare only 2 bytes (or words) of data, the CMPS (compare string) instruction is capable of comparing two arrays of data located in memory locations pointed at by the SI and DI registers. These instructions are very powerful and can be used in many applications, as will be shown shortly.

Use of SI and DI, DS and ES in string instructions

For string operations to work, designers of the CPU must set aside certain registers for specific functions. These registers must permanently provide the source and destination operands. This is exactly what the 80x86 has done. In 8088/86 microprocessors, the SI and DI registers always point to the source and destination operands, respectively. Now the question is: Which segments are they combined with to generate the 20-bit physical address? To generate the physical address, the 8088/86 always uses SI as the offset of the DS (data segment) register and DI as the offset of ES (extra segment). This is the default mode. It must be noted that the ES register must be initialized for the string operation to work.

Byte and word operands in string instructions

In each of the string instructions, the operand can be a byte or a word. They are distinguished by the letters B (byte) and W (word) in the instruction mnemonic. Table 6-3 provides a summary of all the string instructions. Each one will be discussed separately in the context of examples.

Table 6-3: String Operation Summary

Instruction	Mnemonic	Destination	Source	Prefix
move string byte	MOVSB	ES:DI	DS:SI	REP
move string word	MOVSW	ES:DI	DS:SI	REP
store string byte	STOSB	ES:DI	AL	REP
store string word	STOSW	ES:DI	AX	REP
load string byte	LODSB	AL	DS:SI	none
load string word	LODSW	AX	DS:SI	none
compare string byte	CMPSB	ES:DI	DS:SI	REPE/REPNE
compare string word	CMPSW	ES:DI	DS:SI	REPE/REPNE
scan string byte	SCASB	ES:DI	AL	REPE/REPNE
scan string word	SCASW	ES:DI	AX	REPE/REPNE

DF, the direction flag

To process operands located in consecutive memory locations requires that the pointer be incremented or decremented. In string operations this is achieved by the direction flag. Of the 16 bits of the flag register (D0 - D15), bit 11 (D10) is set aside for the direction flag (DF). It is the job of the string instruction to increment or decrement the SI and DI pointers, but it is the job of the programmer to specify the choice of increment or decrement by setting the direction flag to high or low. The instructions CLD (clear direction flag) and STD (set direction flag) are specifically designed for that.

CLD (clear direction flag) will reset (put to zero) DF, indicating that the string instruction should increment the pointers automatically. This automatic incrementation sometimes is referred to as *autoincrement*.

STD (set the direction flag) performs the opposite function of the CLD instruction. It sets DF to 1, indicating to the string instruction that the pointers SI and DI should be decremented automatically.

REP prefix

The REP (repeat) prefix allows a string instruction to perform the operation repeatedly. Now the question is: How many times is it repeated? REP assumes that CX holds the number of times that the instruction should be repeated. In other words, the REP prefix tells the CPU to perform the string operation and then decrements the CX register automatically. This process is repeated until CX becomes zero. To understand some of the concepts discussed so far, look at the following example.

Example 6-13

Using string instructions, write a program that transfers a block of 20 bytes of data.

Solution:

```
in the data segment:
DATA1 DB            'ABCDEFGHIJKLMNOPQRST'
      ORG           30H
DATA2 DB            20 DUP (?)

In the code segment:
    ASSUME CS:CODESG,DS:DATSEG,SS:STASG,ES:DATSEG
    MOV     AX,DATSEG
    MOV     DS,AX               ;INITIALIZE THE DATA SEGMENT
    MOV     ES,AX               ;INITIALIZE THE EXTRA SEGMENT
    CLD                         ;CLEAR DIRECTION FLAG FOR AUTOINCREMENT
    MOV     SI,OFFSET DATA1     ;LOAD THE SOURCE POINTER
    MOV     DI,OFFSET DATA2     ;LOAD THE DESTINATION POINTER
    MOV     CX,20               ;LOAD THE COUNTER
    REP     MOVSB               ;REPEAT UNTIL CX BECOMES ZERO
```

In Example 6-13, after the transfer of every byte by the MOVSB instruction, both the SI and DI registers are incremented automatically once only (notice CLD). The REP prefix causes the CX counter to be decremented and MOVSB is repeated until CX becomes zero. Notice in the ASSUME statement that both DS and ES are defined. A different segment for the ES could have been used. In that case ES had to be initialized both in the coding and in the ASSUME statement.

An alternative solution for Example 6-13 would change only two lines of code:

```
    MOV     CX,10
    REP     MOVSW
```

In this case the MOVSW will transfer a word (2 bytes) at a time and increment the SI and DI registers each twice. REP will repeat that process until CX becomes zero. Notice the CX has the value of 10 in it since 10 words is equal to 20 bytes.

STOS and LODS instructions

The STOSB instruction stores the byte in the AL register into memory locations pointed at by ES:DI and increments (if DF = 0) DI once. If DF = 1, then DI is decremented. The STOSW instruction stores the contents of AX in memory locations ES:DI and ES:DI+1 (AL into ES:DI and AH into ES:DI+1), then increments DI twice (if DF = 0). If DF = 1, DI is decremented twice.

The LODSB instruction loads the contents of memory locations pointed at by DS:SI into AL and increments (or decrements) SI once if DF = 0 (or DF = 1). LODSW loads the contents of memory locations pointed at by DS:SI into AL and DS:SI+1 into AH. The SI is incremented twice if DF = 0. Otherwise, it is decremented twice. LODS is never used with a REP prefix.

Testing memory using STOSB and LODSB

The following example uses string instructions STOSB and LODSB to test an area of RAM memory.

Example 6-14

Write a program that:
(1) Uses STOSB to store byte AAH into 100 memory locations,
(2) Uses LODS to test the contents of each location to see if AAH was there. If the test fails, the system should display the message "bad memory".

Solution:
Assuming that ES and DS have been assigned in the ASSUME directive, the following is from the code segment:

```
        ;PUT PATTERN AAAAH IN TO 50 WORD LOCATIONS
        MOV   AX,DTSEG            ;INITIALIZE
        MOV   DS,AX               ;DS REG
        MOV   ES,AX               ;AND ES REG
        CLD                       ;CLEAR DF FOR INCREMENT
        MOV   CX,50               ;LOAD THE COUNTER (50 WORDS)
        MOV   DI,OFFSET MEM_AREA  ;LOAD THE POINTER FOR DESTINATION
        MOV   AX,0AAAAH           ;LOAD THE PATTERN
        REP   STOSW               ;REPEAT UNTIL CX=0
        ;BRING IN THE PATTERN AND TEST IT ONE BY ONE
        MOV   SI,OFFSET MEM_AREA  ;LOAD THE POINTER FOR SOURCE
        MOV   CX,100              ;LOAD THE COUNT (COUNT 100 BYTES)
AGAIN:  LODSB                     ;LOAD INTO AL FROM DS:SI
        XOR   AL,AH               ;IS PATTERN THE SAME?
        JNZ   OVER                ;IF NOT THE SAME THEN EXIT
        LOOP  AGAIN               ;CONTINUE UNTIL CX=0
        JMP   EXIT                ;EXIT PROGRAM
OVER:   MOV   AH,09               ;{ DISPLAY
        MOV   DX, OFFSET MESSAGE  ;{ THE MESSAGE
        INT   21H                 ;{ ROUTINE
EXIT:   ...
```

In the program in Example 6-14, first AAH is written into 100 locations by using word-sized operand AAAAH and a count of 50. In the test part, LODS brings in the contents of memory locations into AL one by one, and each time it is eXclusive-ORed with AAH (AH register has hex value of AA). If they are the same, ZF = 1 and the process is continued. Otherwise, the pattern written there by the previous routine is not there and the program will exit. This, in concept, is somewhat similar to the routine used in the IBM PC's BIOS except that the BIOS routine is much more involved and uses several different patterns of data for the test and it can be used to test any part of RAM, either the main RAM or the video RAM.

REPZ and REPNZ prefixes

These prefixes can be used with the CMPS and SCAS instructions for testing purposes. They are explained below.

REPZ (repeat zero), which is the same as REPE (repeat equal), will repeat the string operation as long as the source and destination operands are equal (ZF = 1) or until CX becomes zero.

REPNZ (repeat not zero), which is the same as REPNE (repeat not equal), will repeat the string operation as long as the source and destination operands are not equal (ZF = 0) or until CX become zero. These two prefixes will be used in the context of applications after the explanation of the CMPS and SCANS instructions.

CMPS (compare string) allows the comparison of two arrays of data pointed at by the SI and DI registers. One can test for the equality or inequality of data by use of the REPE or REPNE prefixes, respectively. The comparison can be performed a byte at a time or a word at time by using CMPSB or CMPSW.

For example, if comparing "Euorop" and "Europe" for equality, the comparison will continue using the REPE CMPS as long as the two arrays are the same.

```
;from the data segment:
DATA1  DB      'Europe'
DATA2  DB      'Euorop'
;from the code segment:
          CLD                          ;DF=0 for increment
          MOV    SI,OFFSET DATA1       ;SI=DATA1 offset
          MOV    DI,OFFSET DATA2       ;DI=DATA2 offset
          MOV    CX,06                 ;load the counter
          REPE   CMPSB                 ;repeat until not equal or CX=0
```

In the case above, the two arrays are to be compared letter by letter. The first characters pointed at by SI and DI are compared. In this case they are the same ('E'), so the zero flag is set to 1 and both SI and DI are incremented. Since ZF = 1, the REPE prefix repeats the comparison. This process is repeated until the third letter is reached. The third letters "o" and "r" are not the same; therefore, ZF is reset to zero and the comparison will stop. ZF can be used to make the decision as shown in the following example.

Example 6-15

Assuming that there is a spelling of "Europe" in an electronic dictionary and a user types in "Euorope", write a program that compares these two and displays the following message, depending on the result:
1. If they are equal, display "The spelling is correct".
2. If they are not equal, display "Wrong spelling".

Solution:

```
DAT_DICT        DB      'Europe'
DAT_TYPED       DB      'Euorope'
MESSAGE1        DB      'The spelling is correct','$'
MESSAGE2        DB      'Wrong spelling','$'

;from the code segment:
          CLD                               ;DF=0 FOR INCREMENT
          MOV    SI,OFFSET DAT_DICT         ;SI=DATA1 OFFSET
          MOV    DI,OFFSET DAT_TYPED        ;DI=DATA2 OFFSET
          MOV    CX,06                      ;LOAD THE COUNTER
          REPE   CMPSB                      ;REPEAT AS LONG AS EQUAL OR UNTIL CX=0
          JE     OVER                       ;IF ZF=1 THEN DISPLAY MESSAGE1
          MOV    DX,OFFSET MESSAGE2         ;IF ZF=0 THEN DISPLAY MESSAGE2
          JMP    DISPLAY
OVER:     MOV    DX,OFFSET MESSAGE1
DISPLAY:  MOV    AH,09
          INT    21H
```

One could juggle around the code in Example 6-15 to make it more efficient and use fewer jumps, but for the sake of clarity it is presented in this manner.

CMPS can be used to test inequality of two arrays using "REPNE CMPSB". For example, when comparing the following social security numbers, the comparison will continue to the last digit since no two digits in the same position are the same.

231-24-7659   564-77-1338

SCAS (scan string)

The SCASB string instruction compares each byte of the array pointed at by ES:DI with the contents of the AL register, and depending on which prefix of REPE or REPNE is used, a decision is made for equality or inequality. For example, in array "Mr. Jones", one can scan for the letter "J" by loading the AL register with character "J" and then using the "REPNE SCASB" operation to look for that letter.

```
in the data segment:
DATA1  DB      'Mr. Gones'

and in the code segment:
       CLD                              ;DF=0 FOR INCREMENT
       MOV    DI,OFFSET DATA1           ;DI=ARRAY OFFSET
       MOV    CX,09                     ;LENGTH OF ARRAY
       MOV    AL,'G'                    ;SCANNING FOR THE LETTER 'G'
       REPNE SCASB                      ;REPEAT THE SCANNING IF NOT EQUAL OR
                                        ;UNTIL THE CX IS ZERO
```

In the example above, the letter "G" is compared with "M". Since they are not equal, DI is incremented and CX is decremented, and the scanning is repeated until the letter "G" is found or the CX register is zero. In that example, since "G" is found, ZF is set to 1 (ZF = 1), indicating that there is a letter "G" in the array.

Replacing the scanned character

SCASB can be used to search for a character in an array, and if it is found, it will be replaced with the desired character.

Example 6-16

Write a program that scans the name "Mr. Gones" and replaces the "G" with the letter "J", then displays the corrected name.

Solution:
The following assumes that ES and DS have been assigned in the ASSUME directive.

```
in the data segment:
DATA1      DB      'Mr. Gones','$'

and in the code segment:
           MOV    AX,DTSEG
           MOV    DS,AX
           MOV    ES,AX
           CLD                          ;DF=0 FOR INCREMENT
           MOV    DI,OFFSET DATA1       ;ES:DI=ARRAY OFFSET
           MOV    CX,09                 ;LENGTH OF ARRAY
           MOV    AL,'G'                ;SCANNING FOR THE LETTER 'G'
           REPNE  SCASB                 ;REPEAT THE SCANNING IF NOT EQUAL OR
           JNE    OVER                  ;UNTIL CX IS ZERO.  JUMP IF Z=0
           DEC    DI                    ;DECREMENT TO POINT AT 'G'
           MOV    BYTE PTR [DI],'J'     ;REPLACE 'G' WITH 'J'
OVER:      MOV    AH,09                 ;DISPLAY
           MOV    DX,OFFSET DATA1       ;THE
           INT    21H                   ;CORRECTED NAME
```

In string operations, after each execution, the pointer is incremented (that is, if DF = 0). Therefore, in the example above, DI must be decremented, causing the pointer to point to the scanned character and then replace it.

XLAT instruction and look-up tables

There is often a need in computer applications for a table that holds some important information. To access the elements of the table, 8088/86 microprocessors provide the XLAT (translate) instruction. To understand the XLAT instruction, one must first understand tables. The table is commonly referred to as a *look-up table*. Assume that one needs a table for the values of x^2, where x is between 0 and 9. First the table is generated and stored in memory:

```
SQUR_TABLE  DB      0,1,4,9,16,25,36,49,64,81
```

Now one can access the square of any number from 0 to 9 by the use of XLAT. To do that, the register BX must have the offset address of the look-up table, and the number whose square is sought must be in the AL register. Then after the execution of XLAT, the AL register will have the square of the number. The following shows how to get the square of 5 from the table:

```
MOV   BX,OFFSET SQUR_TABLE     ;load the offset address of table
MOV   AL,05                    ;AL=05 will retrieve 6th element
XLAT                           ;pull out of table the element
                               ;and put in AL
```

After execution of this program, the AL register will have 25 (19H), the square of 5. It must be noted that for XLAT to work, the entries of the look-up table must be in sequential order and must have a one-to-one relation with the element itself. This is because of the way XLAT works. In actuality, XLAT is one instruction, which is equivalent to the following code:

```
SUB   AH,AH          ;AH=0
MOV   SI,AX          ;SI=000X
MOV   AL,[BX+SI]     ;GET THE SIth ENTRY FROM BEGINNING
                     ;OF THE TABLE POINTED AT BY BX
```

In other words, if there was no XLAT instruction, the code above would do the same thing, and this is the way many RISC processors perform this operation. Now why would one want to use XLAT to get the square of a number from a look-up table when there is the MUL instruction? The answer is that MUL takes longer.

Code conversion using XLAT

In many microprocessor-based systems, the keyboard is not an ASCII type of keyboard. One can use XLAT to translate the hex keys of such keyboards to ASCII. Assuming that the keys are 0 - F, the following is the program to convert the hex digits of 0 - F to their ASCII equivalents.

```
data segment:
ASC_TABL    DB      '0','1','2','3','4','5','6','7','8'
            DB      '9','A','B','C','D','E','F'
HEX_VALU    DB      ?
ASC_VALU    DB      ?

code segment:
            MOV   BX,OFFSET ASC_TABL  ;BX= TABLE OFFSET
            MOV   AL,HEX_VALU         ;AL=THE HEX DATA
            XLAT                      ;GET THE ASCII EQUIVALENT
            MOV   ASC_VALU,AL         ;MOVE IT TO MEMORY
```

Review Questions

1. In string operations, register _____ is used to point to the source operand and register _____ is used to point to the destination operand.
2. SI is used as an offset into the _____ segment, and DI is used as an offset into the _____ segment.
3. The _____ flag, bit _____ of the flag register, is used to tell the CPU whether to increment or decrement pointers in repeated string operations.
4. State the purpose of instructions CLD and STD.
5. If a string instruction is repeatedly executed because of a REP prefix, how does the CPU know when to stop repeating it?
6. In the following program segment, what condition will cause the REPNZ to fail?

```
MOV    SI, OFFSET DATA1
MOV    DI, OFFSET DATA2
MOV    CX,LENGTH
REPNZ  CMPSB
```

SUMMARY

Signed number representation in the 8086/88 is achieved by using the MSB (most significant bit) as a sign bit. In a byte operand, the sign bit is D7, and in a word operand, the sign bit is D15. A sign bit of zero indicates a positive number, and a sign bit of 1 indicates a negative number. Negative numbers are represented in 2's complement. Signed addition and subtraction instructions use the same instructions as unsigned addition and subtraction: ADD and SUB. However, signed multiplication and division use the instructions IMUL and IDIV instead of MUL and DIV. In signed number arithmetic, the programmer must check for the overflow problem. An overflow occurs when either there is a carry into the MSB, or there is a carry out and no carry into the MSB. The overflow problem can be avoided by use of the sign extension instructions CBW and CWD.

Arithmetic shift instructions work similarly to the logic shift instructions except that the arithmetic shift instructions must take the sign bit into account. Therefore, they copy the sign bit into the shifted bits. The compare (CMP) instruction works the same for signed numbers as it does for unsigned numbers, but different conditional jump instructions are used after the CMP in programs.

The 80x86 has many instructions that operate on strings of data. These instructions include STOS and LODS instructions to store and load data and the SCAS scanning instruction. String operations use registers DI and SI as pointers to data in the extra and data segments. These instructions can be repeated by using any of the various forms of the REP prefix. Whether the pointers DI and SI will be incremented or decremented with each repetition depends on the setting of the direction flag. There is also an instruction for table processing, the XLAT instruction.

PROBLEMS

1. Show how the 80x86 computer would represent the following numbers and verify each with DEBUG.
   (a) -23   (b) +12   (c) -28H   (d) +6FH
   (e) -128   (f) +127   (g) +365   (h) -32 767
2. Find the overflow flag for each case and verify the result using DEBUG.
   (a) (+15)+(-12)   (b) (-123)+(-127)   (c) (+25h)+ (+34)
   (d) (-127) + (+127)   (e) (+1000) + (-1000)
3. Sign-extend the following and write simple programs in DEBUG to verify them.
   (a) -122   (b) -999h   (c) +17h
   (d) +127   (e) -129

4. Modify Program 6-2 to find the highest temperature. Verify your program.
5. Which instructions are used to set and reset the direction flag? State the purpose of the direction flag.
6. The REP instruction can be used with which of the following instructions?
   (a) MOVSB   (b) MOVSW   (c) CMPSB
   (d) LODSB   (e) STOSW   (f) SCASW
7. In Problem 6-6, state the source and destination operand for each instruction.
8. Write and verify a program that transfers a block of 200 words of data.
9. Use instructions LODSx and STOSx to mask the 3 from a set of 50 ASCII digits, and transfer the result to a different memory location. This involves converting from ASCII to unpacked BCD, then storing it at a different location; for example,

                             source   destination
   ASCII for '5'   0011 0101   0000 0101
10. Which prefix is used for the inequality case for CMPS and SCAS instructions?
11. Write a program that scans the initials "IbM" and replaces the lowercase "b" with uppercase "B".
12. Using the timing chart in Appendix B.2, compare the clock count of the instruction XLAT and its equivalent to see which is more efficient.
13. Write a program using a look-up table and XLAT to retrieve the y value in the equation $y = x^2 + 2x + 5$ for x values of 0 to 9.

ANSWERS TO REVIEW QUESTIONS

Section 6.1: Signed Number Arithmetic Operations
1. d7, d15
2. 16H = $0001\ 0110_2$ in 2's complement: $1110\ 1010_2$
3. -128 to +127; -32,768 to +32,767 (decimal)
4. an overflow is a carry into the sign bit; a carry is a carry out of the register
5. the CBW instruction sign extends the sign bit of a byte into a word; the CWD instruction sign extends the sign bit of a word into a doubleword
   F6H sign extended into AX = FFF6H
   124C sign extended into DX AX would be DX = 0000 and AX = 124CH.
6. IMUL, IDIV
7. SHR shifts each bit right one position and fills the MSB with zero
   SAR shifts each bit right one position and fills the MSB with the sign bit
   in each; the LSB is shifted into the carry flag
8. (a) JLE will jump if OF is the inverse of SF, or if ZF = 1
   (b) JG will jump if OF equals SF, or if ZF = 0

Section 6.2: String and Table Operations
1. SI, DI
2. data, extra
3. direction flag, bit 11 or D10
4. CLD clears DF to 0; STD sets DF to 1
5. when CX = 0
6. if CX = 0 or the point at which DATA1 and DATA2 are not equal

CHAPTER 7

MODULES, AND MODULAR AND C PROGRAMMING

OBJECTIVES

Upon completion of this chapter, you will be able to:

» Discuss the advantages of modular programming
» Break large programs into modules and code the modules and calling program
» Declare names that are defined in other modules by use of the EXTRN directive
» Declare names that are used in other modules by use of the PUBLIC directive
» Link subprograms together into one executable program
» Code segment directives to link data, code, or stack segments from different modules into one segment
» Code programs using the full segment definitions
» List the various methods of passing parameters to modules and discuss the advantages and disadvantages of each
» Code programs passing the parameters via registers, memory, or stack
» Code Assembly language within C programs by using inline coding
» Code Assembly language modules for C programs
» Describe the C calling convention for parameter passing
» Link Assembly language modules with C programs

In this chapter the concept of modules is presented along with rules of writing modules and linking them together. Some very useful modules will be given, along with the methods of passing parameters among various modules. In the final section we show how to combine Assembly language programs with C programs.

SECTION 7.1: WRITING AND LINKING MODULES

Why modules?

It is common practice in writing software packages to break down the project into small modules and distribute the task of writing those modules among several programmers. This not only makes the project more manageable but also has other advantages, such as:

1. Each module can be written, debugged, and tested individually.
2. The failure of one module does not stop the entire project.
3. The task of locating and isolating any problem is easier and less time consuming.
4. One can use the modules to link with high-level languages such as C, Pascal, or BASIC.
5. Parallel development shortens considerably the time required to complete a project.

In this section we explain how to write and link modules to create a single executable program.

Writing modules

In previous chapters, a main procedure was written that called many other subroutines. In those examples, if one subroutine did not work properly, the entire program would have to be rewritten and reassembled. A more efficient way to develop software is to treat each subroutine as a separate program (or module) with a separate filename. Then each one can be assembled and tested. After testing each program and making sure that each works, they can all be brought together (linked) to make a single program. To enable these modules to be linked together, certain Assembly language directives must be used. Among these directives, the two most widely used are EXTRN (external) and PUBLIC. Each is discussed below.

EXTRN directive

The EXTRN directive is used to notify the assembler and linker that certain names and variables which are not defined in the present module are defined externally somewhere else. In the absence of the EXTRN directive, the assembler would show an error since it cannot find where the names are defined. The EXTRN directive has the following format:

```
EXTRN name1:type               ;each name can be in a separate EXTRN
EXTRN name2:type
EXTRN name1:type,name2:type    ;or many can be listed in the same EXTRN
```

External procedure names can be NEAR, FAR, or PROC (which will be NEAR for small models or FAR for larger models). The following are the types for data names, with the number of bytes indicated in parentheses: BYTE (1), WORD (2), DWORD (4), FWORD (6), QWORD (8), or TBYTE (10).

PUBLIC directive

Those names or parameters defined as EXTRN (indicating that they are defined outside the present module) must be defined as PUBLIC in the module where they are defined. Defining a name as PUBLIC allows the assembler and linker to match it with its EXTRN counterpart(s). The following is the format for the PUBLIC directive:

```
PUBLIC name1              ;each name can be in a separate directive
PUBLIC name2

PUBLIC name1, name2       ;or many can be listed in the same PUBLIC
```

Example 7-1 should help to clarify these concepts. It demonstrates that for every EXTRN definition there is a PUBLIC directive defined in another module. In Example 7-1 the EXTRN and PUBLIC directives were related to the name of a FAR procedure.

END directive in modules

In Example 7-1, notice the entry and exit points of the program. The entry point is MAIN and the exit point is "END MAIN". Modules that are called by the main module have the END directive with no label or name after it. Notice that SUBPROG1 and SUBPROG2 each have the END directive with no labels after them.

Example 7-1

Assume there is a program that constitutes the main routine, and two smaller subroutines named SUBPROG1 and SUBPROG2. The subprograms are called from the main routine. The following shows the use of directives EXTRN and PUBLIC:

Solution:
```
;-------------------------------------------------------------------
;one file will contain the main module:
            EXTRN    SUBPROG1:FAR
            EXTRN    SUBPROG2:FAR
CODSG7_1  SEGMENT
MAIN        PROC     FAR
            ASSUMECS;CODSG7_1,DS:....,SS:....,ES:...

            ...
            CALL     SUBPROG1
            CALL     SUBPROG2

            ...
            MOV      AH,4CH
            INT      21H
MAIN        ENDP
CODSG7_1  ENDS
            END      MAIN


;-------------------------------------------------------------------
;--------------- and in a separate file: --------------------------
            PUBLIC  SUBPROG1
CODSEG1   SEGMENT
SUBPROG1  PROC FAR
            ASSUME  CS:CODSEG1

            ...
            RET
SUBPROG1  ENDP
CODSEG1   ENDS
            END


;-------------------------------------------------------------------
  ;--------------- and in another file: ---------------------------
            PUBLIC  SUBPROG2
CODSEG2   SEGMENT
SUBPROG2  PROC FAR
            ASSUME  CS:CODSEG2

            ...
            RET
SUBPROG2  ENDP
CODSEG2   ENDS
            END
```

Linking modules together into one executable unit

Assuming that each program module in Example 7-1 is assembled separately and saved under the filenames EXAMPLE1.OBJ, PROC1.OBJ, and PROC2.OBJ, the following shows how to link them together in MASM in order to generate a single executable code:

C> LINK EXAMPLE1.OBJ + PROC1.OBJ + PROC2.OBJ

Program 7-1 shows how the EXTRN and PUBLIC directives can also be applied to data variables. In Program 7-1, the main module contains a data segment and a stack segment, but the subroutine modules do not. Each module can have its own data and stack segment. While it is entirely permissible and possible that the modules have their own data segments if they need them, generally there is only one stack that is defined in the main program and must be defined so that it is combined with the system stack . In all programs so far, this was not done for the sake of simplicity, and that is the reason the LINK program generated the "warning :no stack segment" message. Later in this chapter we show how to eliminate that error message and to combine many segments of different modules to generate one uniform segment for each of code, data, and stack.

Use the program shells in Example 7-1 to:
1. Add two words.
2. Multiply two words.
Each one should be performed by a separate module. The data is defined in the main module, and the add and multiply modules have no data segment of their own.

```
TITLE    PROG7-1   DEMONSTRATES MODULAR PROGRAMMING
PAGE 60,132
            EXTRN    SUBPROG1:FAR
            EXTRN    SUBPROG2:FAR
            PUBLIC   VALUE1, VALUE2, SUM, PRODUCT
;--------------------------
STSEG       SEGMENT
            DB       64 DUP (?)
STSEG       ENDS
;--------------------------
DTSEG       SEGMENT
VALUE1      DW       2050
VALUE2      DW       500
SUM         DW       2 DUP (?)
PRODUCT     DW       2 DUP (?)
DTSEG       ENDS
;--------------------------
CODSG_A     SEGMENT
MAIN        PROC   FAR
            ASSUME CS:CODSG_A,DS:DTSEG,SS:STSEG
            MOV      AX,DTSEG
            MOV      DS,AX
            CALL     SUBPROG1        ;CALL SUBPROG TO ADD VALUE1 + VALUE2
            CALL     SUBPROG2        ;CALL SUBPROG TO MUL VALUE1 * VALUE2
            MOV      AH,4CH
            INT      21H             ;GO BACK TO DOS
MAIN        ENDP
CODSG_A     ENDS
            END    MAIN
```

Program 7-1: Main Module

```
;THIS PROGRAM FINDS THE SUM OF TWO EXTERNALLY DEFINED WORDS
;AND STORES THE SUM IN A LOCATION DEFINED BY THE CALLING MODULE
TITLE       SUBPROG1   PROGRAM TO ADD TWO WORDS
PAGE        60,132
            EXTRN    VALUE1:WORD
            EXTRN    VALUE2:WORD
            EXTRN    SUM:WORD
            PUBLIC   SUBPROG1
CODSG_B   SEGMENT
SUBPROG1 PROC    FAR
            ASSUME CS:CODSG_B
            SUB     BX,BX              ;INITIALIZE CARRY COUNT
            MOV     AX,VALUE1
            MOV     DX,VALUE2
            ADD     AX,DX              ;ADD VALUE1 + VALUE2
            ADC     BX,00              ;ACCUMULATE CARRY
            MOV     SUM,AX             ;STORE SUM
            MOV     SUM+2,BX           ;STORE CARRY
            RET
SUBPROG1 ENDP
CODSG_B   ENDS
            END
```

Program 7-1: Module 2

```
;THIS PROGRAM FINDS THE PRODUCT OF TWO EXTERNALLY DEFINED WORDS
;AND STORES THE PRODUCT IN A LOCATION DEFINED BY THE CALLING MODULE
TITLE       SUBPROG2   PROGRAM TO MULTIPLY TWO WORDS
PAGE        60,132
            EXTRN    VALUE1:WORD
            EXTRN    VALUE2:WORD
            EXTRN    PRODUCT:WORD
            PUBLIC   SUBPROG2
CODSG_C   SEGMENT
SUBPROG2 PROC    FAR
            ASSUME CS:CODSG_C
            MOV     AX,VALUE1
            MOV     CX,VALUE2
            MUL     CX                 ;MULTIPLY VALUE1 * VALUE2
            MOV     PRODUCT,AX    ;STORE PRODUCT
            MOV     PRODUCT+2,DX ;STORE PRODUCT HIGH WORD
            RET
SUBPROG2 ENDP
CODSG_C   ENDS
            END
```

Program 7-1: Module 3

Analysis of Program 7-1

Notice in the main module that each of the two subroutines were declared with the EXTRN directive, indicating that these procedures would be defined in another file. The external subroutines were defined as FAR in this case. In the files where each subroutine is defined, it is declared as PUBLIC, so that other programs can call it. In the main module, the names VALUE1, VALUE2, SUM, and PRODUCT were defined as PUBLIC, so that other programs could access these data items. In the subprograms, these data items were declared as EXTRN. These three programs would be linked together as follows:

C> LINK PROG7-1.OBJ + SUBPROG1.OBJ + SUBPROG2.OBJ

The linker program resolves external references by matching PUBLIC and EXTRN names. The linker program will search through the files specified in the LINK command for the external subroutines. Notice that the filenames are unrelated to the procedure names. "MAIN" is contained in file "PROG7-1.OBJ".

SEGMENT directive

In previous chapters, when a segment was defined, no other attributes were mentioned after it. It was simply written

```
name            SEGMENT
```

This kind of definition of segments was acceptable since there was only one of each of code, data, and stack segments. However, when there are many modules to be linked together, the segment definition must be adjusted. The complete segment definition used widely in modular programming is as follows:

```
name            SEGMENT  alignment  combine type   class name
```

Appendix C (see SEGMENT) gives a complete description of the fields of the SEGMENT directive. A brief explanation of each field is given below.

The *alignment* field indicates whether a segment should start on a byte, word, paragraph, or page boundary. For example, if WORD is given in the alignment field, the segment will start at the next available word. When WORD boundary is used, if a previous segment ended at offset 0048H, the next segment will start at 004AH. The default alignment is PARA, meaning that each segment will start on a paragraph boundary. A paragraph in DOS is defined as 16 bytes; therefore, each segment will start on a 16-byte boundary. When PARA is used, if the previous segment ended at 0048H, the next segment would begin at the next paragraph boundary, which is 0050H. Paragraph boundaries end in 0; they are evenly divisible by 16 (10H).

The *combine type* field indicates to the linker whether segments of the same type should be linked together. Typical options for combine type are STACK or PUBLIC. An example below shows how to use this field in the stack segment definition to combine the stack segment of a program with the system stack to eliminate the "Warning: no stack segment" message generated by the linker. If the combine type is PUBLIC, the linker will combine that segment with other segments of the same type in other modules. This can be used to combine code segments with various names under a single name.

The *class name* field has four options: 'CODE', 'STACK', 'DATA', and 'EXTRA'. It must be enclosed in single quotes. It is used in combining segments of the same type from various modules.

Complete stack segment definition

The following stack segment definition in the main module will eliminate the "Warning: no stack segment" message generated by the linker:

```
name            SEGMENT    PARA    STACK 'STACK'
```

Complete data and code segment definitions

The following is a data segment definition that can be used if no other module has defined any data segment:

```
name            SEGMENT    PARA   'DATA'
```

If any other module has defined a data segment then PUBLIC should be placed in between the PARA and 'DATA'. The following are the code and data segment definitions to combine segments from different modules:

```
name            SEGMENT    PARA    PUBLIC 'CODE'
name            SEGMENT    PARA    PUBLIC 'DATA'
```

One additional point that must be made clear is that in order to combine various segments from different modules into one segment, the segment names must be the same. This is demonstrated in Example 7-2.

Program 7-2 uses the complete segment definition to redefine all the segments of Program 7-1. An analysis of how the segments are combined as shown in the link map follows the program. The code segments were not made PUBLIC in this example.

```
TITLE      PROG7-2        PROG7-1 REWRITTEN WITH FULL SEGMENT DEFINITION
PAGE       60,132
           EXTRN    SUBPROG1:FAR
           EXTRN    SUBPROG2:FAR
           PUBLIC    VALUE1, VALUE2, SUM, PRODUCT
;-------------------------
STSEG      SEGMENT  PARA STACK 'STACK'
           DB       100 DUP(?)
STSEG      ENDS
;-------------------------
DTSEG      SEGMENT   PARA 'DATA'
VALUE1     DW       2050
VALUE2     DW       500
SUM        DW       2 DUP (?)
PRODUCT    DW       2 DUP (?)
DTSEG      ENDS
;-------------------------
CODSG_A    SEGMENT  PARA 'CODE'
MAIN       PROC    FAR
           ASSUME CS:CODSG_A,DS:DTSEG,SS:STSEG
           MOV      AX,DTSEG
           MOV      DS,AX
           CALL     SUBPROG1       ;CALL SUBPROG TO ADD VALUE1 + VALUE2
           CALL     SUBPROG2       ;CALL SUBPROG TO MUL VALUE1 * VALUE2
           MOV      AH,4CH
           INT      21H            ;GO BACK TO DOS
MAIN       ENDP
CODSG_A    ENDS
           END      MAIN
```

Program 7-2: Main Module

```
;THIS PROGRAM FINDS THE SUM OF TWO EXTERNALLY DEFINED WORDS
;AND STORES THE SUM IN A LOCATION DEFINED BY THE CALLING MODULE
TITLE      SUBPROG1   PROGRAM TO ADD TWO WORDS
PAGE       60,132
           EXTRN    VALUE1:WORD
           EXTRN    VALUE2:WORD
           EXTRN    SUM:WORD
           PUBLIC   SUBPROG1
CODSG_B    SEGMENT   PARA 'CODE'
SUBPROG1   PROC    FAR
           ASSUME CS:CODSG_B
           SUB      BX,BX          ;INITIALIZE CARRY COUNT
           MOV      AX,VALUE1
           MOV      DX,VALUE2
           ADD      AX,DX          ;ADD VALUE1 + VALUE2
           ADC      BX,00          ;ACCUMULATE CARRY
           MOV      SUM,AX         ;STORE SUM
           MOV      SUM+2,BX       ;STORE CARRY
           RET
SUBPROG1   ENDP
CODSG_B    ENDS
           END
```

Program 7-2: Module 2

```
;THIS PROGRAM FINDS THE PRODUCT OF TWO EXTERNALLY DEFINED WORDS
;AND STORES THE PRODUCT IN A LOCATION DEFINED BY THE CALLING MODULE
TITLE        SUBPROG2   PROGRAM TO MULTIPLY TWO WORDS
PAGE         60,132
             EXTRN     VALUE1:WORD
             EXTRN     VALUE2:WORD
             EXTRN     PRODUCT:WORD
             PUBLIC    SUBPROG2
CODSG_C  SEGMENT  PARA 'CODE'
SUBPROG2 PROC    FAR
             ASSUME CS:CODSG_C
             MOV       AX,VALUE1
             MOV       CX,VALUE2
             MUL       CX              ;MUL VALUE1 * VALUE2
             MOV       PRODUCT,AX      ;STORE PRODUCT
             MOV       PRODUCT+2,DX ;STORE PRODUCT HIGH WORD
             RET
SUBPROG2 ENDP
CODSG_C  ENDS
             END


     Start   Stop    Length  Name                    Class
     00000H  00063H  00064H  STSEG                   STACK
     00070H  0007BH  0000CH  DTSEG                   DATA
     00080H  00092H  00013H  CODSG_A                 CODE
     000A0H  000B5H  00016H  CODSG_B                 CODE
     000C0H  000D0H  00011H  CODSG_C                 CODE
```

Program 7-2: Module 3 and the Link Map

Analysis of Program 7-2 link map

The link map shows the start and end of each segment. Notice that each segment starts at a 16-byte boundary: 00070H, 00080H, etc. The code segment for the main module has the name "CODSG_A", starts at 00080H, and ends at 00092H, taking a total of 00013H bytes. It was classified as 'CODE'. The next code segment is defined under the name "CODSG_B". Notice that it starts at the 16-byte boundary 000A0H since it was defined as PARA. This means that from 00093H to 0009FH is unused. Similarly, the third module starts at 000C0H. Notice that each code segment is separate. They can all be merged together into one segment by using the PUBLIC option. This is shown in Example 7-2. To merge the code segments together, each code segment must have the same name and be declared PUBLIC.

Example 7-2

Show the link map for Program 7-2 rewritten to combine code segments (use PARA boundaries) using directive:
```
CDSEG    SEGMENT   PARA PUBLIC 'CODE'
```

Solution:
```
     Start   Stop    Length  Name                    Class
     00000H  00063H  00064H  STSEG                   STACK
     00070H  0007BH  0000CH  DTSEG                   DATA
     00080H  000D0H  00051H  CDSEG                   CODE
```

The following are the SEGMENT directives using word boundaries:
```
STSEG    SEGMENT   WORD STACK 'STACK'
DTSEG    SEGMENT   WORD 'DATA'
CDSEG    SEGMENT   WORD PUBLIC 'CODE'
```

The following is the link map when the program used WORD boundaries:
```
     Start   Stop    Length  Name                    Class
     00000H  00063H  00064H  STSEG                   STACK
     00064H  0006FH  0000CH  DTSEG                   DATA
     00070H  000AAH  0003BH  CDSEG                   CODE
```

Modular programming and use of the new segment definition

In this section we give an example of modular programming for those who are using the new segment definition. This section can be skipped without loss of continuity. Example 7-3 rewrites Example 7-1 to define segments using the new segment definition.

Example 7-3

Modular program shells for the new segment directives.

The main file will contain:

```
                .MODEL SMALL
                .STACK 64
                .DATA
                ....
                ....
                .CODE
                EXTRN   SUBPROG1:NEAR
                EXTRN   SUBPROG2:NEAR
MAIN:           MOV     AX,@DATA        ;this is the program entry point
                MOV     DS,AX
                CALL    SUBPROG1
                CALL    SUBPROG2
                MOV     AH,4CH
                INT     21H
                END     MAIN            ;this is the program exit point


;------------- and in a separate file: -------------------------------------

                .MODEL  SMALL
                .CODE
                PUBLIC  SUBPROG1
SUBPROG1 PROC
                ...
                RET
SUBPROG1 ENDP
                END


;------------- and in another file: -------------------------------------

                .MODEL  SMALL
                .CODE
                PUBLIC  SUBPROG2
SUBPROG2 PROC
                ...
                RET
SUBPROG2 ENDP
                END
```

Notice that in the main module of Example 7-3, the name MAIN has a colon after it and is used for the first executable instruction. This is the entry point of the program. The exit point of the program is indicated by the same label, which must be named in the END directive. No program can have more than one entry and exit point. The label MAIN was chosen in this instance, but of course any name could have been chosen. Remember that the END directives in other modules do not have a label after the word "END". Program 7-3 is the same as Program 7-1, rewritten for the new segment definition. Compare the two programs to see the ease of the new segment definition. When using the simplified segment definition shown in Example 7-3, procedures will default to NEAR for small or compact models and FAR for medium, large, or huge models.

```
TITLE          PROG7-3 MODULAR PROGRAMMING WITH NEW SEGMENT DEFINITION
PAGE           60,132
               .MODEL SMALL
               .STACK 64
               .DATA
               PUBLIC VALUE1, VALUE2, SUM, PRODUCT
VALUE1     DW      2050
VALUE2     DW      500
SUM        DW      2 DUP (?)
PRODUCT    DW      2 DUP (?)
;-------------------------
               .CODE
               EXTRN SUBPROG1:NEAR
               EXTRN SUBPROG2:NEAR
MAIN:      MOV     AX,@DATA
           MOV     DS,AX
           CALL    SUBPROG1         ;CALL SUBPROG TO ADD VALUE1 + VALUE2
           CALL    SUBPROG2         ;CALL SUBPROG TO MUL VALUE2 * VALUE2
           MOV     AH,4CH
           INT     21H              ;GO BACK TO DOS
           END     MAIN
```

Program 7-3: Main Module

```
;THIS PROGRAM FINDS THE SUM OF TWO EXTERNALLY DEFINED WORDS
;AND STORES THE SUM IN A LOCATION DEFINED BY THE CALLING MODULE
TITLE          SUBPROG1  PROGRAM TO ADD TWO WORDS
PAGE           60,132
               .MODEL SMALL
               EXTRN VALUE1:WORD
               EXTRN VALUE2:WORD
               EXTRN SUM:WORD
               .CODE
               PUBLIC SUBPROG1
SUBPROG1 PROC   NEAR
           SUB     BX,BX            ;INITIALIZE CARRY COUNT
           MOV     AX,VALUE1
           MOV     DX,VALUE2
           ADD     AX,DX            ;ADD VALUE1 + VALUE2
           ADC     BX,00            ;ACCUMULATE CARRY
           MOV     SUM,AX           ;STORE SUM
           MOV     SUM+2,BX         ;STORE CARRY
           RET
SUBPROG1 ENDP
           END
```

Program 7-3: Module 2

```
;THIS PROGRAM FINDS THE PRODUCT OF TWO EXTERNALLY DEFINED WORDS
;AND STORES THE PRODUCT IN A LOCATION DEFINED BY THE CALLING MODULE
TITLE          SUBPROG2  PROGRAM TO MULTIPLY TWO WORDS
PAGE           60,132
               .MODEL SMALL
               EXTRN VALUE1:WORD
               EXTRN VALUE2:WORD
               EXTRN PRODUCT:WORD
               .CODE
               PUBLIC SUBPROG2
SUBPROG2 PROC   NEAR
           MOV     AX,VALUE1
           MOV     CX,VALUE2
           MUL     CX               ;MULTIPLY VALUE1 * VALUE2
           MOV     PRODUCT,AX       ;STORE PRODUCT
           MOV     PRODUCT+2,DX     ;STORE PRODUCT HIGH WORD
           RET
SUBPROG2 ENDP
           END
```

Program 7-3: Module 3

Review Questions

1. List three advantages of modular programming.
2. The _____ directive is used within a module to indicate that the named variable can be used by another module.
3. The _____ directive is used within a module to indicate that the named variable was defined in another module.
4. How does the system determine the entry and exit points of a program consisting of more than one module?
5. What is a paragraph?
6. Write the directive that will define the stack segment so that it will be combined with the system stack.
7. If a word-sized data item named TOTAL is being used in a module but the data item was defined in another module, code the directive to define TOTAL in the module.
8. If PARA were used for the alignment type of a code segment that ended at 56H, where would the next code segment begin?
9. Write the code segment directives for a calling program and a module so that they will be combined into one code segment.

SECTION 7.2: SOME VERY USEFUL MODULES

In this section we show the development of two very useful modules. First, programs are developed that convert from hex to decimal, and vice versa. Then they are rewritten as modules that can be called from any program. Finally, the calling program is written.

Binary (hex)-to-ASCII (decimal) conversion

The result of arithmetic operations is, of course, in binary. To display the result in decimal, the number is first converted to decimal, and then each digit is tagged with 30H to put it in ASCII form so that it can be displayed or printed. The first step is to convert the binary number to decimal. Look at the following example, which converts 34DH to decimal.

```
34DH = (3 x 16^2)  + (4 x 16^1)  + (D=13 x 16^0)
     = (3 x 256)  + (4 x 16)  + (13 x 1)
     = 768        + 64        + 13
     = 845
```

Another method to convert a hex number to decimal is to divide it repeatedly by 10 (0AH), storing each remainder, until the quotient is less than 10. The following steps would be performed:

```
34DH / A = 84 remainder 5
84H  / A = 8  remainder 4
8 ( < A, so the process stops)
Taking the remainders in reverse order gives: 845 decimal
```

Program 7-4 shows the conversion process for a word-sized (16-bit) number using the method of repeated division demonstrated above. Since a word-sized hex number is between 0 and FFFFH, the result in decimal can be as high as 65535. Therefore, a string length of 5 should be sufficient to hold the result. The binary number to be converted is in data item BINNUM. Notice in Program 7-4 that as each decimal digit (the remainder) is placed in DL, it is tagged with 30H to convert it to ASCII. It is then placed in a memory area called ASCNUM. The ASCII digits are placed in memory so that the lowest digit is in high memory, as is the convention of ASCII storage in DOS.

```
TITLE           PROG7-4     CONVERT BINARY TO ASCII
PAGE            60,132
STSEG           SEGMENT PARA STACK 'STACK'
                DB      64 DUP (?)
STSEG           ENDS
;--------------------------
DTSEG           SEGMENT
BINNUM          DW      246DH
                ORG     10H
ASCNUM          DB      5 DUP ('0')
DTSEG           ENDS
;--------------------------
CDSEG           SEGMENT 'CODE'
B2ASC_CON PROC  FAR
                ASSUME CS:CDSEG,DS:DTSEG,SS:STSEG
                MOV     AX,DTSEG
                MOV     DS,AX
                MOV     BX,10               ;BX=10 THE DIVISOR
                MOV     SI,OFFSET ASCNUM    ;SI = BEGINNING OF ASCII STRING
                ADD     SI,5                ;ADD LENGTH OF STRING
                DEC     SI                  ;SI POINTS TO LAST ASCII DIGIT
                MOV     AX,BINNUM           ;LOAD BINARY (HEX) NUMBER
BACK:           SUB     DX,DX               ;DX MUST BE 0 IN WORD DIVISION
                DIV     BX                  ;DIVIDE HEX NUMBER BY 10 (BX=10)
                OR      DL,30H              ;TAG '3' TO MAKE IT ASCII
                MOV     [SI],DL             ;MOVE THE ASCII DIGIT
                DEC     SI                  ;DECREMENT POINTER
                CMP     AX,0                ;CONTINUE LOOPING WHILE AX > 0
                JA      BACK
                MOV     AH,4CH
                INT     21H                 ;GO BACK TO DOS
B2ASC_CON ENDP
CDSEG           ENDS
                END     B2ASC_CON
```

Program 7-4

ASCII (decimal)-to-binary (hex) conversion

When a user keys in digits 0 to 9, the keyboard provides the ASCII version of the digits to the computer. For example, when the key marked 9 is pressed, in reality the keyboard provides its ASCII version 00111001 (39H) to the system. In Chapter 3 we showed how in some cases, such as addition, the numbers can be processed in ASCII and there is no need to convert them to hex (binary). However, in the majority of cases the number needs to be converted to hex in order to be processed by the CPU. Look at the example of converting decimal 482 to hex. The following shows the steps to convert this number to hex:

$482 / 16^2 = 482 / 256 = 1$
$482 - (1 \times 256) = 226$ $226 / 16^1 = 226 / 16 = 14 = E$
$226 - (14 \times 16) = 2$
482 decimal = 1E2 hexadecimal

However, a computer would use a different method since it works in binary arithmetic, not decimal. First the 30H would be masked off each ASCII digit. Then each digit is multiplied by a weight (a power of 10) such as 1, 10, 100, or 1000 and they are then added together to get the final hex (binary) result. Converting decimal 482 to hex involves the following steps. First a user types in '482' through the PC ASCII keyboard, yielding 343832, the ASCII version of 482. Then the following steps are performed:

$2 \times 1 \quad = \quad\quad = \quad\quad 2$
$8 \times 10 \quad = \quad 80 = \quad 50H$
$4 \times 100 = 400 = \underline{190H}$
$\quad\quad\quad\quad\quad\quad\quad\quad 1E2$ hexadecimal

Program 7-5 converts an ASCII number to binary. It assumes the maximum size of the decimal number to be 65535. Therefore, the maximum hex result is FFFFH, a 16-bit word. It begins with the least significant digit, masks off the 3, and multiplies it by its weight factor. Register CX holds the weight, which is 1 for the least significant digit. For the next digit CX becomes 10 (0AH), for the next it becomes 100 (64H), and so on. The program assumes that the least significant ASCII digit is in the highest memory location of the data. This is consistent with the conventions of storing ASCII numbers with the most significant digit in the lower memory address and the least significant digit in the highest memory address. For example, placing '749' at memory offset 200 gives offset 200 = (37), 201 = (34), and 202 = (39). DOS 21H function 0A also places ASCII numbers this way.

```
TITLE          PROG7-5   CONVERT ASCII TO BINARY
PAGE           60,132
STSEG          SEGMENT PARA STACK 'STACK'
               DB      64 DUP (?)
STSEG          ENDS
;--------------------------
DTSEG          SEGMENT
TEN            DW      10
ASCNUM         DB      '09325'
STRLEN         DB      5
               ORG     10H
BINNUM         DW      0
DTSEG          ENDS
;--------------------------
CDSEG          SEGMENT
ASC2B_CON PROC  FAR
               ASSUME CS:CDSEG,DS:DTSEG,SS:STSEG
               MOV     AX,DTSEG
               MOV     DS,AX
               SUB     DI,DI                ;CLEAR DI FOR THE BINARY(HEX) RESULT
               MOV     SI,OFFSET ASCNUM     ;SI = BEGINNING OF ASCII STRING
               MOV     BL,STRLEN            ;BL = LENGTH OF ASCII STRING
               SUB     BH,BH                ;BH=0 USE BX IN BASED INDEX MODE
               DEC     BX                   ;BX IS OFFSET TO LAST DIGIT
               MOV     CX,1                 ;CX = WEIGHT FACTOR
AGAIN:         MOV     AL,[SI+BX]           ;GET THE ASCII DIGIT
               AND     AL,0FH               ;STRIP OFF '3'
               SUB     AH,AH                ;CLEAR AH FOR WORD MULTIPLICATION
               MUL     CX                   ;MULTIPLY BY THE WEIGHT
               ADD     DI,AX                ;ADD IT TO BINARY (HEX)RESULT
               MOV     AX,CX                ;MULTIPLY THE WEIGHT FACTOR
               MUL     TEN                  ;  BY TEN
               MOV     CX,AX                ;  FOR NEXT ITERATION
               DEC     BX                   ;DECREMENT DIGIT POINTER
               JNS     AGAIN                ;JUMP IF COUNTER >= 0
               MOV     BINNUM,DI            ;SAVE THE BINARY(HEX)RESULT
               MOV     AH,4CH
               INT     21H                  ;GO BACK TO DOS
ASC2B_CON ENDP
CDSEG          ENDS
               END     ASC2B_CON
```

Program 7-5

Programs 7-4 and 7-5 have been written and tested with sample data, and now can be changed from programs into modules that can be called by any program.

Binary-to-ASCII module

Program 7-6 is the modularize Program 7-4. The procedure is declared as public, so it can be called by another program. All values used are declared external since the data will be provided by the calling program. Therefore, this module does not need its own data segment. Notice the following points about the module:

1. Since this module will be called by another module, no entry point and exit point were given. Therefore, the END directive does not have the label B2ASC_CON.
2. The module must return to the caller and not DOS as was the case in Program 7-5.
3. This module does not need its own data or stack segments.

```
TITLE           PROG7-6    BINARY TO DECIMAL CONVERSION MODULE
PAGE            60,132
;this module converts a binary (hex) number up to FFFFH to decimal
;  then makes it displayable (ASCII)
;CALLING PROGRAM SETS
;  AX = BINARY VALUE TO BE CONVERTED TO ASCII
;  SI = OFFSET ADDRESS WHERE ASCII VALUE TO BE STORED
                PUBLIC  B2ASC_CON
CDSEG           SEGMENT  PARA PUBLIC 'CODE'
B2ASC_CON PROC    FAR
                ASSUME  CS:CDSEG
                PUSHF                       ;STORE REGS CHANGED BY THIS MODULE
                PUSH   BX
                PUSH   DX
                MOV    BX,10                ;BX=10 THE DIVISOR
                ADD    SI,4                 ;SI POINTS TO LAST ASCII DIGIT
B2A_LOOP:  SUB    DX,DX                ;DX MUST BE 0 IN WORD DIVISION
                DIV    BX                   ;DIVIDE HEX NUMBER BY 10 (BX=10)
                OR     DL,30H               ;TAG '3' TO REMAINDER TO MAKE IT ASCII
                MOV    [SI],DL              ;MOVE THE ASCII DIGIT
                DEC    SI                   ;DECREMENT POINTER
                CMP    AX,0                 ;CONTINUE LOOPING WHILE AX > 0
                JA     B2A_LOOP
                POP    DX                   ;RESTORE REGISTERS
                POP    BX
                POPF
                RET
B2ASC_CON ENDP
CDSEG           ENDS
                END
```

Program 7-6

```
TITLE           PROG7-7  ASCII TO BINARY CONVERSION MODULE
PAGE            60,132
;this module converts any ASCII number between 0 to 65535 to binary
;CALLING PROGRAM SETS
;  SI = OFFSET OF ASCII STRING
;  BX = STRING LENGTH - 1 (USED AS INDEX INTO ASCII NUMBER)
;THIS MODULE SETS
;  AX = BINARY NUMBER
;------------------------
                EXTRN   TEN:WORD
                PUBLIC  ASC2B_CON
CDSEG           SEGMENT PARA PUBLIC 'CODE'
ASC2B_CON PROC  FAR
                ASSUME CS:CDSEG
                PUSHF                       ;STORE REGS CHANGED IN    THIS MODULE
                PUSH   DI
                PUSH   CX
                SUB    DI,DI                ;CLEAR DI FOR THE BINARY(HEX) RESULT
                MOV    CX,1                 ;CX = WEIGHT FACTOR
A2B_LOOP:  MOV    AL,[SI+BX]           ;GET THE ASCII DIGIT
                AND    AL,0FH               ;STRIP OFF '3'
                SUB    AH,AH                ;CLEAR AH FOR WORD MULTIPLICATION
                MUL    CX                   ;MULTIPLY BY THE WEIGHT
                ADD    DI,AX                ;ADD IT TO BINARY (HEX) RESULT
                MOV    AX,CX                ;MULTIPLY THE WEIGHT FACTOR
                MUL    TEN                  ;  BY TEN
                MOV    CX,AX                ;  FOR NEXT ITERATION
                DEC    BX                   ;DECREMENT DIGIT POINTER
                JNS    A2B_LOOP             ;JUMP IF OFFSET >= 0
                MOV    AX,DI                ;STORE BINARY NUMBER IN AX
                POP    CX                   ;RESTORE FLAGS
                POP    DI
                POPF
                RET
ASC2B_CON ENDP
CDSEG           ENDS
                END
```

Program 7-7

SECTION 7.2: SOME VERY USEFUL MODULES   185

ASCII-to-binary module

Program 7-7 is the modularized version of Program 7-5. Notice the following points about the module:

1. TEN is defined in the calling program.
2. This module must return to the caller and not DOS.

Calling module

Program 7-8 shows the calling program for the module that converts ASCII to binary. This program sets up the data segment, inputs the ASCII data from the keyboard, places it in memory, then calls the routine to convert the number to binary. Finally, the hex result is stored in memory.

```
TITLE       PROG7-8   CALLING PROGRAM TO CONVERT ASCII TO BINARY
PAGE        60,132
            PUBLIC TEN
STSEG       SEGMENT PARA STACK  'STACK'
            DB      64 DUP (?)
STSEG       ENDS
;-------------------------------------------------------------------------------
DTSEG       SEGMENT
ASC_AREA    LABEL   BYTE
MAX_LEN     DB      6
ACT_LEN     DB      ?
ASC_NUM     DB      6 DUP (?)
            ORG     10H
BINNUM      DW      0
PROMPT1     DB      'PLEASE ENTER A 5 DIGIT NUMBER','$'
TEN         DW      10
DTSEG       ENDS
;-------------------------------------------------------------------------------
CDSEG       SEGMENT
            EXTRN ASC2B_CON:FAR
MAIN        PROC    FAR
            ASSUME CS:CDSEG,DS:DTSEG,SS:STSEG
            MOV     AX,DTSEG
            MOV     DS,AX
            ;DISPLAY THE PROMPT
            MOV     AH,09
            MOV     DX,OFFSET PROMPT1
            INT     21H
            ;INPUT STRING
            MOV     AH,0AH
            MOV     DX,OFFSET ASC_AREA
            INT     21H
            MOV     SI,OFFSET ASC_NUM
            MOV     BH,00
            MOV     BL,ACT_LEN
            DEC     BX
            CALL    ASC2B_CON
            MOV     BINNUM,AX       ;SAVE THE BINARY (HEX) RESULT
            MOV     AH,4CH
            INT     21H             ;GO BACK TO DOS
MAIN        ENDP
CDSEG       ENDS
            END     MAIN
```

Program 7-8

Review Questions

1. Show a step-by-step analysis of Program 7-4 with data F624H. Show the sequence of instructions and the data values.
2. Show a step-by-step analysis of Program 7-5 with data '1456'. Show the sequence of instructions and the data values.

SECTION 7.3: PASSING PARAMETERS AMONG MODULES

Occasionally, there is a need to pass parameters among different Assembly language modules or between Assembly language and BASIC, Pascal, or C language programs. The parameter could be fixed values, variables, arrays of data, or even pointers to memory. Parameters can be passed from one module to another through registers, memory, or the stack. In this section we explore passing parameters between Assembly language modules.

Passing parameters via registers

When there is a need to pass parameters among various modules, one could use the CPU's registers. For example, if a main routine is calling a subroutine, the values are placed in the registers in the main routine and then the subroutine is called upon to process the data. In such cases the programmer must clearly document the registers used for the incoming data and the registers that are expected to have the result after the execution of the subroutine. In Chapter 4 this concept was demonstrated with INT 21H and INT 10H. Program 7-8 demonstrated this method. In that program, registers BX and SI were set to point to certain data items before the module was called, and the called module placed its result in register AX prior to returning to the calling routine.

Passing parameters via memory

Although parameter passing via registers is widely used in many of the DOS and BIOS interrupt function calls, the limited number of registers inside the CPU is a major limitation associated with this method of parameter passing. This makes register management a cumbersome task. One alternative is to pass parameters via memory by defining an area of RAM and passing parameters to these RAM locations. DOS and IBM BIOS use this method frequently. The problem with passing parameters to a fixed area of memory is that there must be a universal agreement to the address of the memory area in order to make sure that modules can be run on hardware and software of various companies. This kind of standardization is hard to come by. The only reason that BIOS and DOS use an area of memory for passing parameters is because IBM and Microsoft worked closely together to decide the memory addresses. Another option, and indeed the most widely used method of passing parameters, is via the stack, as discussed next. Passing parameters via the stack makes the parameters both register and memory independent.

Passing parameters via the stack

The stack is a very critical part of every program and playing with it can be risky. When a module is called, it is the stack that holds the address where the program must return after execution. Therefore, if the contents of the stack are altered, the program can crash. This is the reason that working with the stack and passing parameters through it must be understood very thoroughly before one embarks on it.

Program 7-9, on the following page, demonstrates this method of parameter passing and is written with the following requirements. The main module gets three word-sized operands from the data segment, stores them on the stack, and then calls the subroutine. The subroutine gets the operands from the stack, adds them together, holds the result in a register, and then returns control to the main module. The main module stores the result of the addition. Following the program is a detailed stack contents analysis that will show how the parameters are stored on the stack by the main routine and retrieved from the stack by the called routine.

```
TITLE        PROG7-9  PASSING PARAMETERS VIA THE STACK
PAGE         60,132
             EXTRN    SUBPROG6:FAR
;--------------------------
STSEG        SEGMENT  PARA STACK 'Stack'
             DB       64 DUP (?)
STSEG        ENDS
;--------------------------
DTSEG        SEGMENT  PARA 'Data'
VALUE1       DW       3F62H
VALUE2       DW       1979H
VALUE3       DW       25F1H
RESULT       DW       2 DUP (?)
DTSEG        ENDS
;--------------------------
CDSEG        SEGMENT  PARA PUBLIC 'Code'
MAIN         PROC  FAR
             ASSUME CS:CDSEG,DS:DTSEG,SS:STSEG
             MOV      AX,DTSEG
             MOV      DS,AX
             PUSH     VALUE3          ;SAVE VALUE3 ON STACK
             PUSH     VALUE2          ;SAVE VALUE2 ON STACK
             PUSH     VALUE1          ;SAVE VALUE1 ON STACK
             CALL     SUBPROG6        ;CALL THE ADD ROUTINE
             MOV      RESULT,AX       ;STORE
             MOV      RESULT+2,BX     ; THE RESULT
             MOV      AH,4CH
             INT      21H
MAIN         ENDP
CDSEG        ENDS
             END      MAIN
```

Program 7-9: Main Module

```
;---------------- in a separate file: --------------------------
TITLE        SUBPROG6   MODULE TO ADD THREE WORDS BROUGHT IN FROM THE STACK
PAGE         60,132
             PUBLIC    SUBPROG6
CDSEG        SEGMENT   PARA PUBLIC 'Code'
SUBPROG6 PROC   FAR
             ASSUME CS:CDSEG
             SUB      BX,BX           ;CLEAR BX FOR CARRIES
             PUSH     BP              ;SAVE BP
             MOV      BP,SP           ;SET BP FOR INDEXING
             MOV      AX,[BP]+6       ;MOV VALUE1 TO AX
             MOV      CX,[BP]+8       ;MOV VALUE2 TO CX
             MOV      DX,[BP]+10      ;MOV VALUE3 TO DX
             ADD      AX,CX           ;ADD VALUE2 TO VALUE1
             ADC      BX,00           ;KEEP THE CARRY IN BX
             ADD      AX,DX           ;ADD VALUE3
             ADC      BX,00           ;KEEP THE CARRY IN BX
             POP      BP              ;RESTORE BP BEFORE RETURNING
             RET      6               ;RETURN AND ADD 6 TO SP TO BYPASS DATA
SUBPROG6 ENDP
CDSEG        ENDS
             END
```

Program 7-9: Module 2

Stack contents analysis for Program 7-9

To clarify the concept of parameter passing through the stack, the following is a step-by-step analysis of the stack pointer and stack contents. Assume that the stack pointer has the value SP = 17FEH before the "PUSH VALUE3" instruction in the main module is executed.

1. VALUE3 = 25F1H is pushed and SP = 17FC (remember little endian: low byte to low address and high byte to high address).
2. VALUE2 = 1979H is pushed and then SP = 17FA.
3. VALUE1 = 3F62H is pushed and then SP = 17F8.

4. CALL SUBPROG6 is a FAR call; therefore, both CS and IP are pushed onto the stack, making SP = 17F4. If it had been a near call, only IP would have been saved.

5. In the subprogram module, register BP is saved by PUSHing BP onto the stack, which makes SP = 17F2. In the subprogram, BP is used to access values in the stack. First SP is copied to BP since only BP can be used in indexing mode with the stack segment (SS) register. In other words, "MOV AX,[SP+4]" will cause an error. "MOV AX,[BP]+6" loads VALUE1 into AX. [BP]+6 = 17F2+6 = 17F8, which is exactly where VALUE1 is located. Similarly, BP+8 = 17F2+8 = 17FA is the place where VALUE2 is located, and BP+10 = 17F2H+10 = 17FCH is the location of VALUE3.

6. After all the parameters are brought into the CPU by the present module and are processed (in this case added), the module restores the original BP contents by POPping BP from stack. Then SP = 17F4.

17F0		
17F1		
17F2	BP	
17F3		
17F4	IP	
17F5		
17F6	CS	
17F7		
17F8	62	VALUE1
17F9	3F	
17FA	79	VALUE2
17FB	19	
17FC	F1	VALUE3
17FD	25	
17FE		

Program 7-9 Stack Contents Diagram

7. RET 6: this is a new instruction. The RETurns shown previously did not have numbers right after them. The "RET n" instruction means first to POP CS:IP (IP only if the CALL was NEAR) off the top of the stack and then add n to the SP. As can be seen from the Program 7-9 diagram, after popping CS and IP off the stack, the stack pointer is incremented four times, making SP = 17F8, and then adding 6 to it to bypass the six locations of stack where the parameters are stored makes the SP = 17FEH, its original value. Now what would happen if the program had a RET instruction instead of the "RET 6"? The problem is that every time this subprogram is executed it will cause the stack to lose six locations. If that had been done in the example above, when the same routine is called again the stack starts at 17F8 instead of 17FE. If this practice of losing some area of the stack continues, eventually the stack could be reduced to a point where the program would run out of stack and crash.

Review Questions

1. List one advantage and one disadvantage of each method of parameter passing.
   (a) via register (b) via stack (c) via memory
2. Assume that we would like to access some parameters from the stack. Which of the following are correct ways of accessing the stack?
   (a) MOV AX,[BP]+20 (b) MOV AX,[SP]+20
   (c) MOV AX,[BP+DI] (d) MOV AX,[SP+SI]

SECTION 7.4: COMBINING ASSEMBLY LANGUAGE AND C PROGRAMS

Although Assembly language is the fastest language available for a given CPU, it cannot be run on different CPUs. For example, Intel's 80x86 Assembly programs cannot be run on Motorola's 68000 series computers since the opcode, mnemonics, register names, and size are totally different. Therefore, a portable language is needed.

Why C?

Although the dream of a universal language among the peoples of the world is still unrealized, C language is becoming the universal language among all the various CPUs. Today, a large portion of programs written for computers, from PCs to supercomputers such as CRAY, are in C language. C is such a universal programming language that it can be run on any CPU architecture with little or no modification. It is simply recompiled for that CPU. The fact that C is such a portable language is making it the dominant language of programmers. However, C is not as fast as Assembly language. Combining C and Assembly language takes advantage of C's portability and Assembly's speed. Today it is very common to see a software project written using 70 to 80% C and the rest Assembly language.

There are two ways to mix C and Assembly. One is simply to insert the Assembly code in C programs, which is commonly referred to as *inline assembly*. The second method is to make the C language call an external Assembly language procedure. In this section we first discuss how to do inline assembly coding and then show a C language program calling an Assembly procedure. Readers without a C programming background can bypass this section without loss of continuity. This section covers both Microsoft's Quick C and Borland's Turbo C++.

Inserting 80x86 assembly code into C programs

In this section we discuss inlining with Borland's Turbo C. Microsoft C inline coding is very similar to Borland's, but early versions do not support it. For other C compilers, consult that C manual. The following code demonstrates how to change the cursor position to row = 10, column = 20 in a C program. In Borland's Turbo C, "#pragma inline" informs the compiler of inline Assembly code before the first use of Assembly instructions. After that, Assembly instructions are prefaced with "asm", which is a reserved word. Microsoft's C uses the preface "_asm". The following shows two variations of Borland's format for inline assembly.

```
/* version 1: using keyword asm before each line of inline code */
#pragma inline
main ()
{
asm      mov ah,2;       /* each line should end with semicolon or <CR> */
asm      mov bh,0;
asm      mov dl,20;      /* comments must be C style, not ";" assembly style */
asm      mov dh,10;
asm      int 10h;
}


/* version 2: using the keyword asm before a block of inline code */
#pragma inline
main ()
{
asm     {
mov ah,2
mov bh,0
mov dl,20
mov dh,10
int 10h
        }
}
```

As shown above, each line of inline code is prefaced by the keyword "asm", or a block of inline code is prefaced by "asm". Each line must end in a semicolon or newline, and any comments must be in the correct form for C.

Example 7-4, on the following page, shows two programs that display a string of data. Solution A uses C language exclusively. Solution B uses Borland's Turbo C with inline Assembly code. Notice that in mixing C with Assembly code, Assembly directives such as OFFSET in "MOV DX,OFFSET MESSAGE" are not recognizable by C.

xample 7-5 also shows inline assembly. The inline code sets the cursor at row = 10 and column = 20 and then displays a string of data using a combination of Borland C and Assembly.

Example 7-4

Solution A: A C language program

```
#include <stdio.h>
main ( )
{
            printf("The planet Earth. \n");
}
```

Solution B: Turbo C with inline Assembly

```
#pragma inline
char const *MESSAGE = "The planet Earth.\n$";
main ()
{
  asm   mov ah,9
  asm   mov dx, MESSAGE
  asm   int 21h
}
```

Example 7-5

Borland C and inline Assembly code

```
#pragma inline
main ()
{
int const row = 10;
int const column = 20;
char  const *MESSAGE = "The planet Earth. \n$";

asm      {
mov ah,2
mov bh,0
mov dl,column
mov dh,row
int 10h              /* set cursor position */
mov ah,09
mov dx,MESSAGE
int 21h              /* display message */
        }
}
```

C programs that call Assembly procedures

Although inline assembly is fast and easy, in real-life applications it is common to write Assembly language subroutines and then make them available for C to call as if calling a C function. What is referred to in C language terminology as a *function* is called a *procedure (subroutine)* in Assembly language. Before embarking on writing Assembly routines to be used with C, one must first understand how parameters are passed from C to Assembly language. All high-level languages, such as C, BASIC, FORTRAN, and Pascal, pass parameters to subroutines (functions) that they are calling via the stack. Some of them pass the value itself (C, Pascal), while some others pass the address of the value (BASIC, FORTRAN). In BASIC, only the offset address is passed, while in FORTRAN both the segment and offset addresses are passed. Even the order in which they pass parameters differs among high-level languages. The terminology *calling convention* refers to the way that a given language passes parameters to the subroutines it calls. The following describes the C calling convention.

Example 7-6

```
extern cursor (int, int);
main ( )
{
cursor (15,12);
printf("This program sets the cursor");
}


;------------- in cursor.asm: ----------------------------------
        .MODEL          SMALL
        .CODE
        PUBLIC          _CURSOR
;this procedure is written to be called by a C program
_CURSOR          PROC
                PUSH BP                  ;save the BP (it is being altered)
                MOV  BP,SP               ;use BP as indexing into stack
                MOV  DH,[BP+4]           ;get the x (row) value from stack
                MOV  DL,[BP+6]           ;get the y (column) value from stack
                MOV  AH,02               ;set registers for INT call
                MOV  BH,00
                INT  10H
                POP  BP                  ;restore BP
                RET
_CURSOR          ENDP
```

C calling convention

How does C pass parameters to functions? It is extremely important to understand this since failure to do so can cause getting the wrong data from the stack when trying to access it through the Assembly subroutine. The following describes the C calling convention for mixing C with MASM Assembly language. An Assembly language procedure to be called by C must follow these rules:

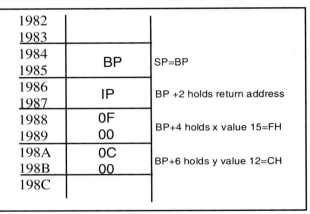

Example 7-6 Stack Contents Diagram

1. The parameters are passed by value to the stack in reverse order of encountering them. For example, in the function prog (x,y,z), first z is passed, then y, and so on.
2. After parameters are passed in reverse order, C also saves the address (CS,IP). If C is compiled in SMALL or COMPACT memory model (or if the procedure is NEAR) only the IP is saved. If C is compiled for MEDIUM, LARGE, or HUGE (or the procedure is FAR), both CS and IP are passed to the stack (CS is passed first, then IP).
3. BP must be saved on the stack and then the parameters must be accessed by the BP register and displacement, since BP is the offset of the stack segment (SS) register.
4. The last instruction should be RET with no number after it, since it is the job of C to restore the stack to its original place when it takes back control.
5. Any name shared publicly with C must be prefaced with underscore, and only the first eight characters of the name are recognized by C.
6. C passes the parameters by value except for arrays, which are passed by reference.
7. If C is compiled in MEDIUM, HUGE, or LARGE model, use the FAR option for the Assembly language procedure. If C is compiled with the SMALL model, use the NEAR option for the Assembly language procedure.

To understand the concepts above, assume that there is a C function named cursor (x,y), where x and y are the column and row values, respectively. Example 7-6 shows how x and y are passed to the stack and then accessed by Assembly code. The step-by-step sequence of the stack contents is shown also.

When C calls the cursor function, it saves y first, then x, and then the return address IP, and finally, gives control to the Assembly code. The first instruction of the assembly procedure must be saving the BP register, "PUSH BP". The last instruction must be the RET instruction.

Notice that the first two instructions of the procedure must always be saving BP and moving SP to BP. Similarly, the last two instructions must be popping BP and RET. The body of Assembly code goes in between them. This way of accessing arguments in the stack is standard, and saving any other registers will have no effect on displacement calculation as long as the number of PUSH and POP instructions are equal.

Example 7-7 shows the cursor routine rewritten to save all registers altered by the routine. The stack contents analysis is shown in the diagram.

Example 7-7

```
        .MODEL SMALL
        .CODE
        PUBLIC _CURSOR
        ;this procedure is written to be called by C language
_CURSOR PROC
        PUSH    BP              ;save the BP since contents are altered
        MOV     BP,SP
        PUSH    AX              ;push regs altered by this module
        PUSH    DX
        PUSH    BX
        MOV     DH,[BP+4]       ;get x the row value from stack
        MOV     DL,[BP+6]       ;get y the column value from stack
        MOV     AH,02           ;set up for INT call
        MOV     BH,00
        INT     10H
        POP     BX              ;restore registers
        POP     DX
        POP     AX
        POP     BP
        RET
_CURSOR ENDP
        END
```

How parameters are returned to C

In the preceding section we describe how arguments are passed from C to the stack and from there to an Assembly procedure. What happens if a C function expects to receive an argument? When C expects an argument from an Assembly procedure, it expects to find the returned parameter in certain register(s), depending on the size of the parameters as shown in Table 7-1.

197E	BL	BX
197F	BH	
1980	DL	DX
1981	DH	
1982	AL	AX
1983	AH	
1984	BP	SP=BP
1985		
1986	IP	BP +2 holds return address
1987		
1988	0F	BP+4 holds x value 15=FH
1989	00	
198A	0C	BP+6 holds y value 12=CH
198B	00	

Example 7-7 Stack Contents Diagram

Table 7-1: Returned Values from Assembly Procedures

Register	Size	C Data Type
AL	1 byte	char, short
AX	2 bytes	int
DX:AX	4 bytes	long

In Table 7-1 the register indicates the register used for the return value. If the value returned is a pointer (address), AX will hold IP if it is NEAR and DX:AX will hold CS:IP if it is FAR. This is illustrated in Example 7-8, where the sum of x, y, and z is returned to C through DX and AX as expected by C. DX has the higher word and AX the lower word. In the stack frame illustration, first notice that since the procedure is FAR, both CS and IP are saved on the stack. Therefore, to access the C arguments, it is necessary to use BP+6, BP+8, and BP+10 displacements.

As a rule, if the Assembly procedure is NEAR, the last argument passed by C is accessed by the displacement of BP+4, and if it is FAR, it is accessed by BP+6 displacement. In order not to be bothered by these rules, new assemblers have become more user friendly, as shown in the next topic.

Example 7-8

Three values of int size are passed by a C function to an Assembly procedure. The assembly code adds them together and returns the total sum back to C, which displays the result.

```
extern unsigned long sum (int, int, int);
{
main()
printf("The sum is equal to %u", sum (500,6500,200));
}
The following is sum.asm

            .MODEL MEDIUM
            .CODE
            PUBLIC _SUM
            ;this far procedure gets three words form stack and adds
            ;them together.  At the end DX:AX has the total sum
_SUM        PROC    FAR
            PUSH    BP              ;save BP
            MOV     BP,SP           ;use it as SP
            SUB     AX,AX           ;clear AX
            MOV     DX,AX           ;and DX
            ADD     AX,[BP+6]       ;add the first
            ADC     DX,0            ;add the carry
            ADD     AX,[BP+8]       ;add the second
            ADC     DX,0            ;add the carry
            ADD     AX,[BP+10]      ;add the third
            ADC     DX,0            ;add the carry
            POP     BP              ;restore BP
            RET                     ;go back to C
_SUM        ENDP
            END
```

New assemblers and linking with C

In recent years some Assemblers have made linking with C much easier. Using MASM 5.1, or TASM 1.0 and higher, ends the need to worry about the displacement or about beginning the names common to C and Assembly with an underscore or about saving BP. The program above is rewritten on the following page. Notice the C letter in directive ".MODEL SMALL, C".

Address		
17F0		
17F1		
17F2	BP	SP=BP
17F3		
17F4	IP	
17F5		
17F6	CS	
17F7		
17F8		x value pointed at by BP+6
17F9		
17FA		y value pointed at by BP+8
17FB		
17FC		z value pointed at by BP+10
17FD		

Example 7-8 Stack Contents Diagram

This automatically makes the assembler calculate [BP+n] for all the parameters. Compare these two programs to see the convenience of the new assemblers. Example 7-8 in the new format follows.

```
                        .MODEL MEDIUM, C
                        .CODE
                        PUBLIC          SUM
                        ;this far procedure gets three words form stack and adds
                        ;them together.  At the end DX:AX has the total sum
        SUM             PROC  FAR        DATA1:WORD, DATA2:WORD, DATA3:WORD
                        SUB    AX,AX ;CLEAR AX
                        MOV    DX,AX ;CLEAR DX
                        ADD    AX,DATA1
                        ADC    DX,0
                        ADD    AX,DATA2
                        ADC    DX,0
                        ADD    AX,DATA3
                        ADC    DX,0
                        RET
        SUM             ENDP
                        END
```

Passing array addresses from C to the stack

The C language passes variables to the stack by value and arrays by a pointer. In other words, the offset address of the array is pushed onto the stack if the memory model is SMALL or MEDIUM; otherwise, both the segment and offset address of the array are pushed. Example 7-9 illustrates this point. It uses a C language array to define daily wages for a five-day week, using an unsigned int (0 to 255 range values) data definition. It then uses Assembly code to add them and return the total sum back to C to be displayed.

Example 7-9

```
int  wages [5] = {154, 169, 98, 129, 245};
extern unsigned short weekpay(int wages[]);
main()
{
printf("Weekly pay = %u", weekpay(wages));
}

weekpay.asm is as follows:
                .MODEL MEDIUM
                .CODE
                PUBLIC          _WEEKPAY
                ;this procedure add five bytes together.
                ;At the end AX has the total sum
_WEEKPAY PROC  FAR
                PUSH BP                 ;save BP
                MOV    BP,SP
                PUSH SI                 ;save SI
                SUB    AX,AX            ;
                MOV    CX,5
                MOV    SI,[BP+6]        ;
AGAIN:          ADD    AL,[SI]          ;add a day's wages
                ADC    AH,0
                INC    SI               ;increment pointer to next wage
                INC    SI
                LOOP  AGAIN
                POP    SI
                POP    BP
                RET
_WEEKPAY  ENDP
                END
```

Linking assembly language routines with C

The following steps describe how to link Microsoft Quick C with MASM assembly language routines.

1. Make sure that the assembly language procedure declares the procedure as PUBLIC. The procedure name should begin with underscore. For example, if the procedure is called "sum" in the C program, it should be "_sum" in the assembly language routine. Make the assembly language procedure NEAR for small model and FAR for medium model.
2. In the C program, declare the procedure as external.
3. Assemble the assembly language program with MASM to produce the object file: for example, module1.obj.
4. Compile the C program to produce the object file: for example, prog1.obj. Note that when using the command line compiler QCL, the system defaults to producing a small model. When in the Quick C integrated environment, the default is the medium model.
5. Link them together to produce the executable file.

> C> link prog1.obj + module1.obj

In Borland C++, they can be linked together as follows:

> C> bcc prog1.c module1.asm

The "bcc" command will compile the C program, use the TASM assembler to assemble the assembly language program, and then link them together. Note that Borland C is case sensitive. If your procedure is called "_SUM" in the assembly language program and "sum" in the C program, the linker will not be able to link them together. Make the procedure name lowercase in the Assembly language program. If you are using Borland C++, it is recommended not to use the "cpp" filename extension since this will cause the function name to be mangled, and therefore the linker will not be able to find the function. If you must use the "cpp" extension, you must compile the C program with the /S option to obtain an assembly language listing, then see how the function name was mangled and use that name in your assembly language program. For example, the function name "sum" was listed as "@sumq$iii". Therefore, all references to "sum" in the assembly language program had to be changed to "@sumq$iii" in order to allow the program to be linked with the C++ program.

Review Questions

1. A C program can either call an Assembly language program or use _____ coding where the Assembly language code is inserting into the C program.
2. Describe the C convention for passing parameters to functions.

SUMMARY

Modular programming involves breaking down a project into independent subprograms. Each subprogram accomplishes a specific set of tasks. Good programming practices dictate that the input and output variables to each subprogram are clearly documented. Variables within subprograms are defined by EXTRN and PUBLIC directives. These provide the means by which the computer can locate variables. Various methods for passing parameters are used, including passing by register, by memory, or by the stack.

The C programming language has gained widespread popularity because of the ease with which code can be ported from one machine to another. However, it is often desirable to include Assembly language programs because of the increased speed that can be gained. Assembly language routines can be called by C programs, or the Assembly language code can be coded directly into the C program by a technique called inline coding.

PROBLEMS

1. Fill in the blanks in the following program. The main program defines the data and calls another module to add 5 bytes of data, then saves the result. *Note:* Some blanks may not need anything.

```
                .MODEL SMALL
                .STACK 100H
                .DATA
                PUBLIC      _____,_____
DATA1           DB          25,12,34,56,98
RESULT          DW          ?
                .CODE
                EXTRN       _____:FAR
HERE:           MOV   AX,@DATA
                MOV   DS,AX
                CALL  SUM
                MOV   AH,4CH
                INT   21H
                END   _____
```

   In another file there is the module for summing 5 bytes of data:

```
                .MODEL  SMALL
                _____DATA1:BYTE
                _____RESULT:WORD
COUNT           EQU    5
                .CODE
                _____SUM
SUM             PROC   _____
                MOV   BX,OFFSET DATA1
                SUB   AX,AX
                MOV   CX,COUNT
_____:         ADD   AL, BYTE PTR [BX]
                ADC   AH,0
                INC   BX
                LOOP  AGAIN
                MOV   RESULT,AX
                RET
_____          ENDP
                END   _____
```

2. If a label or parameter is not defined in a given module, it must be declared as _____.

3. If a label or parameter is used by other modules, it must be declared as _____ in the present module.

4. List the options for the EXTRN directive when it is referring to a procedure.

5. List the options for the EXTRN directive when it is referring to a data item.

6. List the options for the PUBLIC directive when it is referring to a procedure.

7. List the options for the PUBLIC directive when it is referring to a data item.

8. Convert Program 4-1 to the modular format, making each of the INT subroutines a separate module. Each module should be NEAR. Assemble and test the program.

9. Assume that there are four separate modules with segment names of CODSG_1, CODSG_2, CODSG_3, and CODSG_4. The program entry point is 00040 for CODSG_1, as shown in the following link map.

Start	Stop	Length	Name
00040H	-----	0000BH	CODSG_1
-----	-----	00014H	CODSG_2
-----	-----	00025H	CODSG_3
-----	-----	00041H	CODSG_4

   (a) Fill in the blanks assuming that all segments were defined as PARA.
   (b) Fill in the blanks assuming that all segments were defined as WORD.

---

10. Assume that all four segments in Problem 9 were defined as
    CDSEG   SEGMENT PARA PUBLIC 'CODE"
    Write the link map for the code segments.
11. Compare the link map of the full segment definition with the traditional segment definition. Does the sequence of the segments have any bearing on the link map? If so, explain why.
12. Write a program that accepts two unsigned numbers (each less than 999) from the keyboard, converts them to hex, takes the average, and displays the result on the monitor. Use the hex-to-decimal and ASCII-to-hex conversion modules in the text.
13. Write a program (similar to Program 7-2) with the following components.
    (a) In the main program, two values are defined: 1228 and 52400.
    (b) The main program calls two separate modules, passing the values by stack.
    (c) In the first module, the two numbers are multiplied and the result is passed back to the main module.
    (d) The second module performs division of the two numbers (52400 /122) and passes both the quotient and remainder back to the main program to be stored.
    (e) Analyze the stack and its contents for each module if SP = FFF8H immediately before the first CALL instruction in the main module.
14. Modify Program 7-3 to push the offset addresses of the data. Diagram the stack.
15. Write an inline assembly program to set the cursor to row 14, column 27, and then display the message "This is a test".
16. Modify Example 7-8 to add twelve monthly salaries. The total yearly salary cannot be higher than $65,535.

ANSWERS TO REVIEW QUESTIONS

Section 7.1: Writing and Linking Modules
1. (1) each module can be developed individually, allowing parallel development of modules, which shortens development time, (2) easier to locate source of bugs, (3) these modules can be linked with high-level languages such as C
2. PUBLIC   3. EXTRN
4. the module that is the entry and exit point will have a label after the END statement
5. a paragraph consists of 16 bytes and begins on an address ending in 0H
6. name   SEGMENT PARA STACK 'STACK'   7. EXTRN   TOTAL:WORD
8. 60H   9. name   SEGMENT   PARA   PUBLIC 'CODE'

Section 7.2: Some Very Useful Modules
1. 1st iteration: AX=F624   F624/A = 189D   remainder DL=2
   2nd iteration:AX=189D   189D/A=0276   remainder DL=1
   3rd iteration: AX=0276   0276/A=003F   remainder DL=0
   4th iteration:AX=003F   003F/A=6   remainder DL=3
   5th iteration:AX=0006   0006/A=0   remainder DL=6
   AX is now zero, so the conversion is complete: $F624H=63012_{10}$
2. 1st iteration: AL=36   06x1=6   DI=6
   2nd iteration:AL=35   05xA=32   DI=6+32=38
   3rd iteration: AL=34   04x64=190   DI=38+1C8
   4th iteration:AL=31   01x03E8=03E8   DI=1C8+03E8=05B0
   5th iteration:AL=30   0x2710=0   DI=05B0
   BX has been decremented from 4 to 0, is now -1, so the conversion is complete
   01456_{10}=05B0H

Section 7.3: Passing Parameters among Modules
1. (a) by register; one advantage is the execution speed of registers; one disadvantage is that there are a limited number of registers available so that not many values can be passed
   (b) by stack; one advantage is it does not use up available registers; one disadvantage is that errors in processing the stack can cause the system to crash
   (c) by memory; one advantage is a large area available to store data; one disadvantage is that the program
would   not be portable to other computers
2. (a) and (c) are correct, (b)and (d) are not correct because SP cannot be used in indexing mode with SS

Section 7.4: Combining Assembly Language and C Programs
1. inline
2. parameters are passed by value except for arrays which are passed by reference; parameters are passed in reverse order of argument list; after arguments are pushed onto the stack, C pushed CS:IP for FAR procedures or IP for NEAR procedures

CHAPTER 8

32-BIT PROGRAMMING FOR 386 AND 486 MACHINES

OBJECTIVES

Upon completion of this chapter, you will be able to:

» Discuss the major differences between the 8086/286 and the 80386/486
» List the registers of the 80386/486 machines
» Diagram the register sizes available in the 386/486
» Describe the difference between real and protected modes
» Explain the difference in register usage between the 8086/286 and 386/486
» Discuss how the increased register size of the 386/486 relates to an increase memory range
» Diagram how the "little endian" storage convention of 80x86 machines stores doubleword-sized operands
» Code programs for 386/486 machines using extended registers and new directives
» Code arithmetic statements using the extended registers of the 386/486
» Describe the factors resulting in the increased performance of 386/486 over previous generations of microprocessors

All programs discussed so far were intended for 16-bit machines such as 8088, 8086, and 80286 IBM and compatible computers. Although those programs will run on 80386- and 80486-based machines with much improved speed, the true power of 386 and 486 microprocessors shows up when they are switched to protected mode. What is protected mode? As mentioned in Chapter 1, the 386 and 486 can operate in two modes: real mode and protected mode. In real mode they function essentially the same as 8086/286 machines with the exception that 32-bit registers are available. They still have a capacity of addressing a maximum of 1 megabyte of memory. More important, they run all MS-DOS programs without any modification. In protected mode they can access up to 4 gigabytes of memory, but they also require a very complex operating system, one of whose tasks is to assign a privilege level of 0 to 3 (0 being the highest) to each program run on the CPU. At this time only the Unix operating system is taking advantage of protected mode of both the 386 and 486 microprocessors. In March 1992, IBM introduced OS/2 version 2.0, designed specifically for 386 systems. This is a 32-bit version of the OS/2 operating system written to take advantage of protected mode of 386 and higher microprocessors. This is in contrast to OS/2 version 1, which was designed for 16-bit 80286 protected mode. The combination of 32-bit processing power and an operating system with *multitasking* and *multiuser* capability makes the 386 and 486 computers comparable to the minicomputers of the 1970s at a fraction of the cost. The term *multiuser* refers to a system that can support more than one terminal/keyboard at a time. *Multitasking* refers to systems that can execute more than one program at a time.

In this chapter we discuss the characteristics of 386 and 486 microprocessors in real mode that affect programming. Then some program examples will be given that use the 32-bit capability of these machines. Finally, a timing comparison of several programs run across 80x86 machines will be given in order to appreciate the speed of 386/486-based computers. A full discussion of protected mode and all capabilities of these processors is not included since this would demand an entire volume by itself.

SECTION 8.1: 80386/80486 MACHINES IN REAL MODE

In this section we concentrate on some of the most important differences between the 8086/286 and 386/486 in real mode. One major difference is the register size. While in the 8086/286 the maximum register size is 16 bits wide, in the 386/486 the maximum size of registers has been extended to 32 bits. All register names have been changed to reflect this extension. Therefore, AX has become EAX, BX is now EBX, and so on, as illustrated below and outlined in Table 8-1. For example, the 386/486 contains registers AL, AH, AX, and EAX with 8, 8, 16, and 32 bits, respectively. In the 86/286, register AX is accessible either as AL or AH or AX, while in the 386/486, register EAX can be accessed only as AL or AH or AX or EAX. In other words, the upper 16 bits of EAX are not accessible as a separate register. The same rule applies to EBX, ECX, and EDX. Registers DI, SI, BP, and SP have become EDI, ESI, EBP, and ESP, respectively. That means the 386/486 can access DI, EDI, SI, ESI, BP, EBP, SP, and ESP. All of these registers are accessible in real mode.

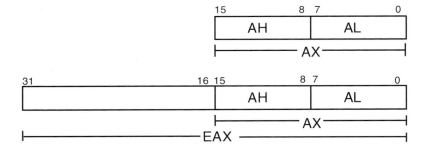

In addition to the CS, DS, SS, and ES segment registers, there are also two new segment registers which are accessible in real mode: FS and GS. With the addition of these new segment registers, there are a total of six segment registers, making it possible to access 384K bytes ($6 \times 64 = 384$), since each segment register can access up to 64K bytes of memory. Again, all these registers are accessible in real mode. Although both the flag register and IP are extended to 32 bits, only the lower 16 bits are available in real mode. To access all 32 bits of these registers, one must switch to protected mode. There are several control registers (CR0, CR1, CR2, and CR3) in protected mode but only bit 0 of CR0 is available in real mode. Bit 0 of CR0 is the protection-enable bit. When power is applied to the 386/486, it selects real mode automatically and PE (bit 0 of CR0) is low. To switch from real mode to protected mode, this bit must be set to 1. Again, only the Unix and OS/2 operating systems use protected mode at this time. As far as MS-DOS is concerned, up to version 5 is not using the protected mode of the 386/486. This might change with future versions of MS-DOS.

Table 8-1: Registers of the 80386/486 by Category

Category	Bits	Register Names
General	32	EAX,EBX,ECX,EDX
	16	AX,BX,CX,DX
	8	AH,AL,BH,BL,CH,CL,DH,DL
Pointer	32	ESP (extended SP), EBP (extended BP)
	16	SP (stack pointer), BP (base pointer)
Index	32	ESI (extended SI), EDI (extended DI)
	16	SI (source index), DI (destination index)
Segment	16	CS (code segment), DS (data segment), SS (stack segment), ES (extra segment) FS (extra segment), GS (extra segment)
Instruction	32	EIP (extended instruction pointer)
Flag	32	EFR (extended flag register)
Control	32	CR0, CR1, CR2, CR3

Note: Only bit 0 of CR0 is available in real mode. All other control registers are available in protected mode only.

General registers are pointers in 386/486

Another major change from 86/286 to 386/486 is the ability of general registers such as EAX, ECX, and EDX to be used as pointers. As shown in previous chapters, AX, CX, and DX could not be used as pointers. For example, an instruction such as "MOV CL,[AX]" would have cause an error in the 86/286 CPU since only BX, SI, DI, and BP were allowed to be used as pointers to memory. This has changed starting with the 80386 microprocessor. In the 386/486 CPU, the following instructions are perfectly legal:

```
MOV   AX,[ECX]
ADD   SI,[EDX]
OR    EBX,[EAX]+20
```

It must be noted that when EAX, ECX, or EDX are used as offset addresses, DS is the default segment register. That means that SS is the default segment register for ESP and EBP, CS for EIP, and DS is for all other registers. The segment override symbol (:) can be used to change the default segment register as shown next.

```
MOV   AX,FS:[ECX]   ;move contents of FS:ECX to AX
```

Calculation of physical addresses in real mode is the same as for the 86/286 as discussed in Chapter 1. In the example above, the physical addresses can be calculated by shifting left the segment register FS one hex digit and adding it to offset ECX. For example, if FS = 12E0 and ECX = 00000120, the physical address specified by FS:ECX would be 14000H (12E00 + 0120 = 14000H).

Table 8-2 summarizes addressing modes for the 386/486. There are additional addressing modes available for 386 and higher CPUs which will be covered in future volumes.

Table 8-2: Addressing Modes for the 80386/486

Addressing Mode	Operand	Default Segment
Register	register	none
Immediate	data	none
Direct	[OFFSET]	DS
Register indirect	[BX]	DS
	[SI]	DS
	[DI]	DS
	[EAX]	DS
	[EBX]	DS
	[ECX]	DS
	[EDX]	DS
	[ESI]	DS
	[EDI]	DS
Based relative	[BX]+disp	DS
	[BP]+disp	SS
	[EAX]+disp	DS
	[EBX]+disp	DS
	[ECX]+disp	DS
	[EDX]+disp	DS
	[EBP]+disp	SS
Indexed relative	[DI]+disp	DS
	[SI]+disp	DS
	[EDI]+disp	DS
	[ESI]+disp	DS
Based indexed relative	[R1][R2]+disp where R1 and R2 are any of the above	If BP is used, segment is SS; otherwise, DS is the segment

Note:
In based indexed relative addressing, disp is optional.

386/486 maximum memory range in real mode: 1M

There is a dilemma in the 386/486 working under DOS in real mode. If in real mode the maximum range of memory is 1M (00000 to FFFFFH), what happens if a 32-bit register is used as an offset into the segment? The range of the 32-bit offset is 00000000H to FFFFFFFFH; therefore, using a 32-bit register as an offset will place the address range beyond 1M. This is a situation that the programmer must avoid in 386/486 computers working with DOS version 5 and lower. For example, to execute the instruction "MOV AX,[ESI]", the programmer must make the upper 16 bits of ESI all zeros. This means that the segment offset range in real mode 386/486 under DOS is 0000 to FFFFH. The following are some cases of legal and illegal codings for real mode of the 386/486 under DOS.

```
ADD    EAX,[BX]              ;LEGAL
ADD    ECX,[DX]              ;ILLEGAL! EDX CAN BE USED
                            ;AS POINTER BUT NOT DX
MOV    AX,WORD PTR [ECX]    ;LEGAL
ADD    EBX,[EDX]            ;LEGAL
```

Accessing 32-bit registers with commonly used assemblers

In Assembly language the directive ".386" is used to access the 32-bit registers of 386/486 computers in real mode under DOS and to employ the new instructions of the 386 microprocessor. Every new generation of 80x86 has some new instructions that do not execute on lower processors, meaning that they are upwardly compatible. In other words, using the ".386" directive in a program means that the program must be run only on 386 and higher (486 and 586) computers and cannot be run on 8088/86- and 286-based computers. In contrast, all programs in previous chapters were written in a way that they could be run on any 80x86 computer. The following are additional assembler directives, which indicate the type of microprocessor supported by Microsoft's assembler (MASM) and Borland's Turbo assembler (TASM).

MASM	TASM	Meaning
.86	P8086	will run on any 80x86 computer (default)
.286	P286	will run on any 286 and higher computer; also allows use of new 286 instructions
.386	P386	will run on any 386 and higher computer; also allows use of new 386 instructions
.486	P486	will run on any 486 and higher computer; also allows use of new 486 instructions

Program 8-1 demonstrates the use of the ".386" directive and the 80386 32-bit instructions. The simplified segment definition was used. The program used the 32-bit register EAX to add and subtract values of various size to demonstrate 32-bit programming of the 386/486 under DOS. Now the question is how to run this program and see the register contents in 386/486 machines. Unfortunately, the DEBUG utility used in earlier chapters cannot be used since it shows only the 16-bit registers. In many assemblers, including MASM and TASM, there are advanced debugging tools that one can use to see the execution of the 386/486 programs. In the case of MASM, the CodeView utility, and for TASM, the Turbo Debugger, are tools that allow one to monitor the execution of the 386/486 in addition to 8086/88 and 286 programs.

Below is shown a trace of Program 8-1, using Microsoft's CodeView program. To examine the 32-bit registers in CodeView, press F2 to display registers; then select the Options menu from the top of the screen, and a drop-down menu appears. Select "386" from the drop-down menu to display the registers in 32-bit format.

Write a program using the 32-bit registers of the 386 to add the values 100000, 200000, and 40000. Then subtract from the total sum the values 80000, 35000, and 250. Place the result in memory locations allocated using the DD, doubleword directive, used for 32-bit numbers.

```
TITLE     ADD AND SUBTRACT USING 32-BIT REGISTERS IN 386 MACHINES
PAGE      60,132
          .MODEL SMALL
          .386
          .STACK 200H
          .DATA
RESULT    DD        ?
          .CODE
BEGIN:    MOV       AX.@DATA
          MOV       DS,AX
          SUB       EAX,EAX
          ADD       EAX,100000      ;EAX = 186A0H
          ADD       EAX,200000      ;EAX = 186A0H + 30D40 H =  493E4H
          ADD       EAX,40000       ;EAX = 493E4H + 9C40H = 53020H
          SUB       EAX,80000       ;EAX = 53020H - 13880H = 3F7A0H
          SUB       EAX,35000       ;EAX = 3F7A0H - 88B8H = 36EE8H
          SUB       EAX,250         ;EAX = 36338H - FAH = 36DEEH = 224750 decimal
          MOV       RESULT,EAX
          MOV       AH,4CH
          INT       21H
          END       BEGIN
```

Program 8-1

```
4833:0000 B83648        MOV    AX,4836                      EAX=00036DEE
4833:0003 8ED8          MOV    DS,AX                        EBX=00000000
4833:0005 662BC0        SUB    EAX,EAX                      ECX=00000000
4833:0008 6605A0860100  ADD    EAX,000186A0                 EDX=00000000
4833:000E 6605400D0300  ADD    EAX,00030D40                 ESP=00000200
4833:0014 6605409C0000  ADD    EAX,00009C40                 EBP=00000000
4833:001A 662D80380100  SUB    EAX,00013880                 ESI=00000000
4833:0020 662DB8880000  SUB    EAX,000088B8                 EDI=00000000
4833:0026 662DFA000000  SUB    EAX,000000FA                 DS=....4836
                                                            ES=....4823
4833:0030 B44C          MOV    AH,4C                        FS=....0000
4833:0032 CD21          INT    21                           GS=....0000
4833:0034 0000          ADD    Byte Ptr [BX+SI],AL          SS=....4837
4833:0036 0000          ADD    Byte Ptr [BX+SI],AL          CS=....4833
4833:0038 0000          ADD    Byte Ptr [BX+SI],AL          IP=0000002C
4833:003A 0000          ADD    Byte Ptr [BX+SI],AL
4833:003C 0000          ADD    Byte Ptr [BX+SI],AL          NV UP
4833:003E 0000          ADD    Byte Ptr [BX+SI],AL          EI NG
                                                            NZ AC
>t                                                          PE NC
>t
>t                                                          DS:0004
>                                                           00000000
```

Program 8-1: CodeView Screen of Program Execution

Little endian revisited

In analyzing how the 386/486 stores 32-bit data in memory or loads a 32-bit operand into a register, recall the little endian convention: The low byte goes to the low address and the high byte to the high address. For example, an instruction such as "MOV RESULT,EAX" in Program 8-1 will store the data in this way:

OFFSET	CONTENTS
RESULT	d0-d7
RESULT+1	d8-d15
RESULT+2	d16-d23
RESULT+3	d24-d31

Example 8-1

Assuming that SI=1298 and EAX = 41992F56H, show the contents of memory locations after the instruction "MOV [SI],EAX".

Solution: (in HEX)
  DS:1298 = (56)
  DS:1299 = (2F)
  DS:129A = (99)
  DS:129B = (41)

Review Questions

1. In the 80386/486, the bits of register EDX can be accessed either as DL, bits __ to __, or DH, bits __ to __, or DX, bits __ to __, or EAX, bits __ to __.
2. In the 386/486 segment size is ____ bytes.
3. What is real mode? What is protected mode?
4. True or false: The instruction "MOV DX,[AX]" is illegal in the 8086 but "MOV DX,[EAX]" is legal in the 386/486.
5. What is the default segment register when EAX is used as a pointer?
6. What is the purpose of the ".386" directive?
7. If DI = 148F and EBX = 6B2415F9, show the contents of memory after the instruction "MOV [DI],EBX" is executed.

SECTION 8.2: SOME SIMPLE 386/486 PROGRAMS

One way to increase the processing power of the microprocessor is to widen the register size. This allows processing large numbers as a whole rather than breaking them into smaller chunks to fit into small registers. The 32-bit registers have become standard in all recent microprocessors. Powerful supercomputers use 64-bit registers. In this section we show revisions of some earlier programs using the 32-bit capability of the 386/486 machines to see the impact of the wider registers in programming. By comparing 32-bit versions of these programs with the 16-bit versions, one can see the increased efficiency of 32-bit coding. The impact on speed is discussed in the final section.

Adding 16-bit words using 32-bit registers

Program 3-1b used 16-bit registers for adding several words of data. The sum was accumulated in one register and another register was used to add up the carries. This is not necessary when using 32-bit registers. First, refresh your memory by looking at Program 3-1b and then examine Program 8-2, a 32-bit version of the same program, written for 386/486 CPUs.

```
TITLE        REVISION OF PROGRAM 3-1B USING 32-BIT REGISTERS
PAGE         60,132
             .MODEL SMALL
             .386
             .STACK 200H
             .DATA
DATA1   DD   27345,28521,29533,30105,32375
SUM     DD   ?
COUNT   EQU  5
             .CODE
BEGIN:  MOV  AX,@DATA
        MOV  DS,AX
        MOV  CX,COUNT           ;CX is loop counter
        MOV  SI,OFFSET DATA     ;SI is data pointer
        SUB  EAX,EAX            ;EAX will hold sum
BACK:   ADD  EAX,DWORD PTR[SI]  ;add next word to EAX
        ADD  SI,4               ;SI points to next dword
        DEC  CX                 ;decrement loop counter
        JNZ  BACK               ;continue adding
        MOV  SUM,EAX            ;store sum
        MOV  AH,4CH
        INT  21H
        END  BEGIN
```

Program 8-2

Rewrite Program 3-2 in Chapter 3 to add two 8-byte operands using 32-bit registers.

```
TITLE        ADD TWO 8-BYTE NUMBER USING 32-BIT REGISTERS IN THE 386
PAGE         60,132
             .MODEL SMALL
             .386
             .STACK 200H
             .DATA
DATA1   DQ   548FB9963CE7H
        ORG  0010H
DATA2   DQ   3FCD4FA23B8DH
        ORG  0020H
DATA3   DQ   ?
             .CODE
BEGIN:  MOV  AX,@DATA
        MOV  DS,AX
        CLC                     ;clear carry before first addition
        MOV  SI,OFFSET DATA1    ;SI is pointer for operand1
        MOV  DI,OFFSET DATA2    ;DI is pointer for operand2
        MOV  BX,OFFSET DATA3    ;BX is pointer for the sum
        MOV  CX,02              ;CX is the loop counter
BACK:   MOV  EAX,DWORD PTR [SI] ;move the operand to EAX
        ADC  EAX,DWORD PTR [DI] ;add the  operand to EAX
        MOV  DWORD PTR [BX],EAX ;store the sum
        INC  SI                 ;point to next dword of operand1
        INC  SI
        INC  SI
        INC  SI
        INC  DI                 ;point to next dword of operand2
        INC  DI
        INC  DI
        INC  DI
        INC  BX
        INC  BX                 ;point to next dword of sum
        INC  BX
        INC  BX
        LOOP BACK               ;if not finished, continue adding
        MOV  AH,4CH
        INT  21H                ;go back to DOS
        END  BEGIN
```

Program 8-3a

Adding multiword data in 386/486 machines

In Program 3-2, two multiword numbers were added using 16-bit registers. Each number could be as large as 8 bytes wide. That program required a total of four iterations. Using the 32-bit registers of the 386/46 requires only two iterations, as shown in Program 8-3a on the previous page. This loop version of the multiword addition program is very long and inefficient. It can be made more efficient by saving the flag register that holds the carry bit of the first 32-bit addition on the stack and then adding four to each pointer instead of incrementing the pointers 4 times. The loop is shown below in Program 8-3b.

```
;this revision of Program 3-1a shows how to save the flags
;      before updating the pointers
    BACK:    MOV     EAX,DWORD PTR [SI]     ;move the operand to EAX
             ADC     EAX,DWORD PTR [DI]     ;add the  operand to EAX
             MOV     DWORD PTR [BX],EAX     ;store the sum
             PUSHF                          ;save the flags
             ADD     SI,4                   ;point to next dword of operand1
             ADD     DI,4                   ;point to next dword of operand2
             ADD     BX,4                   ;point to next dword of sum
             POPF                           ;restore the flags
             LOOP    BACK                   ;if not finished, continue adding
```

Program 8-3b

Due to the high penalty associated with branch instructions such as the LOOP and Jcondition instructions in the 386/486, it is better to use the non-loop version of this program, shown in Program 8-4.

First notice that the data is stored exactly the same way as in the loop version of the program. Data directive DQ is used to set up storage for the 8-byte numbers. First, the lower dword (4 bytes) of DATA1 is moved into EAX, and the lower dword of DATA2 is added to EAX. Then the upper dword of DATA1 is moved into EBX, and the upper dword of DATA2 is added to EBX, with any carry that may have been generated in the addition of the lower dwords. EAX now holds the lower 4 bytes of the result, and EBX holds the upper 4 bytes of the result.

Program 8-4 is much more efficient than using the loop concept. To see why and for a discussion of the impact of branching instructions on the performance of programs in the 80386/486, see Section 8.3.

```
    TITLE       ADD TWO 8-BYTE NUMBERS USING 32-BIT REGISTERS IN THE 386  (NO-LOOP VERSION)
    PAGE        60,132
                .MODEL SMALL
                .386
                .STACK  200H
                .DATA
    DATA1       DQ      548FB9963CE7H
                ORG     0010H
    DATA2       DQ      3FCD4FA23B8DH
                ORG     0020H
    DATA3       DQ      ?
                .CODE
    BEGIN:      MOV     AX,@DATA
                MOV     DS,AX
                MOV     EAX,DWORD PTR DATA1      ;move lower dword of DATA1 into EAX
                ADD     EAX,DWORD PTR DATA2      ;add lower dword of DATA2 to EAX
                MOV     EBX,DWORD PTR DATA1+4    ;move upper dword of DATA1 into EBX
                ADC     EBX,DWORD PTR DATA2+4    ;add upper dword of DATA2 to EBX
                MOV     DWORD PTR DATA3,EAX      ;store lower dword of result
                MOV     DWORD PTR DATA3+4,EBX    ;store upper dword of result
                MOV     AH,4CH
                INT     21H
                END     BEGIN
```

Program 8-4

Multiplying a 32-bit operand by a 16-bit operand in the 386/486

As a final example of the power of 32-bit registers in 386/486 machines, in this section we look at the multiplication of a 32-bit operand by a 16-bit operand. Comparing the 386/486 version with the 86/286 version of this program clearly reveals the coding efficiency of the 32-bit register of the 386/486 systems. First look at the 386/486 version of the multiplication of a 32-bit operand by a 16-bit operand, shown in Program 8-5. Notice that the 16-bit operand is placed in a 32-bit register in order to perform 32-bit arithmetic.

Multiplying a 32-bit register:

EAX

by a 32-bit operand:

The product is stored in:

| EDX | EAX |

Figure 8-1. 386/486 Multiplication

Write a program using the 386/486 to multiply a 32-bit operand by a 16-bit operand.

```
TITLE      MULTIPLICATION OF DOUBLE WORD BY WORD USING 386/486
PAGE       60,132
           .MODEL SMALL
           .386
           .STACK  200H
           .DATA
DATA1   DD      500000          ;MULTIPLICAND (UP TO 32-BIT SIZE DATA)
DATA2   DD      50000           ;MULTIPLIER (UP TO 16-BIT SIZE)
RESULT  DQ      ?               ;PRODUCT (UP TO 48-BIT SIZE)
           .CODE
MAIN:   MOV     AX,@DATA
        MOV     DS,AX
        MOV     EAX,DATA1               ;32-BIT OPERAND
        MUL     DWORD PTR DATA2         ;TIMES 16-BIT OPERAND
        MOV     DWORD PTR RESULT,EAX    ;SAVE THE RESULT
        MOV     DWORD PTR RESULT+4,EDX
        MOV     AH,4CH
        INT     21H
        END     MAIN
```

Program 8-5

To appreciate the processing power of the 32-bit registers of the 386/486, the next topic shows a revision of Program 8-5, using the 16-bit registers of the 8086/286 processors.

32-bit by 16-bit multiplication using 8086/286 registers

For the sake of clarity in the following discussion, word size W1 and W2 will be used to represent the 32-bit multiplicand. To multiply that by the 16-bit operand W3, the following algorithm must be followed. Assume that all values are in hex.

```
              W2    W1          multiplicand
         x           W3         multiplier
              ----------------
              W3xW1             a 32-bit result
     +    W3xW2                 a 32-bit result must be shifted left  one hex
              ----------------  position, then added
              X3 X2 X1          a 48-bit result (X1, X2, X3 are word size)


         W1    DW    _____
         W2    DW    _____    ;W2:W1 IS A 32-BIT MULTIPLICAND
         W3    DW    _____    ;W3 IS A 16-BIT MULTIPLIER
```

```
X1      DW      ?
X2      DW      ?               ;X3X2X1 THE 48-BIT PRODUCT RESULT
X3      DW      ?
        ...
        MOV     AX,W1   ;GET THE LOW WORD
        MUL     W3      ;MULTIPLY
        MOV     X1,AX   ;SAVE THE LOW WORD OF THE PRODUCT
        MOV     X2,DX   ;SAVE THE HIGH WORD OF THE PRODUCT
        MOV     AX,W2   ;GET THE HIGH WORD
        MUL     W3      ;MULTIPLY
        ADD     X2,AX   ;ADD THE MIDDLE 16-BIT WORD
        ADC     DX,0    ;PROPAGATE THE CARRY TO DX
        MOV     X3,DX   ;SAVE THE HIGH WORD RESULT
```

Now after understanding the process above, Program 8-6 will show how it is actually coded. First, a DD directive is used to define a 32-bit data instead of using DW twice. Similarly, since there is no directive to define a 48-bit data, the DQ (define quad word) directive is used, which defines a 64-bit operand. The unused bits become zeros.

```
TITLE       MULTIPLICATION OF DOUBLEWORD BY WORD USING 86/286
PAGE        60,132
            .MODEL SMALL
            .STACK 200H
            .DATA
DATA1   DD      500000                      ;MULTIPLICAND (UP TO 32-BIT SIZE DATA)
DATA2   DW      50000                       ;MULTIPLIER (UP TO 16-BIT SIZE)
RESULT  DQ      ?                           ;PRODUCT (UP TO 48-BIT SIZE)
            .CODE
MAIN:   MOV     AX,@DATA
        MOV     DS,AX
        MOV     AX,WORD PTR DATA1           ;GET LOW WORD OF MULTIPLICAND
        MUL     WORD PTR DATA2              ;MULTIPLY THE MULTIPLIER
        MOV     WORD PTR RESULT,AX          ;SAVE LOW WORD OF THE PRODUCT
        MOV     WORD PTR RESULT + 2,DX      ;SAVE MIDDLE WORD OF PRODUCT
        MOV     AX,WORD PTR DATA1 + 2       ;GET THE HIGH WORD OF MULTIPLICAND
        MUL     WORD PTR DATA2              ;MULTIPLY THE MULTIPLIER
        ADD     WORD PTR RESULT + 2 ,AX     ;ADD THE MIDDLE 16-BIT WORD
        ADC     DX,0                        ;PROPAGATE THE CARRY TO DX
        MOV     WORD PTR RESULT + 4,DX      ;SAVE THE HIGH WORD RESULT
        MOV     AH,4CH
        INT     21H
        END     MAIN
```

Program 8-6

Comparing these two programs, one can see why the 32-bit registers have become the standard for all new generation of microprocessors.

Review Questions

1. Compare the number of iterations for adding two 8-byte numbers for the following CPUs.
   (a) 8085 (a 8-bit) CPU
   (b) 8086/88/286
   (c) 386/486
   (d) Cray supercomputer (64-bit system)
2. What data directives are used to define 32-bit and 64-bit operands?
3. What directive is used in MASM to inform the assembler that the program is using 386 instructions? In TASM?

SECTION 8.3: 80x86 PERFORMANCE COMPARISON

The newer generations of the 80x86 family not only have powerful mainframe features such as protection capabilities, but they also execute the instructions of previous generations much faster. In the preceding section it was seen how efficient the 32-bit coding can be. In this section we compare the performance of the 80x86 family of processors. To do that, the number of clock cycles (ticks) that each instruction of a given program takes to execute for the 8086, 286, 386, and 486 CPUs will be examined. To fully understand the remaining material in this section, it is necessary to review the introduction to Appendix B, Section B.2. The clock cycles table in Appendix B does not show the total time taken for each processor to execute. This is because such a calculation in terms of microseconds or milliseconds depends on the hardware design of the system, primarily on the factors of working frequency and memory design. Such hardware discussions and their impact on the performance of the computer are beyond the scope of this book but will be discussed in Volume 2 of this series. Comparing the performance of the 80x86 family can take one of two approaches:

1. Taking a program written for the 8086 and calculating the number of clocks taken to execute it, unchanged, on each of Intel's 8086, 80286, 386, and 486 microprocessors.
2. Modifying the same program for 32-bit processing of the 386/486 and then calculating the total number of clocks to execute it for the 386 and 486 microprocessors.

Running an 8086 program across the 80x86 family

Intel has employed some very advanced techniques in pipelining to enhance the processing power of 386 and 486 microprocessors. For example, many instructions that took four or five clocks to execute on the 8086, take only one or two clocks on the 386 and 486 machines. This is shown next.

Problem 3-1b showed a program that calculated the total sum of five words of data. Since the loop is the most time-consuming part of this program, below is shown a comparison of the total number of clocks taken for one iteration across all of Intel's 80x86 processors. The number of clocks for each instruction is taken from Appendix B.

		8086	286	386	486
BACK: ADD	AX,[SI]	14	7	6	2
ADC	BX,0	4	3	2	1
INC	SI	2	2	2	1
INC	SI	2	2	2	1
DEC	CX	2	2	2	1
JNZ	BACK	16/4	7/3	7/3	3/1
total clocks per iteration		40	23	21	9

To calculate the total clocks for the five iterations, simply multiply the total number of clocks for one iteration by 5 and then adjust it for the last iteration, since the number of clocks for no jump in the last iteration is less than for jump in previous iterations. To adjust it, subtract the difference between the jump and no jump clock. For example, the total clocks for the five iterations in the 8086 column is $40 \times 5 = 200$, so adjusting for the last iteration involves subtracting 12 ($16 - 4 = 12$) from 200, which results in 188 clocks. The same procedure followed for the 80286, results in a total clocks of $(23 \times 5) - 4 = 111$.

The data above shows clearly the power of the newer generation of the 80x86 family. The same program originally written for 8086 machines runs twice as fast on Intel's 386 and four times faster on the 486 microprocessor. This plus the fact that 386/486 microprocessors have 32-bit data buses transferring data in and out of the CPU makes the case for the 386/486 even stronger.   Now the question is how much faster will it run if the program is rewritten to utilize the 32-bit processing power of the 386/486 CPU. This is shown next. Program 8-2 showed the 32-bit version of the same program. The iteration section of the program and the number of clocks for the 386 and 486 are as follows:

```
                                           386      486
BACK:  ADD    EAX,DWORD PTR [SI]            6        2
       ADD    SI,4                          2        1
       DEC    CX                            2        1
       JNZ    BACK                          7/3      3/1

total clocks per iteration                 17       7
```

Multiplying for the five iterations gives $(5 \times 17) - 4 = 81$ clocks for the 386 and $(5 \times 7) - 2 = 33$ clocks for the 486. By comparing the results above, one might conclude that rewriting all 16-bit programs for the 32-bit registers of the 386/486 is about 25% faster. That is true for some applications but not all. For example, examine the case of adding multibyte operands shown next. Compare the performance of Program 3-2 run across 80x86 CPUs. The following times assumed two clock cycles for m (memory fetch).

```
                  8086      286       386        486
BACK:  MOV AX,[SI]  10        5         4          1
       ADC AX,[DI]  14        7         6          2
       MOV [BX],AX  10        3         2          1
       INC SI        2        2         2          1
       INC SI        2        2         2          1
       INC DI        2        2         2          1
       INC DI        2        2         2          1
       INC BX        2        2         2          1
       INC BX        2        2         2          1
       LOOP BACK   17/5    (10)/4    (13)/11      7/6

total per iteration  53       37        37         17
for four iterations: 200     142       146         67
```

Now compare this result with the 32-bit version of the same program. The modified version was discussed in the preceding section (Program 8-4) and the clock count is as follows:

```
                                           386      486
     MOV    EAX,DWORD PTR DATA1             4        1
     ADD    EAX,DWORD PTR DATA2             6        2
     MOV    EBX,DWORD PTR DATA1+4           4        1
     ADC    EBX,DWORD PTR DATA2+4           6        2
     MOV    DWORD PTR DATA3,EAX             2        1
     MOV    DWORD PTR DATA3+4,EBX           2        1

total clocks for the entire operation:     24       8
```

In the 386, the clock count is reduced from 146 to 24, and for the 486 it is reduced from 67 to 8. Using the same hardware but changing the software to take advantage of the 32-bit capability of the 386/486 sped up the processing power 6-fold (146 divided by 24) and 8.5-fold (67 divided by 8), respectively, for the 386 and 486.   The discussion above clearly indicates there is a very heavy penalty associated with branching in the advanced processors. It also shows that if one wants to spend the resources and rewrite the old 16-bit programs for the new 32-bit architecture, it can be well worth the effort.

Review Questions

1. Compare the execution clocks (refer to Appendix B) for "ADD BX,AX" (ADD reg,reg) for the 8086, 286, 386, and 486 CPUs.
2. Using the 8086 as a base, show the increase in speed as a percentage for each processor in Question 1.
3. For instruction JNZ, compare the branch penalty for the 8086, 286, and 386. Assume that m=2.
   (a) in clocks   (b) in percent (notake/take $\times$ 100)

SUMMARY

The 386/486 CPUs represent a major inprovement over the 8086/286 in several areas. Not only are they much faster in terms of execution speed, they also have much better processing power because they are 32-bit machines. They are also capable of accessing an address range of 4 gigabytes of memory. The 386/486 was designed in such a way that all programs written for the 8086/286 will run on it with no modification. Other changes in the 386/486 include two additional segment registers and the ability to use general registers as pointers.

PROBLEMS

1. In a 386/486 program, show the content of each register indicated in parentheses after execution of the instruction.
   (a) MOV EAX,9823F4B6H   (AL,AH,AX and EAX)
   (b) MOV EBX,985C2H   (BL,BH,BX,EBX)
   (c) MOV EDX,2000000   (DL,DH,DX,EDX)
   (d) MOV ESI,120000H   (SI,ESI)
2. Show the destination and its contents in each of the following cases.
   (a) MOV   EAX,299FF94H
       ADD   EAX,34FFFFH
   (b) MOV   EBX,500 000
       ADD   EBX,700 000
   (c) MOV   EDX,40 000 000
       SUB   EDX,1 500 000
   (d) MOV   EAX,39393834H
       AND   EAX,0F0F0F0FH
   (e) MOV   EBX,9FE35DH
       XOR   EBX,0F0F0F0H
3. Using the little endian convention show the contents of the destination in each case.
   (a) MOV [SI],EAX   ;ASSUME SI=2000H AND EAX=9823F456H
   (b) MOV [BX],ECX   ;ASSUME BX,348CH AND ECX=1F23491H
   (c) MOV EBX,[DI]   ;ASSUME DI=4044H WITH THE
                                ;FOLLOWING DATA. ALL IN HEX.
   DS:4044=(92)
   DS:4045=(6D)
   DS:4046=(A2)
   DS:4047=(4C)
4. Compare the clock count for the 80x86 microprocessor in each case:
   (a) Write a program for the 8086/286 to transfer 50 words of data, one word (16 bits) at a time. Do not use string instructions.
   (b) Modify the program in part (a) to transfer 2 words (32 bits) at a time and calculate the clock count for the 386 and 486.
   In both parts (a) and (b), the clock count should be calculated for one iteration and for all iterations.
5. Instruction DAA, described in Chapter 3, works only on the AL register, regardless of which of Intel's 80x86 microprocessors is used. Write a program that adds

two multibyte packed BCD numbers, each 10 bytes wide (use the DT directive) and compare the clock count for one iteration if it is run on Intel's 8086, 286, 386, and 486 CPUs.

ANSWERS TO REVIEW QUESTIONS

Section 8.1: 80386/80486 Machines in Real Mode
1. 0 to 7, 8 to 15, 0 to 15, 0 to 31
2. 64K bytes
3. real mode is similar to the operation of 8086 machines; protected mode assigns a priority to programs and has other advanced features that take advantage of the 386's power
4. true
5. DS
6. allows use of 386 instructions
7. DS:148F = F9,   DS:1490 = 15,   DS:1491 = 24,   DS:1492 = 6B

Section 8.2: Some Simple 386/486 Programs
1. (a) 8; (b) 4; (c) 2; (d) 1
2. DD, DQ
3. .386, P386

Section 8.3: 80x86 Performance Comparison
1. 8086: 3   286: 2   386: 2   486: 1
2. 286 is a 33% improvement over 8086
   386 is a 0% improvement over 286
   486 is a 100% improvement over 386
3. (a) 8086: 8   286: 6   386: 6
   (b) 8086: 400   286: 300   386: 300

APPENDIX A: DEBUG PROGRAMMING

DEBUG is a program included in the MS-DOS and PC-DOS operating systems that allows the programmer to monitor a program's execution closely for debugging purposes. Specifically, it can be used to examine and alter the contents of memory, to enter and run programs, and to stop programs at certain points in order to check or even change data. This appendix provides a tutorial introduction to the DEBUG program. You will learn how to enter and exit DEBUG, how to enter, run, and debug programs, how to examine and alter the contents of registers and memory, plus some additional features of DEBUG that prove useful in program development. Numerous examples of Assembly language programming in DEBUG are given throughout and the appendix closes with a quick reference summary of the DEBUG commands.

First, a word should be said about the examples in this appendix. Within examples, what you should type in will be represented in italic caps:

ITALICS CAPS REPRESENT WHAT THE USER TYPES IN

and the response of the DEBUG program will be in bold caps:

BOLD CAPS REPRESENT THE COMPUTER RESPONSE

The examples in this appendix assume that the DEBUG program is in drive A and that your programs are on drive B. If your system is set up differently, you will need to keep this in mind when typing in drive specifications (such as "B:"). It is strongly suggested that you type in the examples in DEBUG and try them for yourself. The best way to learn is by doing!

SECTION A.1: ENTERING AND EXITING DEBUG

To enter the DEBUG program, simply type its name at the DOS level:

A>*DEBUG <return>*
-

"DEBUG" may be typed in either uppercase or lowercase. Again let us note that this example assumes that the DEBUG program is on the diskette in drive A. After "DEBUG" and the carriage return (or enter key) is typed in, the DEBUG prompt "-" will appear on the following line. DEBUG is now waiting for you to type in a command.

Now that you know how to enter DEBUG, you are ready to learn the DEBUG commands. The first command to learn is the quit command, to exit DEBUG.

The quit command, Q, may be typed in either uppercase or lowercase. This is true for all DEBUG commands. After the Q and carriage return have been entered, DEBUG will return you to the DOS level. This is shown in Example A-1, on the following page.

Example A-1: Entering and Exiting DEBUG

```
A>DEBUG <return>
-Q <return>
A>
```

SECTION A.2: EXAMINING AND ALTERING THE CONTENTS OF REGISTERS

The register command allows you to examine and/or alter the contents of the internal registers of the CPU. The R command has the following syntax:

R   <register name >

The R command will display all registers unless the optional <register name> field is entered. In the latter case, only the register named will be displayed.

Example A-2: Using the R Command to Display All Registers

```
A>DEBUG <return>
-R <return>

AX=0000 BX=0000 CX=0000 DX=0000 SP=FFEE BP=0000 SI=0000 DI=0000
DS=0C44 ES=0C44 SS=0C44 CS=0C44 IP=0100   NV UP DI PL NZ NA PO NC
0C44:0100 0000     ADD    [BX+SI],AL          DS:0000=CD
-
```

After the R and carriage return are typed in, DEBUG responds with three lines of information. The first line displays the general-purpose, pointer, and index registers' contents. The second line displays the segment registers' contents, the instruction pointer's current value, and the flag register bits. The codes at the end of line two, "NV UP DI ... NC", indicate the status of eight of the bits of the flag register. The flag register and its representation in DEBUG are discussed in Section A.6. The third line shows some information useful when you are programming in DEBUG. It shows the instruction pointed at by CS:IP. The third line on your system will vary from what is shown above. For the purpose at hand, concentrate on the first two lines. The explanation of the third line will be postponed until later in this appendix.

When you enter DEBUG initially, the general-purpose registers are set to zero and the flag bits are all reset. The contents of the segment registers will vary depending on the system you are using, but all segment registers will have the same value, which is decided by the DOS operating system. For instance, notice in Example A-2 above that all segment registers contain 0C44H. It is strongly recommended not to change the contents of the segment registers since these values have been set by the operating system. *Note:* In a later section of this appendix we show how to load an Assembly language program into DEBUG. In that case the segment registers are set according to the program parameters and registers BX and CX will contain the size of the program in bytes.

If the optional register name field is specified in the R command, DEBUG will display the contents of that register and give you an opportunity to change its value. This is seen next in Example A-3.

Example A-3: Using the R Command to Display/Modify Register

(a) Modifying the contents of a register

```
-R CX
CX 0000
:FFFF
-R CX
CX  FFFF
:
```

(b) DEBUG pads values on the left with zero

```
-R AX
AX 0000
:1
-R AX
AX 0001
:21
-R AX
AX 0021
:321
-R AX
AX 0321
:4321
-R AX
AX 4321
:54321
     ^ Error
```

(c) Entering data into the upper byte

```
-R DH
BR Error
-R DX
DX 0000
:4C00
-
```

Part (a) of Example A-3 first showed the R command followed by register name CX. DEBUG then displayed the contents of CX, which were 0000, and then displayed a colon ":". At this point a new value was typed in, and DEBUG prompted for another command with the "-" prompt. The next command verified that CX was indeed altered as requested. This time a carriage return was entered at the ":" prompt so that the value of CX was not changed.

Part (b) of Example A-3 showed that if fewer than four digits are typed in, DEBUG will pad on the left with zeros. Part (c) showed that you cannot access the upper and lower bytes separately with the R command. If you type in any digit other than 0 through F (such as in "2F0G"), DEBUG will display an error message and the register value will remain unchanged.

See Section A.6 for a discussion of how to use the R command to change the contents of the flag register.

SECTION A.3: CODING AND RUNNING PROGRAMS IN DEBUG

In the next few topics we explore how to enter simple Assembly language instructions, and assemble and run them. The purpose of this section is to familiarize the reader with using DEBUG, not to explain the Assembly language instructions found in the examples.

A, the Assemble command

The assemble command is used to enter Assembly language instructions into memory.

A   <starting address>

The starting address may be given as an offset number, in which case it is assumed to be an offset into the code segment, or the segment register can be specified explicitly. In other words, "A 100" and "A CS:100" will achieve the same results. When this command is entered at the command prompt "-", DEBUG will begin prompting you to enter Assembly language instructions. After an instruction is typed in and followed by <return>, DEBUG will prompt for the next instruction. This process is repeated until you type a <return> at the address prompt, at which time DEBUG will return you to the command prompt level. This is shown in part (a) of Example A-4.

Before you type in the commands of Example A-4, be aware that one important difference between DEBUG programming and Assembly language programming is that DEBUG assumes that all numbers are in hex, whereas most assemblers assume that numbers are in decimal unless they are followed by "H". Therefore, the Assembly language instruction examples in this section do not have "H" after the numbers as they would if an assembler were to be used. For example, you might enter an instruction such as "MOV AL,3F". In an Assembly language program written for MASM, for example, this would have been typed as "MOV AL,3FH".

Example A-4: Assemble, Unassemble, and Go Commands

(a) Assemble command

```
-A 100
103D:0100 MOV AX,1
103D:0103 MOV BX,2
103D:0106 MOV CX,3
103D:0109 ADD AX,BX
103D:010B ADD AX,CX
103D:010D INT 3
103D:010E
-
```

(b) Unassemble command

```
-U 100 10D
103D:0100 B80100        MOV     AX,0001
103D:0103 BB0200        MOV     BX,0002
103D:0106 B90300        MOV     CX,0003
103D:0109 01D8          ADD     AX,BX
103D:010B 01C8          ADD     AX,CX
103D:010D CC            INT     3
-
```

(c) Go command

```
-R
AX=0000  BX=0000  CX=0000  DX=0000  SP=CFDE  BP=0000  SI=0000  DI=0000
DS=103D  ES=103D  SS=103D  CS=103D  IP=0100   NV UP DI PL NZ NA PO NC
103D:0100 B80100        MOV     AX,0001
-G
AX=0006  BX=0002  CX=0003  DX=0000  SP=CFDE  BP=0000  SI=0000  DI=0000
DS=103D  ES=103D  SS=103D  CS=103D  IP=010D   NV UP DI PL NZ NA PE NC
103D:010D CC            INT     3
-
```

As you type the instructions in, DEBUG converts them to machine code. If you type in an instruction incorrectly such that DEBUG cannot assemble it, DEBUG will give you an error message and prompt you to try again. Again, keep in mind that the value for the code segment may be different on your machine when you run Example A-4. Notice that each time DEBUG prompts for the next instruction, the offset has been updated to the next available location. For example, after typing in the first instruction at offset 0100, DEBUG converted this to machine language, stored it in bytes 0100 to 0102, and prompted the user for the next instruction, which will be stored at offset 0103. *Note:* Do not assemble beginning at an offset lower than 100. The first 100H (256) bytes are reserved by DOS and should not be used by your programs. This is the reason that examples in this book use "A 100" to start assembling instructions after the first 100H bytes.

U, the unassemble command: looking at machine code

The unassemble command displays the machine code in memory along with their equivalent Assembly language instructions. The command can be given in either format shown below.

```
U       <starting address > <ending address>
U       <starting address > < L number of bytes>
```

Whereas the assemble instruction takes Assembly language instructions from the keyboard and converts them to machine code which it stores in memory, the unassemble instruction does the opposite. Unassemble takes machine code stored in memory and converts it back to Assembly language instructions to be displayed on the monitor. Look at part (b) of Example A-4 on the preceding page. The unassemble command was used to unassemble the code that was entered in part (a) with the assemble command. Notice that both the machine code and Assembly instructions are displayed. The command can be entered either with starting and ending addresses, as was shown in Example A-4: "U 100 10D", or it can be entered with a starting address and a number of bytes in hex. The same command in the second format would be "U 100 LD", which tells DEBUG to start unassembling at CS:100 for D bytes. If the U command is entered with no addresses after it: "U <return>", then DEBUG will display 32 bytes beginning at CS:IP. Successively entering "U <return>" commands will cause DEBUG to display consecutive bytes of the program, 32 bytes at a time. This is an easy way to look through a large program.

G, the go command

The go command instructs DEBUG to execute the instructions found between the two given addresses. Its format is

```
G       < = starting address> <stop address(es)>
```

If no addresses are given, DEBUG begins executing instructions at CS:IP until a breakpoint is reached. This was done in part (c) of Example A-4 on the preceding page. Before the instructions were executed, the R command was used to check the values of the registers. Since CS:IP pointed to the first instruction, the G command was entered, which caused execution of instructions up until "INT 3", which terminated execution. After a breakpoint is reached, DEBUG displays the register contents and returns you to the command prompt "-". Up to 10 stop addresses can be entered. DEBUG will stop execution at the first of these break-points that it reaches. This can be useful for programs that could take several different paths.

Example A-5: Various Forms of the Go Command

The program is first assembled:

```
-A 100
103D:0100 MOV AX,1
103D:0103 MOV BX,2
103D:0106 MOV CX,3
103D:0109 ADD AX,BX
103D:010B ADD AX,CX
103D:010D INT 3
103D:010E
```

(a) Go command in form "G"

```
-G
AX=0006 BX=0002 CX=0003 DX=0000 SP=CFDE BP=0000 SI=0000 DI=0000
DS=103D ES=103D SS=103D CS=103D IP=010D  NV UP DI PL NZ NA PE NC
103D:010D CC         INT    3
-
```

(b) Go command in form "G = start address"

```
-G =100
AX=0006 BX=0002 CX=0003 DX=0000 SP=CFDE BP=0000 SI=0000 DI=0000
DS=103D ES=103D SS=103D CS=103D IP=010D  NV UP DI PL NZ NA PE NC
103D:010D CC         INT    3
-
```

(c) Go command form "G = start address ending address"

```
-G =100 109
AX=0001 BX=0002 CX=0003 DX=0000 SP=CFDE BP=0000 SI=0000 DI=0000
DS=103D ES=103D SS=103D CS=103D IP=0109  NV UP DI PL NZ NA PE NC
103D:0109 01D8        ADD    AX,BX
-
```

(d) Go command format "G   address"

```
-R IP
 IP 0109
  :0100
-G 109
AX=0001 BX=0002 CX=0003 DX=0000 SP=CFDE BP=0000 SI=0000 DI=0000
DS=103D ES=103D SS=103D CS=103D IP=0109  NV UP DI PL NZ NA PE NC
103D:0109 01D8        ADD    AX,BX
-
```

At this point the third line of the register dump has become useful. The purpose of the third line is to show the location, machine code, and Assembly code of the next instruction to be executed. In Example A-5, look at the last line in the register dump given after the G command. Notice at the leftmost part of line three, the value CS:IP. The values for CS and IP match those given in lines one and two. After CS:IP is the machine code, and after the machine code is the Assembly language instruction.

Part (a) of Example A-5 is the same as part (c) of Example A-4. The go command started at CS:IP and executed instructions until it reached instruction "INT 3". Part (b) gave a starting address but no ending address; therefore, DEBUG executed instructions from offset 100 until "INT 3" was reached. This could also have been typed in as "G =CS:100". Part (c) gave both starting and ending addresses. We can see from the register results that it did execute from offset 100 to 109. Part (d) gave only the ending address. When the start address is not given explicitly, DEBUG uses the value in register IP. Be sure to check that value with the register command before issuing the go command without a start address.

T, the trace command: a powerful debugging tool

The trace command allows you to trace through the execution of your programs one or more instructions at a time to verify the effect of the programs on registers and/or data.

T   <= starting address> <number of instructions>

This tells DEBUG to begin executing instructions at the starting address. DEBUG will execute; however, many instructions have been requested in the second field. The default value is 1 if no second field is given. The trace command functions similarly to the go command in that if no starting address is specified, it starts at CS:IP. The difference between this command and the go command is that trace will display the register contents after each instruction, whereas the go command does not display them until after termination of the program. Another difference is that the last field of the go command is the stop address, whereas the last field of the trace command is the number of instructions to execute.

Example A-6 shows a trace of the instructions entered in part (a) of Example A-4. Notice the way that register IP is updated after each instruction to point to the next instruction. The third line of the register display shows the instruction pointed at by IP, that is, the next instruction to be executed. Tracing through a program allows you to examine what is happening in each instruction of the program. Notice the value of AX after each instruction in Example A-6.

Example A-6: Trace Command

```
-T=100 5
 AX=0001 BX=0000 CX=0000 DX=0000 SP=CFDE BP=0000 SI=0000 DI=0000
 DS=103D ES=103D SS=103D CS=103D IP=0103  NV UP DI PL NZ NA PO NC
 103D:0103 BB0200     MOV    BX,0002

 AX=0001 BX=0002 CX=0000 DX=0000 SP=CFDE BP=0000 SI=0000 DI=0000
 DS=103D ES=103D SS=103D CS=103D IP=0106  NV UP DI PL NZ NA PO NC
 103D:0106 B90200     MOV    CX,0003

 AX=0001 BX=0002 CX=0003 DX=0000 SP=CFDE BP=0000 SI=0000 DI=0000
 DS=103D ES=103D SS=103D CS=103D IP=0109  NV UP DI PL NZ NA PO NC
 103D:0109 01D8       ADD    AX,BX

 AX=0003 BX=0002 CX=0003 DX=0000 SP=CFDE BP=0000 SI=0000 DI=0000
 DS=103D ES=103D SS=103D CS=103D IP=010B  NV UP DI PL NZ NA PE NC
 103D:010B 01C8       ADD    AX,CX

 AX=0006 BX=0002 CX=0003 DX=0000 SP=CFDE BP=0000 SI=0000 DI=0000
 DS=103D ES=103D SS=103D CS=103D IP=010D  NV UP DI PL NZ NA PE NC
 103D:010D CC         INT    3
-
```

The same trace as shown in Example A-6 could have been achieved with the command "-T 5", assuming that IP = 0100. Experiment with the various forms of the trace command. "T" with no starting or count fields will execute one instruction starting at CS:IP. If no first field is given, CS:IP is assumed. If no second field is given, 1 is assumed.

If you trace a large number of instructions, it may scroll upward off the screen faster than you can read it. <Ctrl-num lock > can be used to stop the scrolling temporarily. To resume the scrolling, enter any key. This works not only on the trace command, but for any command that displays information to the screen.

Example A-7: Moving Data into 8- and 16-bit Registers

```
A>DEBUG
-R
AX=0000 BX=0000 CX=0000 DX=0000 SP=CFDE BP=0000 SI=0000 DI=0000
DS=103D ES=103D SS=103D CS=103D IP=0100   NV UP DI PL NZ NA PO NC
103D:0100 B664        MOV     DH,64
-A 100

103D:0100 MOV AL,3F
103D:0102 MOV BH,04
103D:0104 MOV CX,FFFF
103D:0107 MOV CL,BH
103D:0109 MOV CX,1
103D:010C INT 3
103D:010D
-T =100 5
AX=003F BX=0000 CX=0000 DX=0000 SP=CFDE BP=0000 SI=0000 DI=0000
DS=103D ES=103D SS=103D CS=103D IP=0102   NV UP DI PL NZ NA PO NC
103D:0102 B704        MOV     BH,04

AX=003F BX=0400 CX=0000 DX=0000 SP=CFDE BP=0000 SI=0000 DI=0000
DS=103D ES=103D SS=103D CS=103D IP=0104   NV UP DI PL NZ NA PO NC
103D:0104 B9FFFF      MOV     CX,FFFF

AX=003F BX=0400 CX=FFFF DX=0000 SP=CFDE BP=0000 SI=0000 DI=0000
DS=103D ES=103D SS=103D CS=103D IP=0107   NV UP DI PL NZ NA PO NC
103D:0107 88F9        MOV     CL,BH

AX=003F BX=0400 CX=FF04 DX=0000 SP=CFDE BP=0000 SI=0000 DI=0000
DS=103D ES=103D SS=103D CS=103D IP=0109   NV UP DI PL NZ NA PO NC
103D:0109 B90100      MOV     CX,0001

AX=003F BX=0400 CX=0001 DX=0000 SP=CFDE BP=0000 SI=0000 DI=0000
DS=103D ES=103D SS=103D CS=103D IP=010C   NV UP DI PL NZ NA PO NC
103D:010C CC          INT     3
-
```

Example A-8 shows some common programming errors in moving data into registers. The DEBUG assemble command catches this type of error when an instruction is entered and it tries to assemble it. In instruction "MOV DS,1200" the error is that immediate data cannot be moved into a segment register. The other errors involve move instructions, where the first and second operands do not match in size.

Example A-8: Common Errors in Register Usage

```
A>DEBUG
-A 100
103D:0100 MOV AL,FF3
          ^ Error
103D:0100 MOV AX,12345
             ^ Error
103D:0100 MOV DS,1200
             ^ Error
103D:0100 MOV SI,DH
          ^ Error
103D:0100 MOV AX,BH
             ^ Error
103D:0100 MOV AL,BX
             ^ Error
103D:0100
-Q
A>
```

Example A-9: Assembling and Unassembling a Program

```
A>DEBUG
-R
AX=0000 BX=0000 CX=0000 DX=0000 SP=CFDE BP=0000 SI=0000 DI=0000
DS=1132 ES=1132 SS=1132 CS=1132 IP=0100   NV UP DI PL NZ NA PO NC
1132:0100 BED548     MOV    SI,48D5
-A 100
1132:0100 MOV AL,57
1132:0102 MOV DH,86
1132:0104 MOV DL,72
1132:0106 MOV CX,DX
1132:0108 MOV BH,AL
1132:010A MOV BL,9F
1132:010C MOV AH,20
1132:010E ADD AX,DX
1132:0110 ADD CX,BX
1132:0112 ADD AX,1F35
1132:0115
-U 100 112
1132:0100 B057         MOV    AL,57
1132:0102 B686         MOV    DH,86
1132:0104 B272         MOV    DL,72
1132:0106 89D1         MOV    CX,DX
1132:0108 88C7         MOV    BH,AL
1132:010A B39F         MOV    BL,9F
1132:010C B420         MOV    AH,20
1132:010E 01D0         ADD    AX,DX
1132:0110 01D9         ADD    CX,BX
1132:0112 05351F       ADD    AX,1F35
-
```

The program above is stored starting at CS:IP of 1132:0100. This logical address corresponds to physical address 11420 (11320 + 0100). Refer to Chapter 1 for a discussion of physical versus logical addresses in 80x86 CPUs.

SECTION A.4: DATA MANIPULATION IN DEBUG

Next are described three DEBUG commands that are used to examine or alter the contents of memory.

F   the fill command fills a block of memory with data
D   the dump command displays contents of memory to the screen
E   the enter command examines/alters the contents of memory

F, the fill command: filling memory with data

The fill command is used to fill an area of memory with a data item. The syntax of the F command is as follows:

F   <starting address > <ending address> <data>
F   <starting address > < L number of bytes > <data>

This command is useful for filling a block of memory with data, for example to initialize an area of memory with zeros. Normally, you will want to use this command to fill areas of the data segment, in which case the starting and ending addresses would be offset addresses into the data segment. To fill another segment, the register should precede the offset. For example, the first command below would fill 16 bytes, from DS:100 to DS:10F with FF. The second command would fill a 256-byte block of the code segment, from CS:100 to CS:1FF with ASCII 20 (space).

F 100 10F FF
F CS:100 1FF 20

Example A-10 demonstrates the use of the F command. The data can be a series of items, in which case DEBUG will fill the area of memory with that pattern of data, repeating the pattern over and over. For example:

F 100 L20 00 FF

The command above would cause 20 hex bytes (32 decimal) starting at DS:100 to be filled alternately with 00 and FF.

D, the dump command: examining the contents of memory

The dump command is used to examine the contents of memory. The syntax of the D command is as follows:

D   <start address > <end address>
D   <start address > < L number of bytes>

The D command can be entered with a starting and ending address, in which case it will display all the bytes between those locations. It can also be entered with a starting address and a number of bytes (in hex), in which case it will display from the starting address for that number of bytes. If the address is an offset, DS is assumed. The D command can also be entered by itself, in which case DEBUG will display 128 consecutive bytes beginning at DS:100. Then next time "D" is entered by itself, DEBUG will display 128 bytes beginning at wherever the last display command left off. In this way, one can easily look through a large area of memory, 128 bytes at a time.

Example A-10: Filling and Dumping a Block of Memory

(a) Fill and dump commands

```
A>DEBUG
-F 100 14F 20
-F 150 19F 00
-D 100 19F
103D:0100  20 20 20 20 20 20 20 20-20 20 20 20 20 20 20 20
103D:0110  20 20 20 20 20 20 20 20-20 20 20 20 20 20 20 20
103D:0120  20 20 20 20 20 20 20 20-20 20 20 20 20 20 20 20
103D:0130  20 20 20 20 20 20 20 20-20 20 20 20 20 20 20 20
103D:0140  20 20 20 20 20 20 20 20-20 20 20 20 20 20 20 20
103D:0150  00 00 00 00 00 00 00 00-00 00 00 00 00 00 00 00  ...............
103D:0160  00 00 00 00 00 00 00 00-00 00 00 00 00 00 00 00  ...............
103D:0170  00 00 00 00 00 00 00 00-00 00 00 00 00 00 00 00  ...............
103D:0180  00 00 00 00 00 00 00 00-00 00 00 00 00 00 00 00  ...............
103D:0190  00 00 00 00 00 00 00 00-00 00 00 00 00 00 00 00  ...............
-
```

(b) Filling and dumping selected memory locations

```
-F 104 10A FF
-D 104 10A
103D:0104  FF FF FF FF-FF FF FF                              .......
-D 100 10F
103D:0100  20 20 20 20 FF FF FF FF-FF FF FF 20 20 20 20 20   .......
-
```

(c) Filling and dumping code segment memory

```
-F CS:100 12F 20
-D CS:100 12F
103D:0100  20 20 20 20 20 20 20 20-20 20 20 20 20 20 20 20
103D:0110  20 20 20 20 20 20 20 20-20 20 20 20 20 20 20 20
103D:0120  20 20 20 20 20 20 20 20-20 20 20 20 20 20 20 20
-
```

Example A-10, on the preceding page, demonstrates use of the fill and dump commands. Part (a) shows two fill commands to fill areas of the data segment, which are then dumped. Part (b) was included to show that small areas of memory can be filled and dumped. Part (c) shows how to fill and dump to memory from other segments. Keep in mind that the values for DS and CS may be different on your machine.

It is important to become thoroughly familiar with the format in which DEBUG dumps memory. Example A-11 provides further practice in dumping areas of memory.

Example A-11: Using the Dump Command to Examine Machine Code

```
-U 100 112
1132:0100 B057          MOV    AL,57
1132:0102 B686          MOV    DH,86
1132:0104 B272          MOV    DL,72
1132:0106 89D1          MOV    CX,DX
1132:0108 88C7          MOV    BH,AL
1132:010A B39F          MOV    BL,9F
1132:010C B420          MOV    AH,20
1132:010E 01D0          ADD    AX,DX
1132:0110 01D9          ADD    CX,BX
1132:0112 05351F        ADD    AX,1F35
-D CS:100 11F
1132:0100  B0 57 B6 86 B2 72 89 D1-88 C7 B3 9F B4 20 01 D0  0W6.2r.Q.G3.4 .P
1132:0110  01 D9 05 35 1F 19 83 3E-E3 45 00 74 12 53 56 BB  .Y.5t..cE.t.SV;
-
```

Example A-11 shows a program being unassembled that had been loaded previously into DEBUG. Below that, the portion of the code segment containing the program is dumped. Notice that the machine codes are stored one after another continuously. It is important to become thoroughly familiar with the way DEBUG dumps memory. The following is one line from Example A-11:

```
1132:0100  B0 57 B6 86 B2 72 89 D1-88 C7 B3 9F B4 20 01 D0  0W6.2r.Q.G3.4 .P
```

The line begins with the address of the first byte displayed on that line, in this case 1132:0100, with 1132 representing the contents of CS and 0100 being the offset into the code segment. After the address, 16 bytes of data are displayed followed by a display of those items. Bytes that contain ASCII characters will display the characters. If the contents of a byte are not an ASCII code, it is not displayable and will be represented by ".". The first byte displayed above is offset 0100, the second offset 0101, the third offset 0102, and so on, until the last byte on that line, which is offset 010F.

```
OFFSET:    100 101 102 103 104 105 106 107-108 109 10A 10B 10C 10D 10E 10F

1132:0100  B0  57  B6  86  B2  72  89  D1-  88  C7  B3  9F  B4  20  01  D0
```

The addresses displayed are logical addresses. The logical address of 1132:0100 above would correspond to physical address 11420 (11320 + 0100 = 11420).

E, the enter command: entering data into memory

The fill command was used to fill a block with the same data item. The enter command can be used to enter a list of data into a certain portion of memory. The syntax of the E command is as follows:

```
E        <address > <data list>
E        <address>
```

Example A-12: Using the E Command to Enter Data into Memory

(a) Entering data with the E command

```
-E 100 'John Snith'
-D 100 10F
103D:0100  4A 6F 68 6E 20 53 6E 69-74 68 20 20 20 20 20 20  John Snith
```

(b) Altering data with the E command

```
-E 106
103D:0106  6E.6D
-D 100 10F
103D:0100  4A 6F 68 6E 20 53 6D 69-74 68 20 20 20 20 20 20  John Smith
```

(c) Another way to alter data with the E command,
    hitting the space bar to go through the data a byte at a time

```
-E 100
103D:0100 4A.  6F.  68.  6E.  20.  53.  6E.6D
-D 100 10F
103D:0100  4A 6F 68 6E 20 53 6D 69-74 68 20 20 20 20 20 20  John Smith
-
```

(d) Another way to alter data with the E command

```
-E 107
103D:0107 69.-
103D:0106 6E.6D
-
```

Part (a) of Example A-12 showed the simplest use of the E command, entering the starting address, followed by the data. That example showed how to enter ASCII data, which can be enclosed in either single or double quotes. The E command has another powerful feature: the ability to examine and alter memory byte by byte. If the E command is entered with a specific address and no data list, DEBUG assumes that you wish to examine that byte of memory and possibly alter it. After that byte is displayed, you have four options:

1. You can enter a new data item for that byte. DEBUG will replace the old contents with the new value you typed in.
2. You can hit <return>, which indicates that you do not wish to change the value.
3. You can hit the space bar, which will leave the displayed byte unchanged but will display the next byte and give you a chance to change that if you wish.
4. You can enter a minus sign, "-", which will leave the displayed byte unchanged but will display the previous byte and give you a chance to change it.

Look at part (b) in Example A-12. The user wants to change "Snith" to "Smith". After the user typed in "E 106", DEBUG responded with the contents of that byte, 6E, which is ASCII for n, and prompted with a ".". Then the user typed in the ASCII code for "m", 6D, and entered carriage return and then dumped the data to see if the correction was made. Part (c) of Example A-12 showed another way to make the same correction. The user started at memory offset 100 and pressed that space bar continuously until the desired location was reached. Then he made the correction and pressed carriage return.

Finally, part (d) showed a third way the same correction could have been made. In this example, the user accidentally entered the wrong address. The address was one byte past the one that needed correction. The user entered a minus sign, which caused DEBUG to display the previous byte on the next line. Then the correction was made to that byte. Try these examples yourself since the E command will prove very useful in debugging your future programs.

The E command can be used to enter numerical data as well:

E 100 23 B4 02 4F

Example A-13 gives an example of entering code with the assemble command, entering data with the enter command, and running the program. This use of the E command is common in program testing and debugging. Example A-14 shows the little endian storage convention of 80x86 microprocessors.

Example A-13: Entering Data and Code and Running a Program

```
A>DEBUG
-A 100
103D:0100 MOV AL,00
103D:0102 ADD AL,[0200]
103D:0106 ADD AL,[0201]
103D:010A ADD AL,[0202]
103D:010E ADD AL,[0203]
103D:0112 ADD AL,[0204]
103D:0116 INT 3
103D:0117
-E DS:0200 25 12 15 1F 2B
-D DS:0200 020F
103D:0200  25 12 15 1F 2B 02 00 E8-51 FF C3 E8 1E F6 74 03   %...+..hQ.Ch.vt.
-G =100 116
AX=0096  BX=0000  CX=0000  DX=0000  SP=CFDE  BP=0000  SI=0000  DI=0000
CS=103D  ES=103D  SS=103D  CS=103D  IP=0116   OV UP DI NG NZ AC PE NC
103D:0116 CC        INT    3
-
```

Example A-14: How the 80x86 Stores Words: Little Endian

(a) Moving a word from memory into a register

```
A>DEBUG
-D 6820 LF
103D:6820  26 00 EA 27 CF 5B 48 22-0D 00 B8 15 45 00 EA 20   &.j'O[H"..8.E.j
-A 100
103D:0100 MOV BX,[6826]
103D:0104 INT 3
103D:0105
-T
AX=0000  BX=2248  CX=0000  DX=0000  SP=CFDE  BP=0000  SI=0000  DI=0000
DS=103D  ES=103D  SS=103D  CS=103D  IP=0104   NV UP DI PL NZ NA PO NC
103D:0104 CC        INT    3
-
```

(b) Moving a word from a register into memory

```
-D 200 20F
103D:0200  F2 FF 0E 0B 37 B8 FF FF-50 E8 B3 08 83 C4 02 20   R...78..Ph3..D.
-A 100
103D:0100 MOV BX,1234
103D:0103 MOV [200],BX
103D:0107 INT 3
103D:0108
-G =100
AX=0000  BX=1234  CX=0000  DX=0000  SP=CFDE  BP=0000  SI=0000  DI=0000
DS=103D  ES=103D  SS=103D  CS=103D  IP=0107   NV UP DI PL NZ NA PO NC
103D:0107 CC        INT    3
-D 200 LF
103D:0200  34 12 0E 0B 37 B8 FF FF-50 E8 B3 08 83 C4 02 20   4...78..Ph3..D.
-
```

In Example A-14, part (a), the direct addressing mode was used to move the two bytes beginning at offset 6826 to register BX. Looking at the dump shows that location 6826 contains 48 and the following byte at offset 6827 contains 22. These bytes were moved into register BX in low byte to low byte, high byte to high byte order. The contents of lower memory location 6826, which were 48, were moved to the low byte, BL. The contents of higher memory location 6827, which were 22, were moved to the high byte, BH. In part (b), value 1234H was moved into register BX and then stored at offset 200. Notice that offset address 200 contains the lower byte 34 and the higher offset address 201 contains the upper byte 12.

SECTION A.5: EXAMINING THE STACK IN DEBUG

In this sections we explore the implementation of the stack in 80x86 Assembly language programming and how the stack can be examined through DEBUG. This section should be covered after Section 1.5 in Chapter 1.

Pushing onto the stack

Example A-15 demonstrates how the stack is affected by PUSH instructions. First the assemble command is used to enter instructions that load three registers with 16-bit data, initialize the stack pointer to 1236H, and push the three registers onto the stack. Then the instructions are executed with the go command and the contents of the stack examined with the dump command. The following shows the contents of the stack area after each push instruction, assuming that SP = 1236 before the first push. Notice that the stack grows "upward" from higher memory locations toward lower memory locations. After each push, the stack pointer is decremented by 2.

```
SP = 1236
After "PUSH AX"
      103D:1230  00 00 00 00 B6 24 00 00-00 00 00 00 00 00 00 00
SP = 1234
After "PUSH DI"
      103D:1230  00 00 C2 85 B6 24 00 00-00 00 00 00 00 00 00 00
SP = 1232
After "PUSH DX"
      103D:1230  93 5F C2 85 B6 24 00 00-00 00 00 00 00 00 00 00
SP = 1230
```

Example A-15: Pushing Onto the Stack

```
A>DEBUG
-A 100
103D:0100 MOV AX,24B6
103D:0103 MOV DI,85C2
103D:0106 MOV DX,5F93
103D:0109 MOV SP,1236
103D:010C PUSH AX
103D:010D PUSH DI
103D:010E PUSH DX
103D:010F INT 3
103D:0110
-F 1230 123F 00
-D 1230 LF
103D:1230  00 00 00 00 00 00 00 00-00 00 00 00 00 00 00 00  ...............
-G =100
AX=24B6  BX=0000  CX=0000  DX=5F93  SP=1230  BP=0000  SI=0000  DI=85C2
DS=103D  ES=103D  SS=103D  CS=103D  IP=010F   NV UP DI PL NZ NA PO NC
103D:010F CC        INT    3
-D 1230 123F
103D:1230  93 5F C2 85 B6 24 00 00-00 00 00 00 00 00 00 00  ._B.6$.........
```

Popping the stack

Example A-16 demonstrates the effect of pop instructions on the stack. The trace shows that after each pop is executed, the stack pointer SP is incremented by 2. As the stack is popped, it shrinks "downward" toward the higher memory addresses.

Example A-16: Popping the Stack Contents into Registers

```
-A 100
103D:0100 MOV SP,18FA
103D:0103 POP CX
103D:0104 POP DX
103D:0105 POP BX
103D:0106 INT 3
103D:0107
-E SS:18FA 23 14 6B 2C 91 F6
-D 18FA 18FF
103D:18FA  23 14 6B 2C 91 F6                         #.k,.v
-R IP
IP 010F
:0100
-T
AX=24B6  BX=0000  CX=0000  DX=5F93  SP=18FA  BP=0000  SI=0000  DI=85C2
DS=103D  ES=103D  SS=103D  CS=103D  IP=0103   NV UP DI PL NZ NA PO NC
103D:0103 59        POP    CX
-T
AX=24B6  BX=0000  CX=1423  DX=5F93  SP=18FC  BP=0000  SI=0000  DI=85C2
DS=103D  ES=103D  SS=103D  CS=103D  IP=0104   NV UP DI PL NZ NA PO NC
103D:0104 5A        POP    DX
-T
AX=24B6  BX=0000  CX=1423  DX=2C6B  SP=18FE  BP=0000  SI=0000  DI=85C2
DS=103D  ES=103D  SS=103D  CS=103D  IP=0105   NV UP DI PL NZ NA PO NC
103D:0105 5B        POP    BX
-T
AX=24B6  BX=F691  CX=1423  DX=2C6B  SP=1900  BP=0000  SI=0000  DI=85C2
DS=103D  ES=103D  SS=103D  CS=103D  IP=0106   NV UP DI PL NZ NA PO NC
103D:0106 CC        INT    3
-
```

SECTION A.6: EXAMINING/ALTERING THE FLAG REGISTER IN DEBUG

The discussion of how to use the R command to examine/alter the contents of the flag register was postponed until this section, so that program examples that affect the flag bits could be included. Table A-1, on the following page, gives the codes for 8 bits of the flag register which are displayed whenever a G, T, or R DEBUG command is given.

If all the bits of the flag register were reset to zero, as is the case when DEBUG is first entered, the following would be displayed for the flag register:

NV UP DI PL NZ NA PO NC

Similarly, if all the flag bits were set to 1, the following would be seen:

OV DN EI NG ZR AC PE CY

Example A-17 shows how to use the R command to change the setting of the flag register.

Example A-17: Changing the Flag Register Contents

```
-R F
NV UP DI PL NZ NA PO NC -DN OV NG
-R F
OV DN DI NG NZ NA PO NC -
-
```

Example A-17 on the preceding page showed how the flag register can be examined, or examined and then altered. When the R command is followed by "F", this tells DEBUG to display the contents of the flag register. After DEBUG displays the flag register codes, it prompts with another "-" at the end of the line of register codes. At this point, flag register codes may be typed in to alter the flag register, or a simple carriage return may be typed in if no changes are needed. The register codes may be typed in any order.

Table A-1: Codes for the Flag Register

Flag	Code When Set (=1)	Code When Reset (= 0)
OF overflow flag	OV (overflow)	NV (no overflow)
DF direction flag	DN (down)	UP (up)
IF interrupt flag	EI (enable interrupt)	DI (disable interrupt)
SF sign flag	NG (negative)	PL (plus, or positive)
ZF zero flag	ZR (zero)	NZ (not zero)
AF auxiliary carry flag	AC (auxiliary carry)	NA (no auxiliary carry)
PF parity flag	PE (parity even)	PO (parity odd)
CF carry flag	CY (carry)	(NC (no carry)

Impact of instructions on the flag bits

Example A-18, on the following page, shows the effect of ADD instructions on the flag register. The ADD in Part (a) involved byte addition. Adding 9C and 64 results in 00 with a carry out. The flag bits indicate that this was the result. Notice the zero flag is now ZR, indicating that the result is zero. In addition, the carry flag was set, indicating the carry out. The ADD in part (b) involves word addition. Notice that the sign flag was set to NG after the ADD instruction was executed. This is because the result, CAE0, in its binary form will have a 1 in bit 15, the sign bit. Since we are dealing with unsigned addition, we interpret this number to be positive CAE0H, not a negative number. This points out the fact that the microprocessor treats all data the same. It is up to the programmer to interpret the meaning of the data. Finally, look at the ADD in part (c). Adding AAAAH and 5556H gives 10000H, which results in BX = 0000 with a carry out. The zero flag indicates the zero result (BX = 0000), while the carry flag indicates that a carry out occurred.

Hexarithmetic command

This command is like an on-line hex calculator that performs hex addition and subtractions. Its format is

H   <number 1> <number 2>

When this command is entered at the DEBUG "-" prompt, DEBUG will display their sum followed by their difference (number 1 - number 2).

Procedure command

This command has a syntax similar to the trace command:

P   < = start address> <number of instructions>

It is used to execute a loop, call, interrupt or repeat string operation as if it were a single instruction instead of tracing through every instruction in that procedure.

Example A-18: Observing Changes in the Flag Register

```
(a)

A>DEBUG
-A 100
103D:0100 MOV AL,9C
103D:0102 MOV DH,64
103D:0104 ADD AL,DH
103D:0106 INT 3
103D:0107
-T 3
AX=009C BX=0000 CX=0000 DX=0000 SP=CFDE BP=0000 SI=0000 DI=0000
DS=103D ES=103D SS=103D CS=103D IP=0102   NV UP DI PL NZ NA PO NC
103D:0102 B664      MOV     DH,64

AX=009C BX=0000 CX=0000 DX=6400 SP=CFDE BP=0000 SI=0000 DI=0000
DS=103D ES=103D SS=103D CS=103D IP=0104   NV UP DI PL NZ NA PO NC
103D:0104 00F0      ADD     AL,DH

AX=0000 BX=0000 CX=0000 DX=6400 SP=CFDE BP=0000 SI=0000 DI=0000
DS=103D ES=103D SS=103D CS=103D IP=0106   NV UP DI PL ZR AC PE CY
103D:0106 CC        INT     3
-


(b)

-A 100
103D:0100 MOV AX,34F5
103D:0103 ADD AX,95EB
103D:0106 INT 3
103D:0107
-T =100 2
AX=34F5 BX=0000 CX=0000 DX=6400 SP=CFDE BP=0000 SI=0000 DI=0000
DS=103D ES=103D SS=103D CS=103D IP=0103   NV UP DI PL NZ NA PO NC
103D:0103 05EB95    ADD     AX,95EB

AX=CAE0 BX=0000 CX=0000 DX=6400 SP=CFDE BP=0000 SI=0000 DI=0000
DS=103D ES=103D SS=103D CS=103D IP=0106   NV UP DI NG NZ AC PO NC
103D:0106 CC        INT     3
-


(c)

-A 100
103D:0100 MOV BX,AAAA
103D:0103 ADD BX,5556
103D:0107 INT 3
103D:0108
-G =100 107
AX=34F5 BX=0000 CX=0000 DX=6400 SP=CFDE BP=0000 SI=0000 DI=0000
DS=103D ES=103D SS=103D CS=103D IP=0107   NV UP DI PL ZR AC PE CY
103D:0107 CC        INT     3
-
```

Example A-19, on the following page, shows how to code a simple program in DEBUG, set up the desired data, and execute the program. This program includes a conditional jump that will decide whether to jump based on the value of the zero flag. This example also points out some important differences between coding a program in DEBUG and coding a program for an assembler such as MASM. First notice the JNZ instruction. If this were an Assembly language program, the instruction might be "JNZ LOOP_ADD", where the label LOOP_ADD refers to a line of code. In DEBUG we simply JNZ to the address. Another important difference is that an Assembly language program would have separate data and code segments. In Example A-19, the test data was entered at offset 0200, and consequently, BX was set to 0200 since it is being used as a pointer to the data. In an Assembly language program, the data would have been set up in the data segment and the instruction might have been "MOV BX,OFFSET DATA1" where DATA1 is the label associated with the data directive that stored the data.

Example A-19: Tracing through a Program to Add 5 Bytes

```
A>DEBUG
-A 100
103D:0100 MOV CX,05
103D:0103 MOV BX,0200
103D:0106 MOV AL,0
103D:0108 ADD AL,[BX]
103D:010A INC BX
103D:010B DEC CX
103D:010C JNZ 0108
103D:010E MOV [0205],AL
103D:0111 INT 3
103D:0112
-E 0200 25 12 15 1F 2B
-D 0200 020F
103D:0200  25 12 15 1F 2B 9A DE CE-1E F3 20 20 20 20 20 20  %...+.^n.
-G =100 111
AX=0096 BX=0205 CX=0000 DX=0000 SP=CFDE BP=0000 SI=0000 DI=0000
DS=103D ES=103D SS=103D CS=103D IP=0111   NV UP DI PL ZR NA PE NC
103D:0111 CC        INT   3


-D 0200 020F
103D:0200  25 12 15 1F 2B 96 DE CE-1E F3 20 20 20 20 20 20  %...+.^n.
```

Example A-20: Data Transfer Program in DEBUG

```
A>DEBUG
-A 100
103D:0100 MOV SI,0210
103D:0103 MOV DI,0228
103D:0106 MOV CX,6
103D:0109 MOV AL,[SI]
103D:010B MOV [DI],AL
103D:010D INC SI
103D:010E INC DI
103D:010F DEC CX
103D:0110 JNZ 0109
103D:0112 INT 3
103D:0113
-E 0210 25 4F 85 1F 2B C4
-D 0210 022F
103D:0210  25 4F 85 1F 2B C4 43 0C-01 01 01 00 02 FF FF FF  %O..+DC........
103D:0220  FF FF FF FF FF FF FF FF-FF FF FF FF 45 0D CA 2A  ...........E.J*
-G =100
AX=00C4 BX-0000 CX=0000 DX=0000 SP=CFDE BP=0000 SI=0216 DI=022E
DS=103D ES=103D SS=103D CS=103D IP=0112   NV UP DI PL ZR NA PE NC
103D:0112 CC        INT   3
-D 0210 022F
103D:0210  25 4F 85 1F 2B C4 43 0C-01 01 01 00 02 FF FF FF  %O..+DC........
103D:0220  FF FF FF FF FF FF FF FF-25 4F 85 1F 2B C4 CA 2A  ........%O..+DJ*
-
```

SECTION A.7: ADDITIONAL DEBUG DATA MANIPULATION COMMANDS

The following commands are often useful in manipulating the data in your programs.

M, the move command: copying data from one location to another

The move command is used to copy data from one location to another. The original location will remain unchanged. The syntax of this command is

M   <starting address> <ending address> <destination address>

M   <starting address> <L number of bytes> <destination address>

In other words, this command will place a copy of the data found from starting address to ending address at the destination address. Part (a) in Example A-21, on the following page, gives an example of using the move command. This command copied the data found in locations 130 to 13f to location 140. The same result could have been achieved by "M 130 LF 140".

C, the compare command: checking blocks of data for differences

The compare command is used to check two areas of memory and display bytes that contain different data. If the two blocks are identical, DEBUG will simply display the command prompt "-". The syntax of the command is

C   <starting address> <ending address> <compare address>
C   <starting address> < L number of bytes> <compare address>

In other words, this command will compare the data found from the starting address to the ending address with the data found beginning at the compare address and will display any bytes which differ. Part (b) in Example A-21 contains examples of using the compare command. The first command compared from offsets 130 to 134 with memory beginning at location 140. Since no differences were found, DEBUG responded with the command prompt "-". That command could also have been entered as "C 130 L5 140". The next command compared from offsets 130 to 134 with memory beginning at location 150 and printed all five locations since all of them differed.

Example A-21: Move, Search, and Compare Commands

(a) Move command

```
-F 130 13F FF
-D 130 15F
103D:0130  FF FF FF FF FF FF FF FF-FF FF FF FF FF FF FF FF ...............
103D:0140  00 00 00 00 00 00 00 00-00 00 00 00 00 00 00 00 ...............
103D:0150  00 00 00 00 00 00 00 00-00 00 00 00 00 00 00 00 ...............
-M 130 13F 140
-D 130 15F
103D:0130  FF FF FF FF FF FF FF FF-FF FF FF FF FF FF FF FF ...............
103D:0140  00 00 00 00 00 00 00 00-00 00 00 00 00 00 00 00 ...............
103D:0150  00 00 00 00 00 00 00 00-00 00 00 00 00 00 00 00 ...............
```

(b) Compare command

```
-C 130 134 140
-C 130 134 150
103D:0130  FF  00  103D:0150
103D:0131  FF  00  103D:0151
103D:0132  FF  00  103D:0152
103D:0133  FF  00  103D:0153
103D:0134  FF  00  103D:0154
```

(c) Search command

```
-S 150 15F FF
-S 130 133 FF
103D:0130
103D:0131
103D:0132
103D:0133
-
```

S, the search command: search a block of memory for a data item

The search command is used to search a block of data for a specific data value. If the item is not found, DEBUG simply displays the command prompt "-". Otherwise, all locations where the data item was found will be displayed. The syntax is:

```
S       <starting address>  <ending address>  <data>
S       <starting address>  <L number of bytes>  <data>
```

DEBUG will search from the starting to the ending address to find data. Look at part (c) of Example A-21. This example searched from locations 150 to 15F for FF and did not find it. The next command searched from 130 to 133 for FF and printed all four addresses since all four contained FF. The following command would have achieved the same result: "S 130 L4 FF". The data may be a list of data items, in which case DEBUG will search for that pattern of data.

SECTION A.8: LOADING AND WRITING PROGRAMS

The write and load commands below are used to save a program onto disk and load a previously saved program from disk into DEBUG. They both require a thorough familiarity with advanced DOS concepts.

W, the write command: saving instructions on disk

The write command is used to save instructions onto a disk. Its format is

```
W       <starting address> <drive number> <starting sector> <sectors>
```

Writing to specific sectors is not recommended since a thorough familiarity with the way information is stored on drives is needed. Writing to the wrong sector could damage the disk's directory, rendering it useless. Example A-23 shows how to use the W command without any parameters to save code on a disk, after the N command had been used to set up a filename.

L, the load command: loading instructions from disk

The load command performs the opposite function of the write command: It loads from disk into memory starting at the specified address. Its syntax is

```
L       <starting address> <drive number> <starting sector> <sectors>
```

After the load, registers BX CX will hold the size of the program in bytes. Using the load command with all its options requires a thorough understanding of disk storage and it is not recommended for beginning students. However, the L command may be used after the name command in a simple format, shown below.

N, the name command: used to load a file from disk

The name command can be used with the load command to load a program into DEBUG.

```
-N <filename>
-L
```

The name command above sets up the filename to be loaded by the load command. An alternative way to load a program into DEBUG is when you initially enter the DEBUG program:

```
-DEBUG <filename>
```

Example A-22: Loading an Assembled Program into DEBUG

(a) Loading with the name and load commands

```
-N B:\PROGRAMS\PROG1.EXE
-L
-
```

(b) Loading on entering DEBUG

```
A>DEBUG B:\PROGRAMS\PROG1.EXE
-
```

Example A-23 first shows how to save code that has been entered in DEBUG. The code entered is the code for Example A-19. After the code has been entered with the A command, registers BX and CX must be set up to contain the number of bytes to be saved. CX is set to 12 to save 12 bytes, BX is the high word and in this case should be zero. The N command sets up the drive and filename to be used, then the W command writes the code to disk. Note that the filename extension must be "com" because "exe" files cannot be saved in this manner. The rest of Example A-23 shows how to load saved code into DEBUG. The N command sets up the file reference and the L command loads the code into DEBUG.

Example A-23: Saving and Loading Code

```
C>DEBUG
-A 100
12B0:0100 MOV CX,05
12B0:0103 MOV BX,0200
12B0:0106 MOV AL,0
12B0:0108 ADD AL,[BX]
12B0:010A INC BX
12B0:010B DEC CX
12B0:010C JNZ 0108
12B0:010E MOV [0205],AL
12B0:0111 INT 3
12B0:0112
-R CX
CX 0000
:12
-r
AX=0000 BX=0000 CX=0012 DX=0000 SP=CFDE BP=0000 SI=0000 DI=0000
DS=12B0 ES=12B0 SS=12B0 CS=12B0 IP=0100   NV UP DI PL NZ NA PO NC
12B0:0100 B90500        MOV    CX,0005
-N B:EX19.COM
-W
Writing 0012 bytes
-Q

C>DEBUG
-N B:EX19.COM
-L
-R
AX=0000 BX=0000 CX=0012 DX=0000 SP=FFFE BP=0000 SI=0000 DI=0000
DS=12CC ES=12CC SS=12CC CS=12CC IP=0100   NV UP DI PL NZ NA PO NC
12CC:0100 B90500        MOV    CX,0005
-u cs:100 111
12CC:0100 B90500              MOV    CX,0005
12CC:0103 BB0002              MOV    BX,0200
12CC:0106 B000               MOV    AL,00
12CC:0108 0207               ADD    AL,[BX]
12CC:010A 43                 INC    BX
12CC:010B 49                 DEC    CX
12CC:010C 75FA               JNZ    0108
12CC:010E A20502             MOV    [0205],AL
12CC:0111 CC                 INT    3
-
```

Table A-2: Summary of DEBUG Commands

Function	Command Options		
Assemble	A	<starting address>	
Compare	C	<start address> <end address> <compare address>	
	C	<start address> < L number of bytes> <compare address>	
Dump	D	<start address> <end address>	
	D	<start address> < L number of bytes>	
Enter	E	<address> <data list>	
	E	<address>	
Fill	F	<start address> <end address> <data>	
	F	<start address> < L number of bytes> <data>	
Go	G	< = start address> <end address(es)>	
Hexarith	H	<number 1> <number 2>	
Load	L	<start address> <drive> <start sector> <sectors>	
Move	M	<start address> <end address> <destination>	
	M	<start address> < L number of bytes> <destination>	
Name	N	<filename>	
Procedure	P	< = start address> <number of instructions>	
Register	R	<register name>	
Search	S	<start address> <end address> <data>	
	S	<start address> < L number of bytes> <data>	
Trace	T	< = start address> <number of instructions>	
Unassemble	U	<start address> <end address>	
	U	<start address> < L number of bytes>	
Write	W	<start address> <drive> <start sector> <sectors>	

Notes:
1. All addresses and numbers are given in hex.
2. Commands may be entered in lowercase or uppercase, or a combination.
3. Ctrl-c will stop any command.
4. Ctrl-numlock will stop scrolling of command output. To resume scrolling, enter any key.

APPENDIX B: 80x86 INSTRUCTIONS AND TIMING

In the first section of this appendix, we list the instructions of the 8086, give their format and expected operands, and describe the function of each instruction. Where pertinent, programming examples have been given. These instructions will operate on any 8086 or higher IBM-compatible computer. There are additional instructions for higher microprocessors (80186 and above); however, these instructions are not given in this list. The second section is a list of clock counts for each instruction across the 80x86 family.

SECTION B.1: THE 8086 INSTRUCTION SET

AAA   ASCII Adjust after Addition

Flags: Affected: AF and CF. Unpredictable: OF, SF, ZF, PF.
Format: AAA
Function: This instruction is used after an ADD instruction has added two digits in ASCII code. This makes it possible to add ASCII numbers without masking off the upper nibble "3". The result will be unpacked BCD in AL with carry flag set if needed. This instruction adjusts only on the AL register. AH is incremented if the carry flag is set.

Example 1:
```
MOV    AL,31H          ;AL=31 THE ASCII CODE FOR 1
ADD    AL,37H          ;ADD 37 (ASCII FOR 7) TO AL;  AL=68H
AAA                    ;AL=08 AND CF=0
```

In the example above, ASCII 1 (31H) is added to ASCII 7 (37H). After the AAA instruction, AL will contain 8 in BCD and CF = 0. The following example shows another ASCII addition and then the adjustment:

Example 2:
```
MOV    AL,'9'          ;AL=39 ASCII FOR 9
ADD    AL,'5'          ;ADD 35 (ASCII FOR 5) TO AL THEN AL=6EH
AAA                    ;NOW AL=04 CF=1
OR     AL,30H          ;converts result to ASCII
```

AAD   ASCII Adjust before Division

Flags: Affected: SF, ZF, PF. Unpredictable: OF, AF, CF.
Format: AAD
Function: Used before the DIV instruction to convert two unpacked BCD digits in AL and AH to binary. A better name for this would be BCD to binary conversion before division. This allows division of ASCII numbers. Before the AAD instruction is executed, the ASCII tag of 3 must be masked from the upper nibble of AH and AL.

Example:
```
MOV   AX,3435H            ;AX=3435 THE ASCII FOR 45
AND   AX,0F0FH            ;AX=0405H UNPACKED BCD FOR 45
AAD                       ;AX=002DH HEX FOR 45
MOV   DL,07               ;DL=07
DIV   DL                  ;2DH DIV BY 07 GIVES AL=06,AH=03
OR    AX,3030H            ;AL=36=QUOTIENT AND AH=33=REMAINDER
```

AAM   ASCII Adjust after Multiplication

Flags: Affected: AF, CF. Unpredictable: OF, SF, ZF, PF.

Format: AAM

Function: Again, a better name would have been BCD adjust after multiplication. It is used after the MUL instruction has multiplied two unpacked BCD numbers. It converts AX from binary to unpacked BCD. AAM adjusts only AL, and any digits greater than 9 are stored in AH.

Example:
```
MOV   AL,'5'         ;AL=35
AND   AL,0FH         ;AL=05 UNPACKED BCD FOR 5
MOV   BL,'4'         ;BL=34
AND   BL,0FH         ;BL=04 UNPACKED BCD FOR 4
MUL   BL             ;AX=0014H=20 DECIMAL
AAM                  ;AX=0200
OR    AX,3030H       ;AX=3230 ASCII FOR 20
```

AAS   ASCII Adjust after Subtraction

Flags: Affected: AF, CF. Unpredictable: OF, SF, ZF, PF.

Format: AAS

Function: After the subtraction of two ASCII digits, this instruction is used to convert the result in AL to packed BCD. Only AL is adjusted, the value in AH will be decremented if the carry flag is set.

Example:
```
MOV   AL,32H         ;AL=32 ASCII FOR 2
MOV   DH,37H         ;DH=37 ASCII FOR 7
SUB   AL,DH          ;AL-DH=32-37=FBH WHICH IS -5 IN 2'S COMP
                     ;CF=1 INDICATING A BORROW
AAS                  ;NOW AL=05 AND CF=1
```

ADC   Add with Carry

Flags: Affected: OF, SF, ZF, AF, PF, CF.

Format: ADC dest,source;dest = dest + source + CF

Function: If CF=1 prior to this instruction, then after execution of this instruction, source is added to destination plus 1. If CF = 0, source is added to destination plus 0. Used widely in multibyte and and multiword additions.

ADD   Signed or Unsigned ADD

Flags: Affected: OF, SF, ZF, AF, PF, CF.

Format: ADD dest,source;dest = dest + source

Function: Adds source operand to destination operand and places the result in destination. Both source and destination operands must match (e.g., both byte size or word size) and only one of them can be in memory.

Unsigned addition:

In addition of unsigned numbers, the status of CF, ZF, SF, AF, and PF may change, but only CF, ZF, and AF are of any use to programmers. The most important of these flag is CF. It becomes 1 when there is carry from D7 out in 8-bit (D0 - D7) operations, or a carry from D15 out in 16-bit (D0 - D15) operations.

Example 1:
```
MOV   BH,45H        ;BH=45H
ADD   BH,4FH        ;BH=94H (45H+4FH=94H)
                    ;CF=0,ZF=0,SF=1,AF=1,and PF=0
```

Example 2:
```
MOV   AL,FEH        ;AL=FEH
MOV   DL,75H        ;DL=75H
ADD   AL,DL         ;AL=FE+75=73H
                    ;CF=1,ZF=0,AF=0,SF=0,PF=0
```

Example 3:
```
MOV   DX,126FH      ;DX=126FH
ADD   DX,3465H      ;DX=46D4H (126F=3465=46D4H)
                    ;CF=0,ZF=0,AF=1,SF=0,PF=1

MOV   BX,0FFFFH
ADD   BX,1          ;BX=0000 (FFFFH+1=0000)
                    ;AND CF=1,ZF=1,AF=1,SF=0,PF=1
```

Signed addition:

In addition of signed numbers, the status of OF, ZF, and SF must be noted. Special attention should be given to the overflow flag (OF) since this indicates if there is an error in the result of the addition. There are two rules for setting OF in signed number operation. The overflow flag is set to 1:

1. If there is a carry from D6 to D7 and no carry from D7 out in an 8-bit operation or a carry from D14 to D15 and no carry from D15 out in a 16-bit operation
2. If there is a carry from D7 out and no carry from D6 to D7 in an 8-bit operation or a carry from D15 out but no carry from D14 to D15 in a 16-bit operation

Notice that if there is a carry both from D7 out and from D6 to D7, then OF = 0 in 8-bit operations. In 16-bit operations, OF = 0 if there is both a carry out from D15 and a carry from D14 to D15.

Example 4:
```
MOV   BL,+8         ;BL=0000 1000
MOV   DH,+4         ;DH=0000 0100
ADD   BL,DH         ;BL=0000 1100 SF=0,ZF=0,OF=0,CF=0
```
Notice SF = D7 = 0 since the result is positive and OF = 0 since there is neither a carry from D6 to D7 nor any carry beyond D7. Since OF = 0, the result is correct [(+8) + (+4) = (+12)].

Example 5:
```
MOV   AL,+66        ;AL=0100 0010
MOV   CL,+69        ;CL=0100 0101
ADD   CL,AL         ;CL=1000 0111 = -121 (INCORRECT)
                    ;CF=0,SF=1,ZF=0, AND OF=1
```

In Example 5, the correct result is +135 [(+66) + (+69) = (+135)], but the result was -121. The OF = 1 is an indication of this error. Notice that SF = D7 = 1 since the result is negative; OF = 1 since there is a carry from D6 to D7 and CF=0.

Example 6:
```
MOV    AL,-12        ,;AL=1111 0100
MOV    BL,+18        ;BL=0001 0010
ADD    BL,AL         ;BL=0000 0110 (WHICH IS +6 )
                     ;SF=0,ZF=0,OF=0, AND CF=1
```

Notice above that $OF = 0$ since there is a carry from D6 to D7 and a carry from D7 out.

Example 7:
```
MOV    AH,-30        ;AH=1110 0010
MOV    DL,+14        ;DL=0000 1110
ADD    DL,AH         ;DL=1111 0000 (WHICH IS -16 AND CORRECT)
                     ;AND SF=1,ZF=0,OF=0, AND CF=0
```
$OF = 0$ since there is no carry from D7 out nor any carry from D6 to D7.

Example 8:
```
MOV    AL,-126       ;AL=1000 0010
MOV    BH,-127       ;BH=1000 0001
ADD    AL,BH         ;AL=0000 0011 (WHICH IS +3 AND WRONG)
                     ;AND SF=0,ZF=0 AND OF=1
```
$OF = 1$ since there is carry from D7 out but no carry from D6 to D7.

AND   Logical AND

X Y	X AND Y
0 0	0
0 1	0
1 0	0
1 1	1

Flags: Affected: $CF = 0$, $OF = 0$, SF, ZF, PF.
Unpredictable: AF.
Format: AND dest,source
Function: Performs logical AND on the operands, bit by bit, storing the result in the destination.

Example:
```
MOV    BL,39H ;BL=39
AND    BL,09H ;BL=09
;39    0011 1001
;09    0000 1001
;--    ---------
;09    0000 1001
```

CALL   Call a Procedure

Flags: Unchanged.
Format: CALL proc;transfer control to procedure
Function: Transfers control to a procedure. RET is used to return control to the instruction after the call. There are two types of CALLs: NEAR and FAR. If the target address is within the same code segment, it is a NEAR call. If the target address is outside the current code segment, it is a FAR CALL. Each is described below.

NEAR CALL: If calling a near procedure (the procedure is in the same code segment as the CALL instruction) then the content of the IP register (which is the address of the instruction after the CALL) is pushed onto the stack and SP is decremented by 2. Then IP is loaded with the new value which is the offset of the procedure. At the end of the procedure when the RET is executed, IP is popped off the stack, which returns control to the instruction after the CALL. There are three ways to code the address of the called NEAR procedure:

1. Direct:
```
        CALL    proc1
        ...
proc1   PROC NEAR
        ...
        RET
proc1   ENDP
```

2. Register indirect:
```
        CALL    [SI]        ;transfer control to address in SI
```

3. Memory indirect:
```
        CALL    WORD PTR [DI]       ;DI points to the address that
                                    ;contains IP address of proc
```

FAR CALL: When calling a far procedure (the procedure is in a different segment than the CALL instruction), the SP is decremented by 4 after CS:IP of the instruction following the CALL is pushed onto the stack. CS:IP is then loaded with the segment and offset address of the called procedure. In pushing CS:IP onto the stack, CS is pushed first and then IP. When the RETF is executed, CS and IP are restored from the stack and execution continues with the instruction following the CALL. The following addressing modes are supported:

1. Direct (but outside the present segment):
```
        CALL    proc1
        ...
proc1   PROC FAR
        ...
        RETF
proc1   ENDP
```

2. Memory indirect:
```
        CALL    DWORD PTR [DI]  ;transfer control to CS:IP where
                                ;DI and DI+1 point to location of CS and
                                ;DI+2 and DI+4 point to location of IP
```

CBW   Convert Byte to Word

Flags: Unchanged.
Format: CBW
Function: Copies D7 (the sign flag) to all bits of AH. Used widely to convert a signed byte in AL into a signed word to avoid the overflow problem in signed number arithmetic.

Example:
```
MOV   AX,0
MOV    AL,-5              ;AL=(-5)=FB in 2's complement
                         ;AX = 0000 0000 1111 1011
CBW                      ;now AX=FFFB
                         ;AX = 1111 1111 1111 1011
```

CLC   Clear Carry Flag

Flags: Affected: CF.
Format: CLC
Function: Resets CF to zero (CF = 0).

CLD   Clear Direction Flag

Flags: Affected: DF.
Format: CLD
Function: Resets DF to zero ($DF = 0$). In string instructions if $DF = 0$, the pointers are incremented with each execution of the instruction. If $DF = 1$, the pointers are decremented. Therefore, CLD is used before string instructions to make the pointers increment.

CLI   Clear Interrupt Flag

Flags: Affected: IF.
Format: CLI
Function: Resets IF to zero, thereby masking external interrupts received on INTR input. Interrupts received on NMI input are not blocked by this instruction.

CMC   Complement Carry Flag

Flags: Affected: CF.
Format: CMC
Function: Changes CF from 0 to 1 or from 1 to 0.

CMP   Compare Operands

Flags: Affected: OF, SF, ZF, AF, PF, CF.
Format: CMP dest,source;sets flags as if "SUB dest,source"
Function: Compares two operands of the same size. The source and destination operands are not altered. Performs comparison by subtracting the source operand from the destination and sets flags as if SUB were performed. The relevant flags are as follows:

	CF	ZF	SF	OF
dest > source	0	0	0	SF
dest = source	0	1	0	SF
dest < source	1	0	1	inverse of SF

CMPS/CMPSB/CMPSW   Compare Byte or Word String

Flags: Affected: OF, SF, ZF, AF, PF, CF.
Format: CMPSx
Function: Compares strings a byte or word at a time. DS:SI is used to address the first operand; ES:DI is used to address the second. If $DF = 0$, it increments the pointers SI and DI. If $DF = 1$, it decrements the pointers. It can be used with prefix REPE or REPNE to compare strings of any length. The comparison is done by subtracting the source operand from the destination and sets flags as if SUB were performed.

CWD   Convert Word to Doubleword

Flags: Unchanged.
Format: CWD
Function: Converts a signed word in AX into a signed doubleword by copying the sign bit of AX into all the bits of DX. Often used to avoid the overflow problem in signed number arithmetic.

Example:
```
MOV  DX,0
MOV   AX,-5          ;AX=(-5)=FFFB in 2's complement
;DX = 0000H
CWD
;DX = FFFFH
```

DAA   Decimal Adjust after Addition

Flags: Affected: SF, ZF, AF, PF, CF, OF.
Format: DAA
Function: This instruction is used after addition of BCD numbers to convert the result back to BCD. It adds 6 to the lower 4 bits of AL if it is greater than 9 or if AF = 1. Then it adds 6 to the upper 4 bits of AL if it is greater than 9 or if CF = 1.

Example 1:
```
MOV   AL,47H         ;AL=0100 0111
ADD   AL,38H         ;AL=47H+38H=7FH.   invalid BCD
DAA                  ;NOW AL=1000 0101 (85H IS VALID BCD)
```

In this example, since the lower nibble was larger than 9, DAA added 6 to AL. If the lower nibble is less than 9 but AF = 1, it also adds 6 to the lower nibble.

Example 2:
```
MOV   AL,29H         ;AL=0010 1001
ADD   AL,18H         ;AL=0100 0001 INCORRECT RESULT
DAA                  ;AL=0100 0111 A VALID BCD FOR 47H.
```

The same thing can happen for the upper nibble.

Example 3:
```
MOV   AL,52H         ;AL=0101 0010
ADD   AL,91H         ;AL=1110 0011 AN INVALID BCD
DAA                  ;AL=0100 0011 AND CF=1
```

Again the upper nibble can be smaller than 9 but because CF = 1, it must be corrected.

Example 4:
```
MOV   AL,94H         ;AL=1001 0100
ADD   AL,91H         ;AL=0010 0101 INCORRECT RESULT
DAA                  ;AL=1000 0101 A VALID BCD FOR 85 AND CF=1
```

It is entirely possible that 6 is added to both high and low nibble.

Example 5:
```
MOV   AL,54H         ;AL=0101 0100
ADD   AL,87H         ;AL=1101 1011 INVALID BCD
DAA                  ;AL=0100 0001 AND CF=1 (141 IN BCD)
```

DAS   Decimal Adjust after Subtraction

Flags: Affected: SF, ZF, AF, PF, CF. Unpredictable: OF.
Format: DAS
Function: This instruction is used after subtraction of BCD numbers to convert the result to BCD. If the lower 4 bits of AL represent a number greater than 9 or if AF = 1, then 6 is subtracted from the lower nibble. If the upper 4 bits of AL is now greater than 9 or if CF = 1, 6 is subtracted from the upper nibble.

Example:
```
MOV   AL,45H       ;AL=0100 0101 BCD for 45
SUB   AL,17H       ;AL=0010 1110 AN INVALID BCD
DAS               ;AL=0010 1000 BCD FOR 28(45-17=28)
```

For more examples of problems associated with BCD arithmetic, see DAA.

DEC   Decrement

Flags: Affected: OF, SF, ZF, AF, PF. Unchanged: CF.
Format: DEC dest;dest = dest - 1
Function: Subtracts 1 from the destination operand. Note that CF (carry/borrow) is unchanged even if a value 0000 is decremented and becomes FFFF.

DIV   Unsigned Division

Flags: Unpredictable: OF, SF, ZF, AF, PF, CF.
Format: DIV source;divide AX or DX:AX by source
Function: Divides either an unsigned word (AX) by a byte or an unsigned doubleword (DX:AX) by a word. If dividing a word by a byte, the quotient will be in AL and the remainder in AH. If dividing a doubleword by a word, the quotient will be in AX and the remainder in DX. Divide by zero causes interrupt type 0.

ESC   Escape

Flags: Unchanged.
Format: ESC
Function: This instruction facilitates the use of math coprocessors (such as the 8087) which share data and address buses with the microprocessor. ESC is used to pass an instruction to a coprocessor and is usually treated as NOP (no operation) by the main processor.

HLT   Halt

Flags: Unchanged.
Format: HLT
Function: Causes the microprocessor to halt execution of instructions. To get out of the halt state, activate an interrupt (NMI or INTR) or RESET.

IDIV   Signed Number Division

Flags: Unpredictable: OF, SF, ZF, AF, PF, CF.
Format: IDIV source;divide AX or DX:AX by source
Function: This division function divides either a signed word (AX) by a byte or a signed doubleword (DX:AX) by a word. If dividing a word by a byte, the signed quotient will be in AL and the signed remainder in AH. If dividing a doubleword by a word, the signed quotient will be in AX and the signed remainder in DX. Divide by zero causes interrupt type 0.

IMUL   Signed Number Multiplication

Flags: Affected: OF, CF. Unpredictable: SF, ZF, AF, PF.
Format: IMUL source ;AX = source $\times$ AL or DX:AX = source $\times$ A X
Function: Multiplies a signed byte or word source operand by a signed byte or word in AL or AX with the result placed in AX or DX:AX.

IN   **Input Data from Port**

Flags: Unchanged.
Format: IN accumulator,port   ;input byte or word into AL or AX
Function: Transfers a byte or word to AL or AX from an input port
specified by the second operand. The port address can be direct or register indirect:

1. Direct: the port address is specified directly and cannot be larger than
FFH.

Example 1:
IN   AL,99H   ;BRING A BYTE INTO AL FROM PORT 99H

Example 2:
IN   AX,78H   ;BRING A WORD FROM PORT ADDRESSES 78H
                        ;AND 79H. THE BYTE FROM PORT 78 GOES
                        ;TO AL AND BYTE FROM PORT 79H TO AH.

2. Register indirect: the port address is kept by the DX register. Therefore,
it can be as high as FFFFH.

Example 3:
MOV DX,481H   ;DX=481H
IN   AL,DX   ;BRING THE BYTE TO AL FROM THE PORT
                        ;WHOSE ADDRESS IS POINTED BY DX

Example 4:
IN   AX,DX   ;BRING A WORD FROM PORT ADDRESS OF
                        ;POINTED BY DX. THE BYTE FROM PORT
                        ;DX GOES TO AL AND BYTE FROM PORT
                        ;DX+1 TO AH.

INC   **Increment**

Flags: Affected: OF, SF, ZF, AF, PF. Unchanged: CF.
Format: INC destination;dest = dest + 1
Function: Adds 1 to the register or memory location specified by the
operand. Note that CF is not affected even if a value FFFF is incremented to 0000.

INT   **Interrupt**

Flags: Affected: IF, TF.
Format: INT type;transfer control to INT type
Function: Transfers execution to one of the 256 interrupts. The vector
address is specified by the type number, which cannot be greater than FFH (0 to FF
= 256 interrupts).

The following steps are performed for the interrupt:

1. SP is decremented by 2 and the flags are pushed onto the stack.
2. SP is decremented by 2 and CS is pushed onto the stack.
3. SP is decremented by 2 and the IP of the next instruction after the
interrupt is pushed onto the stack.
4. Multiplies the type number by 4 to get the address of the vector table.
Starting at this address, the first 2 bytes are the value of IP and the next 2 bytes are
the value for CS of the interrupt handler (interrupt handler is also called interrupt
service routine).
5. Resets IF and TF.

Interrupts are used to get the attention of the microprocessor. In the 8086/88 there are a total of 256 interrupts: INT 00, INT 01, INT 02, ... , INT FF. As mentioned above, the address that an interrupt jumps to is always four times the value of the interrupt number. For example, INT 03 will jump to memory address 0000CH ($4 \times 03 = 12 = 0C$ HEX). Table B-1 is a partial list of the interrupts and is commonly referred to as the interrupt vector table.

Table B-1: Interrupt Vector Table

INT # (hex)	Physical Address	Logical Address
INT 00	00000	0000:0000
INT 01	00004	0000:0004
INT 02	00008	0000:0008
INT 03	0000C	0000:000C
INT 04	00010	0000:0010
INT 05	00014	0000:0014
....	.....	....
INT FF	003FC	0000:03FC

Every interrupt has a program associated with it called the interrupt service routine (ISR). When an interrupt is invoked, the CS:IP address of its ISR is retrieved from the vector table (shown above). The lowest 1024 bytes ($256 \times 4 = 1024$) of RAM are set aside for the interrupt vector table and must not be used for any other function.

Example: Find the physical and logical addresses of the vector table associated with (a) INT 14H and (b) INT 38H.
Solution:
(a) The physical address for INT 12H is 00050H-00053H
($4 \times 14H = 50H$). That gives the logical address of 0000:0050H - 0000:0053H.
(b) The physical address for INT 38H is 000E0H - 000E3H, making the physical address 0000:00E0H - 0000:00E3H.

The difference between INTerrupt and CALL instructions

The following are some of the differences between the INT and CALL FAR instructions:

1. While a CALL can jump to any location within the 1-megabyte address range (00000 - FFFFF) of the 8088/86 CPU, "INT nn" jumps to a fixed location in the vector table as discussed earlier.
2. While the CALL is used by the programmer at a predetermined point in a program, a hardware interrupt can come in at any time.
3. A CALL cannot be masked (disabled), but "INT nn" can be masked.
4. While a "CALL FAR" automatically saves on the stack only the CS:IP of the next instruction, "INT nn" saves the FR (flag register) in addition to the CS:IP.
5. While at the end of the procedure that has been CALLed the RETF (return FAR) is used, for "INT nn" the instruction IRET (interrupt return) is used.

The 256 interrupts can be categorized into two different groups: hardware and software interrupts.

Hardware interrupts

The 8086/88 microprocessors have two pins set aside for inputting hardware interrupts. They are INTR (interrupt request) and NMI (nonmaskable interrupt). Although INTR can be ignored through the use of software masking, NMI cannot be masked using software. These interrupts are activated externally by putting 5 volts on the hardware pins of NMI or INTR. Intel has assigned INT 02 to NMI. When it is activated it will jump to memory location 00008 to get the address (CS:IP) of the interrupt service routine (ISR). Memory locations 00008, 00009, 0000A, and 0000B contain the 4-byte CS:IP. There is no specific location in the vector table assigned to INTR because INTR is used to expand the number of hardware interrupts and should be allowed to use any "INT nn" instruction that has not been assigned previously. In the IBM PC, one Intel 8259 PIC (programmable interrupt controller) chip is connected to INTR to add a total of eight hardware interrupts to the microprocessor. IBM PC/AT, PS/2 80286, 80386, and 80486 computers use two 8259 chips to allow up to 15 hardware interrupts. The design of hardware interrupts and the use of the 8259 are covered in Volume 2 of this series.

Table B-2: IBM PC Interrupt System

Interrupt	Logical Address	Physical Address	Purpose
0	00E3:3072	03EA2	Divide error
1	0600:08ED	068ED	Single step (trace command in DEBUG)
2	F000:E2C3	FE2C3	Nonmaskable interrupt
3	0600:08E6	068E6	Breakpoint
4	0700:0147	00847	Signed number arithmetic overflow
5	F000:FF54	FFF54	Print screen (BIOS)
10	F000:F065	FF065	Video I/O (BIOS)
...	...	...	...
21	relocatable	---	DOS function calls
...	...	...	...

Software interrupts

These interrupts are called software interrupts since they are invoked as a result of the execution of an instruction and no external hardware is involved. In other words, these interrupts are invoked by executing an "INT nn" instruction such as the DOS function call "INT 21H" or video interrupt "INT 10H" shown in Chapter 4. These interrupts can be invoked by a program at any time, the same as any other instruction. Many of the interrupts in this category are used by the DOS operating system and IBM BIOS to perform the essential tasks that every computer must provide to the system and the user. Also within this group of interrupts are predefined functions associated with some of the interrupts. They are "INT 00" (divide error), "INT 01" (single step), "INT 03" (breakpoint), and "INT 04" (signed number overflow). Each one is described below. These interrupts are shown in Table B-1. Looking at Table B-1, one can say that aside from "INT 00" to "INT 04", which have predefined functions, the rest of the interrupts, from "INT 05" to "INT FF", can be used to implement either software or hardware interrupts.

Functions associated with "INT 00" to "INT 03"

As mentioned earlier, interrupts "INT 00" to "INT 03" have predefined functions and cannot be used in any other way. The function of each is described next.

INT 00 (divide error)

This interrupt, sometimes referred to as a conditional or exception interrupt, is invoked by the microprocessor whenever there is a condition that it cannot take care of, such as an attempt to divide a number by zero. "INT 00" is invoked by the microprocessor whenever there is an attempt to divide a number by zero. In the IBM PC and compatibles, the service subroutine for this interrupt is responsible for displaying the message "DIVIDE ERROR" on the screen if a program such as the following is executed:

```
MOV AL,25      ; put 25 into AL
MOV BL,00      ; put 00 into BL
DIV BL         ; divide 25 by 00
```

This interrupt is also invoked if the quotient is too large to fit into the assigned register when executing a DIV instruction, as described in Chapter 3.

INT 01 (single step)

There is often a need to execute a given program one instruction at a time and then inspect the registers (possibly memory as well) to see what is happening inside the CPU. This is commonly referred to as single-stepping. IBM and Microsoft call it TRACE in the DEBUG program. To allow the implementation of single-stepping, Intel has set aside "INT 01" specifically for that purpose. For the Trace command in DEBUG after execution of each instruction, the CPU jumps automatically to physical location 00004 to fetch the 4 bytes for CS:IP of the interrupt service routine. One of the functions of this ISR is to dump the contents of the registers onto the screen.

INT 02 (nonmaskable interrupt)

This interrupt is used in the PC to indicate memory errors, among other problems.

INT 03 (breakpoint)

While in single-step mode, one can inspect the CPU and system memory after execution of each instruction. A breakpoint allows one to do the same thing, after execution of a group of instructions rather than after each instruction. Breakpoints are put in at certain points of a program to monitor the flow of the program and to inspect the results after certain instructions. The CPU executes the program to the breakpoint and stops. One can proceed from breakpoint to breakpoint until the program is complete. With the help of single-step and breakpoints, programs can be debugged and tested more easily. The Intel 8086/88 CPUs have set aside "INT 03" for the sole purpose of implementing breakpoints. When the instruction "INT 03" is placed in a program the CPU will execute the program until it encounters "INT 03", and then it stops. One interesting point about this interrupt is that it is a one-byte instruction, in contrast to all other interrupt instructions, "INT nn", which are two-byte instructions. This allows the user to insert 1 byte of code and remove it to proceed with the execution of the program. The opcode for INT 03 is "CC".

IBM PC and DOS assignment of interrupts

When the IBM PC was being developed, the designers at IBM had to coordinate the assignment of the 256 available interrupts for the 8086/88 with Microsoft, the developer of the DOS operating system, lest a conflict occur between the BIOS and DOS interrupt designations. The result of cooperation in assigning interrupts to IBM BIOS subroutines and DOS function calls is shown in Table B-2. The table gives a partial listing of interrupt numbers from 00 to FF, the logical address of the service subroutine for each interrupt, their physical addresses, and the purpose of each interrupt. It must be mentioned that depending on the computer and the DOS version, some of the logical addresses could be different from Table B-2.

How to get the vector table of any PC

One can get the vector table of any IBM PC/XT, PC/AT, PS/2, PS/1, or any 80x86 IBM-compatible computer and inspect the logical address assigned to each interrupt. To do that use DEBUG's DUMP command "-D 0000:0000", as shown next.

```
A>debug
-D 0000:0000
0000:0000  E8 56 2B 02 56 07 70 00-C3 E2 00 F0 56 07 70 00   ...........
0000:0010  56 07 70 00 54 FF 00 F0-47 FF 00 F0 47 FF 00 F0   ...........
```

Note: The contents of the memory locations could be different, depending on the DOS version.

Example: From the dump above, find the CS:IP of the service routine associated with INT 5.

Solution: To get the address of "INT 5", calculate the physical address of 00014H ($5 \times 4 = 00014H$). The contents of these locations are $00014 = 54$, $00015 = FF$, $00016 = 00$, and $00016 = F0$. This gives $CS = F000$ and $IP = FF54$.

INTO   Interrupt on Overflow

Flags: Affected: IF, TF.
Format: INTO
Function: Transfers execution to an interrupt handler written for overflow if OF (overflow flag) has been set. Intel has set aside INT 4 for this purpose. Therefore, if $OF = 1$ when INTO is executed, the CPU jumps to memory location 00010H ($4 \times 4 = 16 = 10H$). The contents of memory locations 10H, 11H, 12H, and 13H are used as IP and CS of the interrupt handler procedure. This instruction is widely used to detect overflow in signed number addition. In signed number operations, OF becomes 1 in two cases:

1. Whenever there is a carry from d6 to d7 in 8-bit operations and no carry from D7 out (or in 16-bit operations when there is carry from d14 to d15 and $CF = 0$)
2. When there is carry from from D7 out and no carry from D6 to D7 (or in the case of 16-bit operation when there is a carry from D15 out and no carry from D14 to D15)

IRET   Interrupt Return

Flags: Affected: OF, DF, IF, TF, SF, ZF, AF, PF, CF.
Format: IRET
Function: Used at the end of an interrupt service routine (interrupt handler), this instruction restores all flags, CS, and IP to the values they had before the interrupt so that execution may continue at the next instruction following the

INT instruction. While the RET instruction is used at the end of the subroutine associated with the CALL instruction, IRET must be used for the subroutine associated with the "INT XX" instruction or the hardware interrupt handler.

JUMP Instructions

The following instructions are associated with jumps (both conditional and unconditional). They are categorized according to their usage rather than alphabetically.

J condition

Flags: Unchanged.
Format: Jxx target;jump to target upon condition
Function: Used to jump to a target address if certain conditions are met. The target address cannot be more than -128 to +127 bytes away. The conditions are indicated by the flag register. The condition that determines whether the jump takes place, can be categorized into three groups,

(1) flag values,
(2) the comparison of unsigned numbers, and
(3) the comparison of signed numbers.
Each is explained next.

1. "J condition" where the condition refers to flag values. The status of each bit of flag register has been decided by execution of instructions prior to the jump. The following "J condition" instructions check if a certain flag bit is raised or not.

JC	Jump Carry	jump if $CF=1$
JNC	Jump No Carry	jump if $CF=0$
JP	Jump Parity	jump if $PF=1$
JNP	Jump No Parity	jump if $PF=0$
JZ	Jump Zero	jump if $ZF=1$
JNZ	Jump No Zero	jump if $ZF=0$
JS	Jump Sign	jump if $SF=1$
JNS	Jump No Sign	jump if $SF=0$
JO	Jump Overflow	jump if $OF=1$
JNO	Jump No Overflow	jump if $OF=0$

Notice that there is no "J condition" instruction for AF.

2. "J condition" where the condition refers to the comparison of unsigned numbers. After a compare (CMP dest,source) instruction is executed, CF and ZF indicate the result of the comparison, as follows:

	CF	ZF
destination > source	0	0
destination = source	0	1
destination < source	1	0

Since the operands compared are viewed as unsigned numbers, the following "J condition" instructions are used.

JA	Jump Above	jump if $CF=0$ and $ZF=0$
JAE	Jump Above or Equal	jump if $CF=0$
JB	Jump Below	jump if $CF=1$
JBE	Jump Below or Equal	jump if $CF=1$ or $ZF=1$
JE	Jump Equal	jump if $ZF=1$
JNE	Jump Not Equal	jump if $ZF=0$

3. "J condition" where the condition refers to the comparison of signed numbers. In the case of the signed number comparison, although the same instruction, "CMP destination,source", is used, the flags used to check the result are as follows:

destination > source	OF=SF or ZF=0
destination = source	ZF=1
destination < source	OF inverse of SF

Consequently, the "J condition" instructions used are different. They are as follows:

JG	Jump Greater	jump if ZF=0 or OF=SF
JGE	Jump Greater or Equal	jump if OF=SF
JL	Jump Less	jump if OF≠SF
JLE	jump Less or Equal	jump if ZF=1 or OF≠SF
JE	jump if Equal	jump if ZF = 1

There is one more "J condition" instruction:
JCXZ ;Jump if CX is Zero. ZF is ignored.

All "J condition" instructions are short jumps, meaning that the target address cannot be more than -128 bytes backward or +127 bytes forward from the IP of the instruction following the jump. What happens if a programmer needs to use a "J condition" to go to a target address beyond the -128 to +127 range? The solution is to use the "J condition" along with the unconditional JMP instruction, as shown next.

```
            ADD    BX,[SI]
            JNC    NEXT
            JMP    TARGET1
NEXT:       ....
            ...
TARGET1     :ADD   DI,10
            ...
```

JMP   Unconditional Jump

Flags: Unchanged.
Format: JMP [directives] target;Jump to target address
Function: This instruction is used to transfer control unconditionally to a new address. The difference between JMP and CALL is that the CALL instruction will return and continue execution with the instruction following the CALL, whereas JMP will not return. The target address could be within the current code segment, which is called a near jump, or outside the current code segment, which is called a far jump. Within each category there are many ways to code the target address, as shown next.

1. Near jump
(a) direct short jump: In this jump the target address must be within -128 to +127 bytes of the IP of the instruction after the JMP. This is a 2-byte instruction. The first byte is the opcode EBH and the second byte is the signed number displacement, which is added to the IP of the instruction following the JMP to get the target address. The directive SHORT must be coded, as shown next:

```
            JMP  SHORT OVER
            ...
OVER:       ...
```

If the target address is beyond the -128 to +127 byte range and the SHORT directive is coded, the assembler gives an error.

(b) Direct jump: This is a 3-byte instruction. The first byte is the opcode E9H and the next two bytes are signed number displacement value. The displacement is added to the IP of the instruction following the JMP to get the target address. The displacement can be in the range -32768 to +32767. In the absence of the SHORT directive, the assembler in its first pass always uses this kind of JMP, and then in the second pass if the target address is within the -128 and +127 byte range, it uses the NOP opcode 90H for the third byte. This is the reason to code the directive SHORT if it is known that the target address of the JMP is within the short range.

(c) Register indirect jump: In this jump the target address is in a register as shown next:

```
JMP     DI  ;jump to the address found in DI
```

Any nonsegment register can be used for this purpose.

(d) Memory indirect jump: In this jump the target address is in a memory location whose address is pointed at by a register:

```
JMP     WORD PTR [SI] ;jump to the address found at the address in SI
```

The directive WORD PTR must be coded to indicate this is a near jump.

2) Far jump

In a far JMP, the target address is outside the present code segment; therefore, not only the offset value but also the segment value of the target address must be given. A far jump is a 5-byte instruction: the opcode EAH and 4 bytes for the offset and segment of the target address. The following shows the two methods of coding the far jump.

(a) Direct far jump: This requires that both CS and IP be updated. One way to do that is to use the LABEL directive:

```
            JMP     TARGET2
            ...
TARGET2     LABEL FAR
ENTRY:          ...
```

This is exactly what IBM has done in BIOS of the IBM PC/XT when the computer is booted. When the power to the PC is turned on, the 8088/86 CPU begins to execute at address FFFF:0000H. IBM uses a FAR jump to make it go to location F000:E05BH, as shown next:

```
                    ;CS=FFFF and IP=0000
0000 EA5BE000F0     JMP     RESET
                    ;CS=F000
                    ORG     0E05BH
E05B    RESET       LABEL   FAR
E05B    START:
E05B                CLI
E05C                    ...
```

The EXTRN and PUBLIC directives also can be used for the same purpose.

(b) Memory indirect far jump: The target address (both CS:IP) is in a memory location pointed to by the register:

```
JMP    DWORD  PTR [BX]
```

The DWORD and PTR directives must be used to indicate that it is a far jump.

LAHF   Load AH from Flags

Flags: Unchanged.
Format: LAHF
Function: Loads the lower 8 bits of the flag register into AH.

LDS   Load Data Segment Register

Flags: Unchanged.
Format: LDS dest,source;load dest and DS starting at source
Function: Loads into destination (which is a register) the contents of two memory locations indicated by source and loads DS with the contents of the two succeeding memory locations. This is useful for accessing a new data segment and its offset.

Example: Assume the following memory locations with the contents:
```
;DS:1200=(46)
;DS:1201=(10)
;DS:1202=(38)
;DS:1203=(82)
LDS    DI,[1200]         ;now DI=1046 and DS=8238.
```

LEA   Load Effective Address

Flags: Unchanged.
Format: LEA dest,source;dest = OFFSET source
Function: Loads into the destination (a 16-bit register) the effective address of a direct memory operand.

Example 1:
```
       ORG    0100H
DATA   DB     34,56,87,90,76,54,13,29

       ...
       ;to access the sixth element:
       LEA    SI,DATA+5      ;SI=100H+5=105 THE EFFECTIVE ADDRESS
       MOV    AL,[SI]        ;GET THE SIXTH ELEMENT
```

Example 2:
```
       ;if BX=2000H and SI=3500H
       LEA    DX,[BX][SI]+100H
       ;DX=effective address=2000+3500+100=5600H
```

The following two instructions show two different ways to accomplish the same thing:

```
       MOV SI,OFFSET DATA ;advantage: executes faster
       LEA SI,DATA
```

LES   **Load Extra Segment Register**

Flags: Unchanged.
Format: LES dest,source;load dest and ES starting at source
Function: Loads into destination (a register) the contents of two memory locations indicated by the source and loads ES with the contents of the two succeeding memory locations. Useful for accessing a new extra segment and its offset. This instruction is similar to LDS except that the ES and its offset are being loaded.

LOCK   **Lock System Bus Prefix**

Flags: Unchanged.
Format: LOCK;used as a prefix before instructions
Function: Used in microcomputer systems with more than one processor to prevent another processor from gaining control over the system bus during execution of an instruction.

LODS/LODSB/LODSW   **Load Byte or Word String**

Flags: Unchanged.
Format: LODSx
Function: Loads AL or AX with a byte or word from the memory location pointed to by DS:SI. If $DF = 0$, SI will be incremented to point to the next location. If $DF = 1$, SI will be decremented to point to the next location. SI is incremented/decremented by 1 or 2, depending on whether it is a byte or word string.

LOOP   **Loop until CX=0**

Flags: Unchanged.
Format: LOOP target;DEC CX, then jump to target if CX not 0
Function: Decrements CX by 1, then jumps to the offset indicated by the operand if CX not zero, otherwise continues with the next instruction below the LOOP. This instruction is equivalent to

```
DEC  CX
JNZ  target
```


LOOPE/LOOPZ   **LOOP if Equal / Loop if Zero**

Flags: Unchanged.
Format: LOOPx target;DEC CX, jump to target if $CX \neq 0$ and ZF=1
Function: Decrements CX by 1, then jumps to location indicated by the operand if CX is not zero and ZF is 1, otherwise continues with the next instruction after the LOOP. In other words, it gets out of the loop only when CX becomes zero or when $ZF = 0$.

Example:
Assume that 200H memory locations from offset 1680H should contain 55H. LOOPE can be used to see if any of these locations does not contain 55H:

```
         MOV   CX,200          ;SET UP THE COUNTER
         MOV   SI,1680H        ;SET UP THE POINTER
BACK:    CMP   [SI],55H        ;COMPARE THE 55H WITH MEMO LOCATION
                               ;POINTED AT BY SI
         INC   SI              ;INCREMENT THE POINTER
         LOOPE BACK            ;CONTINUE THE PROCESS UNTIL CX=0 OR
                               ;ZF=0. IN OTHER WORDS EXIT IF ONE
                               ;LOCATION DOES NOT HAVE 55H
```

LOOPNE/LOOPNZ   LOOP While CF Not Zero and ZF Equal Zero

Flags: Unchanged.
Format: LOOPxx target;DEC CX, then jump if CX and ZF not zero
Function: Decrements CX by 1, then jumps to location indicated by the operand if CX and ZF are not zero, otherwise continues with the next instruction below the LOOP. In other words it will exit the loop if CX = zero or ZF = 1.

Example:
Assume that the daily temperatures for the last 30 days have been stored starting at memory location with offset 1200H. LOOPE can be used to find the first day that had a 90-degree temperature.

```
            MOV     CX,30         ;SET UP THE COUNTER
            MOV     DI,1200H      ;SET UP THE POINTER
AGAIN:      CMP     [DI],90
            INC     DI
            LOOPNE AGAIN
```

MOV   Move

Flags: Unchanged.
Format: MOV dest,source;copy source to dest
Function: Copies a word or byte from a register, memory location, or immediate number to a register or memory location. Source and destination must be of the same size and cannot both be memory locations.

MOVS/MOVSB/MOVSW   Move Byte or Word String

Flags: Unchanged.
Format: MOVSx
Function: Moves byte or word from memory location pointed to by DS:SI to memory location pointed to by ES:DI. If DF = 0, both pointers are incremented; otherwise, they are decremented. The SI and DI are incremented/decremented by 1 or 2 depending on whether it is a byte or word string. When used with the REP prefix, CX is decremented each time until CX is zero.

MUL   Unsigned Multiplication

Flags: Affected: OF, CF. Unpredictable: SF, ZF, AF, PF.
Format: MUL source;AX = source $\times$ AL or DX:AX = source $\times$ AX
Function: Multiplies an unsigned byte or word indicated by the operand by a unsigned byte or word in AL or AX with the result placed in AX or DX:AX.

NEG   Negate

Flags: Affected: OF, SF, ZF, AF, PF, CF.
Format: NEG dest;negates operand
Function: Performs 2's complement of operand. Effectively reverses the sign bit of the operand. This instruction should only be used on signed numbers.

NOP   No Operation

Flags: Unchanged.
Format: NOP
Function: Performs no operation. Sometimes used for timing delays to waste clock cycles. Updates IP to point to next instruction following NOP.

NOT   Logical NOT

Flags: Unchanged.
Format: NOT dest ;dest = 1's complement of dest
Function: Replaces the operand with its negation (the 1's complement). Each bit is inverted.

OR   Logical OR

Flags: Affected: CF=0, OF=0, SF, ZF, PF. Unpredictable: AF.
Format: OR dest,source;dest = dest OR source
Function: Performs logical OR on the bits of two operands, replacing the destination operand with the result. Often used to turn a bit on.

X	Y	X OR Y
0	0	0
0	1	1
1	0	1
1	1	1

OUT   Output Byte or Word

Flags: Unchanged.
Format: OUT dest,acc;transfer acc to port dest
Function: Transfers a byte or word from AL or AX to an output port specified by the first operand.   Port address can be direct or register indirect as shown next:
1. Direct: port address is specified directly and cannot be larger than FFH.

Example 1:
```
OUT    68H,AL ;SEND OUT A BYTE FROM AL TO PORT 68H
or
OUT    34H,AX ;SEND OUT A WORD FROM AX TO PORT
              ;ADDRESSES 34H AND 35H.  THE BYTE
              ;FROM AL GOES TO PORT 34H AND
              ;THE BYTE FROM AH GOES TO PORT 35H
```

2. Register indirect: port address is kept by the DX register.   Therefore, it can be as high as FFFFH.

Example 2:
```
MOV    DX,64B1H        ;DX=64B1H
OUT    DX,AL           ;SENT OUT THE BYTE IN AL TO THE PORT
                       ;WHOSE ADDRESS IS POINTED TO BY DX
or
OUT    DX,AX           ;SEND OUT A WORD FROM AX TO PORT
                       ;ADDRESS POINTED TO DX.  THE BYTE
                       ;FROM AL GOES TO PORT DX AND AND BYTE
                       ;FROM AH GOES TO PORT DX+1.
```

POP   POP Word

Flags: Unchanged.
Format: POP dest;dest = word off top of stack
Function: Copies the word pointed to by the stack pointer to the register or memory location indicated by the operand and increments the SP by 2.

POPF   POP Flags off Stack

Flags: OF, DF, IF, TF, SF, ZF, AF, PF, CF.
Format: POPF
Function: Copies bits previously pushed onto the stack with the PUSHF instruction into the flag register. The stack pointer is then incremented by 2.

PUSH   PUSH Word

Flags: Unchanged.
Format: PUSH source;PUSH source onto stack
Function: Copies the source word to the stack and decrements SP by 2.

PUSHF   PUSH Flags onto stack

Flags: Unchanged.
Format: PUSHF
Function: Decrements SP by 2 and copies the contents of the flag register to the stack.

RCL/RCR Rotate Left through Carry and Rotate Right through Carry

Flags: Affected: OF, CF.
Format: RCx dest,n;dest = dest rotate right/left n bit positions
Function: Rotates the bits of the operand right or left. The bits rotated out of the operand are rotated into the CF and the CF is rotated into the opposite end of the word or byte. *Note*: "n" must be 1 or CL.

RET   Return from a Procedure

Flags: Unchanged.
Format: RET [n];return from procedure
Function: Used to return from a procedure previously entered by a CALL instruction. The IP is restored from the stack and the SP is incremented by 2. If the procedure was FAR, then RETF (return FAR) is used, and in addition to restoring the IP, the CS is restored from the stack and SP is again incremented by 2. The RET instruction may be followed by a number that will be added to the SP after the SP has been incremented. This is done to skip over any parameters being passed back to the calling program segment.

ROL/ROR Rotate Left and Rotate Right

Flags: Affected: OF, CF.
Format: ROx dest,n;rotate dest right/left n bit positions
Function: Rotates the bits of a word or byte indicated by the second operand right or left. The bits rotated out of the word or byte are rotated back into the word or byte at the opposite end. *Note*: "n" must be 1 or CL.

SAHF   Store AH in Flag Register

Flags: Affected: SF, ZF, AF, PF, CF.
Format: SAHF
Function: Copies AH to the lower 8 bits of the flag register.

SAL/SAR Shift Arithmetic Left/ Shift Arithmetic Right

Flags: Affected: OF, SF, ZF, PF, CF. Unpredictable: AF.
Format: SAx dest,n;shift signed dest left/right n bit positions
Function: Shifts a word or byte left /right. SAR/ SAL arithmetic shifts are used for signed number shifting. In SAL, as the operand is shifted left bit by bit, the LSB is filled with 0s and the MSB is copied to CF. In SAR, as each bit is shifted right, the LSB is copied to CF and the empty bits filled with the sign bit (the MSB). SAL/SAR essentially multiply/divide destination by a power of 2 for each bit shift. *Note*: "n" must be 1 or CL.

SBB   Subtract with Borrow

Flags: Affected: OF, SF, ZF, AF, PF, CF.
Format: SBB dest,source;dest = dest - CF - source
Function: Subtracts source operand from destination, replacing destination. If CF =1, it subtracts 1 from the result; otherwise, it executes like SUB.

SCAS/SCASB/SCASW   Scan Byte or Word String

Flags: Affected: OF, SF, ZF, AF, PF, CF.
Format: SCASx
Function: Scans a string of data pointed by ES:DI for a value that is in AL or AX. Often used with the REPE/REPNE prefix. If DF is zero, the address is incremented; otherwise, it is decremented.

SHL/SHR Shift Left/Shift Right

Flags: Affected: OF, SF, ZF, PF, CF. Unpredictable: AF.
Format: SHx dest,n;shift unsigned dest left/right n bit positions
Function: These are logical shifts used for unsigned numbers, meaning that the sign bit is treated as data. In SHR, as the operand is shifted right bit by bit and copied into CF, the empty bits are filled with 0s instead of the sign bit as is the case for SAR. In the case of SHL, as the bits are shifted left, the MSB is copied to CF and empty bits are filled with 0, which is exactly the same as SAL. In reality, SAL and SHL are two different mnemonics for the same opcode. SHL/SHR essentially multiply/divide the destination by a power of 2 for each bit position shifted. *Note*: "n" must be 1 or CL.

STC   Set Carry Flag

Flags: Affected: CF.
Format: STC
Function: Sets CF to 1.

STD   Set Direction Flag

Flags: Affected: DF.
Format: STD
Function: Sets DF to 1.   Used widely with string instructions. As explained in the string instructions, if DF = 1, the pointers are decremented.

STI   Set Interrupt Flag

Flags: Affected: IF.
Format: STI
Function: Sets IF to 1, allowing the hardware interrupt to be recognized through the INTR pin of the CPU.

STOS/STOSB/STOSW   Store Byte or Word String

Flags: Unchanged.
Format: STOSx
Function: Copies a byte or word from AX or AL to a location pointed by ES:DI and updates DI to point to the next string element. The pointer DI is incremented if DF is zero; otherwise, it is decremented.

SUB   Subtract

Flags: Affected: OF, SF, ZF, AF, PF, CF.
Format: SUB dest,source;dest = dest - source
Function: Subtracts source from destination and puts the result in the destination. Sets the carry and zero flag according to the following:

	CF	ZF	
dest >source	0	0	the result is positive
dest=source	0	1	the result is 0
dest < source	1	0	the result is negative in 2's comp

The steps for subtraction performed by the internal hardware of the CPU are as follows:

1. Takes the 2's complement of the source
2. Adds this to the destination
3. Inverts the carry and changes the flags accordingly

The source operand remains unchanged by this instruction.

TEST   Test Bits

Flags: Affected: OF, SF, ZF, PF, CF. Unpredictable: AF.
Format: TEST dest,source;performs dest AND source
Function: Performs a logical AND on two operands, setting flags but leaving the contents of both source and destination unchanged.   While the AND instruction changes the contents of the destination and the flag bits, the TEST instruction changes only the flag bits.

Example:
Assume that D0 and D1 of port 27 indicate conditions A and B, respectively, if they are high and only one of them can be high at a given time. The TEST instruction can be used as follows:

```
        IN    AL,PORT_27
        TEST  AL,0000 0001B        ;CHECK THE CONDITION A
        JNZ   CASE_A               ;JUMP TO INDICATE CONDITION A
        TEST  AL,0000 0010B        ;CHECK FOR CONDITION B
        JNZ   CASE_B               ;JUMP TO INDICATE CONDITION B
        ....                       ;THERE IS AN ERROR SINCE NEITHER
        ....                       ;   A OR B HAS OCCURRED.
CASE_A: ....
        ....
CASE_B: ....
```

WAIT **Puts Processor in WAIT State**

Flags: Unchanged.
Format: WAIT
Function: Causes the microprocessor to enter an idle state until an external interrupt occurs. This is often done to synchronize it with another processor or with an external device.

XCHG **Exchange**

Flags: Unchanged.
Format: XCHG dest,source;swaps dest and source
Function: Exchanges the contents of two registers or a register and a memory location.

XLAT **Translate**

Flags: Unchanged.
Format: XLAT
Function: Replaces contents of AL with the contents of a look-up table whose address is specified by AL. BX must be loaded with the start address of the look-up table and the element to be translated must be in AL prior to the execution of this instruction. AL is used as an offset within the conversion table. Often used to translate data from one format to another, such as ASCII to EBCDIC.

XOR **Exclusive OR**

Flags: Affected: CF = 0, OF = 0, SF, ZF, PF.
Unpredictable: AF.
Format: XOR dest,source
Function: Performs a logical Exclusive OR on the bits of two operands and puts the result in the destination. "XOR AX,AX" can be used to clear AX.

X	Y	X XOR Y
0	0	0
0	1	1
1	0	1
1	1	0

SECTION B.2: INSTRUCTION TIMING

In this section of the appendix we provide clock counts for all the instructions of Intel's 8086, 286, 386, and 486 microprocessors. The clock count is the number of clocks that it takes the instruction to execute. They are extracted from Intel's reference manuals on these microprocessors. The number of clocks for each instruction is given with the assumption that the instruction is already fetched into the CPU. The actual clock count can vary depending on the memory hardware design of the system. Note the following points when calculating the clock counts for a given CPU.

1. In calculating the total clock cycles for the 8086/88, one must add the extra clocks associated with the effective address (EA) provided in Table B-3.

2. In calculating the time required for the 8086, 286, and 386SX microprocessors, its 16-bit external data bus must be taken into consideration. In addition, whether the operand address is odd or even must be considered. To reduce the time required to fetch data from memory, these CPUs require that the data be aligned on even address boundaries. If addresses are not on even boundaries, an extra 4 clock-cycle penalty is added when fetching a 16-bit operand. Look at the following examples, assuming that DS = 2500H and BX = 3000H.

```
MOV     AX,[BX];total clocks = 10 + 5
```

Since the physical address is 25000H+3000H=28000H, an even address, and the data bus in the 8086 is 16 bits wide, the contents of memory locations 28000H and 28001H will be fetched into the CPU in one memory cycle. In all 80x86 microprocessors, the low byte goes to the low address and the high byte to the high address. In the example above, the contents of memory location 28000H will go to register AL and 28001H to AH. If $BX = 3005H$, the physical address would be 25000H + 3005H = 28005H, an odd location, and the clocks required would be as follows due to the extra 4 clock penalty for nonaligned data.

```
MOV AX,[BX]   ;total clocks=10+4+5
```

In the instruction above the contents of memory location 28005 are moved to AL and 28006H to AH. In actuality, the way the 8086 accesses memory is that in the first memory cycle, the 16-bit data from 28004H and 28005H is accessed on the D0-D15 data bus and then the 16-bit data of memory locations 28006H and 28007H is fetched in the second memory cycle using the 16-bit data bus. In other words, although memory locations 28004H, 28005H, 28006H, and 28007H were addressed by the 8086 in two consecutive memory cycles, only the contents of 28005H and 28006H are used; the contents of memory locations 28004H and 28007H are discarded. For this reason the data must be word (16-bit) aligned in the 16-bit data bus microprocessors. What happens if an odd address is accessed in the 8086? It still will take only one memory cycle consisting of 4 clocks. For example, in "MOV AH,[BX]" with $BX = 3005H$ and $DS = 25000H$, the contents of memory locations 28004H and 28005H both are accessed with one memory cycle, but only the contents of address 28005H are fetched into register AH.

3. In the 8088 microprocessor, the time required to execute an instruction can vary from the 8086 since the data bus is only 8 bits in the 8088. A 16-bit operand would require two memory cycles (each consisting of 4 clock cycles) to move the operand in or out of the microprocessor: for example,

```
MOV     AL,[BX] ;total clocks = 10 + 5

MOV     AX,[BX];total clocks = 10 + 4 + 5
```

4. For conditional jumps and LOOP instructions, the first number is the number of clocks if the jump is successful (jump is taken) and the second number is for when the jump is not taken (noj = no jump). For example, in the 8086 column for the JNZ instruction has "16,noj 4" for the clock count. The 16 is the clock cycle for the case when the jump is taken. If there is no jump, the clock is 4.

5. The clock number for the 80386SX is the same as the 80386, except for accessing 32-bit operands, for which an extra 2 clocks should be added since the data bus in the 80386SX is 16-bit and the memory cycle time of the 80386SX is 2 clocks.

6. An extra 2 clocks must be added for the 80286 and 80386SX if a 16-bit word operand is not aligned and also for the 386 if a 32-bit operand is not aligned at the 32-bit boundary. See the discussion above in point 2.

7. The number of clocks given for the 80486 microprocessor is for situations when the operand is in the cache memory of the 486 chip; otherwise, extra clocks should be added for the cache miss penalty. For the list of the cache miss penalties, refer to Intel's "i486 Microprocessor Programming Reference Manual".

8. PM (privilege mode) instruction timings are for situations when the CPU is switched protected mode.

9. The "m" (often seen in 286 and 386 instructions) represents the number of components associated with the next instruction to be executed. The value of m varies because the size of the instruction located at the target address can vary. Generally, m can be averaged to 2.

10. The "n" represents the number of repetitions of a given instruction.

11. Due to the ever-advancing architectural design of the 286/386/486 microprocessors, the total clock count for a given program cannot be 100% right. For this reason a 10% margin of error should be taken into consideration when calculating the total clock count of a given program.

12. With every new generation of 80x86, new instructions are added; therefore, there is no clock count for the prior generations. This indicated by "--".

Table B-3: Clock Cycles for Effective Address

Addressing Mode	Operand	CLK
Direct	label	6
Register indirect	[BX]	5
	[SI]	5
	[DI]	5
	[BP]	5
Based relative	[BX]+disp	9
	[BP]+disp	9
Indexed relative	[DI]+disp	9
	[SI]+disp	9
Based indexed	[BX][SI]	7
	[BX][DI]	7
	[BP][SI]	8
	[BP][DI]	8
Based indexed relative	[BX][SI]+disp	11
	[BX][DI]+disp	11
	[BP][SI]+disp	12
	[BP][DI]+disp	12

Note:
These times assume no segment override. If a segment override is used, 2 clock cycles must be added.

A summary of the clock cycles for various Intel microprocessors, by instruction, is given in Table B-4.

Table B-4: Clock Cycles for Various Intel Microprocessors by Instruction

Code	Description	8086	80286	80386	80486
AAA	ASCII adjust for addition	8	3	4	3
AAD	ASCII adjust for division	60	14	19	14
AAM	ASCII adjust for multiplication	83	16	17	15
AAS	ASCII adjust for subtraction	8	3	4	3
ADC	Add with carry				
	reg to reg	3	2	2	1
	mem to reg	9+EA	7	6	2
	reg to mem	16+EA	7	7	3
	immed to reg	4	3	2	1
	immed to mem	17+EA	7	7	3
	immed to acc	4	3	2	1
ADD	Addition				
	reg to reg	3	2	2	1
	mem to reg	9+EA	7	6	2
	reg to mem	16+EA	7	7	3
	immed to reg	4	3	2	1
	immed to mem	17+EA	7	7	3
	immed to acc	4	3	2	1
AND	Logical AND				
	reg to reg	3	2	2	1
	mem to reg	9+EA	7	6	2
	reg to mem	16+EA	7	7	3
	immed to reg	4	3	2	1
	immed to mem	17+EA	7	7	3
	immed to acc	4	3	2	1
ARPL	Adjust RPL (requested privilege level)				
	reg to reg	--	10	20	9
	reg to mem	--	11	21	9
BOUND	Check array bounds	--	13noj	10noj	7noj
BSF	Bit scan forward				
	reg to reg	--	--	10+3n	6/42
	mem to reg	--	--	10+3n	7/43
BSR	Bit scan reverse				
	reg to reg	--	--	10+3n	6/103
	mem to reg	--	--	10+3n	7/104
BSWAP	Byte swap	--	--	--	1
BT	Bit test				
	reg to reg	--	--	3	3
	reg to mem	--	--	12	8
	immed to reg	--	--	3	3
	immed to mem	--	--	6	3
BTC/ BTR/ BTS	Bit test complement/ Bit test reset/ Bit test set				
	reg to reg	--	--	6	6
	reg to mem	--	--	13	13
	immed to reg	--	--	6	6
	immed to mem	--	--	8	8

Table B-4: Clock Cycles for Various Intel Microprocessors by Instruction (continued)

Code	Description	8086	80286	80386	80486
CALL	Call a procedure				
	intrasegment direct	19	7+m	7+m	3
	intrasegment indirect				
	through register	16	7+m	7+m	5
	instrasegment indirect				
	through memory	21+EA	11+m	10+m	5
	intersegment direct	28	13+m	17+m	18
	486: to same level				20
	486: thru Gate to same level				35
	486: to inner level, no parameters				69
	486: to inner level, x parameter (d) words				77+4x
	486: to TSS				37+TS
	486: thru Task Gate				38+TS
	intersegment direct PM	--	26+m	34+m	
	intersegment indirect	37+EA	16+m	22+m	17
	486: to same level				20
	486: thru Gate to same level				35
	486: to inner level, no parameters				69
	486: to innter level, x parameter (d) words				77+4x
	486: to TSS				37+TS
	486: thru Task Gate				38+TS
	intersegment indirect PM	--	29+m	38+m	
CBW	Convert byte to word	2	2	3	3
CDQ	Convert double to quad	--	--	2	
CLC	Clear carry flag	2	2	2	2
CLD	Clear direction flag	2	2	2	2
CLI	Clear interrupt flag	2	3	3	5
CLTS	Clear task switched flag	--	2	5	7
CMC	Complement carry flag	2	2	2	2
CMP	Compare				
	reg to reg	3	2	2	1
	mem to reg	9+EA	6	6	2
	reg to mem	9+EA	7	5	2
	immed to reg	4	3	2	1
	immed to mem	10+EA	6	5	2
	immed to acc	4	3	2	1
CMPS/	Compare string/				
CMPSB/	Compare byte string/				
CMPSW	Compare word string				
	not repeated	22	8	10	8
	REPE/REPNE CMPS/CMPSB/CMPSW	9+22/rep	5+9/rep	5+9/rep	7+7c
CMPXCHG	Compare and exchange				
	reg with reg	--	--	--	6
	reg with mem	--	--	--	7/10
CWD	Convert word to doubleword	5	2	2	3
CWDE	Convert word to extended double	--	--	3	3
DAA	Decimal adjust for addition	4	3	4	2
DAS	Decimal adjust for subtraction	4	3	4	2

Table B-4: Clock Cycles for Various Intel Microprocessors by Instruction (continued)

Code	Description	8086	80286	80386	80486
DEC	Decrement by 1				
	16-bit reg	3	2	2	1
	8-bit reg	3	2	2	1
	memory	15+EA	7	6	3
DIV	Unsigned division				
	8-bit reg	80-90	14	14	16
	16-bit reg	144-162	22	22	24
	double	--	--	--	40
	8-bit mem	(86-96)+EA	17	17	16
	16-bit mem	(150-168)+EA	25	25	24
	double	--	--	--	40
ENTER	Make stack frame				
	W,0	--	11	10	14
	W,1	--	15	12	17
	dw,db	--	12+4(n-1)	15+4(n-1)	17+3n
ESC	Escape				
	reg	2	9-20	varies	
	mem	8+EA	9-20	varies	
HLT	Halt	2	2	5	4
IDIV	Integer division				
	8-bit reg	101-112	17	19	19
	16-bit reg	165-184	25	27	27
	32-bit reg	--	--	43	43
	8-bit mem	(107-118) +EA	20	22	20
	16-bit mem	(171-190) +EA	28	30	28
	32-bit reg	--	--	46	44
IMUL	Integer multiplication				
	8-bit reg	80-98	13	9-14	13-18
	16-bit reg	128-154	21	9-22	13-26
	32-bit reg	--	--	9-38	13-42
	8-bit mem	(86-104) +EA	16	12-17	13-18
	16-bit mem	(134-160)+EA	24	12-25	13-26
	32-bit reg	--	--	12-41	13-42
	immed to 16-bit reg	--	21	9-34	13-18
	immed x 32-bit reg?	--	21	9-38	13-18
	reg to reg (byte)	--	--	9-38	13-18
	reg to reg (word)	--	--	9-38	13-26
	reg to reg (dword)	--	--	9-38	13-42
	mem to reg (byte)	--	--	12-25	13-18
	mem to reg (word)	--	--	12-25	13-26
	mem to reg (dword)	--	--	12-41	13-42
	reg with imm to reg (byte)	--	--	9-14	13-18
	reg with imm to reg (word)	--	--	9-22	13-26
	reg with imm to reg (dword)	--	--	9-38	13-42
	mem with imm to reg (byte)	--	--	12-17	13-18
	mem with imm to reg (word)	--	--	12-25	13-26
	mem with imm to reg (dword)	--	--	12-41	13-42

Table B-4: Clock Cycles for Various Intel Microprocessors by Instruction (continued)

Code	Description	8086	80286	80386	80486
IN	Input from I/O port				
	fixed port	10	5	12	14
	variable port through DX	8	5	13	14
INC	Increment by 1				
	16-bit reg	3	2	2	1
	8-bit reg	3	2	2	1
	mem	15+EA	7	6	3
INS/	Input from port to string				
INSB/	Input byte				
INSW/	Input word				
INSD	Input double	--	5	15	17
	PM	--	--	9,29	10-32
	REP INS/INSB/INSW	--	5+4/rep	13+6/rep	
	REP INS/INSB/INSW PM	--	--	(7,27)+6/rep	
INT	Interrupt				
	type=3	52	23+m	33	
	type=3 PM	--	(40,78)+m	59,99	
	type3	51	23+m	37	
	type3 PM	--	(40,78)+m	59,99	
INTO	Interrupt if overflow				
	interrupt taken	53	24+m	35	
	interrupt not taken	4	3	3	
	PM	--	(40,78)+m	59,99	
INVD	Invalidate data cache	--	--	--	4
INVLPG	Invalidate TLB entry	--	--	--	12/11
IRET	Return from interrupt	32	17+m	22	15
	PM	--	(31,55)+m	38,82	36
IRETD	Return from interrupt double	--	--	22	20
	PM	--	--	38,82	36
JA/	Jump if above/	16,noj 4	7+m,noj 3	7+m,noj 3	3,noj 1
JNBE	Jump if not below or equal				
JAE/	Jump if above or equal/	16,noj 4	7+m,noj 3	7+m,noj 3	3,noj 1
JNB	Jump if not below/				
JNA	Jump if not above				
JCXZ	Jump if CX is zero	18,noj 6	8+m,noj 4	9+m,noj 5	8,noj 5
JECXZ	Jump if ECX is zero	--	--	--	8,noj 5
JE/	Jump if equal/	16,noj 4	7+m,noj 3	7+m,noj 3	3,noj 1
JZ	Jump if zero				
JG/	Jump if greater	16,noj 4	7+m,noj 3	7+m,noj 3	3,noj 1
JNLE	Jump if not less, or equal				
JGE/	Jump if greater or equal/	16,noj 4	7+m,noj 3	7+m,noj 3	3,noj 1
JNL	Jump if not less				
JL/	Jump if less/	16,noj 4	7+m,noj 3	7+m,noj 3	3,noj 1
JNGE	Jump if not greater, or equal				
JLE/	Jump if less or equal/	16,noj 4	7+m,noj 3	7+m,noj 3	3,noj 1
JNG	Jump if not greater				

Table B-4: Clock Cycles for Various Intel Microprocessors by Instruction (continued)

Code	Description	8086	80286	80386	80486
JMP	Jump				
	intrasegment direct short	15	7+m	7+m	3
	intrasegment direct	15	7+m	7+m	3
	intersegment direct	15	11+m	12+m	17
	PM	--	23+m	27+m	18
	intrasegment indirect				
	through memory	18+EA	11+m	10+m	5
	intrasegment indirect				
	through register	11	7+m	7+m	5
	intersegment indirect	24+EA	15+m	12+m	8
	PM	--	26+m	27+m	18
	direct intersegment				17
	486: to same level				19
	486: thru call gate to same level				32
	486: thru TSS				42+TS
	486: thr Task Gate				43+TS
	indirect intersegment				13
	486: to same level				18
	486: thru call gate to same level				31
	486: thru TSS				41+TS
	486: thr Task Gate				42+TS
JNE/	Jump if not equal/	16,noj 4	7+m,noj 3	7+m,noj 3	3,noj 1
JNZ	Jump if not zero				
JNO	Jump if not overflow	16,noj 4	7+m,noj 3	7+m,noj 3	3,noj 1
JNP/	Jump if not parity/	16,noj 4	7+m,noj 3	7+m,noj 3	3,noj 1
JPO	Jump if parity odd				
JNS	Jump if not sign	16,noj 4	7+m,noj 3	7+m,noj 3	3,noj 1
JO	Jump if overflow	16,noj 4	7+m,noj 3	7+m,noj 3	3,noj 1
JP/	Jump if parity/	16,noj 4	7+m,noj 3	7+m,noj 3	3,noj 1
JPE	Jump if parity even				
JS	Jump if sign	16,noj 4	7+m,noj 3	7+m,noj 3	3,noj 1
LAHF	Load AH from flags	4	2	2	3
LAR	Load access rights				
	reg to reg	--	14	15	11
	mem to reg	--	16	16	11
LDS/	Load pointer using DS/				
LES	Load pointer using ES	16+EA	7	7	6
	PM	--	21	22	12
LFS/	Load far pointer				
LGS/					
LSS		--	--	7	6/12
	PM	--	--	22-25	
LEA	Load effective address	2+EA	3	2	2,noi 1
LEAVE	High level procedure exit	--	5	4	5
LGDT	Load global descriptor table	--	11	11	11
LIDT	Load interrupt desc. table	--	12	11	11
LLDT	Load local desc. table				
	reg	--	17	20	11
	mem	--	19	24	11
LMSW	Load machine status word				
	reg	--	3	10	13
	mem	--	6	13	13

Table B-4: Clock Cycles for Various Intel Microprocessors by Instruction (continued)

Code	Description	8086	80286	80386	80486
LOCK	Lock bus	2	0	0	1
LODS/	Load string/				
LODSB/	Load byte string/				
LODSW	Load word string				
	not repeated	12	5	5	5
	repeated	9+13/rep			7+4c
LOOP	Loop	17,noj 5	8+m,noj 4	11+m	7,noj 6
LOOPE/	Loop if equal/				
LOOPZ	Loop if zero	18,noj 6	8+m,noj 4	11+m	9,noj 6
LOOPNE/	Loop if not equal/				
LOOPNZ	Loop if not zero	19,noj 5	8+m,noj 4	11+m	9,noj 6
LSL	Load segment limit				
	reg to reg	--	14	20,25	10
	mem to reg	--	16	21,26	10
LTR	Load task register				
	reg	--	17	23	20
	mem	--	19	27	20
MOV	Move				
	acc to mem	10	3	2	1
	mem to acc	10	5	4	1
	reg to reg	2	2	2	1
	mem to reg	8+EA	5	4	1
	reg to mem	9+EA	3	2	1
	immed to reg	4	2	2	1
	immed to mem	10+EA	3	2	1
	reg to SS/DS/ES	2	2	2	3/9
	reg to SS/DS/ES PM	--	17	18	
	mem to SS/DS/ES	8+EA	5	5	3/9
	mem to SS/DS/ES PM	--	19	19	3
	segment reg to reg	2	2	2	3
	segment reg to mem	9+EA	3	2	3
	control reg to reg	--	--	6	4
	reg to control reg 0	--	--	10	16
	reg to control reg 2	--	--	4	4
	reg to control reg 3	--	--	5	4
	debug reg 0-3 to reg	--	--	22	10
	debug reg 6-7 to reg	--	--	14	10
	reg to debug reg 0-3	--	--	22	11
	reg to debug reg 6-7	--	--	16	11
	test reg to reg	--	--	12	3,4
	reg to test reg	--	--	12	6,4
MOVS/	Move string/				
MOVSB/	Move byte string/				
MOVSW	Move word string				
	not repeated	18	5	7	7
	REP MOVS/MOVSB/MOVSW	9+17/rep	5+4/rep	8+4/rep	12+3/rep
MOVSX	Move with sign-extend				
	reg to reg	--	--	3	3
	mem to reg	--	--	6	3
MOVZX	Move with zero-extend				
	reg to reg	--	--	3	3
	mem to reg	--	--	6	3

Table B-4: Clock Cycles for Various Intel Microprocessors by Instruction (continued)

Code	Description	8086	80286	80386	80486
MUL	Unsigned multiplication				
	8-bit reg	70-77	13	9-14	13/18
	16-bit reg	118-133	21	9-22	13/26
	double ??	--	--	9-38	13/42
	8-bit mem	(76-83)+EA	16	12-17	13/18
	16-bit mem	(124-139)+EA	24	12-25	13/26
	double ??	--	--	12-41	13/42
NEG	Negate				
	reg	3	2	2	1
	mem	16+EA	7	6	3
NOP	No operation	3	3	3	3
NOT	Logical NOT				
	reg	3	2	2	1
	mem	16+EA	7	6	3
OR	Logical OR				
	reg to reg	3	2	2	1
	mem to reg	9+EA	7	6	2
	reg to mem	16+EA	7	7	3
	immed to acc	4	3	2	1
	immed to reg	4	3	2	1
	immed to mem	17+EA	7	7	3
OUT	Output to I/O port				
	fixed port	10	3	10	16
	fixed port PM	--	--	4,24	11,31
	variable port	8	3	11	16
	variable port PM	--	--	5,25	10,30
OUTS/	Output string to port/				
OUTSB/	Output byte ... /				
OUTSW/	Output word ... /				
OUTSD	Output double ...	--	5	14	17
	PM	--	--	8,28	10,32
	REP OUTS/OUTSB/OUTSW	--	5+4/rep	12+5/rep	
	REP OUTS/OUTSB/OUTSW PM	--	--	(6,26)+5/rep	
POP	Pop word off stack				
	reg	8	5	4	4
	segment reg	8	5	7	3/9
	segment reg PM	--	20	21	9
	memory	17+EA	5	5	6
POPA/	Pop all				9
POPAD	Pop all double	--	19	24	9
POPF	Pop flags off stack	8	5	5	9
POPFD	Pop flags off stack double	--	--	5	
PUSH	Push word onto stack				
	reg	11	3	2	4
	segment reg: ES/SS/CS	10	3	2	3
	segment reg: FS/GS	--	--	2	3
	memory	16+EA	5	5	4
	immed	--	3	2	1
PUSHA	Push All	--	17	18	11
PUSHF/	Push flags onto stack				
PUSHD	Push double flag onto stack	10	3	4	4

Table B-4: Clock Cycles for Various Intel Microprocessors by Instruction (continued)

Code	Description	8086	80286	80386	80486
RCL/	Rotate left through carry/				
RCR	Rotate right through carry/				
	reg with single-shift	2	2	9	3
	reg with variable-shift	8+4/bit	5+n	9	8/30
	mem with single-shift	15+EA	7	10	4
	mem with variable-shift	20+EA+4/bit	8+n	10	9/31
	immed to reg	--	5+n	9	8/30
	immed to mem	--	8+n	10	9/31
RET/	Return from procedure/				
RETF/	Return far/				
RETN	Return near				
	intrasegment	16	11+m	10+m	5
	intrasegment with constant	20	11+m	10+m	5
	intersegment	26	15+m	18+m	18
	intersegment PM	--	25+m,55	32+m,62	13
	intersegment with constant	25	15+m	18+m	33
	intersegment w/constant PM	--	25+m,55	32+m,68	17
	486: imm. to SP	--	--	--	14
	486: to same level	--	--	--	17
	486: to outer level	--	--	--	33
ROL/	Rotate left				
ROR	Rotate right				
	reg with single-shift	2	2	3	3
	reg with variable-shift	8+4/bit	5+n	3	3
	mem with single-shift	15+EA	7	7	4
	mem with variable-shift	20+EA+4/bit	8+n	7	4
	immed to reg	--	5+n	3	2
	immed to mem	--	8+n	7	4
SAHF	Store AH into flags	4	2	3	2
SAL/	Shift arithmetic left/				
SAR/	Shift arighmetic right/				
SHL/	Shift logical left/				
SHR	Shift logical right				
	reg with single-shift	2	2	3	3
	reg with variable-shift	8+4/bit	5+n	3	3
	mem with single-shift	15+EA	7	7	4
	mem with variable-shift	20+EA +4/bit	8+n	7	4
	immed to reg	--	5+n	3	2
	immed to mem	--	8+n	7	4
SBB	Subtract with borrow				
	reg from reg	3	2	2	1
	mem from reg	9+EA	7	7	2
	reg from mem	16+EA	7	6	3
	immed from acc	4	3	2	1
	immed from reg	4	3	2	1
	immed from mem	17+EA	7	7	3
SCAS/	Scan string/				
SCASB/	Scan byte string/				

Table B-4: Clock Cycles for Various Intel Microprocessors by Instruction (continued)

Code	Description	8086	80286	80386	80486
SCASW	Scan word string				
	not repeated	15	7	7	6
	REPE/REPNE SCAS/SCASB/SCASW	9+15/rep	5+8/rep	5+8/rep	7+5/rep
SET	Set conditionally				
	reg	--	--	4	4 or 3
	mem	--	--	5	3 or 4
SGDT	Store global descript. table	--	11	9	10
SIDT	Store interrupt desc. table	--	12	9	10
SLDT	Store local desc. table				
	reg	--	2	2	2
	mem	--	3	2	3
SHLD/	Shift left double precision/				
SHRD	Shift right double				
	reg to reg	--	--	3	2
	mem to mem	--	--	7	3
	reg by CL	--	--	3	3
	mem by CL	--	--	7	4
SMSW	Store machine status word				
	reg	--	2	10	2
	mem	--	3	3	3
	mem PM	--	--	2	
STC	Set carry flag	2	2	2	2
STD	Set direction flag	2	2	2	2
STI	Set interrupt flag	2	2	3	5
STOS/	Store string/				
STOSB/	Store byte string/				
STOSW	Store word string				
	not repeated	11	3	4	5
	REP STOS/STOSB/STOSW	9+10/rep	4+3/rep	5+5/rep	7+4/rep
STR	Store task register				
	reg	--	2	2	2
	mem	--	3	2	3
SUB	Subtraction				
	reg from reg	3	2	2	1
	mem from reg	9+EA	7	7	2
	reg from mem	16+EA	7	6	3
	immed from acc	4	3	2	1
	immed from reg	4	3	2	1
	immed from mem	17+EA	7	7	3
TEST	Test				
	reg with reg	3	2	2	1
	mem with reg	9+EA	6	5	2
	immed with acc	4	3	2	1
	immed with reg	5	3	2	1
	immed with mem	11+EA	6	5	2
VERR	Verify read				
	reg	--	14	10	11
	mem	--	16	11	11
VERW	Verify write				
	reg	--	14	15	11
	mem	--	16	16	11

Table B-4: Clock Cycles for Various Intel Microprocessors by Instruction (continued)

Code	Description	8086	80286	80386	80486
WAIT	Wait while TEST pin				
	not asserted	4	3	6	1-3
WBINVD	Write-back invalid. data cache	--	--	--	5
XADD	Exchange and add				
	reg with reg	--	--	--	3
	reg with mem	--	--	--	4
XCHG	Exchange				
	reg with acc	3	3	3	3
	reg wtih mem	17+EA	5	5	5
	reg with reg	4	3	3	3
XLAT/ XLATB	Translate	11	5	5	4
XOR	Logical exclusive OR				
	reg with reg	3	2	2	1
	mem with reg	9+EA	7	7	2
	reg wtih mem	16+EA	7	6	3
	immed with acc	4	3	2	1
	immed with reg	4	3	2	1
	immed with mem	17+EA	7	7	3

APPENDIX C: ASSEMBLER DIRECTIVES AND NAMING RULES

This appendix consists of two sections. The first section describes some of the most widely used directives in 80x86 Assembly language programming. In the second section Assembly language rules and restrictions for names and labels are discussed and a list of reserved words is provided.

SECTION C.1: 80x86 ASSEMBLER DIRECTIVES

Directives, or as they are sometimes called pseudo-ops or pseudo-instructions, are used by the assembler to help it translate Assembly language programs into machine language. Unlike the microprocessor's instructions, directives do not generate any opcode; therefore, no memory locations are occupied by directives in the final ready to run (exe) version of the assembly program. To summarize, directives give directions to the assembler program to tell it how to generate the machine code; instructions are assembled into machine code to give directions to the CPU at execution time. The following are descriptions of the some of the most widely used directives for the 80x86 assembler. They are given in alphabetical order for ease of reference.

ASSUME

The ASSUME directive is used by the assembler to associate a given segment's name with a segment register. This is needed for instructions that must compute an address by combining an offset with a segment register. One ASSUME directive can be used to associate all the segment registers. For example:

```
ASSUME      CS:name1,DS:name2,SS:name3,ES:name4
```

where name1, name2, and so on, are the names of the segments. The same result can be achieved by having one ASSUME for each register:

```
ASSUME      CS:name1
ASSUME      DS:name2
ASSUME      SS:name3
ASSUME      ES:nothing
ASSUME      nothing
```

The key word "nothing" can be used to cancel a previous ASSUME directive.

DB   (Define Byte)

The DB directive is used to allocate memory in byte-sized increments. Look at the following examples:

```
DATA1  DB      23
DATA2  DB      45,97H,10000011B
DATA3  DB      'The planet Earth'
```

In DATA1 a single byte is defined with initial value 23. DATA2 consists of several values in decimal(45), hex (97H), and binary (10000011B). Finally, in DATA3, the DB directive is used to define ASCII characters. The DB directive is normally used to define ASCII data. In all the examples above, the address location for each value is assigned by the assembler. We can assigned a specific offset address by the use of the ORG directive.

DD   (Define Doubleword)

To allocate memory in 4-byte (32-bit) increments, the DD directive is used. Since word-sized operands are 16 bits wide (2 bytes) in 80x86 assemblers, a doubleword is 4 bytes.

```
VALUE1      DD      4563F57H
RESULT      DD      ?                          ;RESERVE  4-BYTE LOCATION
DAT4        DD      25000000
```

It must be noted that the values defined using the DD directive are placed in memory by the assembler in low byte to low address and high byte to high address order. This convention is referred to as little endian. For example, assuming that offset address 0020 is assigned to VALUE1 in the example above, each byte will reside in memory as follows:

```
DS:20=(57)
DS:21=(3F)
DS:22=(56)
DS:23=(04)
```

DQ   (Define Quadword)

To allocate memory in 8-byte increments, the DQ directive is used. In the 80x86 a word is defined as 2 bytes; therefore, a quadword is 8 bytes.

```
DAT_64B     DQ      5677DD4EE4FF45AH
DAT8        DQ      10000000000000
```

DT   (Define Tenbytes)

To allocate packed BCD data, 10 bytes at a time, the DT directive is used. This is widely used for memory allocation associated with BCD numbers.

```
DATA        DT              399977653419974
```

Notice there is no H for the hexadecimal identifier following the number. This is a characteristic particular to the DT directive. In the case of other directives (DB, DW, DD, DQ), if there is no H at the end of the number, it is assumed to be in decimal and will be converted to hex by the assembler. Remember that the little endian convention is used to place the bytes in memory, with the least significant byte going to the low address and the most significant byte to the high address. DT can also be used to allocated decimal data if "d" is placed after the number:

```
DATA        DT      65535d          ;stores hex FFFF in a 10-byte location
```

DUP   (Duplicate)

The DUP directive can be used to duplicate a set of data a certain number of times instead of having to write it over and over.

```
DATA1      DB    20 DUP (99)        ;DUPLICATE 99 20 TIMES
DATA2      DW    6 DUP (5555H)      ;DUPLICATE 5555H 6 TIMES
DATA3      DB    10 DUP (?)         ;RESERVE 10 BYTES
DATA4      DB    5 DUP (5 DUP (0))  ;25 BYTES  INITIALIZED TO ZERO
DATA5      DB    10 DUP (00,FFH)    ;20 BYTES ALTERNATELY = 00 & FF
```

DW   (Define Word)

To allocate memory in 2-byte (16-bit) increments, the DW directive is used. In the 80x86 family, a word is defined as 16 bits.

```
DATAW_1    DW    5000
DATAW_2    DW    7F6BH
```

Again, in terms of placing the bytes in memory the little endian convention is used with the least significant byte going to the low address and the most significant byte going to the high address.

END

Every program must have an entry point. To identify that entry point the assembler relies on the END directive. The label for the entry and end point must match.

```
HERE: MOV    AX,DATASEG          ;ENTRY POINT OF THE PROGRAM
             ...
             ...
      END    HERE                ;EXIT POINT OF THE PROGRAM
```

If there are several modules, only one of them can have the entry point, and the name of that entry point must be the same as the name put for the END directive as shown below:

```
;from the main program:
             EXTRN  PROG1:NEAR
             ...
MAIN_PRO:    MOV    AX,DATASG          ;THE ENTRY POINT
             MOV    DS,AX
             ...
             CALL   PROG1
             ...
             END    MAIN_PRO           ;THE EXIT POINT

;from the module PROG1:
             PUBLIC:PROG1
PROG1        PROC
             ...
             RET                       ;RETURN TO THE MAIN MODULE
PROG1        ENDP
             END                       ;NO LABEL IS GIVEN
```

Notice the following points:

1. The entry point must be identified by a name. In the example above the entry point is identified by the name MAIN_PRO.
2. The exit point must be identified by the same name given to the entry point, MAIN_PRO.
3. Since a given program can have only one entry point and exit point, all modules called (either from main or from the submodules) must have directive END with nothing after it.

ENDP   (see the PROC directive)

ENDS (see the SEGMENT and STRUCT directives)

EQU   (Equate)

To assign a fixed value to a name, one uses the EQU directive. The assembler will replace each occurrence of the name with the value assigned to it.

```
FIX_VALU      EQU    1200
PORT_A        EQU    60H
COUNT         EQU    100
MASK_1        EQU    00001111B
```

Unlike data directives such as DB, DW, and so on, EQU does not assign any memory storage; therefore, it can be defined at any time at any place, and can even be used within the code segment.

EVEN

The EVEN directive forces memory allocation to start at an even address. This is useful due to the fact that in 8086, 286, and 386SXmicroprocessors, accessing a 2-byte operand located at an odd address takes extra time. The use of the EVEN directive directs the assembler to assign an even address to the variable.

```
              ORG    0020H
DATA_1               DB     34H
              EVEN
DATA_2               DW     7F5BH
```

The following shows the contents of memory locations:

```
DS:0020 = (34)
DS:0021 = (? )
DS:0022 = (5B)
DS:0023 = (7F)
```

Notice that the EVEN directive caused memory location DS:0021 to be bypassed, and the value for DATA_2 is placed in memory starting with an even address.

EXTRN   (External)

The EXTRN directive is used to indicate that certain variables and names used in a module are defined by another module. In the absence of the EXTRN directive, the assembler would search for the definition and give an error when it couldn't find it. The format of this directive is

EXTRN name1:typea [,name2:typeb]

where type will be NEAR or FAR if name refers to a procedure, or will be BYTE, WORD, DWORD, QWORD, TBYTE if name refers to a data variable.

```
;from the main program:
          EXTRN  PROG1:NEAR
          PUBLIC:DATA1
          ...
MAIN_PRO  MOV    AX,DATASG              ;THE ENTRY POINT
          MOV    DS,AX
          ...
          CALL   PROG1
          ...
          END    MAIN_PRO              ;THE EXIT POINT

;PROG1 is located in a different file:
          EXTRN DATA1:WORD
          PUBLIC:PROG1
PROG1     PROC
          ...
          MOV    BX,DATA1
          ...
          RET                          ;RETURN TO THE MAIN MODULE
PROG1     ENDP
          END
```

Notice that the EXTRN directive is used in the main procedure to identify PROG1 as a NEAR procedure. This is needed because PROG1 is not defined in that module. Correspondingly, PROG1 is defined as PUBLIC in the module where it is defined. EXTRN is used in the PROG1 module to declare that operand DATA1, of size WORD, has been defined in another module. Correspondingly, DATA1 is declared as PUBLIC in the calling module.

GROUP

The GROUP directive causes the named segments to be linked into the same 64K byte segment. All segments listed in the GROUP directive must fit into 64K bytes. This can be used to combine segements of the same type, or different classes of segments. An example follows:

```
SMALL_SYS   GROUP         DTSEG,STSEG,CDSEG
```

The ASSUME directive must be changed to make the segment registers point to the group:

```
ASSUME       CS:SMALL_SYS,DS:SMALL_SYS,SS:SMALL_SYS
```

The group will be listed in the list file, as shown below:

Segments and Groups:

N a m e	Length	Align	Combine Class
SMALL_SYS	GROUP		
STSEG	0040	PARA	NONE
DTSEG	0024	PARA	NONE
CDSEG	005A	PARA	NONE

INCLUDE

When there is a group of macros written and saved in a separate file, the INCLUDE directive can be used to bring them into another file. In the program listing (.lst file), these macros will be identified by the symbol "C" (or "+" in some versions of MASM) before each instruction to indicate they are copied to the present file by the INCLUDE directive. See Chapter 5 for examples of using the INCLUDE directive.

LABEL

The LABEL directive allows a given variable or name to be referred to by multiple names. This is often used for multiple definition of the same variable or name. The format of the LABEL directive is

```
name    LABEL  type
```

where type may be BYTE, WORD, DWORD, QWORD. For example, a variable name DATA1 is defined as a word and also needs to be accessed as 2 bytes, as shown in the following:

```
DATA_B       LABEL BYTE
DATA1        DW    25F6H

             MOV   AX,DATA1          ;AX=25F6H
             MOV   BL,DATA_B         ;BL=F6H
             MOV   BH,DATA_B +1      ;BH=25H
```

The following shows the LABEL directive being used to allow accessing a 32-bit data item in 16-bit portions.

```
DATA_16      LABEL WORD
DATDD_4      DD    4387983FH
             ...
             MOV   AX,DATA_16        ;AX=983FH
             MOV   DX,DATA_16 + 2    ;DX=4387H
```

The following shows its use in a JMP instruction to go to a different code segment.

```
             ....
             JMP   PROG_A
             ....
PROG_A       LABEL FAR
INITI:       MOV   AL,12H
             OUT   PORT,AL
```

In the program above the address assigned to the names "PROG_A" and "INITI" are exactly the same. The same function can be achieved by the following:

```
JMP FAR PTR INITI
```

LENGTH

The LENGTH operator returns the number of items defined by a DUP operand. See the SIZE directive for an example.

OFFSET

To access the offset address assigned to a variable or a name one uses the OFFSET directive. For example, the OFFSET directive was used in the following example to get the offset address assigned by the assembler to the variable DATA1:

```
        ORG   5600H
DATA1   DW    2345H
        ...
        MOV   SI,OFFSET DATA1     ;SI=OFFSET OF DATA1 = 5600H
```

Notice that this has the same result as "LEA SI,DATA1".

ORG   (Origin)

The ORG directive is used to assign an offset address for a variable or name. For example, to force variable DATA1 to be locating starting from offset address of 0020, one would write

```
        ORG   0020H
DATA1   DW    41F2H
```

This ensures the offset addresses of 0020 and 0021 with content $0020H = (F2)$ and $0021H = (41)$.

PAGE

The PAGE directive is used to make the ".lst" file print in a specific format. The format of the PAGE directive is

PAGE [lines],[columns]

The default listing (meaning that no PAGE directive is coded) will have 66 lines per page with a maximum of 80 characters per line. This can be changed to 60 and 132 with the directive "PAGE 60,132". The range for number of lines is 10 to 255 and for columns is 60 to 132. A PAGE directive with no numbers will generate a page break.

PROC and ENDP   (Procedure and End Procedure)

Often, a group of Assembly language instructions will be combined into a procedure so that it call be called by another module. The PROC and ENDP directives are used to indicate the beginning and end of the procedure. For a given procedure the name assigned to PROC and ENDP must be exactly the same.

```
name1          PROC  [attribute]
               ...
name1          ENDP
```

There are two choices for the attribute of the PROC: NEAR or FAR. If no attribute is given, the default is NEAR. When a NEAR procedure is called, only IP is saved since CS of the called procedure is the same as the calling program. If a FAR procedure is called, both IP and CS are saved since the code segment of the called procedure is different from the calling program.

PTR   (Pointer)

The PTR directive is used to specify the size of the operand. Among the options for size are BYTE, WORD, DWORD, and QWORD. This directive is used in many different ways, the most common of which are explained below.

1. PTR can be used to allow an override of a previously defined data directive.

```
DATA1          DB    23H,7FH,99H,0B2H
DATA2          DW    67F1H
DATA3          DD    22229999H

               ...
               MOV   AX, WORD PTR DATA1 ;AX=7F23
               MOV   BX, WORD PTR DATA1 + 2 ;BX,B299H
```

Although DATA1 was initially defined as DB, it can be accessed using the WORD PTR directive.

```
               MOV   AL, BYTE PTR DATA2  ;AL=F1H
```

In the above, notice that DATA2 was defined as WORD but it is accessed as BYTE with the help of BYTE PTR. If this had been coded as "MOV AL,DATA2", it would generate an error since the sizes of the operands do not match.

```
               MOV   AX, WORD PTR DATA3      ;AX=9999H
               MOV   DX, WORD PTR DATA3 + 2  ;DX=2222H
```

DATA3 was defined as a 4-byte operand but registers are only 2 bytes wide. The WORD PTR directive solved that problem.

2. The PTR directive can be used to specify the size of a directive in order to help the assembler translate the instruction.

```
               INC   [DI]                    ;will cause an error
```

This instruction was meant to increment the contents of the memory location(s) pointed at by [DI]. How does the assembler know whether it is a byte operand, word operand, or doubleword operand? Since it does not know, it will generate an error. To correct that, use the PTR directive to specify the size of the operand as shown next.

```
               INC   BYTE PTR [SI]     ;increment a byte pointed by SI
        or
               INC   WORD PTR [SI]     ;increment a word pointed by SI
        or
               INC   DWORD PTR [SI]    ;increment a doubleword pointed by SI
```

3. The PTR directive can be used to specify the distance of a jump. The options for the distance are FAR and NEAR.

```
        JMP    FAR   PTR    INTI    ;ensures that it will be a 5-byte instruction
        ...
INITI:  MOV    AX,1200
```

See The LABEL directive to find out how it can be used to achieve the same result.

PUBLIC

To inform the assembler that a name or symbol will be referenced by other modules, it is marked by the PUBLIC directive. If a module is referencing a variable outside itself, that variable must be declared as EXTRN. Correspondingly, in the module where the variable is defined, that variable must be declared as PUBLIC in order to allow it to be referenced by other modules. See the EXTRN directive for examples of the use of both EXTRN and PUBLIC.

SEG   (Segment Address)

The SEG operator is used to access the address of the segment where the name has been defined.

```
DATA1        DW     2341H
             ...
             MOV    AX,SEG DATA1 ;AX=SEGMENT ADDRESS OF DATA1
```

This is in contrast to the OFFSET directive which accesses the offset address instead of the segment.

SEGMENT and ENDS

In full segment definition these two directives are used to indicate the beginning and the end of the segment. They must have the same name for a given segment definition. See the following example:

```
DATSEG       SEGMENT
DATA1  DB    2FH
DATA2  DW    1200
DATA3  DD    99999999H
DATSEG       ENDS
```

There are several options associated with the SEGMENT directive, as follows:

```
name1        SEGMENT [align] [combine] [class]

name1        ENDS
```

ALIGNMENT: When several assembled modules are linked together, this indicates where the segment is to begin. There are many options, including PARA (paragraph = 16 bytes), WORD, and BYTE. If PARA is chosen, the segment starts at the hex address divisible by 10H. PARA is the default alignment. In this alignment, if a segment for a module finished at 00024H, the next segment will start at address 00030H, leaving from 00025 to 0002F unused. If WORD is chosen, the segment is forced to start at a word boundary. In BYTE alignment, the segment starts at the next byte and no memory is wasted. There is also the PAGE option, which aligns segments along the 100H (256) byte boundary. While all these options are supported by many assemblers, such as MASM and TASM, there is another option supported only by assemblers that allow system development. This option is AT. The AT option allows the program to assign a physical address. For example, to burn a program into ROM starting at physical address F0000, code

```
ROM_CODE    SEGMENT    AT F000H
```

Due to the fact that option AT allows the programmer to specify a physical address that conflicts with DOS's memory management responsibility, many assemblers such as MASM will not allow option AT.

COMBINE TYPE: This option is used to merge together all the similar segments to create one large segment. Among the options widely used are PUBLIC and STACK. PUBLIC is widely used in code segment definitions when linking more than one module. This will consolidate all the code segments of the various modules into one large code segment. If there is only one data segment and that belongs to the main module, there is no need to define it as PUBLIC since no other module has any data segment to combine with. However, if other modules have their own data segment, it is recommended that they be made PUBLIC to create a single data segment when they are linked. In the absence of that, the linker would assume that each segment is private and they would not be combined with other similar segments (codes with codes and data with data). Since there is only one stack segment, which belongs to the main module, there is no need to define it as PUBLIC. The STACK option is used only with the stack segment definition and indicates to the linker that it should combine the user's defined stack with the system stack to create a single stack for the entire program. This is the stack that is used at run time (when the CPU is actually executing the program).

CLASS NAME: Indicates to the linker that all segments of the same class should be placed next to each other by the LINKER. Four class names commonly used are 'CODE', 'DATA', 'STACK', and 'EXTRA'. When this attribute is used in the segment definition, it must be enclosed in single apostrophes in order to be recognized by the linker.

SHORT

In a direct jump such as "JMP POINT_A", the assembler has to choose either the 2-byte or 3-byte format. In the 2-byte format, one byte is the opcode and the second byte is the signed number displacement value added to the IP of the instruction immediately following the JMP. This displacement can be anywhere between -128 and +127. A negative number indicates a backward JMP and a positive number a forward JMP. In the 3-byte format the first byte is the opcode and the next two bytes are for the signed number displacement value, which can range from -32,768 to 32,767. When assembling a program, the assembler makes two passes through the program. Certain tasks are done in the first pass and others are left to the second pass to complete. In the first pass the assembler chooses the 3-byte code for the JMP. After the first pass is complete, it will know the target address and fill it in during the second pass. If the target address indicates a short jump (less than 128) bytes away, it fills the last byte with NOP. To inform the assembler that the target address is no more than 128 bytes away, the SHORT directive can be used. Using the SHORT directive makes sure that the JMP is 2-byte instruction and not 3-byte with 1 byte as NOP code. The 2-byte JMP requires 1 byte less memory and is executed faster.

SIZE

The size operator returns the total number of bytes occupied by a name. The three directives LENGTH, SIZE, and TYPE are somewhat related. Below is a description of each one using the following set of data defined in a data segment:

```
DATA1      DQ    ?
DATA2      DW    ?
DATA3      DB    20 DUP (?)
DATA4      DW    100 DUP (?)
DATA5      DD    10 DUP (?)
```

TYPE allows one to know the storage allocation directive for a given variable by providing the number of bytes according to the following table:

```
bytes
1      DB
2      DW
4      DD
8      DQ
10     DT
```

For example:
```
MOV    BX,TYPE DATA2    ;BX=2
MOV    DX,TYPE DATA1    ;DX=8
MOV    AX,TYPE DATA3    ;AX=1
MOV    CX,TYPE DATA5    ;CX=4
```

When a DUP is used to define the number of entries for a given variable, the LENGTH directive can be used to get that number.

```
MOV    CX,LENGTH DATA4    ;CX=64H    (100 DECIMAL)
MOV    AX,LENGTH DATA3    ;AX=14H    (20 DECIMAL)
MOV    DX,LENGTH DATA5    ;DX=0A     (10 DECIMAL)
```

If the defined variable does not have any DUP in it, the LENGTH is assumed to be 1.

```
MOV    BX,LENGTH DATA1    ;BX=1
```

SIZE is used to determine the total number of bytes allocated for a variable that has been defined with the DUP directive. In reality the SIZE directive basically provides the product of the TYPE times LENGTH.

```
MOV    DX, SIZE DATA4    ;DX=C8H=200 decimal (100 x 2=200)
MOV    CX, SIZE DATA5    ;CX=28H=40 decimal (4 x 10=40)
```

STRUC   (Structure)

The STRUC directive indicates the beginning of a structure definition. It is ended with an ENDS directive, whose label matches the STRUC label. Although the same mnemonic ENDS is used for end of segment and end of structure, the assembler knows which is meant by the context. A structure is a collection of data types that can be accessed either collectively by the structure name or individually by the labels of the data types within the structure. A structure type must first be defined and then variables in the data segment may be allocated as that structure type. Looking at the following example, the data directives between STRUC and ENDS declare what structure ASC_AREA looks like. No memory is allocated for such a structure definition. Immediately below the structure definition is the label ASC_INPUT, which is declared to be of type ASC_AREA. Memory is allocated for the variable ASC_INPUT. Notice in the code segment that ASC_INPUT can be accessed either in its entirety or by its component parts. It is accessed as a whole unit in "MOV DX,OFFSET ASC_INPUT". Its component parts are accessed by the variable name followed by a period, then the component's name. For example, "MOV BL,ASC_INPUT.ACT_LEN" accesses the actual length field of ASC_IN-PUT.

```
;from the data segment:
ASC_AREA    STRUC                      ;defines struc for string input
MAX_LEN     DB        6                ; maximum length of input string
ACT_LEN     DB        ?                ; actual length of input string
ASC_NUM     DB        6 DUP (?)        ; input string
ASC_AREA    ENDS                       ;end struc definition
ASC_INPUT   ASC_AREA  <>               ;allocates memory for struc

;from the code segment:
            ...
GET_ASC:    MOV   AH,0AH
            MOV   DX,OFFSET ASC_INPUT
            INT   21H
            ...
            MOV   SI,OFFSET ASC_INPUT.ASC_NUM  ;SI points to ASCII num
            MOV   BL,ASC_INPUT.ACT_LEN          ;BL holds string length
            ...
```

TITLE

The TITLE directive instructs the assembler to print the title of the program on top of each page of the ".lst" file. What comes after the TITLE pseudo-instruction is up to the programmer, but it is common practice to put the name of the program as stored on the disk right after the TITLE pseudo-instruction and then a brief description of the function of the program. Whatever is placed after the TITLE pseudo-instruction cannot be more than 60 ASCII characters (letters, numbers, spaces, punctuation, etc).

TYPE

The TYPE operator returns the number of bytes reserved for the named data object. See the SIZE directive for examples of its use.

SECTION C.2: RULES FOR LABELS AND RESERVED NAMES

Labels in 80x86 Assembly language for MASM 5.1 and higher must follow these rules:

1. Names can be composed of:
    alphabetic characters: A - Z and a - z
    digits: 0 - 9
    special characters: "?" "." "@" "_" "$"

2. Names must begin with an alphabetic or special character. Names cannot begin with a digit.

3. Names can be up to 31 characters long.

4. The special character "." can only be used as the first character.

5. Uppercase and lowercase are treated the same. "NAME1" is treated the same as "Name1" and "name1".

Assembly language programs have five types of labels or names:

1. Code labels, which give symbolic names to instructions so that other instructions (such as jumps) may refer to them

2. Procedure labels, which assign a name to a procedure

3. Segment labels, which assign a name to a segment

4. Data labels, which give names to data items

5. Labels created with the LABEL directive

Code labels

These labels will be followed by a colon and have the type NEAR. This enables other instructions within the code segment to refer to the instruction. The labels can be on the same line as the instruction:

```
            ...
ADD_LP:     ADD  AL,[BX]        ;label is on same line as the instruction
            ...
            ...
            LOOP ADD_LP
```

or on a line by themselves:

```
            ...
ADD_LP:                         ;label is on a line by itself
            ADD  AL,[BX]        ;ADD_LP refers to this instruction
            ...
            ...
            LOOP ADD_LP
```

Procedure labels

These labels assign a symbolic name to a procedure. The label can be NEAR or FAR. When using full segment definition, the default type is NEAR. When using simplified segment definition, the type will be NEAR for compact or small models but will be FAR for medium, large, and huge models. For more information on procedures, see PROC in Section 1 of Appendix C.

Segment labels

These labels give symbolic names to segments. The name must be the same in the SEGMENT and ENDS directives. See SEGMENT in Section 1 of this appendix for more information. Example:

```
DAT_SG       SEGMENT
SUM          DW     ?
DAT_SG       ENDS
```

Data labels

These labels give symbolic names to data items. This allows them to be accessed by instructions. Directives DB, DW, DD, DQ and DT are used to allocate data. Examples:

```
DATA1        DB     43H
DATA2        DB     F2H
SUM          DW     ?
```

Labels defined with the LABEL directive

The LABEL directive can be used to redefine a label. See LABEL in Section 1 of this Appendix for more information.

Reserved Names

The following is a list of reserved words in 80x86 Assembly language programming. These words cannot be used as user-defined labels or variable names.

Register Names:

AH	AL	AX	BH	BL	BP	BX	CH	CL	CS	CX	DH
DI	DL	DS	DX	ES	SI	SP	SS				

Instructions:

AAA	AAD	AAM	AAS	ADC	ADD
AND	CALL	CBW	CLC	CLD	CLI
CMC	CMP	CMPS	CWD	DAA	DAS
DEC	DIV	ESC	HLT	IDIV	IMUL
IN	INC	INT	INTO	IRET	JA
JAE	JB	JBE	JCXZ	JE	JG
JGE	JL	JLE	JMP	JNA	JNAE
JNB	JNBE	JNE	JNG	JNGE	JNL
JNLE	JNO	JNP	JNS	JNZ	JO
JP	JPE	JPO	JS	JZ	LAHF
LDS	LEA	LES	LOCK	LODS	LOOP
LOOPE	LOOPNE	LOOPNZ	LOOPZ	MOV	MOVS
MUL	NEG	NIL	NOP	NOT	OR
OUT	POP	POPF	PUSH	PUSHF	RCL
RCR	REP	REPE	REPNE	REPNZ	REPZ
RET	ROL	ROR	SAHF	SAL	SAR
SBB	SCAS	SHL	SHR	STC	STD
STI	STOS	SUB	TEST	WAIT	XCHG
XLAT	XOR				

Assembler operators and directives

$ * +	- . /	= ?	[]		
ALIGN	ASSUME	BYTE	COMM	COMMENT	DB
DD	DF	DOSSEG	DQ	DS	DT
DW	DWORD	DUP	ELSE	END	ENDIF
ENDM	ENDS	EQ	EQU	EVEN	EXITM
EXTRN	FAR	FWORD	GE	GROUP	GT
HIGH	IF	IFB	IFDEF	IFDIF	IFE
IFIDN	IFNB	IFNDEF	IF1	IF2	INCLUDE
INCLUDELIB	IRP	IRPC	LABEL	LE	LENGTH
LINE	LOCAL	LOW	LT	MACRO	MASK
MOD	NAME	NE	NEAR	NOTHING	OFFSET
ORG	PAGE	PROC	PTR	PUBLIC	PURGE
QWORD	RECORD	REPT	REPTRD	SEG	SEGMENT
SHORT	SIZE	STACK	STRUC	SUBTTL	TBYTE
THIS	TITLE	TYPE	WIDTH	WORD	
.186	.286	.286P	.287	.386	.386P
.387	.8086	.8087	.ALPHA	.CODE	.CONST
.CREF	.DATA	.DATA?	.ERR	.ERR1	.ERR2
.ERRB	.ERRDEF	.ERRDIF	.ERRE	.ERRIDN	.ERRNB
.ERRNDEF	.ERRNZ	.FARDATA	.FARDATA?	.LALL	.LFCOND
.LIST	.MODEL	%OUT	.RADIX	.SALL	.SEQ
.SFCOND	.STACK	.TFCOND	.TYPE	.XALL	.XCREF
.XLIST					

APPENDIX D: DOS INTERRUPT 21H LISTING

This appendix lists many of the DOS 21H interrupts, which are used primarily for input, output, and file and memory management. First, a few notes are given about file management under DOS. There are two commonly used ways to access files in DOS. One is through what is called a file handle, the other is through a FCB, or file control block. These terms are defined in detail below. Function calls 0FH through 28H use FCBs to access files. Function calls 39H through 62H use file handles. Handle calls are more powerful and easier to use. However, FCB calls maintain compatibility down to DOS version 1.10. FCB calls have the further limitation that they reference only the files in the current directory, whereas handle calls reference any file in any directory. FCB calls use the file control block to perform any function on a file. Handle calls use an ASCIIZ string (defined below) to open, create, delete, or rename a file and use a file handle for I/O requests. There are some terms used in the interrupt listing that will be unfamiliar to many readers. DOS manuals provide complete coverage of the details of file managment, but a few key terms are defined below.

ASCIIZ string

This is a string composes of any combination of ASCII characters and terminated with one byte of binary zeros (00H). It is frequently used in DOS 21 interrupt calls to specify a filename or path. The following is an example of an ASCIIZ string that was defined in the data segment of a program:

```
NAME_1      DB      'C:\PROGRAMS\SYSTEM_A\PROGRAM5.ASM',0
```

Directory

DOS keeps track of where files are located by means of a directory. Each disk can be partitioned into one or more directories. The directory listing lists each file in that directory, its starting sector, the number of bytes in the file, the date and time the file was created, and other information that DOS needs to access that file. The familiar DOS command "DIR" lists the directory of the current drive to the monitor.

DTA Disk transfer area

This is essentially a buffer area that DOS will use to hold data for reads or writes performed with FCB function calls. This area can be set up by your program anywhere in the data segment. Function call 1AH tells DOS the location of the DTA. Only one DTA can be active at a time.

FAT File allocation table

Each disk has a file allocation table that gives information about the clusters on a disk. Each disk is divided into sectors, which are grouped into clusters. The size of sectors and clusters varies among the different disk types. For each cluster in the disk, the FAT has a code indicating whether the cluster is being used by a file, is available, is reserved, or has been marked as a bad cluster. DOS uses this information in storing and retrieving files.

FCB File control block

One FCB is associated with each open file. It is composed of 37 bytes of data which give information about a file, such as drive, filename and extension, size of the file in bytes, and date and time it was created. It also stores the current block and record numbers, which serve as pointers into a file when it is being read or written to. DOS INT 21H function calls 0FH through 28H use FCBs to access files. Function 0FH is used to open a file, 16H to create a new file. Function calls 14H - 28H perform read/write functions on the file, and 16H is used to close the file. Typically, the filename information is set up with function call 29H (Parse Filename), and then the address of the FCB is placed in DS:DX and is used to access the file.

File handle

DOS function calls 3CH through 62H use file handles. When a file or device is created or opened with one of these calls, its file handle is returned. The file handle is used thereafter to refer to that file for input, output, closing the file, and so on. DOS has a few predefined file handles that can be used by any Assembly language program. These do not need to be opened before they are used:

Handle value	Refers to
0000	standard input device (typically, the keyboard)
0001	standard output device (typically, the monitor)
0002	standard error output device (typically, the monitor)
0003	standard auxiliary device (AUX1)
0004	standard printer device (PTR1)

PSP Program segment prefix

The PSP is a 256-byte area of memory, reserved by DOS for each program. It provides an area to store shared information between the program and DOS.

AH   Function

00   **Terminate the program**

Additional Call Registers
CS = segment address of
PSP (program segment prefix)

Result Registers
None

Note: Files should be closed previously or data may be lost.

01   **Keyboard input with echo**

Additional Call Registers
None

Result Registers
AL = input character   ASCII

Note: Checks for ctrl-break.

02   **Output character to monitor**

Additional Call Registers
DL = character to be displayed

Result Registers
None

03   **Asynchronous input from auxiliary device (serial device)**

Additional Call Registers
None

Result Registers
AL = input character

04   **Asynchronous character output**

Additional Call Registers
DL = character to be output

Result Registers
None

05   **Output character to printer**

Additional Call Registers
DL = character to be printed

Result Registers
None

06   **Console I/O**

Additional Call Registers
DL = OFFH if input
or character to be
displayed, if output

Result Registers
AL = 0H if no character available
   = character that was input, if
input successful

Note: If input, ZF is cleared and AL will have the character. ZF is set if input
and no character was available.

AH   Function

07   Keyboard input without echo

Additional Call Registers	Result Registers
None	AL = input character

Note: Does not check for ctrl-break.

08   Keyboard input without echo

Additional Call Registers	Result Registers
None	AL = input character

Note: Checks for ctrl-break.

09   String output

Additional Call Registers	Result Registers
DS:DX = string address	None

Note: Displays characters beginning at address until a '$' (ASCII 36) is encountered.

0A   String input

Additional Call Registers	Result Registers
DS:DX = address at which to store string	None

Note: Specify the maximum size of the string in byte 1 of the buffer. DOS will place the actual size of the string in byte 2. The string begins in byte 3.

0B   Get keyboard status

Additional Call Registers	Result Registers
None	AL = 00 if no character waiting = OFFH if character waiting

Note: Checks for ctrl-break.

0C   Reset input buffer and call keyboard input function

Additional Call Registers	Result Registers
AL = keyboard function number 01H, 06H, 07H, 08H or 0AH	None

Note: This function waits until a character is typed in.

AH   Function

0D   Reset disk

Additional Call Registers	Result Registers
None	None

Note: Flushes DOS file buffers but does not close files.

0E   Set default drive

Additional Call Registers	Result Registers
DL = code for drive (0=A, 1=B, 2=C, etc.)	AL = number of logical drives in system

0F   Open file

Additional Call Registers	Result Registers
DS:DX = address of FCB	AL = 00 if successful = OFFH if file not found

Note: Searches current directory for file. If found, FCB is filled.

10   Close file

Additional Call Registers	Result Registers
DS:DX = address of FCB	AL = 00 if successful = OFFH if file not found

Note: Flushes all buffers. Also updates directory if file has been modified.

11   Search for first matching filename

Additional Call Registers	Result Registers
DS:DX = address of FCB	AL = 00 if match is found = OFFH if no match found

Note: Filenames can contain wildcards '?' and '*'.

12   Search for next match

Additional Call Registers	Result Registers
DS:DX = address of FCB	AL = 00 if match found = OFFH if no match found

Note: This call should be used only if previous call to 11H or 12H has been successful.

<u>AH</u>   <u>Function</u>

13   Delete file(s)

<u>Additional Call Registers</u>   <u>Result Registers</u>
DS:DX = address of FCB   AL = 00 if file(s) deleted
                                   = OFFH if no files deleted

Note: Deletes all files in current directory matching filename, provided that they are not read-only. Files should be closed before deleting.

14   Sequential read

<u>Additional Call Registers</u>   <u>Result Registers</u>
DS:DX = address of opened FCB   AL = 00H if read successful
                                   = 01H if end of file and no
                                     data is read
                                   = 02H if DTA is too small to
                                     hold the record
                                   = 03H if partial record read and
                                     end of file is reached

Note: The file pointer, block pointer, and FCB record pointer are updated automatically by DOS.

15   Sequential write

<u>Additional Call Registers</u>   <u>Result Registers</u>
DS:DX = address of opened FCB   AL = 00H if write successful
                                   = 01H if disk is full
                                   = 02H if DTA is too small to
                                     hold the record

Note: The file pointer, block pointer, and FCB record pointer are updated automatically by DOS. The record may not physically be written until a cluster is full or the file is closed.

16   Create/open a file

<u>Additional Call Registers</u>   <u>Result Registers</u>
DS:DX = addr. of unopened FCB   AL = 00H if successful
      = OFFH if unsuccessful

Note: If the file already exists, it will be truncated to length 0.

17   Rename file(s)

<u>Additional Call Registers</u>   <u>Result Registers</u>
DS:DX = address of FCB   AL = 00H if file(s) renamed
                                   = OFFH if file not found
                                   or new name already exists

Note: The old name is in the name position of the FCB; the new name is at the size (offset 16H) position.

AH   Function

18   **Reserved**

19   **Get default drive**

Additional Call Registers	Result Registers
None	AL = 0H for drive A
	= 1H for drive B
	= 2H for drive C

1A   **Specify DTA (disk transfer address)**

Additional Call Registers	Result Registers
DS:DX = DTA	None

Note: Only one DTA can be current at a time. This function must be called before FCB reads, writes, and directory searches.

1B   **Get FAT (file allocation table) for default drive**

Additional Call Registers	Result Registers
None	AL = number of sectors per cluster
	CX = number of bytes per sector
	DX = number of cluster per disk
	DS:BX FAT id

1C   **Get FAT (file allocation table) for any drive**

Additional Call Registers	Result Registers
DL = drive code	AL = number of sectors per cluster
0 for A	CX = number of bytes per sector
1 for B	DX = number of cluster per disk
2 for C	DS:BX FAT id

1D   **Reserved**

1E   **Reserved**

1F   **Reserved**

20   **Reserved**

21   **Random read**

Additional Call Registers	Result Registers
DS:DX = address of opened FCB	AL = 00H if read successful
	= 01H if end of file and no data read
	= 02H if DTA too small for record
	= 03H if end of file and partial read

Note: Reads record pointed at by current block and record fields into DTA.

AH   Function

22   Random write

Additional Call Registers	Result Registers
DS:DX = address of opened FCB	AL = 00H if write successful
= 01H if disk is full	
= 02H if DTA too small for record	

Note: Writes from DTA to record pointed at by current block and record fields.

23   Get file size

Additional Call Registers	Result Registers
DS:DX = addr. of unopened FCB	AL = 00H if file found, number
of records is set in FCB random-	
record field (offset 0021H)	
= 0FFH if no match found	

Note: The FCB should contain the record size before the interrupt.

24   Set random record field

Additional Call Registers	Result Registers
DS:DX = address of opened FCB	None

Note: This sets the random-record field (offset 0021H) in the FCB. It is used prior to switching from sequential to random processing.

25   Set interrupt vector

Additional Call Registers	Result Registers
DS:DX = interrupt handler addr.	None
AL = machine interrupt number	

Note: This is used to change the way the system handles interrupts.

26   Create a new PSP (program segment prefix)

Additional Call Registers	Result Registers
DX = segment addr. of new PSP	None

Note: DOS versions 2.0 and higher recommend not using this service, but using service 4B (exec).

<u>AH</u>   <u>Function</u>

27   **Random block read**

Additional Call Registers _____
DS:DX = address of opened FCB
CX = number records to be read
= 02H if DTA too small for block
= 03H if EOF and partial block read
CX = number of records actually read

Result Registers _____
AL = 00H if read successful
= 01H if end of file and no data read

Note: Set the FCB random record and record size fields prior to the interrupt.
DOS will update the random record, current block, and current record fields after
the read.

28   **Random block write**

Additional Call Registers _____
DS:DX = address of opened FCB
CX = number records to write
= 02H if DTA too small for block
CX = number of records actually written

Result Registers _____
AL = 00H if write successful
= 01H if disk is full

Note: Set the FCB random record and record size fields prior to the interrupt.
DOS will update the random record, current block and current record fields
after the write. If CX = 0 prior to the interrupt, nothing is written to the file and
the file is truncated or extended to the length computed by the random record
and record size fields.

29   **Parse filename**

Additional Call Registers _____
DS:SI = address of command line
ES:DI = address of FCB
AL = parsing flags in bits 0-3
   Bit 0 = 1 if leading separators
   are to be ignored; otherwise
   no scan-off takes place
   Bit 1 = 1 if drive ID in FCB
   will be changed only if drive
   was specified in command line
   Bit 2 = 1 if filename will be
   changed only if filename was
   specified in command line
   Bit 3 = 1 if extension will be
   changed only if extension was
   specified in command line

Result Registers _____
DS:SI = address of first char after
ES:DI = address of first byte of
formatted unopened FCB
AL = 00H if no wildcards were in
filename or extension
= 01H if wildcard found
= 0FFH if drive specifier is invalid

Note: The command line is parsed for a filename, then an unopened FCB is
created at DS:SI. The command should not be used if path names are specified.

AH   Function

2A   Get system date

Additional Call Registers	Result Registers
None	CX = year (1980-2099)
	DH = month (1-12)
	DL = day (1-31)
	AL = day of week code
	(0 = Sunday, ... , 6 = Saturday)

2B   Set system date

Additional Call Registers	Result Registers
CX = year (1980-2099)	AL = 00H if date set
DH = month (1-12)	= 0FFH if date not valid
DL = day (1-31)

2C   Get system time

Additional Call Registers	Result Registers
None	CH = hour (0 .. 23)
	CL = minute (0 .. 59)
	DH = second (0 .. 59)
	DL = hundredth of second
	(0 .. 99)

Note: The format returned can be used in calculations but can be converted to a printable format.

2D   Set system time

Additional Call Registers	Result Registers
CH = hour (0 .. 23)	AL = 00H if time set
CL = minute	= 0FFH if time invalid
DH = second
DL = hundredth of second

2E   Set/reset verify switch

Additional Call Registers	Result Registers
AL = 0 to turn verify off	None
= 1 to turn verify on

Note: If verify is on, DOS will perform a verify every time data is written to disk. An interrupt call to 54H gets the setting of the verify switch.

2F   Get DTA (disk transfer area)

Additional Call Registers	Result Registers
None	ES:BX = address of DTA

<u>AH</u>   <u>Function</u>

30   **Get DOS version number**

<u>Additional Call Registers</u>   <u>Result Registers</u>
None   AL = major version number (0,2,3,etc.)
                                  AH = minor version number

31   **Terminate process and stay resident (KEEP process)**

<u>Additional Call Registers</u>   <u>Result Registers</u>
AL = binary return code   None
                                  DX = memory size in paragraphs

Note: This interrupt call terminates the current process and attempts to place the memory size in paragraphs in the initial allocation block, but does not release any other allocation blocks. The return code in AL can be retrieved by the parent process using interrupt 21 call 4DH.

32   **Reserved**

33   **Ctrl-break control**

<u>Additional Call Registers</u>   <u>Result Registers</u>
AL = 00 to get state of   DL = 00 if ctrl-break check off
    ctrl-break check   = 01 if ctrl-break check on
   = 01 to modify state of
    ctrl-break check
DL = 00 to turn check off
   = 01 to turn check on

Note: When ctrl-break check is set to off, DOS minimizes the times it checks for ctrl-break input. When it is set to on, DOS checks for ctrl-break on most operations.

34   **Reserved**

35   **Get interrupt vector address**

<u>Additional Call Registers</u>   <u>Result Registers</u>
AL = interrupt number   ES:BX = address of interrupt handler

36   **Get free disk space**

<u>Additional Call Registers</u>   <u>Result Registers</u>
DL = drive code   AX = FFFFH if drive code invalid
(0 = default,   = sectors per cluster if valid
 1 = A, 2 = B,etc.)   BX = number of available clusters
                                  CX = bytes per sector
                                  DX = total clusters per drive

AH   Function

37   **Reserved**

38   **Country dependent information**

Additional Call Registers
DS:DX = address of 32-byte
block of memory
AL = function code

Result Registers
None

39   **Create subdirectory (MKDIR)**

Additional Call Registers
DS:DX = address of ASCIIZ path
 name of new subdirectory
AX = 3 if path not found

Result Registers
Carry flag = 0 if successful
= 1 if failed
= 5 if access denied

3A   **Remove subdirectory (RMDIR)**

Additional Call Registers
DS:DX = address of ASCIIZ path
 name of subdirectory
AX = 3 if path not found
= 5 if direotory not empty
= 15 if drive invalid

Result Registers
Carry flag = 0 if successful
= 1 if failed

Note: The current directory cannot be removed.

3B   **Change the current subdirectory (CHDIR)**

Additional Call Registers
DS:DX = address of ASCIIZ path
 name of new subdirectory

Result Registers
Carry flag = 0 if successful
= 1 if failed
AX = 3 if path not found

3C   **Create a file**

Additional Call Registers
DS:DX = address of ASCIIZ path
 and file name
CX = file attribute

Result Registers
Carry flag = 0 if successful
= 1 if failed
AX = handle if successful
= 3 if path not found
= 5 if access denied

Note: Creates a new file if filename does not exist, otherwise truncates the file to
length zero. Opens the file for reading or writing. A 16-bit handle will be returned   in AX if the create was successful.

AH   Function

3D   Open file

Additional Call Registers
DS:DX = addres of ASCIIZ path
and file name
AL = mode flags (see below)

Result Registers
Carry flag = 0 if successful
        = 1 if failed
AX = 16-bit file handle if successful
        = 1 if function number invalid
        = 2 if file not found
        = 3 if path not found
        = 4 if handle not available
        = 5 if access denied
        = OCH if access code invalid

AL mode flag summary:

76543210 (bits)	Result
000	open for read
001	open for write
010	open for read/write
0	reserved
000	give others compatible access
001	read/write access denied to others
010	write access denied to others
011	read access denied to others
100	give full access to others
0	file inherited by child process
1	file private to current process

3E   Close file

Additional Call Registers
BX = file handle

Result Registers
Carry flag = 0 if successful
        = 1 if failed
AX = 6 if invalid handle or file not open

Note: All internal buffers are flushed before the file is closed.

3F   Read from file or device

Additional Call Registers
DS:DX = buffer address
BX = file handle
CX = number of bytes to read

Result Registers
Carry flag = 0 if successful
        = 1 if failed
AX = number of bytes actually read,
        = 5 if access denied
        = 6 if file not open or invalid handle

Note: When reading from the standard device (keyboard), at most one line of text
will be read, regardless of the value of CX.

AH   Function

40   Write to file or device

Additional Call Registers
DS:DX = buffer address
BX = file handle
CX = number of bytes to write

Result Registers
Carry flag = 0 if successful
= 1 if failed
AX = number of bytes actually
    written if successful
= 5 if access denied
= 6 if file not open or invalid handle

Note: If the carry flag is clear and AX is less than CX, a parital record was written or a disk full or other error was encountered.

41   Delete file (UNLINK)

Additional Call Registers
DS:DX = address of ASCIIZ
    file specification

Result Registers
Carry flag = 0 if successful
= 1 if failed
AX = 2 if file not found
= 5 if access denied

Note: This function cannot be used to delete a file that is read-only.   First, change the file's attribute to 0 by using interrupt 21 call 43H, then delete the file. No wildcard characters can be used in the filename. This function works by deleting the directory entry for the file.

42   Move file pointer (LSEEK)

Additional Call Registers
BX = file handle
CX:DX = offset
AL = 0 to move pointer offset
bytes from start of file
= 1 to move pointer offset
    bytes from current location
= 2 to move pointer offset
    bytes from end-of-file

Result Registers
Carry flag = 0 if successful
= 1 if fail
AX = 1 if invalid function number
= 6 if file not open or invalid handle
DX:AX = absolute offset from start of
file if successful

Note: To determine file size, call with AL = 2 and offset = 0.

43   Get or set file mode (CHMOD)

Additional Call Registers
DS:DX = address of ASCIIZ
    file specifier
AL = 0H to get attribute
= 1H to set attribute
CX = attribute if setting
= attribute codes if
    getting (see below)

Result Registers
Carry flag = 0 if successful
= 1 if failed
CX = current attribute if set
AX = 1 if invalid function number
= 2 if file not found
= 3 if file does not exist or
    path not found
= 5 if attribute cannot be changed

AH   Function

43   **Get or set file mode (CHMOD)** (continued from previous page)

```
76543210  attribute code bits
0         reserved
 0        reserved
  x       archive
   0      directory  (do not set with 43H; use extended FCB)
    0     volume-label (do not set with 43H; use ext. FCB)
     x    system
      x   hidden
       x  read-only
```

44   **I/O device control (IOCTL)**

Additional Call Registers	Result Registers
AL = 00H to get device info	AX = number of bytes
= 01H to set device info	transferred if CF=0
= 02H char read device to buffer	otherwise = error code
= 03H char write buffer to device	
= 04H block read device to buffer	
= 05H block write buffer to device	
= 06H check input status	
= 07H check output status	
= 08H test if block device changeable	
= 09H test if drive local or remote	
= 0AH test if handle local or remote	
= 0BH to change sharing retry count	
= 0CH char device I/O control	
= 0DH block device I/O control	
= 0EH get map for logical drive	
= 0FH set map for logical drive	
DS:DX = data buffer	
BX = file handle; CX = number of bytes	

45   **Duplicate a file handle (DUP)**

Additional Call Registers	Result Registers
BX = opened file handle	Carry flag = 0 if successful
	= 1 if failed
	AX = returned handle if successful
	= 4 if no handle available
	= 6 if handle invalid or not open

Note: The two handles will work in tandem; for example, if the file pointer of one handle is moved, the other will also be moved.

AH   Function

46   Force a duplicate of a handle (FORCDUP)

Additional Call Registers
BX = first file handle
CX = second file handle

Result Registers
Carry flag = 0 if successful
= 1 if failed
AX = 4 if no handles available
= 6 if handle invalid or not open

Note: If the file referenced by CX is open, it will be closed first. The second file handle will be forced to point identically to the first file handle. The two handles will work in tandem; for example, if the file pointer of one handle is moved, the other will also be moved.

47   Get current directory

Additional Call Registers
DL = drive code
(0 = default, 1 = A,...)
DS:SI = address of 64-byte buffer

Result Registers
Carry flag = 0 if successful
= 1 if failed
DS:SI = ASCIIZ path specifier
AX = OFH if drive specifier invalid

Note: The returned pathname does not include drive information or the leading "\".

48   Allocate memory

Additional Call Registers
BX = number of paragraphs

Result Registers
Carry flag = 0 if successful
= 1 if failed
AX = points to block if successful
= 7 if memory control blocks destroyed
= 8 if insufficient memory
BX = size of largest block available if failed

49   Free allocated memory

Additional Call Registers
ES = segment address of block
    being released

Result Registers
Carry flag = 0 if successful
= 1 if failed
AX = 7 if memory control blocks destroyed
= 9 if invalid memory block addr in ES

Note: Frees memory allocated by 48H.

<u>AH</u>   <u>Function</u>

4A   **Modify memory allocation (SETBLOCK)**

Additional Call Registers
ES = segment address of block
BX = requested new block size
    in paragraphs

Result Registers
Carry flag = 0 if successful
    = 1 if failed
BX = max available block size
    if failed
AX = 7 if memory control blocks destroyed
    = 8 if insufficient memory
    = 9 if invalid memory block
        address in   ES

Note: Dynamically reduces or expands the memory allocated by a previous call
to interrupt 21 function 48H.

4B   **Load and/or execute program (EXEC)**

Additional Call Registers
DS:DX = address of ASCIIZ path
 and filename to load
ES:BX = address of
  parameter block
AL = 0 to load and execute
= 3 to load, not execute

Result Registers
AX = error code if CF not zero

4C   **Terminate a process (EXIT)**

Additional Call Registers
AL = binary return code

Result Registers
None

Note: Terminates a process, returning control to parent process or to DOS.
A return code can be passed back in AL.

4D   **Get return code of a subprocess (WAIT)**

Additional Call Registers
None

Result Registers
AL = return code
AH = 00 if normal termination
 = 01 if terminated by ctrl-break
 = 02 if terminated by critical
     device error
 = 03 if terminated by call to
     interrupt 21 function 31H

Note: Returns the code sent via interrupt 21 function 4CH. The code can be
returned only once.

<u>AH</u>   <u>Function</u>

4E   **Search for first match (FIND FIRST)**

<u>Additional Call Registers</u>
DS:DX = address of ASCIIZ
file specification
CX = attribute to use in search

<u>Result Registers</u>
Carry flag = 0 if successful
= 1 if failed
AX = error code

Note: The filename should contain one or more wildcard characters. Before this call, a previous call to interrupt 21 function 1AH must set the address of the DTA. If a matching filename is found, the current DTA will be filled in as follows:

Bytes 0 - 20: reserved by DOS for use on subsequent search calls
    21   : attribute found
    22 - 23: file time
    24 - 25: file date
    26 - 27: file size (least significant word)
    28 - 29: file size (most significant word)
    30 - 42: ASCIIZ file specification

4F   **Search for next filename match (FIND NEXT)**

<u>Additional Call Registers</u>
None

<u>Result Registers</u>
Carry flag = 0 if successful
= 1 if failed
AX = error code

Note: The current DTA must be filled in by a previous interrupt 21 4EH or 4FH call. The DTA will be filled in as outlined on interrupt 21 function 4E.

50   **Reserved**

51   **Reserved**

52   **Reserved**

53   **Reserved**

54   **Get verify state**

<u>Additional Call Registers</u>
None

<u>Result Registers</u>
AL = 00 if verify OFF
= 01 if verify ON

Note: The state of the verify flag is changed via interrupt 21 function 2EH.

55   **Reserved**

AH   Function

56   Rename file

Additional Call Registers
DS:DX = address of old ASCIIZ
filename specification
ES:DI = address of new ASCIIZ
filename specification

Result Registers
Carry flag = 0 if successful
= 1 if failed
AX = 2 if file not found
= 3 if path or file not found
= 5 if access denied
= 11H if different device in new name

Note: If a drive specification is used, it must be the same in the old and new filename specifications. However, the directory name may be different, allowing a move and rename in one operation.

57   Get/set file date and time

Additional Call Registers
AL = 00 to get
= 01 to set
BX = file handle
CX = time if setting
DX = date if setting

Result Registers
Carry flag = 0 if successful
= 1 if failed
CX = time if getting
DX = date if getting
AX = 1 if function code invalid
= 6 if handle invalid

Note: The file must be open before the interrupt. The format of date and time is:

TIME:
Bits 0BH-0FH hours (0-23)
    05H-0AH minutes (0-59)
    00H-04H number of 2-
second increments (0-29)

DATE:
Bits 09H-0FH year (rel.1980)
    05H-08H month (0-12)
    00H-04H day (0-31)

58   Get/set allocation strategy

Additional Call Registers
AL = 00 to get strategy
= 01 to set strategy
BX = strategy if setting
    00 if first fit
    01 if best fit
    02 if last fit

Result Registers
Carry flag = 0 if successful
= 1 if failed
AX = strategy if getting
= error code if setting

59   Get extended error information

Additional Call Registers
BX = 00

Result Registers
AX = extended error code
(see Table D-1)
BH = error class
BL = suggested remedy
CH = error locus

Warning! This function destroys the contents of registers CL, DX, SI, DI, BP, DS, and ES. Error codes will change with future version of DOS.

AH   Function

5A   Create temporary file

Additional Call Registers
DS:DX = address of ASCIIZ path
CX = file attribute
(00 if normal, 01 if read-only,
02 if hidden, 04 if system)

Result Registers
Carry flag = 0 if successful
= 1 if failed
AX = handle if successful
= error code if failed
DS:DX = address of ASCIIZ path
specification if successful

Note: Files created with this interrupt function are not deleted when the program terminates.

5B   Create new file

Additional Call Registers
DS:DX = address of ASCIIZ
file specification
CX = file attribute
00 if normal
01 if read-only
02 if hidden
04 if system

Result Registers
Carry flag = 0 if successful
= 1 if failed
AX = file handle if successful
= error code if failed

Note: This function works similarly to interrupt 21 function 3CH; however, this function fails if the file already exists, whereas function 3CH truncates the file to length zero.

5C   Control record access

Additional Call Registers
AL = 00 to lock ,= 01 to unlock
BX = file handle
CX:DX = region offset
SI:DI = region length

Result Registers
Carry flag = 0 if successful
= 1 if failed
AX = error code

Note: Locks or unlocks records in systems that support multitasking or networking.

5D   Reserved

AH AL Function

5E 00 Get machine name

Additional Call Registers
DS:DX = address of buffer

Result Registers
Carry flag = 0 if successful
= 1 if failed
CH = 0 if name undefined
≠ 0 if name defined
CL = NETBIOS number if successful
DS:DX = address of identifier if successful
AX = error code

Note: Returns a 15-byte ASCIIZ string computer identifier.

5E 02 Set printer setup

Additional Call Registers
BX = redirection list index
CX = setup strength length
DS:SI = address of setup string

Result Registers
Carry flag = 0 if successful
= 1 if failed
AX = error code

Note: This function specifies a string that will precede all files sent to the network printer from the local node in a LAN. Microsoft Networks must be running in order to use this function.

5E 03 Get printer setup

Additional Call Registers
BX = redirection list index
ES:DI = address of buffer

Result Registers
Carry flag = 0 if successful
= 1 if failed
AX = error code
CX = length of setup string
ES:DI = setup string if successful

5F 02 Get redirection list

Additional Call Registers
BX = redirection list index
DS:SI = address of 16-byte
 device name buffer
ES:DI = address of 128-byte
 netword name buffer

Result Registers
Carry flag = 0 if successful
= 1 if failed
BH = device status flag
bit 1 = 0 if valid device
 = 1 in invalid device
BL = device type
CX = parameter value
DS:SI = addr. ASCIIZ local device name
ES:DI = addr. ASCIIZ network name
AX = error flag

AH AL Function

5F 03   Redirect device

Additional Call Registers
BL = device type
  03 printer
  04 drive

Result Registers
Carry flag = 0 if successful
= 1 if failed
AX = error code
CX = caller value
DS:SI = address of ASCIIZ
local device name
ES:DI = address of ASCIIZ
network name

Note: Used when operating under a LAN, this function allows you to add devices to the network redirection list.

5F 04   Cancel redirection

Additional Call Registers
DS:SI = address of ASCIIZ
local device name

Result Registers
Carry flag = 0 if successful
= 1 if fail
AX = error code

Note: Used when operating under a LAN, this function allows you to delete devices from the network redirection list.

60   Reserved

61   Reserved

62   Get PSP (program segment prefix) address

Additional Call Registers
None

Result Registers
BX = address of PSP

A summary of the IBM error codes is given in Table D-1.

TABLE D-1: Extended Error Code Information

Code	Error
1	invalid function number
2	file not found
3	path not found
4	too many open files
5	access denied
6	invalid handle
7	memory control blocks destroyed
8	insufficient memory
9	invalid memory block address
10	invalid environment
11	invalid format
12	invalid access code
13	invalid data
14	unknown unit
15	invalid disk drive
16	attempt to remove current directory
17	not same device
18	no more files
19	attempt to write on write-protected diskette
20	unknown unit
21	drive not ready
22	unknown command
23	data error (CRC)
24	bad request structure length
25	seek error
26	unknown media type
27	sector not found
28	printer out of paper
29	write fault
30	read fault
31	general failure
32	sharing violation
33	lock violation
34	invalid disk change
35	FCB unavailable
36	sharing buffer overflow
37-49	reserved
50	network request not supported
51	remote computer not listening
52	duplicate name on network
53	network name not found
54	network busy
55	network device no longer exists
56	net BIOS command limit exceeded
57	network adapter hardware error

TABLE D-1: Extended Error Code Information *(continued)*

Code	Error
58	incorrect response from network
59	unexpected network error
60	incompatible remote adapter
61	print queue full
62	not enough space for print file
63	print file was deleted
64	network name not found
65	access denied
66	network device type incorrect
67	network name not found
68	network name limit exceeded
69	net BIOS session limit exceeded
70	temporarily paused
71	network request not accepted
72	print or disk redirection is paused
73-79	reserved
80	file exists
81	reserved
82	cannot make directory entry
83	fail on INT 24
84	too many redirections
85	duplicate redirection
86	invalid password
87	invalid parameter
88	network device fault

APPENDIX E: BIOS INTERRUPT 10H LISTING

AH   **Function**

00   **Set video mode**

Additional Call Registers	Result Registers
AL = video mode	None

See Table E-2 for a list of available video modes and their definition.

01   **Set cursor type**

Additional Call Registers	Result Registers
CH = beginning line of cursor (bits 0 - 4)	None
CL = ending line of cursor (bits 0 - 4)	

Note: All other bits should be set to zero. The blinking of the cursor is hardware controlled.

02   **Set cursor position**

Additional Call Registers	Result Registers
BH = page number	None
DH = row	
DL = column	

Note: When using graphics modes, BH must be set to zero. Text coordinates of the upper left-hand corner will be (0,0).

03H   **Read cursor position and size**

Additional Call Registers	Result Registers
BH = page number	CH = beginning line of cursor
	CL = ending line of cursor
	DH = row
	DL = column

Note: When using graphics modes, BH must be set to zero.

AH   Function

04H   Read light pen position

Additional Call Registers
None

Result Registers
AH = 0 if light pen not triggered
= 1 if light pen triggered
BX = pixel column
CH = pixel row (modes 04H - 06H)
CX = pixel row (modes 0DH - 13H)
DH = character row
DL = character column

05H   Select active display page

Additional Call Registers
AL = page number
(see Table E-1 below)

Result Registers
None

06   Scroll window up

Additional Call Registers
AL = number of lines to scroll
BH = display attribute
CH = y coordinate of top left
CL = x coordinate of top left
DH = y coordinate of lower right
DL = x coordinate of lower right

Result Registers
None

Note: If AL = 0, the entire window is blanked. Otherwise, the screen will be scrolled upward by the number of lines in AL. Lines scrolling off the top of the screen are lost, blank lines are scrolled in at the bottom according to the attribute in BH.

07   Scroll window down

Additional Call Registers
AL = number of lines to scroll
BH = display attribute
CH = y coordinate of top left
CL = x coordinate of top left
DH = y coordinate of lower right
DL = x coordinate of lower right

Result Registers
None

Note: If AL = 0, the entire window is blanked. Otherwise, the screen will be scrolled down by the number of lines in AL. Lines scrolling off the bottom of the screen are lost, blank lines are scrolled in at the top according to the attribute in BH.

<u>AH</u>   <u>Function</u>

08   **Read character and attribute at cursor position**

<u>Additional Call Registers</u>   <u>Result Registers</u>
BH = display page   AH = attribute byte
                                    AL = ASCII character code

09   **Write character and attribute at cursor position**

<u>Additional Call Registers</u>   <u>Result Registers</u>
AL = ASCII character code
BH = display page
BL = attribute
CX = number of characters to write

Note: Does not update cursor position. Use interrupt 10 Function 2 to set cursor position.

0A   **Write character at cursor position**

<u>Additional Call Registers</u>   <u>Result Registers</u>
AL = ASCII character code   None
BH = display page
BL = graphic color
CX = number of characters to write

Note: Writes character(s) using existing video attribute. Does not update cursor position. Use interrupt 10 Function 2 to set cursor position.

0B   **Set color palette**

<u>Additional Call Registers</u>   <u>Result Registers</u>
BH = 00H to set border or   None
background colors
   = 01H to set palette
BL = palette/color

Note: If BH = 00H and in text mode, this Function will set the border color only. If BH = 00H and in graphics mode, this Function will set background and border colors. If BH = 01H, this Function will select the palette. In 320 x 200 four-color graphics, palettes 0 and 1 are available:

Pixel Colors for Palettes 0 and 1

Pixel	Palette 0	Palette 1
0	background	background
1	green	cyan
2	red	magenta
3	brown/yellow	white

AH   Function

0C   **Write pixel**

Additional Call Registers	Result Registers
AL = pixel value	None
CX = pixel column	
DX = pixel row	
BH = page	

Note: Coordinates and pixel value depend on the current video mode. Setting bit 7 of AL causes the pixel value in AL to be XORed with the current value of the pixel.

0D   **Read pixel**

Additional Call Registers	Result Registers
CX = pixel column	AL = pixel value
DX = pixel row	
BH = page	

0E   **TTY character output**

Additional Call Registers	Result Registers
AL = character	None
BH = page	
BL = foreground color	

Note: Writes character to the display and updates cursor position. TTY mode indicates minimal character processing. ASCII codes for bell, backspace, linefeed, and carriage return are translated into the appropriate action.

0F   **Get video mode**

Additional Call Registers	Result Registers
None	AH = width of screen in characters
	AL = video mode
	BH = active display page

Note: See Table E-2 for a list of possible video modes.

AH AL Function

10 00 SubFunction 00H: set palette register to color correspondence

Additional Call Registers	Result Registers
AL = 00H	None
BH = color	
CL = palette register	
(00H to 0FH)	

10 01 SubFunction 01H: set border color

Additional Call Registers	Result Registers
AL = 01H	None
BH = border color	

10 02 SubFunction 02H: set palette and border

Additional Call Registers	Result Registers
AL = 02H	None
ES:DX = address of color list	

Table E-1: Display Pages for Different Modes and Adapters

Mode	Pages	Adapters			
00H	0 - 7	CGA	EGA	MCGA	VGA
01H	0 - 7	CGA	EGA	MCGA	VGA
02H	0 - 3	CGA			
	0 - 7		EGA	MCGA	VGA
03H	0 - 3	CGA			
	0 - 7		EGA	MCGA	VGA
07H	0 - 7		EGA		VGA
0DH	0 - 7		EGA		VGA
0EH	0 - 3		EGA		VGA
0FH	0 - 1		EGA		VGA
10H	0 - 1		EGA		VGA

All other mode-adapter combinations support only one page.

Table E-2: Video Modes and Their Definition

AL	Pixels	Characters	Char box	Text/ graph	Colors		Aadpter	Max pages	Buffer start
00H	320x200	40 x 25	8x8	text	16	*	CGA	8	B8000h
	320x350	40 x 25	8x14	text	16	*	EGA	8	B8000h
	360x400	40 x 25	9x16	text	16	*	VGA	8	B8000h
	320x400	40 x 25	8x16	text	16	*	MCGA	8	B8000h
01H	320x200	40 x 25	8x8	text	16		CGA	8	B8000h
	320x350	40 x 25	8x14	text	16		EGA	8	B8000h
	360x400	40 x 25	9x16	text	16		VGA	8	B8000h
	320x400	40 x 25	8x16	text	16		MCGA	8	B8000h
02H	640x200	80 x 25	8x8	text	16	*	CGA	8	B8000h
	640x350	80 x 25	8x14	text	16	*	EGA	8	B8000h
	720x400	80 x 25	9x16	text	16	*	VGA	8	B8000h
	640x400	80 x 25	8x16	text	16	*	MCGA	8	B8000h
03H	640x200	80 x 25	8x8	text	16		CGA	8	B8000h
	640x350	80 x 25	8x14	text	16		EGA	8	B8000h
	720x400	80 x 25	9x16	text	16		VGA	8	B8000h
	640x400	80 x 25	8x16	text	16		MCGA	8	B8000h
04H	320x200	40 x 25	8x8	graph	4		CGA	1	B8000h
	320x200	40 x 25	8x8	graph	4		EGA	1	B8000h
	320x200	40 x 25	8x8	graph	4		VGA	1	B8000h
	320x200	40 x 25	8x8	graph	4		MCGA	1	B8000h
05H	320x200	40 x 25	8x8	graph	4	*	CGA	1	B8000h
	320x200	40 x 25	8x8	graph	4	*	EGA	1	B8000h
	320x200	40 x 25	8x8	graph	4	*	VGA	1	B8000h
	320x200	40 x 25	8x8	graph	4	*	MCGA	1	B8000h
06H	640x200	80 x 25	8x8	graph	2		CGA	1	B8000h
	640x200	80 x 25	8x8	graph	2		EGA	1	B8000h
	640x200	80 x 25	8x8	graph	2		VGA	1	B8000h
	640x200	80 x 25	8x8	graph	2		MCGA	1	B8000h
07H	720x350	80 x 25	9x14	text	mono		MDA	8	B0000h
	720x350	80 x 25	9x14	text	mono		EGA	4	B0000h
	720x400	80 x 25	9x16	text	mono		VGA	8	B0000h
08H	reserved								
09H	reserved								
0AH	reserved								
0BH	reserved								
0CH	reserved								
0DH	320x200	40 x 25	8x8	graph	16		EGA	2/4	A0000h
	320x200	40 x 25	8x8	graph	16		VGA	8	A0000h
0EH	640x200	80 x 25	8x8	graph	16		EGA	1/2	A0000h
	640x200	80 x 25	8x8	graph	16		VGA	4	A0000h
0FH	640x350	80 x 25	9x14	graph	mono		EGA	1	A0000h
	640x350	80 x 25	8x14	graph	mono		VGA	2	A0000h
10H	640x350	80 x 25	8x14	graph	4		EGA	1/2	A0000h
	640x350	80 x 25	8x14	graph	16		VGA	2	A0000h
11H	640x480	80 x 30	8x16	graph	2		VGA	1	A0000h
	640x480	80 x 30	8x16	graph	2		MCGA	1	A0000h
12H	640x480	80 x 30	8x16	graph	16		VGA	1	A0000h
13H	320x200	40 x 25	8x8	graph	256		VGA	1	A0000h
	320x200	40 x 25	8x8	graph	256		MCGA	1	A0000h

* color burst off

APPENDIX F: ASCII CODES

Ctrl	Dec	Hex	Ch	Code	Dec	Hex	Ch	Dec	Hex	Ch	Dec	Hex	Ch
^@	0	00		NUL	32	20		64	40	@	96	60	`
^A	1	01	☺	SOH	33	21	!	65	41	A	97	61	a
^B	2	02	☻	STX	34	22	"	66	42	B	98	62	b
^C	3	03	♥	ETX	35	23	#	67	43	C	99	63	c
^D	4	04	♦	EOT	36	24	$	68	44	D	100	64	d
^E	5	05	♣	ENQ	37	25	%	69	45	E	101	65	e
^F	6	06	♠	ACK	38	26	&	70	46	F	102	66	f
^G	7	07	●	BEL	39	27	'	71	47	G	103	67	g
^H	8	08	□	BS	40	28	(	72	48	H	104	68	h
^I	9	09	○	HT	41	29	)	73	49	I	105	69	i
^J	10	0A	◉	LF	42	2A	*	74	4A	J	106	6A	j
^K	11	0B	♂	VT	43	2B	+	75	4B	K	107	6B	k
^L	12	0C	♀	FF	44	2C	,	76	4C	L	108	6C	l
^M	13	0D	♪	CR	45	2D	-	77	4D	M	109	6D	m
^N	14	0E	♫	SO	46	2E	.	78	4E	N	110	6E	n
^O	15	0F	☀	SI	47	2F	/	79	4F	O	111	6F	o
^P	16	10	►	DLE	48	30	0	80	50	P	112	70	p
^Q	17	11	◄	DC1	49	31	1	81	51	Q	113	71	q
^R	18	12	↕	DC2	50	32	2	82	52	R	114	72	r
^S	19	13	‼	DC3	51	33	3	83	53	S	115	73	s
^T	20	14	¶	DC4	52	34	4	84	54	T	116	74	t
^U	21	15	§	NAK	53	35	5	85	55	U	117	75	u
^V	22	16	▬	SYN	54	36	6	86	56	V	118	76	v
^W	23	17	↨	ETB	55	37	7	87	57	W	119	77	w
^X	24	18	↑	CAN	56	38	8	88	58	X	120	78	x
^Y	25	19	↓	EM	57	39	9	89	59	Y	121	79	y
^Z	26	1A	→	SUB	58	3A	:	90	5A	Z	122	7A	z
^[	27	1B	←	ESC	59	3B	;	91	5B	[	123	7B	{
^\	28	1C	∟	FS	60	3C	<	92	5C	\	124	7C	|
^]	29	1D	↔	GS	61	3D	=	93	5D	]	125	7D	}
^^	30	1E	▲	RS	62	3E	>	94	5E	^	126	7E	~
^_	31	1F	▼	US	63	3F	?	95	5F	_	127	7F	⌂

REFERENCES

"Disk Operating System Technical Reference", IBM Corporation, Boca Raton, Florida, c. 1984,1985.

"IBM Personal Computer Hardware Reference Library: Technical Reference", IBM Corporation, Boca Raton, Florida, c. 1984.

"8086/8088 User's Manual Programmer's and Hardware Reference", Intel, Mt. Prospect, IL, c. 1990.

"iAPX 286 Programmer's Reference Manual including The iAPX 286 Numeric Supplement", Intel, Mt. Prospect, IL, c. 1983.

"80386 Programmer's Reference Manual", Intel, Mt. Prospect, IL, c. 1986.

"i486[TM] Processor Programmer's Reference Manual", Intel, Mt. Prospect, IL, c.1989.

INDEX

!

.286 directive,   203
.386 directive,   203
.486 directive,   203
.86 directive,   203
:
    following labels,   50
    segment override operator,   44
;
    before comments,   50

A

AAA instruction,   109, 236
AAD instruction,   110, 236
AAM instruction,   109, 237
AAS instruction,   109, 237
accumulator,   26
ADC instruction,   84 - 85, 237
ADD instruction,   25 - 26, 83,
    207, 237 - 238
addition
    BCD,   104
    binary,   6
    hex,   6 - 7
    signed,   153 - 158, 160, 162
    unsigned,   83 - 86
address bus,   10 - 13
addressing
    effective address,   43
    logical address,   27 - 28, 30, 35
    modes,   41 - 44, 46, 48, 201
    offset address,   27, 203
    physical address,   27 - 28, 30,
        35, 43, 202
    table,   45, 202
AF (auxiliary carry flag),   38 - 39,
    101, 105
AH register,   23, 88, 90 - 92, 119,
    158 - 159
AL register,   23, 88, 90 - 92, 158
alignment field,   177, 280
ALU (arithmetic/logic unit),   11, 21
AND instruction,   93, 239
Apple,   13
arguments in macros,   140

ASCII,   8, 69, 102
    addition,   109
    subtraction,   109
    table,   317
ASCIIZ string,   287
asm file,   54
assemblers,   54
assembling a program,   54
ASSUME directive,   52, 272
auxiliary carry,   38, 101, 105
AX register,   23, 88 - 92, 157 - 159

B

background color,   119, 122, 126
based addressing mode,   43
based indexed addressing mode,
    44
BCD (binary coded decimal),
    72, 101
    addition,   104
    multiplication,   109
    packed BCD,   102
    subtraction,   104 - 105
    unpacked BCD,   102
BH register,   23
binary numbers
    addition,   6
    See also conversion
    format,   2
    subtraction,   87
BIOS (basic input output system),
    33, 119
    programs,   99 - 100
BIOS Interrupts
    See INT 10H
bit,   9
BIU (bus interface unit),   21 - 22
BL register,   23
Borland,   54, 190, 196
BP register,   23, 36
breakpoint,   218
bus,   10
    address bus,   10 - 13
    control bus,   10 - 11
    data bus,   10 - 12
BX register,   23
byte,   9

C

C language, 189
    calling Assembly language routines, 191, 194
    calling convention, 192 - 193, 195
    inline coding, 190
CALL instruction, 66 - 67, 239 - 240, 245
carry, 38
    See also auxiliary carry
CBW instruction, 157, 240
CF (carry flag), 37 - 40, 65, 83, 86, 88, 95 - 97, 110 - 113, 155 - 156, 161
CGA (color graphics adapter), 119, 121 - 122, 124 - 126
CH register, 23
CISC architecture, 14
CL register, 23, 110 - 113
class name field, 177, 281
CLC instruction, 240
CLD instruction, 164, 241
CLI instruction, 241
clock cycles, 236, 261 - 262
CMC instruction, 241
CMP instruction, 96 - 97, 161, 241, 249
CMPS instruction, 167, 241
CMPSB instruction, 164, 167, 241
CMPSW instruction, 164, 167, 241
.CODE directive, 74 - 75
code segment
    See segments
CodeView program, 203 - 204
com file, 76 - 77
combine type field, 177, 281
comments, 50
    in macros, 141
compact
    See memory model
conditional jumps
    See jumps
control bus, 10 - 11
conversion
    ASCII to BCD, 102 - 103
    ASCII to binary, 186
    BCD to ASCII, 104
    binary to ASCII, 182 - 184
    binary to decimal, 2
    decimal to binary, 2
    decimal to hex, 4
    exe to com, 77
    hex to binary, 4
    hex to decimal 4
coprocessors, 20

CPU, 9 - 14
CRAY, 189
crf file, 56
CS register, 23, 27 - 28, 64
cursor
    position, 119 - 121
CWD instruction, 157, 241
CX register, 23

D

DAA instruction, 104 - 105, 242
DAS instruction, 104, 107, 242- 243
data bus, 10 - 12
.DATA directive, 74 - 75
data directives, 69 - 73
data segment
    See segments
data types, 69
DB directive, 69, 272
DD directive, 71, 273
DEBUG program, 55, 214
    A (assemble) command, 217, 222
    C (compare) command, 232 - 233
    D (dump) command, 222 - 224
    E (enter) command, 222, 224 - 226
    F (fill) command, 222 - 223
    G (go) command, 217 - 219
    H (hex) command, 229
    L (load) command, 233
    M (move) command, 231 - 233
    N (name) command, 233 - 234
    P (procedure) command, 229
    Q (quit) command, 214 - 215
    R (register) command, 215 - 216, 228
    S (search) command, 232 - 233
    T (trace) command, 220
    table of commands, 235
    table of flag register codes, 229
    U (unassemble) command, 218, 222
    W (write) command, 232 - 233
DEC instruction, 243
DF (direction flag), 38, 164
DH register, 23
DI register, 23
direct addressing mode, 42
directives, 50 - 51, 53
    See also Appendix C
directory, 287
display
    attribute, 120, 122
    character to monitor, 127
    string to monitor, 127
DIV instruction, 90 - 92, 243

division
    signed,   158
    table,   92, 158
    unsigned,   90 - 92
DL register,   23
DOS,   19, 24, 32 - 33, 35
DOS INT21H Function calls
    See INT 21H
DQ directive,   72, 273
DS register,   23, 29 - 30
DT directive,   72, 273
DTA (disk transfer area),   287
DUP directive,   70, 274
DW directive,   70, 274
DWORD attribute,   173, 277, 279
DX register,   23, 88 - 92, 157 - 159

E

EA (effective address),   259
EGA (enhanced graphics adapter),
    119, 121
END directive,   53, 174, 274
ENDM directive,   140
ENDP directive,   52, 275, 278
ENDS directive,   51, 275, 280
ENIAC,   13
entry point,   51 - 53, 67
EQU directive,   71, 131, 275
ES register,   23, 32
ESC instruction,   243
EU (execution unit),   21 - 22
EVEN directive,   275
exception
    divide error,   90
exe file,   54, 76 - 77
exe2bin program,   77
exit point,   51
extra segment
    See segments
EXTRN directive,   173, 176,
    251, 276

F

FAR attribute,   52, 64, 66 - 67,
    173, 240
FAT (file allocation table),   287
FCB (file control block),   288
file handle,   288
flag register,   23, 37 - 38, 40,
    64, 228 - 230
foreground color,   122
FWORD,   173

G

general purpose registers,   22 - 23
gigabyte,   9
graphics mode,   124 - 126
GROUP directive,   276 - 277

H

hexadecimal
    See also addition
    See also conversion
    representation,   3
    See also subtraction
HLT instruction,   243
huge
    See memory model

I

IDIV instruction,   158, 243
IF (interrupt enable flag),   38
immediate addressing mode,   41
IMUL instruction,   159, 243
IN instruction,   244
INC instruction,   244
INCLUDE directive,   147 - 148,
    277
index registers,   23
indexed addressing mode,   43
inline coding,   190 - 191
input
    from keyboard,   128 - 130, 133
instruction decoder,   12
instruction pointer
    See IP
instruction timing,   259 - 261
    table,   262 - 271
INT 00H divide error,   247
INT 01H single step,   247
INT 02H non-maskable interrupt,
    247
INT 03H breakpoint,   247
INT 10H video function calls,
    119 - 126
    See Appendix E,   311
INT 21H DOS function calls,
    119, 127 - 133, 135 - 136
    See Appendix D,   289
INT instruction,   119, 244 - 245,
    247
Intel,   13, 19 - 20, 22, 27, 31, 37,
    43, 45, 105, 109 - 110, 158, 161,
    189, 210, 246 - 248, 259 - 260, 262

interrupts, 244 - 248
        hardware interrupts, 246
        interrupt vector table, 245
        software interrupts, 246
INTO instruction, 248
IP (instruction pointer) register,
        11, 23, 27 - 28, 64
IRET instruction, 248

J

JA (jump if above), 65 - 66, 249
JAE (jump if above/equal), 65, 249
JB (jump if below), 65 - 66, 249
JBE (jump if below/equal), 65, 249
JC (jump if carry), 65, 249
JCXZ (jump if CX=0), 250
JE (jump if equal), 65, 249
JG (jump if greater), 65, 162, 250
JGE (jump if greater/equal), 65,
        162, 250
JL (jump if less), 65, 162, 250
JLE (jump if less/equal), 65,
        162, 250
JMP (unconditional jump), 66,
        250 - 251
JNA (jump if not above), 65
JNAE (jump if not above/equal),
        65
JNB (jump if not below), 65
JNBE (jump if not below/equal),
        65
JNC (jump if no carry), 65, 249
JNE (jump if not equal), 65, 249
JNG (jump if not greater), 65
JNGE (jump if not greater/equal),
        65
JNL (jump if not less), 65
JNLE (jump if not less/equal),
        65
JNO (jump if no overflow), 65,
        249
JNP (jump if no parity), 65, 249
JNS (jump if no sign), 65, 249
JNZ (jump if not zero), 64 - 65, 249
JO (jump if overflow), 65, 249
JP (jump if parity), 65, 249
JPE (jump if parity even), 65
JPO (jump if parity odd), 65
JS (jump if sign), 65, 249
jumps
        conditional jumps, 64, 162, 249
        far jumps, 251
        short jumps, 64, 250
        table, 65
        unconditional jumps, 66, 250
JZ (jump if zero), 65, 249

K

K (unit of measure), 9
keyboard input
        See input
kilobyte, 9

L

LABEL directive, 133, 277
labels, 50, 67, 284 - 286
LAHF instruction, 252
.LALL directive, 141, 143
large
        See memory model
LDS instruction, 252
LEA instruction, 252
LENGTH directive, 278, 282
LES instruction, 253
link map, 179
LINK program, 54 - 55, 57, 175
linking, 57, 175
        C with Assembly language, 196
little endian, 31, 62, 72, 205
LOCAL directive, 144, 146 -
        147
LOCK instruction, 253
LODS instruction, 253
LODSB instruction, 164 - 165,
        253
LODSW instruction, 164 - 165,
        253
loop, 40
LOOP instruction, 86, 253
LOOPE instruction, 253
LOOPNE instruction, 254
LOOPNZ instruction, 254
LOOPZ instruction, 253
LSB (least significant bit), 95 -
        96, 110 - 113, 161
lst file, 55, 141

M

machine code, 23 - 24, 28 - 29
        See also opcode
macro, 140 - 150
        comments in macros, 141
        invoking macros, 140
        local names, 144, 146 - 147
        macro definition, 140
        macro expansion, 140
MACRO directive, 140
map file, 57, 179

masking bits,   93, 98
MASM program,   54 - 55, 73,
     203
MDA (monochrome display
     adapter),   119
medium
     See memory model
megabyte,   9
memory
     cache memory,   20
     memory map,   32
     range,   19 - 20, 203
     virtual memory,   20
memory model,   74
MGA (monchrome graphics
     adapter),   121
microprocessors,   13, 210
     80286,   19, 208, 210 - 211
     80386,   19 - 20, 200 - 201, 203,
          207 - 208, 210 - 211
     80386SX,   20
     80486,   19 - 20, 200 - 201, 203,
          207 - 208, 210 - 211
     8080/85,   19
     8086,   19, 208, 210 - 211
     8088,   19
     table,   20
Microsoft,   19, 24, 187, 190, 196
MODE
     CO80 command,   126
     LPT1 command,   56
modular programming,   173
modules,   173
     linking,   176
     parameter passing,   187 - 188
Motorola,   13, 105, 189
MOV instruction,   24, 254
MOVS instruction,   254
MOVSB instruction,   164, 254
MOVSW instruction,   164, 254
MSB (most significant bit),   95 -
     96, 110 - 113, 153 - 154, 161
MUL instruction, 89 - 90, 208, 254
multibyte processing ,   86, 88, 105
multiplication
     signed,   159
     table,   90, 159
     unsigned,   89 - 90
multiword processing,   85, 154

N

names
     See labels
NEAR attribute,   52, 64, 66 - 67,
     173, 239

NEG instruction,   254
negative number representation,
     6, 153 - 155
nibble,   9
NOP instruction,   254
NOT instruction,   87, 255

O

obj file,   54 - 55
object code
     See machine code
OF (overflow flag),   38, 65, 155 -
     158
OFFSET directive,   60, 278
opcode,   27 - 28, 41
OR instruction,   93, 255
ORG directive,   69, 278
OUT instruction,   255
output
     string to monitor,   127
overflow,   155 - 158, 160

P

P286 directive,   203
P386 directive,   203
P486 directive,   203
P8086 directive,   203
PAGE directive,   56, 278
PARA attribute,   280
parity,   38, 65
PF (parity flag),   38 - 39, 65
pipelining,   21 - 22
pixel ,   124 - 125
pointer registers,   23
POP instruction,   67, 255
POPF instruction,   256
POP instruction,   34 - 35, 67, 255
POPF instruction,   256
PROC directive,   52, 278
procedure,   52
     See also modules
program counter,   11
protected mode,   20
pseudo-instructions
     See directives
pseudo-operations
     See directives
PSP (program segment prefix),
     288
PTR directive,   89, 279
PUBLIC directive,   173 - 174,
     176, 251, 280
PUSH instruction,   34 - 35, 67, 256
PUSHF instruction,   256

Q

QWORD attribute, 173, 277, 279

R

RAM (random access memory),
  9, 11, 32
  video display RAM, 32 - 33, 120
RCL instruction, 112, 256
RCR instruction, 112, 256
real mode, 20
register addressing mode, 41
register indirect addressing mode,
  42
registers, 11, 22 - 23, 200 - 201,
  205
  table, 23, 201
REP prefix, 164 - 166
reserved names
  table, 285 - 286
RET instruction, 67, 256
RISC architecture, 14
ROL instruction, 111, 256
ROM (read only memory), 9,
  11, 32 - 33
ROR instruction, 110, 256
rotate instructions, 110 - 113,

S

SAHF instruction, 256
SAL instruction, 161, 257
.SALL directive, 141, 143
SAR instruction, 161, 257
SBB instruction, '88, 257
SCAS instruction, 257
SCASB instruction, 164, 168, 257
SCASW instruction, 164, 257
scrolling the screen, 120
SEGMENT directive, 51 - 52,
  177, 280
segments, 26 - 28, 30, 32, 36,
  50 - 53
  alignment, 280
  class, 281
  code segment, 27 - 28, 52, 177
  combine type, 281
  data segment, 29 - 30, 51, 164,
    177
  extra segment, 32, 52, 164
  full segment definition, 74, 177
  overlapping, 36
  overrides, 44 - 45
  segment registers, 23, 27 - 30,
    34 - 35

segments (continued)
  simplified segment definition,
    73 - 75, 180
  stack segment, 35, 51, 62 - 63,
    177
SF (sign flag), 38 - 39, 65, 157
shift instructions, 95 - 96, 161
SHL instruction, 96, 161, 257
SHORT directive, 66, 281
SHR instruction, 95, 257
SI register, 23
sign bit, 153 - 154
sign extension, 157 - 158
signed number
  See also addition, subtraction
  representation, 153 - 154
single-step, 38
SIZE directive, 282
small
  See see memory model
SP register, 23, 34 - 35
SS register, 23, 34 - 35
stack, 33 - 35, 62, 67, 227 - 228
stack segment
  See segments
STC instruction, 257
STD instruction, 164, 257
STI instruction, 257
STOSB instruction, 164 - 165
STOSW instruction, 164 - 165
string instructions, 164 - 170
  table, 164
STRUC directive, 282 - 283
SUB instruction, 87, 258
subprograms
  See modules
subroutines, 67
subtraction
  hex, 7
  signed, 154
  unsigned, 87 - 88

T

table processing, 169
TASM program, 54, 73, 203
TBYTE 173
terabyte, 9
TEST instruction, 258
text mode, 119, 121 - 122, 124
TF (trap flag), 38
tiny
  See memory model
TITLE directive, 56, 283
two's complement, 6, 153
type command, 56
TYPE directive, 281 - 283

V

VGA (video graphics adapter), 119, 121
video
    attribute byte, 122
    graphics mode, 124
    modes, 119, 121
    pixel programming, 125
    resolution, 124 - 125
    screen, 119
    screen handling, 120 - 121, 126
    text mode, 119, 121 - 122, 124

W

WAIT instruction, 259
word, 9
WORD attribute, 173, 277, 279 - 280

X

.XALL directive, 141, 143
XCHG instruction, 259
XLAT instruction, 169, 259
XOR instruction, 94, 259

Z

ZF (zero flag), 38 - 39, 60, 65, 167

WILD and WOOLLY MAMMOTHS

by ALIKI

REVISED EDITION

HarperCollins*Publishers*

*for G. Gregory Turak
and Nicholas Taylor Theodos*

And for all my friends in Ohio—especially Maria Duttera,
Jacquelyn Hoover, Linda Woolard, Allan Pitcock, LeeAnn Lugar,
Rebecca and Lance Clarke, Sharon Low, Cleo Stoner, Bill Hughes
and Sue Grindrod. Thanks for the memories.

Mammoth appreciation to Joseph E. Wallace for his undaunted digging,
and to Virginia and Morton Sand for their impulse.

Wild and Woolly Mammoths
Copyright © 1977, 1996 by Aliki Brandenberg. Printed in the U.S.A. All rights reserved.

Library of Congress Cataloging-in-Publication Data   Aliki.   Wild and woolly mammoths / written and illustrated by Aliki.
p.   cm.   ISBN 0-06-026276-1. — ISBN 0-06-026277-X (lib. bdg.) — ISBN 0-06-446179-3 (pbk.)
1. Woolly mammoth—Juvenile literature.[1. Woolly mammoth. 2. Mammoths. 3. Prehistoric animals. 4. Paleontology.] I. Title.
QE882.P8A43 1996   94-48217   569'.6—dc20   CIP AC

Typography by Elynn Cohen   ❖   Revised Edition
Visit us on the World Wide Web!
http://www.harperchildrens.com

WILD and WOOLLY MAMMOTHS

A wild and woolly beast once roamed
the cold northern part of the earth.
It had two great, curved tusks
and a long, hairy trunk.
Its big bones were covered with tough skin
and an undercoat of soft, woolly fur.
Over that, its long shaggy coat of hair
reached almost to the ground.
It was an ancient kind of elephant
called a woolly mammoth.

Woolly mammoths flourished thousands of years ago.
Long, long before then, when dinosaurs lived,
the earth was hot and swampy.
But temperatures changed.
Parts of the earth grew cold.

In some places in the north, the snow never melted.
It froze over and formed thick sheets of ice called glaciers.
This was the time of the Ice Age.

Many animals died out because of the cold.
Other animals did not die out.
They migrated to warmer places and survived.
Still others remained in the cold north.
Every year, vast herds roamed across the icy plains
of Europe, Asia, and North America.

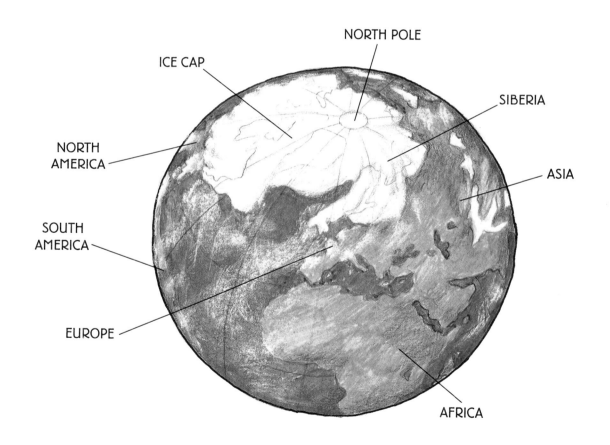

NORTH POLE

ICE CAP

SIBERIA

NORTH
AMERICA

ASIA

SOUTH
AMERICA

EUROPE

AFRICA

Only animals with heavy coats of hair, like the woolly mammoth,
were able to survive the freezing cold.
Their warm covering protected them.

GIANT ELK
(Megaloceros species)

WOOLLY RHINOCEROS
(Coelodonta antiquitatis)

MUSK OX
(Ovibos species)

BISON
(Bison species)

IBEX
(Capra species)

WOOLLY MAMMOTH
(Mammuthus primigenius)

These animals were also protected from the cold by fat.
The woolly mammoth had a hump of fat on its back and
head, and a three-inch layer of fat on its body.

9

It happened long ago
that one of these woolly mammoths
fell into a deep crack in a glacier.
It broke some of its bones and died.
Snow and ice covered its body.
The cold preserved its flesh.

Thirty-nine thousand years passed.
Slowly the weather grew warm again.
The thick layers of ice began to melt.
The Ice Age had ended.

In 1900, the mammoth's body was discovered in Siberia.
Part of it was poking out of the melting ice.
Travelers noticed their dogs sniffing the thawing meat.
The travelers did not know it was a mammoth, but it was.

Scientists found more woolly mammoths frozen in ice.
They found other kinds of mammoths, too, and studied them.
Now they know a great deal about these prehistoric animals.
"Mammoth" means giant, and they were.
Mammoths were the largest land mammals of their time.
They lived in various parts of the world, in diverse climates.

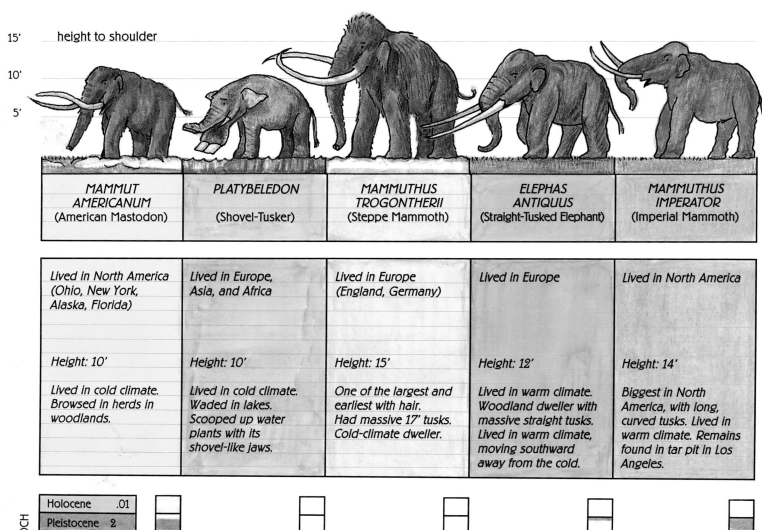

	MAMMUT AMERICANUM (American Mastodon)	PLATYBELEDON (Shovel-Tusker)	MAMMUTHUS TROGONTHERII (Steppe Mammoth)	ELEPHAS ANTIQUUS (Straight-Tusked Elephant)	MAMMUTHUS IMPERATOR (Imperial Mammoth)
	Lived in North America (Ohio, New York, Alaska, Florida)	Lived in Europe, Asia, and Africa	Lived in Europe (England, Germany)	Lived in Europe	Lived in North America
	Height: 10'	Height: 10'	Height: 15'	Height: 12'	Height: 14'
	Lived in cold climate. Browsed in herds in woodlands.	Lived in cold climate. Waded in lakes. Scooped up water plants with its shovel-like jaws.	One of the largest and earliest with hair. Had massive 17' tusks. Cold-climate dweller.	Lived in warm climate. Woodland dweller with massive straight tusks. Lived in warm climate, moving southward away from the cold.	Biggest in North America, with long, curved tusks. Lived in warm climate. Remains found in tar pit in Los Angeles.

height to shoulder
15'
10'
5'

EPOCH

Holocene	.01
Pleistocene	2
Pliocene	5
Miocene	25

MILLIONS OF YEARS AGO

14

Mammoths belonged to the Elephantidae family,
in an ancient group of Proboscidea—a group that includes
mammoths, mastodons, and modern elephants.
They are all animals with long trunks and tusks, hoofs,
and the flat teeth of plant eaters.
Today, only two species of elephants survive—those of Asia and Africa.
They are the last of the proboscideans, which first appeared
more than 50 million years ago.

15' height to shoulder
10'
5'

ELEPHAS FALCONERI (Dwarf Mammoth)	MAMMUTHUS COLUMBI (Columbian Mammoth)	MAMMUTHUS PRIMIGENIUS (Woolly Mammoth)	ELEPHAS MAXIMUS (Modern Indian Elephant)	LOXODONTA AFRICANA (Modern African Elephant)
Lived on Mediterranean islands (Crete, Malta, Cypress, Sardinia)	Lived in southeastern North America (Carolinas, Georgia, Louisiana, Florida, California)	Lived in Europe, North America, Asia	Lives in Asia	Lives in Africa
Height: 3'	Height: 12'	Height: 9'	Height: 8–10'	Height: 13–14'
A dwarf island elephant. Lived in warm climate. Some island species survived for thousands of years after mainland species became extinct.	Had long, twisted tusks. Lived in warm climate in grasslands.	Shaggy, cold-climate tundra dweller. Hunted by early people. Not as big as some elephants, but powerful, and with a massive head.	Warm climate, feeds on leafy vegetation. Threatened by loss of habitat.	Lives in warm climate. Threatened by poachers, who kill it for its ivory tusks.

15

Mammoths traveled in peaceful herds.
In warmer seasons, they moved from grassy plains
to winding rivers, searching for food and water.
They shared their habitat with other plant eaters—
bison, horses, musk oxen, and caribou.
Sometimes they were attacked by smaller, fearless
carnivores—cats, wolves, or bears.
But there was one hunter even more dangerous
than the fierce saber-toothed cat, *Smilodon*.
That was the human hunter.

The mammoth hunters were cave dwellers.
They needed mammoths to live.
They hunted mammoths and other animals
with weapons they made of stone.
So their time is called the Stone Age.

Not long ago, remarkable wall paintings
were discovered in dark, damp caves.
They were made by Stone Age artists.
The paintings show the animals people hunted at that time—
mammoths, camels, bison, aurochs (ancient cattle), and horses.
Many of these animals are now extinct.
Artifacts, too, were found. They were carved in ivory,
bone, and stone, and tell about life long ago.

Horse carved from
mammoth tusk
found in Germany

Bison and plants
carved in bone knife
found in France

Head carved in ivory
found in France

19

More discoveries were made by archaeologists—
scientists who study ancient ruins.
They uncovered the remains of a whole Stone Age village.
They learned many things from this village and others like it.
They found out how mammoth hunters lived, and how
important the mammoth was to them.

In winter, clans lived in caves and in rock shelters,
protected from the cold.
In the spring, the snow began to melt.
The clans moved down to river valleys, where the
mammoths would come to graze.
Men, women, and children worked in groups.
They picked fresh grains, roots, grasses, herbs, and berries.
They collected bones of animals that the river washed down.
They used them to build elaborate shelters, covered
with mud and animal skins.
Then they prepared for the dangerous mammoth hunt.

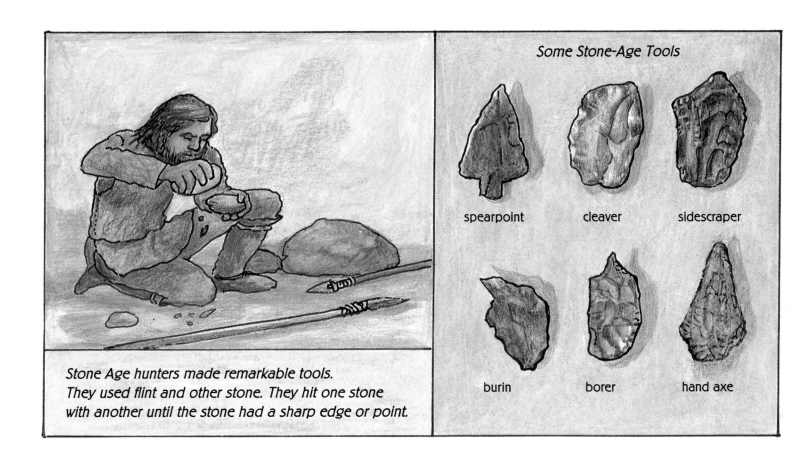

Stone Age hunters made remarkable tools.
They used flint and other stone. They hit one stone
with another until the stone had a sharp edge or point.

Some Stone-Age Tools

spearpoint   cleaver   sidescraper

burin   borer   hand axe

Toolmakers chipped knives, axes, and other tools
out of stone and mammoth bone.
They made razor-sharp spearpoints and attached
them to long, wooden spears.
With these, the hunters would kill the mammoths.
But first they had to find them and trap them.
Often they traveled far from their camps looking for them.

Sometimes the hunters set fires around the herds.
Then they forced the frightened beasts down steep cliffs.
Other hunters waited below to kill the mammoths with their spears.

Sometimes the mammoth hunters dug deep pits. They covered the pits with branches, bones, and earth.

When a mammoth walked over the pit, the cover collapsed, and the mammoth fell in.

It could not escape.
Hunters rolled heavy stones
down on the trapped mammoth
and killed it.

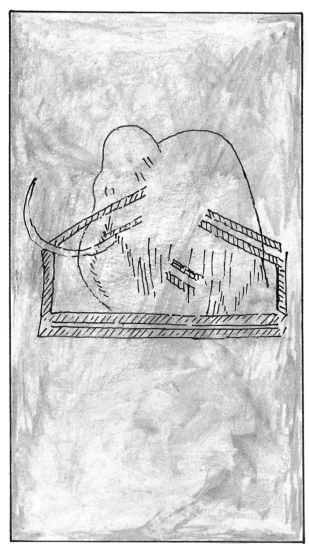

Stone Age wall painting
found in a cave in France.
It shows a mammoth
caught in a pit trap.
Many mammoths that
were discovered showed
that their bones
had been broken,
and they had been
butchered with knives.

Other animals were hunted for food and clothing too,
but a mammoth was a prized catch.
One was big enough to feed many people for a long time.
The group worked as a team to skin and butcher
the giant beast, and they saved nearly all its parts.
It was hard work.
They removed the brains and soft organs.
They cut and sliced the meat into pieces.
They removed the tusks, saved the fat and hide,
collected the bones.
They hauled it all back to their campsite.
Then they probably had a big celebration.

People used the skulls, tusks, and bones
for the foundations of their shelters.
It sometimes took the bones of 95 mammoths
to make one shelter.
They piled the bones around their camp, for ready use.

They used the mammoth's heavy hide as a door flap,
and cut it into strips for cords.
They twisted the long hair into cording for mats,
and used the woolly fur for bedding.
They burned bones for fuel.
They boiled the nourishing fat into a rich brew,
and used the fat for food, drink, medicine,
curing hides, and many other purposes.

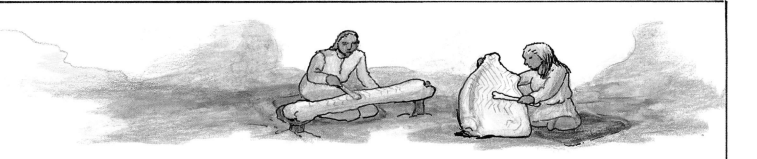

They made musical instruments out of the skull, bones, and tusks.
They used the stomach and intestines
as containers and cooking pots.
They carved the ivory tusks into jewelry, basins, utensils,
needles, buttons, ornaments, and sculptures.

They dried the fresh meat
to preserve it for winter.
They also stored and preserved
fresh meat in deep pits
they dug in the permafrost,
the permanently frozen ground
beneath the thawed, spongy soil.

Mammoth hide was too heavy to be used for clothing. Garments were made mostly of deer and bison skins and furs.

29

Season after season, herds of mammoths
continued to roam the tundras, steppes, and valleys
of the north.
Season after season, hungry cave dwellers
hunted them down.
This could be one reason why they died out.
No one is sure.

Today, elephants and many other animals
are also at risk of dying out.
People are concerned.
Many find ways to protect the animals,
to save them from extinction.

Mammoths were not so lucky.
Now we have only ancient remains
to tell us of their existence.
We can only imagine how it was when
wild and woolly mammoths roamed the earth.